PANIC CITY

PANIC CITY

CRIME AND THE FEAR INDUSTRIES IN JOHANNESBURG

MARTIN J. MURRAY

STANFORD UNIVERSITY PRESS
STANFORD, CALIFORNIA

Stanford University Press
Stanford, California

Portions of this book were previously published in "Policing in Johannesburg after Apartheid," *Social Dynamics* 39, no. 2 (2013): 210–27. Published by Taylor & Francis Ltd. Reused by permission.

Printed in the United States of America on acid-free, archival-quality paper

Library of Congress Cataloging-in-Publication Data

Names: Murray, Martin J., author.
Title: Panic city : crime and the fear industries in Johannesburg / Martin J. Murray.
Description: Stanford, California : Stanford University Press, 2020. | Includes bibliographical references and index.
Identifiers: LCCN 2019019256 (print) | LCCN 2019022135 (ebook) | ISBN 9781503610194 (cloth : alk. paper) | ISBN 9781503611269 (pbk. : alk. paper) | ISBN 9781503611276 (ebook)
Subjects: LCSH: Crime prevention—South Africa—Johannesburg. | Security systems—South Africa—Johannesburg. | Public safety—South Africa—Johannesburg. | Fear of crime—South Africa—Johannesburg.
Classification: LCC HV7434.S62 M87 2020 (print) | LCC HV7434.S62 (ebook) | DDC 364.4096822/15—dc23
LC record available at https://lccn.loc.gov/2019019256
LC ebook record available at https://lccn.loc.gov/2019022135

Cover design by Kevin Barrett Kane
Cover photograph by Felix Lipov
Typeset by Motto Publishing Services in 11/14 Dante MT

Contents

Illustrations

Abbreviations

BAC	Business against Crime
CIU	Central Intervention Unit
CSIR	Centre for Scientific and Industrial Research
CID	City Improvement District
CCC	Combined Chairpersons Committee
CAP	Community Active Protection
CPF	Community Policing Forum
CSO	Community Security Organization
CCTV	Closed Circuit Television
CRA	Craighall Park Residents' Association
ENAT	National Vehicle Identification Database
FTTH	Fibre to the home
GAP	Glenhazel Active Protection
HD	High-definition
IDF	Israeli Defense Force
ICCC	Incident Command and Control Centre
JMPD	Johannesburg Municipal Police Department
MAD	Making a Difference
MSCF	Melville Sector Crime Forum
MSI	Melville Security Initiative
MOU	Memorandum of Understanding
ENAT	National Vehicle Identification Database
PRABOA	Parkhurst Residents and Business Owners Association
PSIRA	Private Security Industry Regulatory Agency
RID	Residential Improvement Districts
SCAP	Sandown-Strathavon CAP
SWAP	Savoy and Waverley CAP
SIA	Security Industry Alliance
SCF	Sector Crime Forum
SANSEA	South African National Security Employers Association
SAPS	South African Police Services
SCCF	Station Crime Combating Forum

TRUs	Tactical Response Units
UTRP	Urban Transformation Research Project
WARM	Westdene, Auckland Park, Rossmore, Richmond, Melville, and Brixton Residents and Ratepayers Association

Preface

> With cities, it is as with dreams: everything imaginable can be dreamed,
> but even the most unexpected dream is a rebus that conceals a desire or,
> its reverse, a fear. Cities, like dreams, are made of desires and fears, even
> if the threat of their discourse is secret, their rules are absurd, their per-
> spectives deceitful, and everything conceals something else.
>
> —Italo Calvino[1]

I

This book explores the imaginative dimension of everyday life in Johannesburg after apartheid through the lens of the subjective perception of
crime, insecurity, and disorder in the public spaces of the city. It does
so by examining the often unacknowledged connections between architecture and the built environment, the organized policing and monitoring of social space, and the shared experience of "ontological insecurity."[2] While city boosters have sought to project an uplifting image
of Johannesburg after apartheid as a thriving cosmopolitan metropolis with world-class aspirations, newspaper accounts, political commentaries, documentary and narrative films, and television programs have
portrayed this sprawling hypermetropolis largely as a dangerous and violent place, haunted by the uncanny specter of the unknown and the unpredictable, with a troubled past and an uncertain future. The disturbing afterlife of white minority rule has reappeared in the distorted shape
of renewed obsession with danger. Crime and the violence associated
with it have become the dominant metaphors for the risks present in
the everyday social experience of urban living. Repeated often enough,
these disturbing images of foreboding and unease congeal into proleptic
projections of insecurity as a permanent condition of city life. Exaggerated or not, shared unease about personal safety and imminent threat
have not only reinforced the widespread belief that the breakdown of social order has reached crisis proportions but also put into motion calls for
the expanded use of disciplinary force to root out crime and disorder.[3]

The central argument of this book is that heightened anxieties about the perils of everyday urban living have spilled over into an obsession with security, in which an oversaturation of ominous signs of vulnerability has produced what amounts to a constant state of collective panic that more often than not identifies the black urban poor as the source of danger. Unease, uncertainty, and suspicion have become the main ingredients that bind the collective experience of urban living in Johannesburg after apartheid around a culture of fear. In a city in which the near-compulsive fixations on crime and violence have insinuated themselves into the social fabric of everyday life, panic preparedness and risk aversion have become the chief planning principles guiding what Mike Davis has termed the "militarization of urban space." This "crusade to secure the city" has found concrete expression in the turn toward proactive (and increasingly aggressive) methods of policing disorder and disciplining urban public space.[4] An obsession with security has inscribed itself in the built environment through such elaborate design features of defensive urbanism as capsular architecture, fortress aesthetics, and citadel formation. This hardening of the urban landscape is embodied in what Nan Ellin has termed the "architecture of fear."[5]

II

One primary aim of this book is to trace the diminishing role of state-sponsored law enforcement in policing the city and to examine the replacement of public policing with private security management in combating crime and disorder in the residential suburban neighborhoods of Johannesburg after the transition to parliamentary democracy. This breakdown the putative state monopoly on the legitimate use of force and violence was neither inevitable nor necessary. In trying to understand these evolving patterns of security governance, this book seeks to contribute to a history of the present, that is, to demonstrate how the concrete circumstances of the retreat of public law enforcement and the expanded role of private security gradually became possible and eventually unavoidable.[6]

This book is less about what public policing agencies and private security companies actually do on the ground than about the force of circumstances that brought these two different organizations into relation with each other. In Johannesburg, novel approaches to the production of security have become perhaps the leading edge of a wholesale shift in thinking about risk management, crime prevention, and safe spaces. At least in theory, a key element in conventional modernist approaches to law enforcement and crime prevention is the belief that the monopoly on organized and official violence should remain in the exclusive hands of the public police force and all those state agencies and branches associated with the criminal justice system. In Johannesburg after apartheid, this principle quickly unraveled. Public policing agencies have suffered from a lack of resources, skills, and training. In the popular imagination, public policing agencies are incapable of maintaining law and order. At best, they are seen as well-meaning but overstretched. At worst, they have acquired a reputation for incompetence, corruption, and brutality. Deep levels of resentment of the public police are definitely holdovers from the apartheid period. But the ways that these policing agencies have operated in the postapartheid period has created new kinds of mistrust and ambivalence. Private security agencies have filled in the gaps, promising to provide security for a price. With their access to the latest technology, their visible display of weaponry, and their reputation for no-nonsense policing, private security companies have seized the upper hand, increasingly eating away at functions that were once exclusively reserved for public law enforcement agencies.[7]

The private security industry is huge and multifaceted. According to industry estimates, the annual turnover for the private security industry is more than R 50 billion ($3.7 billion). Since the early 2000s, the number of private security guards has more than doubled. The private security industry employs close to 500,000 active security officers across South Africa (with a total of 1.5 million registered)—more than twice the size of the public police force and bigger than the public police and military forces combined. Much of this private security business is located in Gauteng, the premier economic hub of South Africa and site of Johannesburg and Pretoria. According to the Private Security Industry Regulatory Authority (PSIRA), more than 40 percent of the estimated 8,650 active security businesses in the country are located in Gauteng.[8] Perhaps the industry's largest branch consists of companies that protect corporate property and assets, that monitor employees working for large corporations, and that provide security for work sites such as mines, factories, and warehouses. The study of these types of private companies is beyond the scope of my research. The primary focus of my book centers on a distinct type of company—the type employed by individual homeowners and residential associations to protect property and ensure individual safety.

III

Tracing the genealogy of security management strategies—both as material products and as allegories for the anxious city—involves deciphering architectural styles as much as ethnographic observation and textual analysis of interview data. Constructed under the influence of siege architecture, the built environment is an active agent in the formation of urban identities. Living in fear behind high walls and security gates, frightened residents have collectively built a shared understanding of the danger lurking outside. What unites suburban residents is a collective paranoia that arises from the perceived threat of crime and violence.

The production of enclosed places—the fortification of private homes, the cordoning off of public streets, and the sequestering of residential neighborhoods—figures prominently in this book. Placemaking involves not only the planning and design of material sites but also the creation of spatialized images that reflect values, sentiments, and beliefs about the city. As the material embodiments of city-building processes, spatial products are infused with powerful messages and symbolic meaning. The production of space consists of more than a serial accumulation of material objects that can be viewed objectively in terms of their style, form, and function. Put more specifically, the built environment constitutes an integral part of the subjective experience of everyday life. As visible and durable objects, spatial products embody both city-building practices and cultural values. The cultures of fear and paranoia that pervade all aspects of everyday life in Johannesburg are the primary driving force behind a broad range of consumer practices related to managing risk and ensuring security.

This book is premised on the view that seemingly ordinary city-building practices, particularly architecture, urban design, and city planning, are not benign or merely technical exercises directed only at replacing worn-out, degraded, and useless places with reworked ones put to the highest and best use, but instead are tactical instruments of power employed to enforce particular visions of urbanity that reflect the vested interests of the powerful at the expense of the powerless. By drawing attention to the ways that power works through the seams and capillaries of urban space, it is possible to expose the unacknowledged complicity of those in architecture, urban design, and city planning with those in real estate in fashioning a fragmented urban landscape that has shut out—whether deliberately or inadvertently, it matters little—the largely black urban poor. Given the feigned innocence and neutrality that often accompany the exercise of power, it is relatively easy to overlook the often hidden motives that architects, designers, and builders harbor when they construct these fortified enclaves. The architectural discourses that accompany the creation of these spatial enclosures legitimate the erection of barriers, walls, and fences on the grounds that the concern for safety is a value of the highest order that displaces considerations of social inclusion. These new building typologies that stress separation and enclosure embody both the architecture of fear and the urbanization of panic. This stress on insecurity and anxiety are themes that do not find themselves in synchronicity with the romanticized, boosterist image of Johannesburg as an emergent world-class city that has taken great strides to shed its odious apartheid past.[9]

IV

> The city is, rather, a *state of mind*, a body of customs and traditions, and of the organized attitudes and sentiments that inhere in these customs and are transmitted with this tradition.
>
> —Robert Park[10]

Classical theories of the modern metropolis typically conceive of the city as a material entity, or a physical presence, marked by boundaries, bisected by lines, and measured in distances. In short, these conventional approaches frame the city as a spatial grid that becomes progressively known through the rigorous application of such instrumental technologies as observing, measuring, mapping, surveying, picturing, and naming. They presume, in other words, that the most revealing aspects of the city lie on the *surface*, that is, embodied in its visible and apparent features. This stress on visibility privileges the display of maps, flow charts, graphs, statistics, surveys, photographs, and moving images as a means of bringing to light the essential characteristics of the city. Anchored in positivist-realist epistemologies that rigidly separate (observable) fact from (normative) value, these conventional approaches look on the cityscape as a legible site of revelation—a bounded, knowable object that becomes known through the assemblage of hard facts, incontrovertible data, and verifiable truths. In this analytic framework, it is not that the city itself is inherently unknowable but that inadequate tools and techniques produce an incomplete knowledge of it.[11]

This trope of visibility remains the central methodological principle guiding such diverse modes of inquiry as positivist social science and ethnographic field research. Yet this almost exclusive reliance on surface appearances—that is, what can be seen as visible objects—ignores other ways of making sense of the city. As Walter Benjamin insightfully pointed out in his brilliant yet unfinished study of the Paris arcades, urban residents do not live merely in a material world but also in their imaginations. The city in the popular imagination, the imagined and imaginary city, exists outside the scopic regimes of visibility. Images of the city—expressed in dreams and desires, fears and nightmares, images and representations—mediate that material existence in powerfully suggestive ways, rendering the city as much a state of mind as an assemblage of material objects and juxtaposition of physical places.[12] This way of comprehending the city dispenses with scopic regimes of visibility in favor of an interpretive reading of the city as a text or script.[13] Approaching the city as an imagined (or imaginary) place, a site of collective memory, or an iconic signifier lays particular stress on the invisible, the hidden from view, the uncanny, the strange (or the strangely familiar), the unknown and unknowable, the immaterial, the opaque, and the fleeting.[14]

V

By and large, scholarly writing in urban studies has focused a great deal of attention on the materiality of cities: the shape of the built environment, the evolution of diverse spatial forms, and the various topographical features that shape the contours of the landscape. As Grady Clay argued some time ago, this conventional way of viewing cities as stage settings and visual compositions has framed urban analysis largely in terms of order and unity, scale and space, light and shadow, and color and texture. This monoperspectival approach to understanding cities amounted to a "kind of tunnel vision" that has downplayed the imaginative dimension of urban living.[15]

The everyday experience of urban living is always and already constituted and structured by histories, stories, and memories—both personal and collective. The physical characteristics of the built environment of cities do not exist apart from the symbolic meanings attached to them. This fluid and porous movement between the material and the immaterial, the real and the imaginary, complicates conventional approaches to understanding urban life that rely on quantifying, measuring, and classifying alone. In so doing, such movement produces the city that comes alive in the popular imagination. This imagined city (or what Robert Park famously called a "state of mind") is fashioned and animated as much by various representations of urban life found in gossip and rumor, apocryphal stories, urban legends, hearsay, myths, fiction writing, documentary film, cinema, television broadcasts, newspaper accounts, visual arts, posted warning signs, and graffiti as by actual places. Popular images of the city—cognitive maps or mental pictures that circulate as tacit understandings—have always played a powerful role in shaping the architectural design of urban space and the contours of the built environment.[16] The phantasmagoric dreamworld produced by these popular images gives rise to the haunting, uncanny, and unsettling qualities of urban life.[17]

Taken together, this diffusion of ideas, thoughts, and opinions—what ordinary people generally accept as commonsense knowledge, whether accurate or not in its details—forms an integral part of the experience of urban living. These ideas inhabit the popular imagination as indisputable social facts, and as such they help to create a climate of public opinion. "If [urban residents] define situations as real," to borrow an old aphorism from W. I. Thomas, "then they are real in their consequences."[18] The palpable power of hearsay and unfounded beliefs derives from their capacity to inspire people to act as though they are unassailable truths or genuinely accurate assessments of social realities.[19] In conversations about the city, there are no innocent narratives. Stories told about the experience of urban living always contain moral judgments, ominous warnings, and prescriptive guidance. Rumors reflect social anxieties and shape subjectivities, fashioning the way urban residents see themselves in relation to others.[20]

The experience of city life consists of an assemblage of overexposed impressions, fleeting afterimages, sensibilities, perceptions, structures of feeling, and modes of thinking that exist in an unstable relationship with the objective reality of social facts and verifiable truth.[21] The intrinsic instability of these impressions means that they can never operate as the unproblematic record of the actual state of affairs. These images allow us to redraw city maps as a semiotic field, or as an aggregation of symbols, codes, and signs invested with almost mythical self-referentiality.[22] It is this disjointed synthesis of the material and immaterial, the real and the imagined, that creates the urban uncanny, or that sense of anxiety about the unknown and the unanticipated.[23]

VI

> In place of the one-to-one fit between evidence and inference—the basis of functional analysis, and the normal procedure in empirical research—[reading the signs] proposes a triadic relationship in which "signifiers" lord it over the "signified," while external reality (the lowly "referent") lurks uneasily in the background, a ghostly presence at the banquet, flitting from table to table, an unwanted guest, refused the right to speak.
> —Raphael Samuel[24]

Cities, in the everyday experience of their inhabitants, are *at one and the same time* actually existing material environments and imagined places, or (to put it another way) categories of thought, depicted in the popular media and in political commentaries, photographs, street maps, professional planning proposals, flowcharts, graphs, and statistics. The *lived* spaces of cities exist as fleeting image, conjecture, and projection as much as they consist of the physical fabric of buildings and streets, bricks and mortar, and concrete and steel.[25] As Jonathan Raban has argued, "The city as we know it, the *soft city* of illusion, myth, aspiration, and nightmare, is as real, perhaps more real, than the *hard city*" of architects, planners, and city builders.[26]

Contrary to the conventional approach to understanding cities in terms of their physical attributes and morphological characteristics, Raban emphasized the subjective qualities of urban experience in which the arbitrariness of signs and the plasticity of images shape the meaning of everyday life. In paying heed to these prescriptions, the point of departure for *Panic City* is a call for a shift in the locus of inquiry from "the study of social facts to that of the symbolic space they inhabit." This insistence on "reading the signs," as Raphael Samuel suggested, "offers a more prismatic way of looking at the city than a positivist-inspired pre-occupation with the facts." It invites us to consider the experience of urban living through the prism of the perceived "truth" of beliefs. In its search for meaning, reading the signs "transfers attention from the study of 'objective' reality to the categories in and through which it is perceived, from collective consciousness to cognitive codes, from social being to the symbolic order."[27]

Yet the hermeneutical study of the production of meaning runs the risk of becoming trapped in the "prison-house of language" in which the descent into discourse "dissolves the real in a web of significations," thereby offering no escape from the labyrinthine maze of words.[28] The point of departure for *Panic City* is that crime and insecurity are at *one and the same time* actual social facts with a real existence on the ground and social constructs, or rhetorical devices, with mythic characteristics. Conversations about crime and danger give voice to fears that mobilize homeowners and neighborhood associations to take action.

Reading the city as an assemblage of signs enables us to unpack the sense of place that urban residents attach to the built environment. Writers as diverse as Walter Benjamin, Georg Simmel, Robert Park, Jonathan Raban, Jean Baudrillard, Roland Barthes, Italo Calvino, Henri Lefebvre, and Michel de Certeau have drawn our attention to how the real and the imaginary comingle in ways that shape our ideas about specific cities. Whatever our point of departure or our angle of vision, what should be evident is that this trope of the city as script or image has a long history. There is nothing particularly novel or postmodern about it. In the 1970s, the discourse of the city as text was an intense debate primarily involving architects, literary critics, and cultural theorists who were struggling to make sense of new directions in city building after the eclipse of modernism. At the start of the twenty-first century, the discourse of the city as image has been commandeered by city boosters, real estate developers, and local officials seeking to use urban spectacle to attract capital investment and to lure tourists. What is central to this place-marketing (or branding) approach to city building is the construction of such aesthetic spaces for cultural consumption as festival marketplaces, refurbished waterfronts, trophy buildings, and iconic museums. As Anna Kligmann has argued, the image of the city has moved from skylines to brandscapes in which buildings function not just as material objects alone but also as advertisements and destinations. In the new ex-

perience economy, sensations, even lifestyles, have replaced material objects as products for consumption.[29]

VII

This book takes the experience of urban living in Johannesburg as its analytic point of departure. The imagining of disorder brought about by
the almost paranoid fixation on crime and violence functions as an unstable system of "floating, unanchored signification[s]."[30] Exploring the
murky intersection between the actual and the imaginary realms of urban life enables me to address questions about how urban residents relate to the ephemeral world of objects, signs, and images that surround
them. In doing so, I seek to understand what it means to inhabit a city
gripped by suspicion and fear. Focusing on the imaginative (or phantasmagoric) dimension of city living provides a useful vantage point from
which to investigate the connections between the steady stream of unsettling images of the "dangerous city" and the spread of a new fortification aesthetic that has come to dominate city-building efforts in Johannesburg after apartheid. The, modern surveillance technologies,
walled-off compounds, obsession with security (apparent in suburban
home design), and suffocation of the conventional public spaces of the
city have become social forces in their own right, dictating the choice
of building typologies, the spatial design of enclosed places, and the aggressive policing of spaces of social congregation.[31]

Imagining the city as a dangerous place inevitably influences ways
of acting in relation to the built environment. This collective sense of
unease has prompted affluent urban residents to experiment with new
spatial strategies designed to isolate them in hideaways cut off from the
public spaces of the city. They have used their fears about the dangerous city to justify their withdrawal into exclusive, fortified enclaves for
residence, work, leisure, and consumption. The steady accretion of such
sequestered places as citadel office complexes, gated residential communities, enclosed shopping malls, festival marketplaces, barricaded
suburban neighborhoods, and other gentrified "shoppertainment" fan-
tasy-scapes have set in motion new patterns of spatial segregation and
social exclusion that have substituted socioeconomic status for the formal racial separation that prevailed under apartheid rule.[32]

As the embodiments of siege architecture, these fortified enclaves can perhaps best be seen as metonyms for the urbanization of panic. They appeal to anxious urban residents who seek to avoid the social heterogeneity of city life, with its chance encounters and mingling across class and race lines. The new spatial enclosures that have proliferated across the urban landscape have created places that contradict the normative ideals of openness, equal accessibility, and freedom of circulation that helped to shape the classical modernist understanding of urban public space.[33] The privatization of social gathering places, policing of boundaries, and restricted access to zones of luxury have combined to partition the urban landscape into a galaxy of fortified enclaves disembedded from the social fabric of the city.[34]

VIII

The haphazard and fragmented urban form of Johannesburg after apartheid has rendered the cityscape difficult to decipher and represent. All sorts of observers, ranging from urban planners to novelists and from municipal authorities to newspaper reporters have struggled to come to terms with the changing features of urban life. Seen from afar, the urban landscape seems indecipherable.[35] In order to grasp the broad social forces that have restructured everyday life in the city, it is sometimes helpful to focus on the incremental and seemingly inconsequential alterations in the quotidian practices that have fundamentally reshaped the experience of urban living. These routine patterns and mundane expectations correspond with what Michel Foucault called the "microphysics of power," an unstable network of practices that insinuate themselves into the cracks and crevices of the everyday social fabric of the city.[36]

Looking at security governance regimes (or extended security networks) from afar—the bird's-eye view—erases the subtle differences that distinguish the many approaches to policing and securing residential neighborhoods. In contrast, the microscopic view enables us to appreciate the improvisational qualities of these experiments with security governance. These "bubbles of security" are sociotemporal "spaces of different size, purpose, and modes of operation," Christine Hentschel has argued. They can be porous or impenetrable, stationary or mobile. These security bubbles can be artificially attached to existing arrangements and incongruously grafted onto "entrenched architectures" of spatial governance, thereby creating (hybrid) layered and overlapping networks. They are uneasy spaces, crisscrossed with "uncertainty and exaggerated expectations." These cocooned spaces have different conditions of existence and expected life spans. They incorporate both private and public spaces, and they bring together both formal and informal modes of governance. Whatever variation exists in terms of scope, scale, or distinct modes of regulation, these bubbles of security share a common purpose: the commitment to safety and the management of risk.[37]

Focusing attention on the cultural process of the fashioning of demonic figures as objects of fear and avoidance or of scorn and ridicule can assist us in illuminating the contested terrain of popular beliefs, myth, and collective memory that swirls around the cityscape. It is not simply what actually exists but what people believe to exist that shapes their understanding of politics, their approach to social action, and their attitude toward the imaginary Other. Social imaginaries act as a metaphorical counterweight—an imaginative alter ego—to the utopian vision of a rainbow nation. To explore these imaginative dimensions of social life does not mean to suggest that the social realities of urban disorder are constructed out of whole cloth or are entirely determined by the system of ideas or language through which they are expressed. In other words, the anxieties of urban living are not simply the outcome of fertile imaginations—social constructions autonomously produced as pure fiction. These sentiments have an actual social history and must be understood within the socioeconomic context of the evolving city—always unfinished and in transition. In the face of the problematic domains of everyday experience, ordinary people simultaneously find refuge in, manipulate, and modify the ways they discuss and interpret the social world around them.[38]

IX

Beyond their morphological forms and physical appearances, cityscapes are products of signification, discourse, and rhetoric.[39] The depictions of urban life found in such diverse sources as novels and popular literature, photojournalism, advertising campaigns, planning manuals, tourist guidebooks, promotional materials, political commentary, the mass media, and everyday conversations create impressions (whether lasting or fleeting) that amount to "cognitive maps" of urban space. The power of these cognitive maps derives from the way they inhabit the imagination, orienting urban residents in space and time and thereby enabling them to vicariously experience places they have never been to.[40]

As with all mediated modes of representation, these cognitive maps of the urban landscape are notoriously slippery and indeterminate. They produce at best partial glimpses of the unbounded experience of urban life. As Michel de Certeau has persuasively argued, to presume a privileged vantage point—the Solar Eye, or the God's-eye view—creates the "fiction of knowledge," or the illusory, unfounded belief that the concrete actuality of the whole city can be captured in a single all-encompassing glance.[41] Yet urban residents routinely engage in the collective fiction of metonymically inferring the whole of the city from its parts.[42] Envisioned through widely divergent vantage points, city images can oscillate between wondrous sites of pleasure and spectacle or frightful places filled with danger.[43]

Reading the signs provides an analytic point of departure for studying the power of belief to trigger social action. Images of urban space always vacillate between "the reassuring solidity of knowingness and the sinister voids of unknowingness." Viewing Johannesburg as an agglomeration of signs requires us to move between surface appearances and disappearances, presences and absences, and the visible and invisible. Probing beneath the visible layers of the known city always yields the unanticipated.[44] In times of uncertainty, spaces of the city are often depicted as chaotic and disorderly, in which "unexpected, unpredictable encounters can easily lead to dreadful dangers."[45] Under circumstances in which the conventional mechanisms for securing the social order fail to function properly, the boundaries of urban space become the contested sites of anxiety and unease. This shadowy terrain—or the "dark side of space," as Anthony Vidler puts it—operates as a telling metaphor for all the possible erosions of urban well-being. As harbingers of the unseen and the unknown, these "dark spaces" act to conceal, in their hidden recesses and opaque margins, "all the objects of fear and phobia that have returned with such insistency to haunt the imaginations" of those urban residents "who have tried to stake out" places of safety and comfort for themselves in the contested urban realm.[46] In the nightmare city, the dark spaces of the city threaten to overwhelm the light spaces by invasion, pollution, and contamination. As Steve Pile puts it, "the city becomes a space of paranoia."[47]

The urban uncanny thus arises at the intersection of what can be confidently known and what remains eerily unknown, or between what can be visualized and what can be only imagined. The uncanniness of urban space finds concrete expression in strangely familiar places, in the opaque worlds of shadow and decay. Uncanny spaces are those that register fear and dread, such as cemeteries, morgues, and mental institutions, as well as those that display urban ruin: abandoned buildings, boarded-up shops, and other derelict structures. The urban uncanny appears in the seemingly endless networks of highways, asphalt arteries, and alleyways that function not as inviting spaces of community but as corridors of flight, anonymous movement, and perpetual transience. To speak of the urban uncanny is to suggest a disenchantment with urban life.[48] The architectural design of enclosed places is thoroughly imbricated with the urban uncanny—the heightened anxiety with what is unknown and unknowable about the city.[49]

X

This book chronicles the origins and development of security initiatives—what I call extended security networks—in the mostly affluent residential suburbs of Johannesburg. The immediate post-1994 moment marked a watershed in policing—a time when old-style mechanisms of repressing political dissent lost any semblance of credibility. Hence, they have given way to a host of experimental initiatives designed to reconcile democratic accountability with the need for crime control. These extended security networks form a kind of mobile technology of urban spatial management that is selectively implemented in diverse settings to achieve the shared objectives of safety and protection. They take shape through hybrid assemblages of social practices, material objects, and regulatory procedures. As a mode of urban governance, extended security networks bring together participating social actors, institutional rules, logistics, expert knowledge, and hard and soft infrastructure—all of which coalesce around the shared goal of risk management.[50]

This book is an attempt at critical engagement—selective, tentative, and provisional—with the capillary micropolitics of everyday policing in the affluent residential neighborhoods of Johannesburg in the decades after the end of apartheid and the transition to parliamentary democracy. It begins with the claim that scholars and political commentators who have concentrated their attention almost exclusively on the big questions of policing and crime control, constitutional rights, and citizenship have largely overlooked the miniscule, incremental modifications to the urban social fabric that have reshaped the ways in which ordinary urban residents experience the city.

Focusing our critical gaze on the microscopic dynamics of everyday policing and security management in the residential neighborhoods enables us to respond more sensitively to the politics of agency as these take shape on the ground, involving as they do the dense web of relations between negotiation and compromise, coercion and force, complicity and affiliation, mimicry and contagion, and resistance and refusal. Restricting the scope of analysis to the unbundling of security services and the retreat of public law enforcement without an acknowledgment of initiatives from below runs the risk of overlooking how the obsessive fixation on crime has spurred neighborhood associations to actively engage in the production of their own security outside of effective state regulation. Contrary to the singular pathway suggested by the rhetoric of neoliberalism, the privatization of security services in Johannesburg has taken place in fits and starts along multiple routes, determined as much by ad hoc experimentation as by deliberate design.

The thinking behind this book combines elements of deductive theorizing with empirically grounded storytelling. Conventional approaches to studying cities typically begin by isolating a single object of study and privileging a particular methodological stance. I do not offer a deductive argument that begins with an a priori theoretical understanding and then proceeds to sift through mountains of information to find empirical evidence to support the original claims. Instead, I construct a topological analysis that examines the patterns of correlation in which heterogeneous elements—regulatory regimes, governance techniques, material forms, institutional rules, and technologies of power—are configured in often unexpected ways.[51] In short, I favor a more robust, eclectic approach that brings together both analytic and synthetic ways of capturing the complexities of urban life.[52] On the analytic side, this book seeks to break down apparently seamless, undifferentiated wholes into discrete parts. On the synthetic side, it tries to piece together disparate fragments into composite wholes as a way of constructing a montage of urban life. In the writing itself, I have employed multiple and fragmentary types of prose narrative (incorporating ethnographic fieldwork, unstructured interviews, embodied observation, and journalistic accounts) in the presentation of the argument.[53] Ethnographic fieldwork involving on-site investigations and personal interactions can often yield surprising and unanticipated findings, in which accidental discoveries that derive from unplanned encounters can produce revelatory moments that steer the conceptual analysis in unexpected directions. In employing this first-person study of social situations, I moved between unobtrusive observation of social interactions and engaged dialogue with key informants. The collection of empirical evidence, the analysis of findings, and the actual writing itself could not proceed without reflexivity. While I began with a loose set of theoretical ideas and analytic categories, I remained open to revising my initial assumptions.[54]

My choice of stories to tell and sites to investigate in no way exhausts the full range of possible areas for scholarly investigation. By piecing together stories about insecurity and fear, aggressive policing techniques, and neighborhood associations as self-mobilized communities into a kind of montage, it is possible to reveal a composite picture of the urban landscape taken as an assembled whole. Arranged with the help of storytelling techniques, these accounts of public policing agencies, private security companies, and neighborhood associations provide critical evidence for my understanding of the urbanization of panic.[55]

Acknowledgments

The origins of this book can be traced to my early impressions of how anxieties about crime and danger have become such permanent fixtures of everyday life in Johannesburg. From the start, I was surprised with how affluent and middle-class residents have taken for granted the creation of formidable perimeter walls, locked security gates, and high-voltage electric fencing. I became curious with how and why this preoccupation with security became so normalized and so much an integral feature of everyday life. During the time I have spent in Johannesburg, I have been followed, robbed, stabbed, and almost carjacked. I have counted more than a dozen crime-related incidents with which I have been somehow connected. My experiences triggered my interest in constructing an analytical account of fear, risk, and obsession with security in the city.

This book draws on many years of thinking about public policing and private security in Johannesburg. The empirical findings are based on numerous research trips to Johannesburg starting in May 2008 and ending in July 2018. Over the course of researching and writing this book, I accumulated a great number of debts (large and small) to others who, in their own peculiar ways, provided assistance of various kinds.

First, I am extremely thankful that Andy Clarno and I decided to work together to do some of our ethnographic field research. During a frantic period of intense research activity (June–July 2012), he and I jointly conducted around fifty interviews with key figures in neighborhood associations, private security companies, and public law enforcement officials. He is absolutely masterful at getting around the city by car. Together, we did all sorts of on-site visits, including to the head offices of private security companies and to the annual meeting of Securex, the continent's leading security and fire trade exhibition held at the Gallagher Convention Centre in Midrand. Andy and I agreed that each of us could use the empirical findings from our joint research efforts in whatever particular ways we saw fit. In writing this book, I have borrowed ideas and virtually whole paragraphs from an article that he and I published in *Social Dynamics*. Our interpretations of the interviews conducted for this book converged in expected ways, but they also diverged in some unexpected ways. Perhaps not so surprisingly, his book is quite different from mine.

This research would not have been possible without the cooperation of the many people whom I interviewed over the course of numerous research trips to Johannesburg. I am grateful for the willingness of dozens of people—including public law enforcement officers, owners and managers of private security companies, key figures in neighborhood associations, and various experts in the field of security—to answer my questions with surprising candor. Although I often did not share their beliefs or specific outlooks, I gained respect for them. What I found strange is that, with one exception, these individuals were never reluctant to talk with me. Members of neighborhood associations invited me to accompany them to weekly or monthly meetings with public police officials at local station houses. Public police officers sometimes took me on nighttime patrols of the inner city. Private security managers and owners are very wary of journalists. Once they learned I was only an academic, they were relieved, allowing me access to their control rooms (with CCTV monitors) and training facilities.

I also owe a debt of gratitude to Alex Wafer, who introduced me to Moses Molefe (not his real name), the head of the Community Policing Forum (CPF) in the inner city. Alex and I conducted a number of walkabouts in Hillbrow, Berea, and Joubert Park, including several nighttime excursions with Moses and the Community Policing Forum. I have benefited in countless ways from the generosity of many individuals and institutions. In particular, I would like to acknowledge the conversations with Danny Nuñes (chair of the Sector Crime Forum in Melville) and the email dialogue with Andrew Pittman, Paul Mills, and Eric van Gils, all associated with the Melville Security Initiative. They provided me with maps of the camera placement in Melville.

I am grateful for the constructive and encouraging support I have received from colleagues at the University of Michigan, especially those in the Department of Afro-American and African Studies, and at Taubman College. I have benefited from the friendship of María Arquero De Alarcón, Omolade Adunbi, Howard Stein, Kelly Askew, Derek Peterson, Danny Herwitz, and Adam Ashforth. I also owe a great debt of gratitude to Olaia Chivite Amigo for her wonderful skills in constructing the maps, figures, and photographic displays in this book. (Data for the maps is copyrighted by OpenStreetMap contributors and can be found at https://www.openstreetmap.org.)

This research would not have been possible without generous financial support of various departments, programs, and individuals at the University of Michigan, including Taubman College (through Associate Dean Geoff Thun), a generous subvention grant from University of Michigan Organized Research (UMOR), and funding at multiple stages from the Department of Afro-American and African Studies. In Johannesburg, I would like to acknowledge the friendship and assistance of Philip Harrison and Yan Yang, Graeme Gotz, Richard Ballard, Keith Breckenridge, Rod Alence, Ingrid Mertins (a filmmaker credited with the highly acclaimed film *Shafted*), Sarah Charlton, Marie Huchzermeyer, Sydney Radebe, and Mfaniseni (Fana) Sihlongonyane. While at Oxford (March–June, 2016), I benefited a great deal from enlightening conversations with Jonny Steinberg, Ian Loader, Lucia Zedner, Idalina Baptista, Colin Bundy, and Miles Larmer. I would like to thank Karina Landman and Willem Badenhurst, who allowed me to make use of several maps that they constructed and that Olaia Chivite Amigo reconfigured to suit my purposes.

I would to thank Alan Harvey, the press director at Stanford University Press, for his initial interest in my book manuscript. I have worked closely with Marcela Cristina Maxfield, acquisitions editor in sociology, and with Sunna Juhn, editorial assistant. I would also like to acknowledge the considerable assistance of Gretchen Otto for work on copyediting. I completed the final stages of this book project while a fellow at the Stellenbosch Institute for Advanced Study (STIAS). I would like to acknowledge the support of the STIAS staff, including the new director, Edward Kirumira, Christoff Pauw (program manager), and Nel-Marie Loock (program administrator), and the friendship of the lively group of fellows assembled there. My brothers, Mark, Dennis, Greg, and Thomas, provide irreverent conversations at least once a year. The hiking has fallen off over the years, and apocryphal stories of doubtful authenticity have overtaken unassailable remembrance. My sons, Jeremy and Andrew, and my daughter, Alida, encouraged me with their presence (both close and distant). As always, my greatest personal debt goes to my wife, Anne Pitcher, who inspired me with her thoughtful interventions at every step along this journey.

PANIC CITY

Introduction

South Africa is one of the most dangerous countries of the world that is not at war.

Helen Epstein, "The Mystery of AIDS in South Africa"[1]

With the end of apartheid and the transition to parliamentary democracy in 1994, urban residents of Johannesburg were buoyed by the promise of political normalization and the hope for racial reconciliation. Yet with the passage of time, the mundane realities of everyday life have gradually overshadowed these great expectations of social stability. With sluggish economic growth and few appreciable benefits trickling down to the urban poor, the "new South Africa" has been inundated with noir visions of chaos and disorder, degeneration and decadence, disintegration and subversion, and invasion and contamination. Urban residents of Johannesburg have been consumed by a heightened anxiety about the uneasiness of everyday living and haunted by inarticulate fears about what the future might bring.

The unsettled circumstances of urban living in Johannesburg after apartheid have proven to be a fertile breeding ground for a variety of "alarmist fantasies" that occasionally spill over into genuine moral panics.[2] As exaggerated expressions of popular mood, moral panics belong to the imaginative dimension of social life. They typically arise at times of political instability and uncertainty, usually after portentous moments of great upheaval when the certitudes of the past have been swept away and new ones are not yet firmly in place. Theories of moral panic do not dismiss concerns over the real dangers of urban living as purely fanciful or illusory. Rather they point to the importance of analyzing sociopolitical, ideological, and discursive frameworks within which certain kinds of seemingly inexplicable behavior come to be interpreted as cause for alarm or as socially threatening.[3] The apprehension and anxiety linked to urban disorder can be accommodated more easily if traced to an identifiable cause and attached to a particular socially stigmatized menace. A feeling of victimhood engenders an urge to identify culprits, real or imagined, and to look for scapegoats on which to place blame for social ills.[4]

It is in this sense that those ordinary urban residents who fear their own victimhood construct cautionary tales about imaginary landscapes inhabited by menacing, spectral figures who are the embodiments of the perils of urban living. This juncture is where (white) class privilege and racial prejudices come together. Popular discourses framed around urban danger—sensationalized in newspaper accounts, theatrical performances, lurid television reports, or popular films and passed along through rumor, urban legend, and gossip—identify unwanted foreigners, international crime syndicates, unemployed urban youth, street-corner drug peddlers, and insalubrious prostitutes as sources of evil, carriers of perdition, and threats to urban order and social stability.[5] Filtered through the always-present lens of racial stereotyping, black lives occupying the streets have become objects of suspicion.[6] These alarmist stories about urban threats give voice to individual and collective anxieties of losing control of the public spaces of the city, and they provide both a convenient excuse for retreat behind fortifications and a justification for urban revanchism.[7]

Regardless of their varied sources of inspiration, moral panics in urban South Africa are not without historical precedent. One can identify similar alarmist fantasies in other places and in other historical periods. For example, municipal health officials in the early twentieth century used the threat of uncontrolled contagious diseases (the so-called sanitation syndrome) to justify forced removals from urban slums and the implementation of residential segregation; the *swaart gevaar* (black swamping) menace provided apartheid social engineers with a convenient excuse for tightening "influx controls" during the 1940s and 1950s; and the securocrats manufactured phobias about the Red Menace and the total (Communist) onslaught as useful rationales for the 1980s political crackdown on the internal anti-apartheid opposition.[8] But what gives these alarmist fantasies that have come to the surface after apartheid their historical specificity is that they have emerged at a time of slow economic growth and intense competition for available jobs, of an AIDS pandemic that has claimed tens of thousands of lives, of unprecedented influx of immigrants from all corners of the world, of a visible and expanding gap between the frightened (largely white) rich and the desperately (largely black) poor, and of an overextended state administration unable to provide basic social services for those who cannot afford to pay. During these times of uncertainty, large numbers of urban residents of Johannesburg have become consumed with apprehension about the invasion of "illegal aliens," the spread of contagious diseases, rising crime rates, and the contamination of drugs.[9]

This new dystopian dread has gone hand in hand with what has amounted to desperate efforts to remake the built environment of the city, to reshape the public spaces of the cityscape, and to redraw boundaries between the "haves" and the "have-nots." The emergence of a new spatial politics of closure and withdrawal has not only reinforced old class and racial divisions and separations but also created new cleavages and fault lines that have decisively cut against the grain of the uplifting political discourse of a more egalitarian, integrated, nonracial future. In their haste to clean up the streetscape, urban planners, city officials, and municipal police have sometimes advanced a city that is more disciplined than governed—that is, a city in which the problems are swept away rather than addressed up front. This obstinate approach has focused on symptoms of urban disorder rather than its underlying causes.[10]

The advent of a new democratic, multiracial order—underwritten by constitutional guarantees and enshrined in the lofty principles of equality, dignity, and freedom—has done little to alter the deeply ingrained structural imbalances of power and to challenge the vast disparities in opportunities and income that have been inherited from the past.[11] The belief that the de jure end of apartheid established a level playing field for the equal enjoyment of formal legal rights across race lines ignores how the "law serves to legitimize the existing social order."[12] Despite the emphasis on "individual autonomy, color-blind constitutionalism, and race-neutrality" embedded in formal legal liberalism, this approach to the practice of law and legal institutions tends to overlook the ways in which racial hierarchies are woven into the social fabric of everyday life. As Joel Modiri has cogently argued, "Life under law after apartheid" has not only reproduced the protection of white privilege but also perpetuated the systematic deprivation of vulnerable black people "through direct and indirect forms of racial marginalization."[13]

The law, legal ideologies, and legal culture are not "above politics" and "free from wider political influences" and pressures "but are in fact implicated in structuring and strengthening existing social arrangements and power relationships."[14] The emphasis in formal legal liberalism on law as objective "results in 'race neutral' laws which can only address the most blatant acts of racial discrimination but do not offer any insight" into the structural inequalities that disproportionately favor entrenched white privilege while simultaneously disadvantaging the black urban poor.[15] The alleged impartiality of the law "normalizes the status quo." Structural inequalities, including massive disparities in income and opportunity, are "enabled by law and tolerated by legal culture."[16]

Imagining Johannesburg as the Scene of the Crime

In Johannesburg after apartheid, the specter of crime and lawlessness has captured the popular imagination.[17] It matters little that the perceived threat of criminal violence is often incommensurate with the real risks to persons and property. For many middle-class residents of the affluent northern suburbs, the central city has become terra incognita, an inscrutable "no-go" zone to be avoided at all cost. The preoccupation with public order, law breaking, and policing is both a commentary on actual danger and risk and a reflection of a sometimes visible and sometimes hidden desire to rid the urban landscape of those considered to be potential criminals.[18]

What should be abundantly clear, especially for anyone who has been the victim of assault, robbery, or rape, is that crime itself (and the violence associated with it) is not socially constructed. It is real. Nevertheless, it can be said that the meanings attached to crime are social constructions.[19] At a time of uncertainty, crime often becomes a grand metaphor for social breakdown, chaos, and decline. Lawlessness becomes a socio-cultural marker for what has gone wrong with the expected order of things. The persistence of rumors, urban legends, and apocryphal stories of danger and foreboding indicate the instability of the boundaries between reality and imagination in the experience of city life. Reading or interpreting urban landscapes as visual or verbal texts, however, requires us to examine cityscapes not only in formal and functional terms but in figural and symbolic ways as well.[20]

The apparent disconnect between the fear of crime (along with the moral panics it invariably engenders) and the actual realities of crime requires some unpacking. What everyone acknowledges—from expert criminologists to public policing agencies in charge of collecting data and keeping statistical records of crime trends and patterns—is that criminality in Johannesburg (particularly residential neighborhoods) is a significant source of disquiet that does not seem to go away. The great difficulty with squaring the fear of crime with the actual realities on the ground is threefold. First, a great deal of crime goes unreported (residents feel, rightly so, that a resolution is very unlikely to come out of reporting a crime at a public police station). This "failure to report crime" is especially the case when black victims are faced with the choice of reporting a crime perpetrated by black assailants or just letting it go. Besides, there is plenty of circumstantial evidence to suggest that public policing agencies, especially in local police stations, notoriously falsely classify reported crimes as less serious than they are in order to ensure that statistics for their precincts do not look too bad in relation to other precincts. Staff promotions and public commendations depend on reducing crime. Second, private security companies operating under contract in residential neighborhoods are reluctant to report every crime (and to classify it under a serious crime category) since they keep their contracts because of their promise to reduce criminality. All private security companies release crime figures and statistics for residential neighborhoods in which they have contracts. They always report that crime has gone down once they were hired, and they never admit that crime has increased. Third, there is the confounding issue of overreporting. Insurance companies require that victims of crime report carjackings, burglaries, destruction of property, and the like. Again, there is plenty of circumstantial evidence to suggest that sometimes alleged "victims of crime" falsely report stolen property (especially automobiles and jewelry) just to "cash in" on fraudulent insurance claims. So in short, although it is possible to arrive at general assessments of crime, one cannot accurately claim, with any degree of reliability, the extent to which crime and crime categories ebb and flow over time, especially when referring to specific residential neighborhoods and police precincts.[21]

Freighted with symbolic meaning, such spatial interventions as private homes retrofitted to resemble fortified enclosures, the erection of physical barriers to close off public streets, high perimeter walls topped with electric fencing, the installation of CCTV cameras, and private security policing of the public streetscape of residential neighborhoods have acquired an excess of meaning as the material embodiments of defensive urbanism. This capsular logic reflects an obsession with security at a time of uncertainty.[22] Instead of fitting organically into the existing social fabric of residential neighborhoods, these spatial interventions are artificially inserted into the suburban landscape in ways that appear to reflect a dystopian impulse.[23] Taken together, these artificial spatial implants constitute the basic building blocks of a new urban configuration that has come into being—a metropolitan agglomeration that resembles what Paul Virilio has referred to as the "City of Panic," or what Lieven de Cauter has called the "capsular logic" of the fortified city.[24]

These spatial interventions seek to establish secure beachheads in an otherwise uncertain and dangerous urban environment. As such, they establish their own rules of engagement, their own extralegal sovereignty, and their own protocols for inclusion and exclusion. They represent virtually self-contained microregimes of spatialized power concentrated in particular locations. These are "imaginary worlds" born out of an obsession with security.[25]

The spatial landscape of Johannesburg consists of a hybrid assemblage of fortified enclaves, securitized residential neighborhoods, and sequestered redoubts cut off from the surrounding streetscape. The "protection services" of private security companies, automated security gates, and high perimeter walls topped with electrified fencing that surround suburban homes have become ubiquitous features in the middle-class residential neighborhoods. The driving force behind this fortification aesthetic can be traced to the (real and perceived) threats linked to crime and disorder.[26] This obsessive fixation on risk and danger did not originate with the formal end to racial segregation and the transition to parliamentary democracy. But the heightened anxieties about the insecurities of urban living have clearly assumed a historical specificity all their own over the past several decades.[27]

Along with other disappearing acts, the gradual fading away of American-style residential suburbs, with their tree-lined avenues, walkable streets, ample social gathering places, assorted commercial shops, and unencumbered views of homes and yards, has become cause for fond remembrance of a romanticized, idyllic past. This "mourning for the impossibility of a mythical return, for the loss of an enchanted world with clear borders and values," as Svetlana Boym has put it, has produced feelings of bewilderment and disorientation.[28] With the passage of time, these collective memories have become even more intense, blending with a sense of betrayal and the felt need to assign blame. Under the aegis of combating crime, new boundaries and fault lines have taken root. Almost overnight, border lines have entrenched themselves around private homes, and barricades have spilled over into residential neighborhoods. These bordering practices, once in place, infiltrate the collective memories of residents, providing a retroactive legitimation for their presence. Because they are so commonplace and routinized, the high walls, automated security gates, CCTV cameras, and proactive private security patrols have become standard features of suburban neighborhoods. For the most part, frightened homeowners have looked upon the piecemeal upgrading of fortification and increasingly draconian policing practices as the normal or "natural" outcome of efforts to combat crime in the residential neighborhoods of Johannesburg.[29]

In their feverish efforts to achieve a sense of security, paranoid homeowners have ironically become virtual prisoners in their own homes, afraid to walk the streets and to venture out after dark. This agoraphobia contributes to a growing sense of isolation, insularity, and individualism, which in turn breeds resentment and paranoia. Those middle-class urban residents who have not left the country have responded to their heightened feelings of unease by doing virtually everything possible to insulate themselves from it. In their frantic quest to ensure their own safety, suburban residents have turned to ever more sophisticated security measures. In the plush, formerly all-white suburbs, almost every house has a fully automated electronic security system with indoor and outdoor sensory detection devices. Frightened homeowners have raised their picturesque garden walls to more formidable heights, topping them with metal spikes and glass shards. They have unfurled reams of razor wire to block exposed perimeters. They have installed electric fencing that shocks when inadvertently touched and have hired armed human shields to screen themselves from the imagined criminals lurking outside and beyond their fortified bunkers. They have erected automated driveway gates, intercom systems, and surveillance cameras. They have added steel-plated security gates to restrict entry into their homes and have divided the interiors into any number of separate secure zones. Anxious suburbanites have enlisted the assistance of private security companies promising both immediate armed response to remote signals from ubiquitous "panic buttons" and full medical assistance in case of injury during an attack. In the sprawling townships, where crime can be even worse, schools, clinics, and other public buildings, as well as those private businesses that can afford it, also have their quota of armed guards and security alarms. In the business and commercial zones of the cityscape, every corporate headquarters complex and all office buildings have adopted their own intricate security arrangements that are subcontracted to private security firms providing everything from electronic monitoring systems to personal bodyguards.[30]

Anxious Urbanism

Johannesburg is a city inundated with suspicion. Nervous residents imagine the urban landscape as an uneven distribution of risks in which *safety* and *security* are relative terms. In the popular imagination, criminal subjects are cast in opposition to the socially constructed "normative identity" of law-abiding citizens who bear witness to the ideal conception of the orderly city and its well-functioning regulatory regimes and hence fully enjoy the rights and "protections of the due process of law."[31] Yet the criminal is not simply some shadowy counterpart to (or mirror opposite of) the law-abiding citizen but is an overdetermined spectral figure who represents all that is impure, unwanted, and disruptive. Criminality represents the antithesis of the rights of property ownership and the personal freedoms of law-abiding citizens. The phantasmagoric specter of criminality provides rhetorical justification for cleansing urban spaces of the unwanted poor.[32]

The specter of violent crime (and the dread that it engenders) has haunted the residential neighborhoods of Johannesburg for at least the past two decades, leaving in its wake a "structure of feeling" that amounts to a deeply embedded existential anxiety about potential risks.[33] These "crime troubles" represent a deeper "ontological insecurity" that is reflected in distrust of public authorities, fear of bodily harm, and suspicion of strangers.[34] The disturbing presence of suspected criminals (real or imagined) unsettles the longed-for stability and integrity of urban living and, as such, seems to embody the mismatch between the utopian ideal of the "good city" and the dystopian reality of disorderly urbanism. With dwindling faith in the effectiveness of public policing agencies to provide effective protection from criminal predations, frightened homeowners in affluent residential neighborhoods have experimented with various risk management strategies, which have made them increasingly dependent on the purchase of ever-more sophisticated security devices and have cemented their reliance on the "protective services" of private security companies.[35]

Unexpected encounters with strangers lurking beyond spatial boundaries of the familiar bring urban residents into contact with the "otherness" of the city. At a time of uncertainty, the seemingly capricious movement of strangers has added new layers of complexity to the idea of the unknown and the unfamiliar in the city. Unknown "others" disrupt and destabilize the expected flow of time associated with familiar places.[36] As John Rundell has argued, "The image of the stranger invariably accompanies the one of the alien, as someone who, whilst coming to live in the city, appears always as the outsider, and thus is always at hand as a subject of and for fear."[37] Banded incongruously together in residential associations in suburban neighborhoods, affluent homeowners have grappled with the strangeness of strangers by turning inward, by blocking out the unfamiliar. Viewed through the introverted lens of the deliberate design of enclosed places, the security-driven logic associated with the architecture of fear has produced the serial repetition of defensible enclaves and "hermetically sealed fortresses" catering to the social insulation, or social imprisonment, of frightened urban residents in their luxury laagers.[38]

Often depicted as disorderly and chaotic, the unfamiliar places of the city indicate where unexpected, unpredictable encounters are freighted with danger. The obsession with unknown figures who traverse urban space appears in "spatial stories" that depict fear and anxiety, threat and vulnerability, and victims and victimhood.[39] The unknown city becomes a dystopian place of paranoia in which the proverbial stranger becomes embodied in the phantomlike figure of the dangerous criminal whose unannounced ghostly presence sows unease and disquiet.[40]

The agoraphobic response to the unprotected open spaces of the city has produced particular social practices in which affluent suburban residents navigate the public streetscape according to rather strict protocols governing their tactics of movement and circulation. They hardly ever venture away from their fortified homes on foot, parking their vehicles behind automated security gates and keeping a vigilant eye on the rearview mirror in case they are followed home. These rules of engagement reflect the militarizing impulses that have come to dominate the production of urban space, in which risk management and crime reduction occupy center stage.[41]

No longer trusting public policing agencies to provide protection from criminal threats and no longer believing in the effectiveness of the criminal justice system to apprehend and punish wrongdoers, anxious residents have turned to private security companies to aggressively respond to unwanted intruders, to systematically police suburban streets, and to discipline criminal suspects.[42] This approach to security management corresponds to what Adi Ophir, Michal Givoni, and Sari Hanafi have called a "logic of inclusive exclusion"—a condition of existence that presupposes not only the exclusion of "unwanted Others" from the protections of the law but also the normalization of the "state of exception." Under these circumstances, suspected "potential criminals" do not enjoy the right to claim rights and are simultaneously exposed to arbitrary violence and the coercive regulation of everyday policing.[43]

In Johannesburg after apartheid, the unbundling of policing services has meant the loosening of dependence on public law enforcement and expanded importance of private security provision. Private security companies have fed on the crime-related moral panic, adding to the unnerving sense of foreboding and the dreaded feeling of being hemmed in by alien and hostile forces. Fear of crime has forced the well-to-do into a hyperinsulated existence that at times resembles urban science fiction, with its *Blade Runner*–like vision of miasmal dystopia.

The abrupt turn toward private security companies that sell protective services has gone hand in hand with the shift to new modes of spatial governance. In their modus operandi, private security companies have shifted from a focus on law enforcement to strategies designed to manage the risk of crime by cleansing urban spaces of would-be or suspected criminals. As Christine Hentschel has persuasively argued, "Governing (through) space has become a sophisticated polyphonic undertaking." In the affluent residential suburbs of northern Johannesburg, hybrid policing arrangements involve a complex triangular relationship between public policing agencies, private security companies, and "responsibilized" citizens grouped together in neighborhood associations. Properly understood, the creation and maintenance of these new regulatory regimes requires a conceptual vocabulary more nuanced than the all-encompassing, blunt language of "neoliberal urbanism," "privatization," and "neo-apartheid."[44] Although the use of these concepts provides some important insights into understanding new modes of security governance in the affluent residential neighborhoods of Johannesburg, painting the urban landscape with such broad brush-strokes fails to grasp the historical specificity of what has happened on the ground and why. The unbundling of public policing and the rise of private security management—which can be called "extended security networks"—has happened not as the result of a deliberate, top-down imposition of new modes of neoliberal urban governance but as a consequence of a great deal of serendipitous improvisation and experimentation without an originating, a priori end point in mind. These new regimes of security governance function as vehicles or expressions for the imbrication and circulation of new kinds of social power that arise from the management of urban space.[45]

In Johannesburg, the retreat of public law enforcement agencies from everyday policing in the public spaces of the city has gone hand in hand with the meteoric rise of private security as the principal mechanism for combatting crime and lawlessness in residential neighborhoods and gated communities, in commercial districts, and in business office parks. This shift in security governance from a system built on public responsibility to one dependent on private service reflects the turn toward state *unmaking*, in which public law enforcement has given way to private crime prevention. The widening terrain of private security governance in the everyday policing of urban space has eroded exclusive state sovereignty and the monopoly in the legitimate use of physical force that public policing agencies have claimed as the normative ideal of modern state making. Fragmented regimes of security governance have reshaped state sovereignty in ways that both suspend the rule of law and intensify the use of arbitrary force.[46] Rather than simply reflecting a simplified kind of neoliberal privatization of policing, the hybrid qualities of these security regimes represents the ambiguous overlapping, the cross contamination, and the collaboration between public law enforcement agencies and private security companies.[47]

In the rhetoric of policy makers, cooperation between public policing agencies and private security companies marks the beginning of the creation of an integrated "policing family" that is better able to reduce crime and prevent disorder.[48] But in practice, the relations between public law enforcement and private security companies are characterized by suspicion and mistrust. The failure of public policing agencies to provide security in sufficient measure to reassure anxious residents of the city has generated a climate of insecurity that has in turn triggered consumer demand for the multiplying products of the private security market.[49]

Yet when referring to extended security networks, it is important not to overemphasize the degree of integration. Although there is considerable overlapping of functions, public law enforcement agencies and private security companies still operate in largely independent spheres, governed by different goals, guidelines, and norms.[50] Skepticism and wariness about each other's motives has prevented the two sides from working together in mutually satisfying ways. Although public law enforcement agencies have pressed for coordination in well-defined public-private policing partnerships, the fusion of public and private policing has not occurred in any sustained way. Some joint partnership-policing initiatives have been implemented, but there is often little cooperation between public law enforcement agencies and private security companies in sustained, working relationships that deal with everyday crime prevention and law enforcement activities.[51]

The Symbolic Meaning of Crime in the Sociocultural Landscape

Spatial strategies of separation operate, both materially and symbolically, by marking boundaries and registering differences, imposing partitions and distances, building barriers, multiplying rules of exclusion, designing spaces of avoidance, and restricting unimpeded movements. It is under these circumstances that the urban residents of Johannesburg try to figure out how to make their way through the labyrinthine passageways that cut over and through the urban landscape.[52]

When middle-class residents of these sequestered enclaves are forced to leave their safety zones, they do so within the protective armor of their cars, dreading every moment they are "out there" in the illegible public spaces of the city, exposed to the mercy of unknown predators who lie in wait for victims. In the popular imagination, these public spaces are the putative "war zones" of the city—no-go areas of crime and violence that threaten the very existence of those seeking a safe haven in their private fortresses. These unsecured places are also the living (and breathing) spaces of the urban poor who have no choice but to face the everyday dangers of the "disorderly city" with little or no protection. The urban poor have filled in the voids, those leftover spaces in the cityscape, abandoned by the anxious middle-class residents who have retreated behind walls, barriers, and fortifications. As a general rule, middle-class residents have dispensed with the utopian ideal of sharing and using the public spaces of the city in equal measure. Only those who do not have a choice are left to fashion their everyday lives in these derelict and dangerous areas.[53]

These conflicting kaleidoscopic images of city life invariably give rise to different perceptions of urban space. Because the evolving urban form of Johannesburg can be viewed from many different angles, focusing on its physical qualities and material embodiments alone does not allow for a comprehensive understanding of the city after apartheid. Urban residents typically experience cities through their spatial practices.[54] Hence, making sense of urban space also requires that we focus attention on those informal rules or normative prescriptions governing the sociospatial routines of everyday life. In other words, it is necessary, as Henri Lefebvre insisted, that we "read," or decipher, the spatial codes that come into existence under historically specific conditions.[55] As urban residents navigate and traverse the cityscape, the practical and metaphorical (along with the real and symbolic) clash with one another. It is out of this confusing conundrum of fleeting confrontations and conflicts, negotiations and compromises that the durable qualities of urban life take shape and crystallize into recognizable patterns. It is out of these intersecting currents that shared meanings are attached to specific places.[56]

PART I

DESTABILIZING THE CIVIC BODY
Agoraphobia and Other (Fantastic)
Obsessions in the New South Africa

1

Nightmare City

Collective paranoia remains a pervasive, endemic feature of everyday life in Johannesburg after apartheid, despite the apparent (and some would say superficial) surface-level normalization of the social order brought about by the formal end to white minority rule and the transition to parliamentary democracy. At a time when the "haves" remain insecure in their privileged status and the "have-nots" harbor deep-seated resentments about their marginality, alarmist fantasies that conjure up frightful images of crime and its victims are bound to play a significant role in influencing what ordinary urban residents perceive to be right or wrong, just or unjust, and virtuous or evil about their city and their country. Whatever their origins and sources of inspiration, these alarmist fantasies are the visible expressions, or the outward signs, of unresolved tensions that reflect deep-seated cleavages along the fault lines of race, class, and national identity. At the heart of these anxieties lies a collective sense of existential dread and uncertainty about the future.[1]

Alarmist fantasies typically come to life in the form of popular beliefs, wild rumors, urban legends, and unsubstantiated opinions that sometimes metamorphose into full-fledged moral panics.[2] The open-ended quality of these stories about crime and victimhood virtually guarantees their wide dissemination across the race, class, and political spectrum of the new South Africa. What matters most in seeking an explanation for why these alarmist fantasies seem to have taken on a life of their own is not the actual truth as to what ordinary people collectively accept as commonsense knowledge, and it is not so much what has actually happened as what they believe has happened that has stirred them into action.[3]

Collective paranoia and the unsettling fears and resentments it breeds typically revolve around conjoined themes of danger and victimization. Disturbing stories of this kind are socially and historically important

for several reasons. Generally speaking, these alarmist fantasies perco-
late to the surface at those unsettled times when conventional expectations about the moral order that bind communities together are dis-
rupted, when the values of fairness seem to be ignored, when existing
boundaries between public and private spaces are trespassed, when established sexual mores are transgressed, when long-standing hierarchies
are challenged, when unwritten rules are cavalierly violated, and when
customary lines of public authority are failing to maintain social order.
In this sense, stories of crime and its victims develop as a reaction to
changing circumstances: the breakdown of those modes of regulation,
supervision, and control that have conventionally held the social order
together in a kind of delicate balance. They indicate that rival interest
groups and various social constituencies have largely retreated from real
and genuine engagement with one another and with the country's problems. They are frequently part of a collective endeavor to identify scapegoats, transfer blame, and rewrite history or deny the past. The power
of these alarmist fantasies to carry symbolic messages depends primarily on their relative autonomy, that is, their ability to strike an imaginative chord with various "publics." All too often, sociocultural groups,
social organizations, and political parties exploit unfounded beliefs, rumors, and popular opinion for their own purposes, using them to mobilize support and deflect criticism.[4]

Alarmist fantasies are discourses, that is, idealizations that are connected with perceptions of social realities. But they do not necessarily imply the linear relation of cause to effect. Stories of violent crime and its
hapless victims originate and are nurtured in historically specific social
sites. Their meanings derive from their social context and, more specifically, from their relationship to the social and political networks in which
they are imbricated. They are embedded in social relations of unequal
power and authority, and individuals and social groups use these stories of crime and its victims in political contests in order to undermine,
modify, or maintain the status quo, sway popular opinion, and achieve
or enhance a position of political or socioeconomic advantage. Alarmist fantasies are not simply unsettling stories that evoke fear and resentment in the abstract. Fashioned out of a dialectic of us versus them, they
not only moralize about concrete situations but also help to shape perceptions of what is real and what is not. In their use of metaphor and imagery (and their reliance on analogical reasoning), stories of conspiracy,

victimization, and betrayal weave together and synthesize complex discourses of race, class, and national identity.[5] In a climate of uncertainty, fear appears under two temporal guises: past and future. Put more precisely, fear becomes "embedded" in the two-dimensional "fields of recollection" of the past and "anticipation" of the uncertain future. Recalling past violent events translates into a source of anxiety about the future.[6]

Untangling the Fact of Fiction and the Fiction of Fact

> Fantasy, abandoned by reason, produces impossible monsters.
>
> —Francisco Goya

One must exercise great caution in taking alarmist fantasies at face value. If we do not seek to distinguish what is said from what exists, these discursive representations can easily monopolize our attention, and the extralinguistic actualities of lived daily experience can be quickly and easily forgotten or passed over as insignificant.[7] In their popular usage, stories of conspiracy, victimization, and betrayal resemble what amounts to a kind of "magical-realist" discourse that inhabits the unstable, fluid space between the actual conditions of everyday life and the imaginary world of make-believe. These stories are neither the unmediated reflection of empirically verifiable fact nor pure fiction. Alarmist fantasies constitute something more than mere hysteria grounded in unfounded belief. They arise from the ambiguities and uncertainties of "not knowing."

Yet to dismiss such anxieties about crime, victimhood, and betrayal as mere rhetorical posturing or to treat them as simply fictionalized fabrications is to confuse the cosmetic with the substantive. Embedded in the symbolic meanings of these alarmist fantasies are traces of the values, assumptions, and operating principles of those who employ them as cultural idioms. Modifications and transformations in these discourses do not provide unmediated evidence of evolving material circumstances that underlie their continued existence. Rather they reveal the changing beliefs of social agents about the material world in which they maneuver.[8]

Exploring these stories of conspiracy, victimization, and betrayal enables us to investigate what ordinary people believe to be true or even just desire to be true and thus may provide helpful clues about what may motivate them to action. Analyzing these discourses may yield little reliable information about actual events and historical processes, but it does offer an opportunity to identify some of the shifting relations of power that have accompanied the making of the new South Africa and to locate emergent sources of social tension that threaten to disrupt the delicately balanced social order in urban landscapes after apartheid. Alarmist fantasies are conveyor belts for popular consciousness beliefs and opinions, however unsubstantiated these might be or however far they diverge from fidelity to empirically grounded evidence. Struggles over how to discursively characterize collective fears and sociocultural uneasiness are essentially power games. It follows that disputes over the use of cultural idioms are contests for power.[9] When South African citizens express anxieties about crime, resentment of foreign immigrants, fear of idle youth, or uneasiness about the declining capacity of public law enforcement and the criminal justice system to protect law-abiding citizens, they are exhibiting their commonsensical understandings about the social world and how it is constituted. These beliefs are sensitive to the material environment but not directly determined by it. These are not fixed, immutable entities, and they never capture the imagination of various publics in identical fashion or in equal measure. Yet some beliefs are more powerful than others, and these are the ones most likely to sway popular opinion, be regarded as commonsense knowledge, and motivate groups to action.[10]

Alarmist fantasies reinforce and, indeed, police moral values. For example, stories about petty thieves, criminal gangs, idle youth, illegal immigrants, drug dealers, homeless squatters, and prostitutes almost always have a moral edge to them, not only identifying what is wrong but prescribing tentative solutions to rectify the situation.[11] Moreover, they typically depict as well as describe. The possible (and plausible) worlds described in rumors, urban legends, and popular beliefs portray real-life experiences. The vision of these fantastic stories metaphorically stands for the sociocultural world of everyday experience. Seen from this perspective, fact and fiction coexist in the same domain, and like so many spices in a soup, they sometimes blend together in surprising ways. When alarmist fantasies are embraced powerfully and vividly by the imagination, they become deeply embedded social facts that shape perceptions of sociocultural reality. Once they are widely shared, they become the potential foundation for further discourse, for collective reference that intensifies the cohesion and identity of social groups, and even for political action.[12]

What makes these alarmist fantasies so slippery, elusive, and difficult to define with any precision is that they do not necessarily correspond to actual events or concrete situations. Ironic as it may seem, it is precisely because these stories lack empirically grounded accuracy, comprehensiveness, and nuanced subtlety that they convey such powerful messages. Whether ordinary urban residents talk of dangerous criminals lurking everywhere, illegal immigrants taking jobs away from the deserving poor, affirmative action policies rewarding incompetence, the difficulties of white job seekers in obtaining work, or corruption corroding the moral fabric of the social order, they are engaged in an active process of establishing a commonsense understanding of the social world. These discursive depictions are not innocent. Apocryphal stories of crime victimization—whose factual content is constantly reconfigured and refashioned in so many different ways that no one can possibly determine the historical veracity of each alleged "fact" (or story)—capture the imagination, mobilize the collective agreement of social groups, and motivate people to undertake purposeful action.[13]

Strictly speaking, to recognize the fact of fiction does not mean to suggest that truthfulness and falsehood are simply indistinguishable linguistic constructs in an infinitely free play of meanings. In weaving together descriptions of events whether real or imagined, these stories of crime and its victims conjure up an entire sociocultural world in the imagination. This vicarious vividness is the foundation of their popular appeal. The power of this kind of expressive communication is that it can sometimes provide a pristine clarity often missing in an eyewitness experience, which is so often muddled and confused. Meaning and experience are continuously intertwined in ways that reveal an intricate reciprocal relationship between extraliterary social reality and forms of expression. Although they bear some connection with the actual conditions of everyday life, alarmist fantasies are typically extrapolated from a few cases or isolated instances to reach sweeping generalizations about the whole situation, thereby transforming historically contingent observations into a seemingly timeless, existential predicament.[14]

Magical Realism and the Spectral City: Inventing Monstrous Figures

The stylized magical realism of contemporary Latin American fiction has its counterpart in the mundane surrealism of faux ethnographic description, a genre epitomized by the sensationalist-driven popular media, in which it is also difficult to separate fact from fiction, actual historical events from hearsay and make-believe, and stories of everyday political drama from the imaginary tales inspired by wild rumors and urban legend.[15] The blurring of actual events (social realities) and fictional accounts creates a kind of mass hysteria and paranoia, a collective hostile gaze in which distrust, suspicion, and hostility stands between "us" and "them."[16] Just like their counterparts in magical-realist discourse, sensationalized accounts of urban danger in Johannesburg rely on a coterie of spectral figures to suggest unease with the everyday chance encounters that are part and parcel of modern urban life. Through lurid television documentaries, sensationalized newspaper stories, political commentaries, official pronouncements, and well-publicized juridical trials as well as through visual images, moralizing tales, and everyday conversation, ordinary urban residents have been subjected to the hyperbolic rhetoric of the invisible danger lurking within. It is through these popular instruments of image making that Fear Incarnate has been grafted onto the already disquieting images of the nomadic poor and homeless, itinerant job seekers, illegal immigrants, prostitutes, idle youth, and other marginalized urban groups. As these and other social imaginaries are identified and classified, they are also stigmatized as demonic figures. As the caricatured personifications of evil, they contaminate the otherwise pristine vision of the idealized "new nation."[17]

Fueled by alarmist fantasies and paranoia, the popular imagination is capable of conjuring up all sorts of spectral, demonic images to give meaning to lived daily experience. These eidolonic phantasmagoria exist in the extradiegetic space between actual persons and fictional characters, between actual persons and ghostlike phantoms. Treating these socially constructed abstractions as objects of inquiry in their own right can give us access to the imaginative dimensions of social life that are often ignored or dismissed by those who uncritically accept the positivistic injunctions of scientific realism. This image making takes place in the intermediate realm between the material realities of everyday life and the mythopoeic invention of pure make-believe. In a literary sense, then, the construction of enigmatic totems of urban danger shares a similar cognitive framework with the creation of science fiction: both are a species of imaginative fantasy that typically relies on an extensive grammar of monstrosity.[18]

As an agent spurring people to action, fear is directed not against what is known but against what is unknown—not against insiders but against outsiders. For middle-class urban residents, conjuring up a whole menagerie of social imaginaries—contemporary folk devils such as idle black youth, illegal aliens, predatory gangs, rapacious drug dealers, wanton prostitutes, and homeless vagabonds—serves to project blame for socioeconomic hardship and political uncertainty onto a largely invisible, malevolent force and, conversely, to not only express a longing for good governance, social justice, and public order but also signal a desire for redemption from annoying urban pathologies.[19] As symbolic representations of Fear Incarnate, social imaginaries come into existence as metaphorical flights of associational fantasy: they not only reflect the object to which they refer but are produced by the discourse that identifies, classifies, and describes them.[20] A suspicious outsider can be "anywhere and anyone, a ghostlike figure in the present, who gives us nightmares about the future." Through their use and reuse, such discursive signifiers recall histories and past fears that are able to "stick to the present."[21]

Like invented traditions, the construction of social imaginaries is a generalizing device that essentially takes place through a process of repetition (stereotyping), formalization (stigmatizing), and ritualization (demonology). For the most part, this social construction involves the transformation of hearsay into conventional wisdom, the extrapolation of direct experience into general rules, and the metamorphosis of opinion into analysis. Yet unlike invented traditions, social imaginaries are never permanent fixtures on the symbolic landscape. Instead, their meanings are contested, negotiated, and altered in their everyday use. When they are stabilized for a time, they tend to metaphorically stand for an actual object to which they simply refer.[22]

The visible presence of idle youth, itinerant job seekers, curbside hawkers, street kids, and ambulatory beggars has become a ubiquitous feature of everyday life in Johannesburg after apartheid. As powerful symbols of urban disorder and decay, these unwanted Others are, both literally and figuratively speaking, "bodies out of place," with nowhere to go without encountering suspicion and hostility.[23] The outward signs of affluence juxtaposed against grim (and sometimes shocking) reminders of urban impoverishment provide ample testimony for how the expectations of the postapartheid social order have remained unrealized. Enduring inequalities coupled with the uneven distribution of opportunities for up-

ward mobility have triggered a great deal of resentment, which has occasionally spilled over into public displays of hostility and frustration,
including xenophobic violence directed against unwanted foreigners.[24]

For affluent residents of Johannesburg who live in stable suburban
neighborhoods, the fear of open spaces is tied to the perceived threats of
risk and harm. An overflow of sensationalist media images and frightening stories of dangerous situations have intermingled with lived experiences, personal memories, and individual histories to produce a collective sense of the risks of urban living. The phantoms of fear that haunt
the cityscape are featured in advertising campaigns warning of house
break-ins and carjackings, in lurid newspaper accounts of murder and
rape, and in popular media reports on crime syndicates, drug dealers,
and underage prostitution. Transmitted by film, television, radio, the internet, and the printed word, such images and narratives fashion representations of the city itself, juxtaposing portraits of enticement and al-
lure with those of peril and menace.[25] Inundated with noir images of the
"dangerous city," affluent urban residents have sought to shield themselves from possible threats of bodily harm.[26]

In unsettled circumstances, sensationalist images and stories typically portray Johannesburg as the quintessential City of Dread, a frightening place suffused with a sense of urgent and apocalyptic anxiety.[27]
Newspaper accounts, television coverage, personal stories, and everyday gossip compete for space in the marketplace of ideas, all proclaiming their commitment to objectivity and veracity. Yet the boundaries
separating truth from fiction and the real from the imaginary are constantly blurred, especially under circumstances in which access to experience is mediated by the "culture of spectacle" that inundates the popular media, seeking to broaden its audience appeal through sensationalist
reporting.[28]

Spatial Stories of Urban Danger

Experiencing Johannesburg involves movement from place to place, and
excursions of almost any sort are fraught with a great deal of anxiety.
Travelers typically rely on anecdotes, rumors, and other stories of the
street to construct their mental maps of the cityscape, dividing the urban landscape into safe places and risky no-go zones. Ordinary inhabitants of the city are constantly confronted with an uncertainty that feeds

on the fear of violence and is rooted in enduring socioeconomic inequalities. Johannesburg is more than a divided city. It is also a bewildering place or, as Achille Mbembe and Sarah Nuttall put it, an "elusive metropolis" that not only *frustrates* representation but also undermines it.[29] The urban landscape consists of a mosaic of ambiguous zones of contact allowing for chance encounters between rich and poor residents in which the outcome of interactions is far from certain.[30]

In contemporary discourses of urban living, the obsession with urban danger is largely constructed around apocryphal stories of menacing figures whose movements through space become a source of anxiety. Such modern-day folk devils as homeless wanderers, jobless vagabonds, roaming gangs, carjackers, petty thieves, and beggars come to life in spatial stories about risk and danger.[31] These spectral figures inhabit the margins of the orderly city, and they are confined to the shadowlands of respectability. They symbolize all that is wrong with the city, and their movements are characterized by such spatial metaphors as *invasions* and *infestations* or *loitering* and *crowding.*[32]

Sometimes what is not known or what is unknowable with any precision assumes a greater significance than what is known. The menacing figures who inhabit the dark in-between spaces of the cityscape are assumed to have sinister motives and are associated with compulsive antisocial behaviors that threaten to bring the city to ruin. In the popular imagination, these unwanted Others have become objects of fear and menace, of scorn and ridicule, and of disdain and dismissal. Their presence becomes a cause for alarm, a justification for anxiety, and an excuse for retreat into fortified enclaves. These ghostlike figures signify strangeness, difference, and the urban uncanny. They are indelibly marked by the stains of impurity. They embody an Otherness that is "out of place" in the orderly city.[33]

As an exercise of the cartographic imagination, anxious urban residents create cognitive maps that categorize the spaces of the city along a continuum ranging from safe to dangerous. A cognitive map is a type of mental picture that enables urban residents to acquire, store, recall, and decode information about the attributes of their metaphorical spatial environment. These mental images are shared, expressive, and highly distorted representations of an actual geographical condition. It is a mental map, in other words, because the objective geographic image has been reshaped by shared assumptions, beliefs, and ideology.[34] These mythological constructions are neither strictly true nor strictly false. Their differences reflect the variability in the political discourses from which they emanate.[35]

At the end of the day, the discursive construction of phantasmagoric Otherness revolves around an aesthetic characterization of what constitutes the appropriate use of property and place in the city. The coercive mechanisms of exclusion from abandoned buildings, sidewalks, and public parks corresponds to a normative assertion of who belongs in the city and who does not. Framed in this way, such popular illegalities as squatting in abandoned buildings, engaging in unauthorized trading, drug dealing, and street prostitution are not structural consequences that emanate from an urban social order characterized by gross inequalities but disruptive threats to municipal order that appear from elsewhere.[36]

On closer inspection, these figural constructions do not have a substantive wholeness that enables us to speak of them in unified categorical terms. These spectral figures reveal themselves to be nothing but phantoms, that is, projected illusions of "a unity that can only exist as image." These simplified caricatures efface both the diversity of circumstances under which these alleged illegitimate usurpers of urban space enter into the city and the various modes of engagement through which they pursue whatever opportunities present themselves.[37] The demonic images attached to unwanted Others effectively deflects attention away from considerations of a rightful place in the city and the legitimacy of competing claims for resources and access to the use of urban space.[38] The specter of rising crime linked with gratuitous violence, the invasion of illegal aliens, the spread of contagious diseases, and the contamination of drugs operates as the source of middle-class anxiety. Yet the perceived danger that the poor and the marginalized Others represent in the conduct of their daily lives stems from their overall condition of desperate need and sheer destitution. Hunger and want always pose threats to the fragile stability and the contrived order of city life.[39]

Crime Talk and the Paradoxes of Urban Living after Apartheid

In their everyday social intercourse, ordinary urban residents have tried to find the best language available with which to describe and interpret their fears about the perils of urban living. To give something a name is to assert, or at least try to assert, imaginative control over it. The stabilized moral order that discourses about urban danger seek to establish is achieved not only by naming categories but by clarifying hierarchical relationships of superiority and inferiority. By establishing classificatory schemes, fixing their meaning and significance, and constructing and discursively patrolling the borders between exclusion and inclusion, alarmist stories told about urban danger help to constitute social imaginaries at the same time as they describe them. The discourse of urban danger attributes real identities and an actual existence to these menacing, phantasmagoric figures.[40]

Words used as descriptive terms and names or fashioned into catchall phrases and shorthand slogans grow and develop with repeated usage. Like all forms of symbolic expression that aid in the communication of abstract ideas, they traverse space and time, conveying messages and eliciting responses. Strung together in sequences, words become stories. Over time, these stories undergo transformation, and in turn they transform those who hear them and engage with them. Their metamorphosis is not a passive record of history but an active embodiment of the genealogy of existing power relations. Because language is intrinsically metaphorical, it becomes possible, or perhaps even inevitable, for the meaning of words to "escape the embrace of lived experience, to detach [themselves] from the fleshy body."[41] What may appear at first glance as mere gossip or hearsay can turn out on closer inspection to be the unwitting bearer of cultural codes that contain and carry forth the hegemony of one point of view over and against its rivals.[42]

The various kinds of casual conversation—spontaneous stories, urban legends, folktales, and even jokes—that have crime and its victims as their subject constitute what can be termed "crime talk." Everyday conversations about crime, risk, and victimhood is a reflection of the uncertainties of urban life. Commonsense knowledge is, of course, formed from the public act of talking—in other words, by idle gossip, rumor, and hearsay. Crime talk consists of narrative fragments and free association about vulnerability, danger, and victimhood. The ceaseless rounds of stories about criminals and their victims provide an evolving set of images and language with which to make sense of unanchored uneasiness. Crime talk does more than simply pass along reliable information; it also circulates and produces stereotypes that provoke fear and thus contributes to the reinforcement of prejudices.[43]

In Johannesburg after apartheid, few subjects have moved so dramatically from the margins of public discourse to the center of heated debate than has the heightened focus on crime and its attendant concerns about personal vulnerability and safety, the qualities of urban life, and the conveniences of daily living. This exchange of ideas about urban danger is, in its popular usage, a social construct, always sinister, with its own history and conventions of thought, imagery, and vocabulary. These ideas do not just reflect real city spaces. They are also imaginative reconstructions that project hopes, desires, and fears onto the symbolic landscape. Like other alarmist fantasies, crime talk is a discourse that has less to do with understanding actual social realities than it has to do with perceptions, attitudes, and beliefs. These ongoing conversations about crime and its victims are contagious. Once one crime story is told, many others are likely to follow, in a sort of endless loop. As a form of literary expression, crime talk is a genre of storytelling. Unlike classical modernist narratives, these are stories without closure, without proper beginnings or endings. What makes these stories peculiar is that they are complex productions, a kind of performance art with many participants both talking and listening but not all of them fully visible or audible. Because they are open to multiple and diverse interpretations, they are without the power to claim unique or closed readings.[44]

Crime talk is not idle chatter. As a type of unconfirmed information passed among individuals and groups, it signals an attempt at collective conversation. Crime talk originates in ambiguous situations and flourishes in times of social unrest and heightened tension. Indeed, it is purposeful and expressive rather than accidental and fortuitous, as it represents the preoccupations of multiple publics seeking to comprehend the exigencies of their imagined precarious situations.[45] Statistically laden and factually accurate accounts of crime and its victims often remain unavailable for popular use until they are cast into narrative forms that highlight their relevance for the conduct of daily life. In this way, crime talk enters into public discourse in the form of rumors, gossip, anecdotes, and vignettes, and it crystallizes into popular beliefs, common knowledge, and shared opinions. As a distinctive kind of exaggerated discourse, crime talk depicts distant, would-be threats as expressions of clear and imminent danger. It is not so much what actually happens as what people believe has happened that stirs them to repeat what they have heard. Encoded with symbolic meaning, these apocryphal micro-stories operate as warning signs, provide moral "object lessons", and offer suggested codes of conduct.[46] Typically embroidered and embellished to fit changing circumstances, crime talk expresses certain imaginative understandings of the city that can easily take on lives of their own, in which rumors metamorphose into what are widely accepted as truthful accounts, and myth masquerades as reality.[47]

Crime talk is a kind of storytelling that not only "preserves the memory of something that happened or at least is believed to have happened" but also claims that something did not "merely happen" but took place "in accordance with the requirements" of a plot that conveys meaning. It is a rhetorical device that assumes a unique narrative privilege, a distinctive poetic license that enables storytellers "to twist the material for effect, to exaggerate, to omit, to draw connections where none are apparent, to silence events that interfere with the storyline, to embellish, to elaborate, to display emotion, to comment, [and] to interpret," even as they claim to be truthfully representing what actually happened. Put another way, "poetic license is a vital feature" of crime talk: it forms an unspoken and often unacknowledged bond that allows storytellers "to maintain an allegiance to the effectiveness of the story" while at the same time claiming to represent the truth of what happened. Armed with poetic license and all the distortions, omissions and exaggerations that it justifies, crime talk aims "at generating a deeper truth, one which gives us greater insight into a situation than the literal truth."[48]

Crime talk forms an integral element of the imaginative dimension of urban living after apartheid. Because it arises out of identifiable situations and yet at the same time it is less bound by the prevailing standards of truthfulness than other kinds of speech, crime talk provides a useful vantage point from which to explore popular attitudes and values often overlooked in conventional political assessments of the transition to parliamentary democracy in postapartheid South Africa. The popular media provide a steady stream of sensational stories chronicling one brutal crime after another visited upon unsuspecting law-abiding citizens. These horrifying accounts of gruesome murder, rape, carjacking, mob violence, physical assaults, robberies, and break-ins are often packed with graphic, lurid details, and the violence accompanying these crimes is typically portrayed as senseless and gratuitous. Yet the real substance and animating force of crime talk originates in the expressive communication of everyday life, or what Arnand Yang has called a "conversation of rumors."[49] All told, rumors tend to breed more rumors, thereby instilling an exaggerated climate of fear and hysteria. Crime talk repeatedly rehearses the tropes of risk, threat, and danger. Whether stories told about crime are apocryphal inventions matters little, because audiences are convinced of their veracity. This storytelling not only reflects social realities but also creates new perceptions of them. What matters more is what people believe to be true. Understood theoretically, crime talk depends on a metonymic line of reasoning, in which the contiguous items in a series—crime, violence, disorder, unruliness, disintegration, crisis, and collapse—do not simply refer, or defer, to one another but become virtually indistinguishable in a seamless web of fear and disenchantment. Taken to its imaginary extremes, crime talk is an apocryphal vision of random violence without interruptions, boundaries, or obstacles.[50]

Ongoing conversations about lawlessness, violence, and crime produce their own subjects and perceptions of what is real, engendering a shared culture of vicarious victimhood in which collective sympathy for individuals who have suffered at the hands of criminals has often generated a compulsive, visceral need for reprisal going beyond notions of justice and increasingly toward acts of revenge.[51] What people gossip about and what stories they tell also reveal how social groups construct a world outside their own immediate experience as meaningful and predictable. In short, everyday casual conversations provide a lens through which to make sense of the intricate processes of practical behavior—what Pierre Bourdieu calls habitus—that structure and shape the ways in which individuals and social groups deal strategically with the social world outside their own personal experiences.[52] Rumor and gossip are direct guides to the molecular, diffuse, and shadowy lines of power, in the sense suggested by Michel Foucault: the complex network of hierarchical relationships that construct the social world, a microuniverse from which there is virtually no escape.[53] Apocryphal stories laying claim to accuracy and truth help to fashion collective identities, to articulate shared memories, and to legitimate the cultural practices of social groups. These operate like the hidden transcripts of daily life.[54]

The purpose of gossiping, rumormongering, and even just talking itself is not to passively deliver information but to actively exchange it. Stories exchanged without regard for verifiable accuracy, and stories amended and altered with every retelling are indeed rumors, but these same stories also reflect how people in their daily lives debate the issues contained within them. Each of these stories taken on its own may prove to be utterly fallacious. But taken together, they form part of a common-sense knowledge, or collective discussion, that reveals how ordinary urban residents think and speak about city life and urban disorder at a time of political uncertainty.[55] In an everyday exchange of information and opinion, crime talk is not only expressive but also productive. The fear and talk of crime not only generate their own commonsense inter-pretations (often simplistic and stereotypical) but also prescribe every-day strategies of protection. Crime stories are a specific kind of narrative that bestows a particular type of knowledge. They attempt to establish some semblance of order and meaning in a social world that seems to have lost coherence and wholeness. Contrary to the firsthand experience of crime, which disrupts meaning and destabilizes the world, the talk of crime symbolically reorders meaning by trying to re-create a stable im-age of the social world. As exercises of the popular imagination, these narratives of crime and violence build partitions and barriers, delineate and enclose spaces, establish distances, differentiate between friend and foe, impose prohibitions and codes of conduct, multiply rules of avoid-ance and exclusion, and restrict movements.[56]

True Lies: Statistics and Crime

> Statistics are like bikinis: what they reveal is interesting. What they con-ceal is vital.
>
> —A. S. K. Joommal[57]

Figures that represent aggregates, percentages, rates, and trends over time give empty abstractions such as murder, robbery, and car theft a sense of concreteness that they do not otherwise possess. As assertions of the real, these figures fill in the gap between what is not known and what passes for commonsense knowledge. Crime statistics operate both as a convenient medium of communication and exchange and as a kind of reified knowledge, whose value expands as it circulates via storytell-ing and rumor.[58]

Like classifying and labeling, counting is not a neutral activity born of detached scientific reasoning. The bureaucratic operations of measure-ment and quantification have long been central features of state-building processes, and as such they reflect the disciplinary power of modern state machineries.[59] In Johannesburg, as elsewhere, figures on crime and its victims are social constructions that generate particular meaningful understandings of urban life. Rather than treating them as true representations of actually existing criminality, crime statistics create images of criminal behavior. At best, one can claim that statistics may indicate some tendencies, patterns, and frequencies of crime. Official statistics about crime should be treated not simply as indicators of criminal behavior and its social distribution but also as organizational products that reflect in part the operational orientations and ideological biases of public law enforcement agencies. As aggregated information that generalizes across artificially conceived notions of space and time, statistics typically conceal as much as they reveal.[60]

Crime statistics produced by law enforcement agencies are subject to a variety of different kinds of distortions A number of important studies have indicated that official police statistics in South Africa were unreliable as accurate measures of crime rates, in part because large numbers of people did not bother to report incidents considered to be less serious.[61] In essence, crime statistics are primarily a rather loose reading of what incidents the public actually reports to the police. A whole assortment of crimes such as petty theft, larceny, and burglary are frequently not reported to public policing agencies because of the widespread lack of faith in the criminal justice system to apprehend and prosecute those allegedly responsible. Women who are the victims of such violent crimes as aggravated assault, rape, and domestic abuse often do not report these incidents to the police for fear of reprisals from the perpetrators. According to an early survey conducted by the South African Institute of Race Relations, only 450 of every 1,000 crimes committed in 1997 were reported to public law enforcement agencies. This percentage has changed little over subsequent decades.[62] In addition, there is plenty of circumstantial evidence to suggest that police officers are often reluctant to open dockets for crimes that they are not confident they can solve. As a consequence, the actual number of crimes committed is much higher than the number that is recorded.[63] Comparable figures are available for other years. Many victims of crimes such as street muggings and attempted robbery typically do not bother to report because they viscerally understand that the perpetrators are unlikely to be apprehended, let alone convicted. In the case of vehicle thefts or break-ins, many insurance companies require car owners to provide a copy of the police report in order to process claims. This rule probably accounts for more accurate statistics for vehicle larceny and house burglaries than for other crimes.[64] In a similar vein, white-collar crimes, such as embezzlement and fraud, are frequently sensationalized in the news media, but these rarely lead to prison sentences.[65]

Reliable crime statistics are nearly impossible to obtain.[66] Distortions appear not only in the collection of crime statistics but also in the classification of criminal acts. Crime figures are difficult to track and compare because state security officials often alter definitions of what constitutes particular type of criminal activity. Guesstimates and conjecture frequently take the place of accurate numbers. The absence of reliable comparable data means that very little can be truthfully said about the patterns, frequencies, and trends of crime over time.[67]

In a similar vein, social analysts have experienced great difficulties in uncovering and reconstructing accurate accounts of the geography of crime, due in part to the paucity and inaccuracy of empirical data but also to the added layers of myth and fabrication. Because crime is not just a social fact but also a metaphor for social breakdown, crime talk is often transformed into a vehicle by which the respectable, property-owning middle classes articulate their fears, define their problems, establish their sociocultural boundaries, frame their agendas, and promote their visions for the future. Consequently, most commentaries and public pronouncements about crime are so embedded in concurrent discourses of control, regulation, and avoidance that any effort to assess its scope and impact are nearly impossible.[68]

The politics of crime often takes the form of conflicts over access to information. Because crime talk carries such a heavy weight of social meaning, it has become a cause célèbre for those who seek to advance the cause of political opposition to the ANC (African National Congress). Crime statistics circulate not simply as information about the state of affairs but as discourse about the effectiveness of municipal governance itself.[69] In early 1998, in the face of mounting hysteria about rising crime, the Ministry of Safety and Security declared a moratorium on the release of crime statistics, classifying this information as an official state secret and announcing that crime figures could be released only every three months at the discretion of the Office of the Minister. Opposition leaders were quick to accuse key state officials and law enforcement agencies of trying to "carefully sanitize the statistics" so as not to cause undue embarrassment for the ANC government. In the midst of this imbroglio, South Africa's private banking sector found itself at odds with official crime pronouncements. Corporate banking officials broke with conventional practice when they released their own bank-related crime statistics. Their figures were at variance with the significantly lower ones issued by the government, and their disclosure came shortly after President Mandela, in his much-publicized opening address to Parliament on 6 February 1998, lashed out at the popular media and critics of the ANC government for distorting the truth, bluntly declaring that those who questioned official pronouncements regarding crime statistics were disloyal and unpatriotic.[70]

With such an astronomical murder rate, daily newspapers have stopped reporting everyday killings and have instead concentrated on only the most gruesome and spectacular crimes. Ironically, these graphic displays of heinous murder that have appeared in mass-circulation daily newspapers have only heightened the sense of hysteria about crime. When high-ranking ANC officials criticized the largely hostile (and white-dominated) popular media for their often sensationalized coverage of the crime danger, opposition politicians, newspaper executives, and civil libertarians reacted strongly against what they regarded as a not-so-veiled effort to muzzle the free press.[71] Lost in the ensuing vitriolic war of words was any reasonable assessment of how the steady diet of sensational stories about criminal violence plays into stereotypes and actually reinforces white prejudice, contributing to a white middle-class backlash against the urban poor as a homogeneous social group.[72]

The real significance of crime statistics lies not so much in their indication of the rise and fall (or the pendular swings) of criminality but in how these numbers reveal the depth of the middle-class hysterical reaction to feelings of personal vulnerability and the extent of the fear of the urban underclasses. The moral panic triggered by apprehension about crime has engendered a clear reorientation of middle-class attitudes toward the unemployed, the casual poor, and the social outcasts who inhabit marginal places in the city. Social anxieties about urban danger have played a significant part in provoking the propertied middle classes to seek out the safety of cloistered places in the city and to frequently turn their backs on the plight of the poor.

In conventional approaches to policing the city, law enforcement agencies chart the criminal character of urban spaces through the collection, classification, and display of the statistical prevalence of crime. This kind of spatial mapping, or cartographic exercise, gives rise to an image of the criminogenic city separated into zones of safety and zones of danger, and to ways of living in the city "informed by a perception of the relative riskiness of particular zones." In contrast to the moral topographies of urban space engineered through conventional modernist policing techniques, new postliberal modes of urban governance seek to reduce risk through strategies of spatial differentiation, separation, and compartmentalization. Such fictional representations of urban life as Ridley Scott's *Blade Runner* effectively capture this ethos in the dreary, dystopian *City of Tomorrow*, in which the urban landscape is divided between the safe places of civility—policed buildings and secured entertainment sites—and "the spaces lying outside the limits of these secure spaces, full of threat, chaos, and danger."[73]

This fictionalized representation is imitated in real life in the kinds of defensive spatialization that have come to shape post-public space: enclosed shopping malls outfitted with their own security systems and private policing, citadel office complexes with restricted access, and gated residential communities protected by perimeter walls, sentry gates, and security guards. This kind of spatial transformation of the urban landscape has signaled the death of the public city, that is, the classically liberal dream of the modern metropolis as open, congregating space—the civic habitat for the entertainment and pleasure of free citizens.[74]

The Power of Discourse to Shape the Imaginary City

> It is not important whether or not the interpretation is correct, if [people] define situations as real, they are real in their consequences.
> —W. I. Thomas and D. I. Thomas, *The Child in America*[75]

It is difficult to disentangle the ordinary routines and discourses that accompany everyday life in the city from the grandiose metaphorical meanings that so freely intermingle with shared beliefs, sensibilities, and desires about the qualities of urban living.[76] Popular perceptions of city life follow well-established image categories of the city as a dangerous place. The term *dangerous* is a compelling figure of speech but one without precise definition. It functions as a kind of wandering signifier that, while not totally empty, can be infused with symbolic meaning to serve the purposes of those who make use of it rhetorically.[77]

The episodic outbursts of excited speculation about crime are not only a normative projection of what constitutes deviance (such as loitering and idleness, drug dealing, prostitution, public drunkenness, and illegal immigration) but also a prescription for moral, social, and ideological boundaries and an assertion of desire for discipline, regulation, and control. Crime talk is a genre of metaphorical expression that condenses some difficult-to-grasp yet unsettling changes in the social and moral order. This understanding is not to neglect the connection that exists between fear and the actual existence of real-life dangers. But it does mean to suggest that everyday talk about crime is usually also a device for identifying, registering, and making sense of a variety of troublesome insecurities. It is neither something apart from the texture of everyday life nor something merely imposed from without by media manipulation. Talk of crime, and the passions and anxieties such communicative exchange discloses, speaks directly to the collective sense that ordinary people have of the habitability of the place in which they live (and of its past, present, and possible future) and its relationship with the surrounding cultural environments and socioeconomic hierarchies.[78] To acknowledge that the actual extent of lawlessness is unknown and even unknowable, that official crime statistics are a kind of fact-making fiction, is not at all to deny the real existence of crime. Ordinary urban residents encounter crime, violence, and lawlessness in visceral terms—in concrete firsthand experience, in anecdotal storytelling and rumor, and in the steady stream of mediated images that, in their repetitive retelling, take on a life of their own.[79] To paraphrase Mary Douglas, crime talk operates as a conduit for communicating and politicizing collective fear only because real danger actually exists.[80]

The combination of anxiety and unease creates a fertile breeding ground for mythical fantasies and distorted perceptions of urban living. The talk of urban danger runs as an obsessive theme in newspapers, political commentaries, popular fiction, and everyday conversation.[81] The sheer magnitude of stories about crime and its hapless victims serve as texts expressing certain imaginative views of the city. This crime talk—what amounts to mystification presenting itself as quasiunderstanding—has come to be organized into a series of tropes ranging from lawlessness and danger to disorderly and chaotic. The discourse of crime lends significance to particular locations. The steady stream of stories about crime and its victims accumulate over time, bearing silent witness to the unsettling sense of urban disorder and producing an imaginary cultural landscape that divides the city into dangerous places to be avoided and safe places to never leave. The discourse of crime and the fear it engenders are symbolic weapons in the battle over urban space. Through recourse to such binary opposites as orderly versus disorderly, sanitary versus dirty, or safe versus dangerous, the urban middle classes have been able to imagine the urban landscape as divided into distinct geographic zones.[82] With the end of apartheid, the speed at which neighborhoods have undergone transformation has meant that the boundaries separating safe spaces from dangerous ones are more difficult to define and maintain. The socioeconomic inequalities that permeate South Africa after apartheid certainly frame everyday violence and criminality. In reality, if deeply entrenched inequalities are important conditions in understanding the high rates of crime, the correlation between poverty and criminality is not sufficient to explain its causes. What one needs to understand is how enduring inequalities, persistent poverty, and limited opportunities for upward mobility reproduce the victimization and criminalization of the poor, the indifference to their plight, the disregard of their civil rights, and their lack of access to justice.[83]

As with other alarmist fantasies, the discourse of lawlessness and crime has contributed to the popular perception of the city as a disorderly, dangerous place that one cautiously enters expecting unpleasant confrontations and random acts of gratuitous and meaningless violence.[84] For all their apparent unnaturalness, disturbing encounters of this sort are perhaps more authentic expressions of city spaces sharply divided along class and racial lines than are the exalted civility that the democratic ideal of urbanity projects. Discourses are not only social products but are also modes of power that have fundamental social effects.[85] Crime talk does not just evoke images of the dangerous city after apartheid or express fears of the deracinated Other. It also reveals a visceral resentment of the putative loss of the city to the unruly underclasses: the unemployed, the beggars and thieves, the homeless, the mentally disturbed, and the unwanted.

The popular media do not simply provide lurid and sensational details about crime and its victims but actively shape the discourse of urban living, provide guidelines for traversing the city landscape, offer cautionary tales about places to avoid, present sentimental views of the past, and serve as vehicles for urban residents to remember, classify, and recount their own encounters with danger. The categories organized around spatial mapping and around counting, classifying, and locating crime serve to construct and discursively patrol the borders between different parts of the city, making the division of the city landscape into safe and dangerous zones a symbolic feature of everyday life in Johannesburg.[86] In reading the regular crime reports in *The Star* (Johannesburg's leading daily newspaper), it is possible to discover a spatial reasoning at work: a way of thinking that not only connects fear, danger, and disorder to particular places but also contrasts the ordered moral economy that the white middle-class suburbs represent with the lawlessness of the inner-city ghettoes. Fashioned in this way, the discourse of crime is a kind of discursive representation of urban space, analogous to an exercise in topographical mapping. Like all cartographic representations of urban space, crime talk is a *contested* practice, thoroughly implicated within molecular relations of power. Yet unlike those cartographic exercises that rely on the idealized homogeneous and continuous space of Euclidian geometry, crime talk is at root a deconstructionist gesture, a kind of discursive mapping that reveals the fissures, fractures, and conflicts of urban space, or what Pierre Bourdieu calls "discontinuous, patchy space." Seen from this angle, the discourse of crime is a practical method of revealing hidden aspects of urban landscapes and bringing them out into the open for popular scrutiny.[87]

The discourse of crime is like a provisional, protean blueprint for the construction of urban dystopias. It does not try to capture the city from a single vantage point but instead oscillates between a number of different positions: between actuality and the imaginary, between what exists and what might exist, and between a documentary-like portrait of urban living and a kind of film noir representation of the underside of city life. Crime talk is embedded in a language of power and avoidance. Despite its origins in middle-class paranoia, this discourse of crime reveals the contradictory senses of the city—the experiences of separation and unity, of hurried movements through the streets and furtive glances over the shoulder, of unwelcome noise and eerie silence, of confusion and bewilderment juxtaposed with legibility and coherence, of exclusion

and constraint as well as mobility and circulation, and of spatial entrap-
ment and unimpeded freedom of movement. Far from providing a commanding vision of the urban landscape, crime talk invents an imaginary
patchwork city, a collage of imagined places known through word-of-
mouth and experienced vicariously through stories of danger.[88]

2

The Anorexic State

It seems that in Jozi [Johannesburg] every pedestrian needs a personal bodyguard to stay alive.
> —Bongani Madondo, "Send Task Force to Save Hillbrow!"[1]

Both literally and metaphorically, public law enforcement agencies represent "the state [apparatus] on the streets."[2] Yet routine police misconduct and ineffectiveness in preventing crime in Johannesburg have produced a tangible distrust of these agencies and the criminal justice system.[3] In the years following the end of apartheid, the dramatic increase in anxiety about crime was directly proportionate to a precipitous decline in the widely held belief in the ability of public policing agencies to effectively deal with lawlessness and criminality. As crime and the violence associated with it gravitated to affluent suburban neighborhoods, criminality acquired a "new visibility,"[4] in which the heightened sense of urgency blended seamlessly with increasingly shrill calls to get "tough on criminals."[5] Rising lawlessness and criminality dovetailed with the already existing insecurity that accompanied the transition to parliamentary democracy, engendering dystopian images of the new democratic order as "bordering on chaos and collapse, moored to narratives of things falling apart, in the face of a government that is ignoring the crime problem, covering things up and that should be doing a lot more."[6]

This loss of faith in the effectiveness and even the willingness of public law enforcement agencies and the criminal justice system to combat crime triggered widespread popular resentment and anger. Fearful residents did not wait for public policing agencies to provide security and instead turned en masse to private solutions to manage the perceived risk of crime. Although the official vision of integrated policing in Johannesburg after apartheid established the foundation for the equitable redistribution of resources and uniform policing regulation across the urban landscape, the multiplication of policing services has tended to produce fragmented and unequal security networks that have unevenly coalesced around place, income, and race.[7]

In a fractured urban security environment in which criminal violence mirrors structural patterns of inequitable socioeconomic opportunities and historical exclusion along race and class racial lines, affluent residents have sought their own solutions to insecurity. Local security initiatives have blossomed across the urban landscape, as coalitions of property owners, merchants and shopkeepers, and residential homeowners' associations have enlisted the services of private security companies to protect their persons and property. By defining threats to personal safety and supplying expensive means to address them, the private security industry has effectively shaped a "'new risk mentality' that generates mushrooming demand for its own products and services."[8] By encouraging the active engagement and participation of local communities in the production of their own security, municipal authorities have paradoxically weakened their own capacity to maintain and manage regulatory power over the singular and uniform provision of public policing services, thereby undermining their own legitimacy.[9]

Unbundling Security Services: Pluralizing the Practice of Policing

In Johannesburg after apartheid, the transformation of security governance has proceeded along two separate and contradictory lines. On the one hand, municipal authorities have made great strides in improving the quality of the public policing system through the racial integration of police services from the lowest to the highest ranks, through the redistribution of personnel and resources toward deprived townships where these were previously scarce, through the reassertion of public (civic) authority over the militarized police that prevailed during the apartheid era, and through the adoption of new strategies of security governance. On the other hand, the implementation of these new strategies of security governance has led to the fragmentation of policing services.[10] Private security companies have come to play an increasingly prominent role in wealthier residential suburbs, whereas poorer areas have come to rely on various kinds of self-mobilized community policing.[11]

The scope of private enterprise policing has expanded at an unprecedented pace in urban South Africa since the early 1990s. Services and tasks that were once virtually monopolized by state agencies—such as protection of private property, the securing and monitoring of safe public spaces, crime prevention and law enforcement, the apprehension of suspected criminals, the investigation of criminal offenses, armed response to emergency situations, mobile patrolling, the housing and transporting of prisoners, and intelligence gathering in criminal cases—have been transferred in varying degrees and through various arrangements to private, profit-making enterprises. Unable to stem the rising tide of criminality within the scope of their limited institutional and financial resources, state-sponsored policing agencies have watched helplessly as their once-exclusive functions have been usurped by others: private security firms, security initiatives attached to residential associations, neighborhood watch organizations, business owners' and property owners' associations, and even vigilante groups operating outside the law and on their own initiative.[12] The increasing commodification of policing services and the unbundling of security provision has resulted in the accelerated fragmentation and pluralization of the panoptic administration of social space.[13] This diversification of security governance has produced a multiplicity of relationships, programs, and techniques, along with a variety of different stakeholders, organizations, and agencies, in which each party claims legitimacy and assumes certain responsibilities for the delivery of security services and technologies.[14]

As a general rule, the binary distinction between public policing agencies and profit-seeking private security companies is simply too broad to capture the tangled spectrum of security arrangements. Rather than working with a dichotomous model that divides public and private policing into hermetically separated spheres, it is more useful to explore how they overlap and are often thoroughly imbricated in the everyday practice of security governance. As Benoît Dupont has argued, "There is as much diversity within the private security industry as there are differences separating public and private security providers."[15] The complex variety of private security arrangements ranges from the formal (defined by legally binding contracts and institutional rules) to the informal (characterized by *ad hoc* and occasional agreements) and from the microsetting of a single residence to the macroscale of several contiguous neighborhoods. In addition, the modes of service delivery vary considerably, depending in part on the quality of protection and type of security packages on offer.[16] For example, the work of private security companies providing proactive public-space policing over entire neighborhoods bears little resemblance to the everyday tasks of informal stationary guards watching over the entrance to a lone commercial establishment. The labyrinthine web of interdependencies that bind together public policing agencies and private security companies in complex networks cannot be easily classified in ways that can be clearly understood.[17]

The exponential growth of the private security industry—characterized three decades ago as a worldwide "silent revolution"[18]—has fundamentally reshaped the character of crime prevention and law enforcement in the post-public city.[19] The rapid development of increasingly complex and differentiated patchworks of protective services makes it more and more difficult to conceive of crime control purely or even principally in terms of the conventional paradigm of state-sponsored public policing. The increased reliance on private security services has undermined the modernist dream-fantasy of creating and maintaining a virtual state monopoly over the legitimate use of force and violence.[20] This unbundling of policing services has produced far-reaching consequences, not only for equal access to safety and security as basic rights for all urban residents but also for the capacity of municipal administration to maintain regulatory powers (and even the semblance of credibility) over what remains one of its core functions.[21] Security provision must now be understood to refer to the whole range of law enforcement practices, crime prevention tactics, and surveillance technologies provided not only by public bodies such as the municipal police or local authorities but also by private security companies that compete in the marketplace.[22]

Inverting Public and Private Policing Functions in the Criminogenic City

The emergence and expansion of a market for private security has fundamentally transformed the terrain of urban governance. The provision of security has increasingly fallen under the sway of private enterprise. Security, protection, and risk management have acquired new meanings at a time when private companies offer these as "services" for sale as marketable commodities in a competitive marketplace. Rather than functioning as public goods or shared resources, they are acquired in the same way as other products that the market distributes. These changes call into question the conventional modes of policing, law enforcement, prosecution, and punishment.[23] A withering array of policing frameworks, formats, and schemes have taken shape over the past several decades in what can be described as a highly segmented market for security products. With the commodification of protection services and security management, policing has been subjected to the twin dynamics of disaggregation and hybridization—the hallmarks of the postmodern urban condition.[24] The fact that so many different policing agencies coexist typically results in a duplication of functions, since the distinctions between their roles are no longer clear and the lines between their objectives have become blurred.[25] As one leading scholar of the private security industry put it, "It is now almost impossible to identify any function or responsibility of the public police which is not, somewhere and under some circumstances, assumed and performed by private police."[26]

Policing has come to resemble a "differentiated patchwork of security provision."[27] The proliferation of policing services has exposed the myth of state sovereignty and its monopoly over crime control and security governance.[28] There is now widespread recognition that policing has become multitiered, fragmented, and dispersed. This pluralization of security provision has resulted in a more complex division of policing labor between an assortment of public law enforcement agencies and private business organizations, operating at multiple scales, with different security functions and under sometimes contradictory regulatory frameworks. In the new world of security governance, alliances of public, parochial, and private agencies and associations coexist, sometimes drawn together in complex assemblages and intricate networks of policing and crime control.[29] Pluralized policing has blurred and confused the conventional dichotomies between public policing as moral, reactive, and punitive and "private security as instrumental, proactive (risk averse) and consensual."[30]

This unbundling of security services and the development of new kinds of hybrid policing reflect the worldwide trend toward the adoption of neoliberal modes of urban governance, including the privatization of municipal assets, the outsourcing of city services, and the formation of public-private partnerships.[31] There is a growing consensus in the scholarly literature that the introduction of new approaches to crime control and law enforcement over the past several decades has profoundly transformed what it means to talk about the provision of urban security.[32] A great deal of scholarly research has highlighted a number of these new developments, including the expansion of private security services, the growing significance of transnational policing practices and the expanded role of expert consultancies, changes in the organization and management of public law enforcement agencies, the impact of new technologies on policing and crime control, and the replacement of conventional disciplinary approaches to crime control with new risk-based (or actuarial) policing strategies.[33] Scholars have described these new approaches to law enforcement and crime control as "post-Keynesian policing," "plural policing," the "extended policing family," "situational crime prevention," "preventative safety (or disorder reduction) partnerships," "'pick 'n' mix' policing for a postmodern age," and even "the end of public policing."[34] Whatever else these labels characterize, they represent efforts to grapple with the shift—sometimes visible and dramatic, other times subtle and messy—from a state-sponsored criminal justice system designed to maximize the efficient production of law enforcement and crime control to the fluid, endlessly mutable operations of the private security industry organized around minimizing risk in a climate of insecurity.[35]

In the conventional understanding of modern policing, state agencies operate as the monopolistic guardians of law and order. In the uncertain age of late modernity, the restructuring and rearticulation of this operating principle has occurred both from above and from below.[36] The erosion of the capacity of state policing agencies to engage in effective crime prevention has paved the way for private security companies, on the one side, and mobilized communities, on the other, to fill in the gaps.[37] The introduction of these new preventative strategies of crime control and public safety cannot be understood as merely an extension of existing criminal justice procedures but as the adoption of an entirely new paradigm. This new infrastructure is oriented toward a different set of objectives—such as crime prevention, personal security, risk reduction, and minimization of fear—that are markedly distinct from the conventional goals of criminal prosecution and punishment under the sanction of state-authorized criminal justice.[38]

The expanded role of private security marks a transition from a hierarchical administration of law enforcement and crime prevention to more network-based forms of lateral decision-making that blur the boundaries between conventional understandings of public and private. The expanded role of private security companies in crime prevention cannot be seen as simply an erosion of state power or legitimacy that inevitably led to the privatization of security provision and the replacement of public policing altogether. Rather, the pluralization of policing has produced new modes of security that have reconfigured the relationships between public policing agencies and private security companies.[39] In the marketplace for consumer goods, the provision of private security has become deeply embedded in a "regime of choice."[40] Private security arrangements serve parochial or club interests, which maintain a narrow drawn focus and thus stand apart from the broader public interest.[41] Seen in this light, the commodification of customized policing services has enabled private organizations and local communities "to pursue their particularistic (and self-defined) security requirements without reference to any conception of the common good or obligations associated with the practice of democratic citizenship."[42] Taken to the extreme, the purchase of privatized security services as club goods points toward the construction of a "neo-feudal world of private orders in which social cohesion and common citizenship have collapsed."[43]

The limitations of public policing as an effective agency in law enforcement have exposed what David Garland has called the "myth of sovereign crime control."[44] The blurring of the conventional boundaries between state-sponsored policing and private security makes it necessary to develop a new vocabulary and a new way of understanding that can enable us to make sense of what amounts to a structural symbiosis between the two.[45] Indeed, a number of critical observers have moved away from a narrow focus on the evolving division of labor between public and private policing and have begun to speak instead in terms of "extended security networks," "security assemblages," "nodal security governance," "liquid security," and "networked security governance."[46] Others have invoked such metaphors as "security quilts" (Ericson), "security webs" (Shamir and Ben-Ar), "reassurance policing" (Crawford and Lister), "policing webs" (Brodeur), "multi-choice policing" (Baker), and "twilight policing" (Diphoorn) to refer to the blurred boundaries between public agencies and private companies in the provision of security.[47]

These new analytic frameworks take for granted the hybrid blending and fragmentation of policing systems and protective services.[48] In this new way of thinking, policing has evolved into a system of "networked nodal governance," or complex latticework of overlapping and intersecting mechanisms that work together to produce public safety and security in ways that go well beyond hard-and-fast distinctions between public law enforcement and private policing. [49] Drawing from the public, private, and voluntary organizations, such networks of security have become the bedrocks of new approaches to urban governance.[50] These mechanisms of "networked nodal governance" transcend the "established conceptual boundaries drawn between 'public' and 'private' agencies, places, and functions."[51]

In carrying out their mandated role in maintaining law and order, public policing agencies must strike a delicate balance between their operational efficiency and democratic accountability to local constituencies who, after all, enjoy rights of citizenship under the rule of law.[52] In contrast, private security companies are primarily obligated to their clients, who pay for protective services with the expectation that they will receive the safekeeping they are promised.[53] The purpose behind public policing is to provide a shared public good that is consumed collectively. In contrast, the aim of private security companies is to profit from selling marketable commodities. As a consequence, these two goals veer in different directions and often come into conflict with one another.[54]

Despite the steady expansion of private security companies into fields conventionally thought to be the exclusive preserve of public policing agencies, it makes little sense to try to squeeze these shifting patterns into a uniform, one-size-fits-all explanatory framework. Concepts such as privatization, marketization, and neoliberalism cannot possibly capture the complexity of these shifting patterns. What has occurred in Johannesburg and elsewhere is not simply the wholesale transfer of security functions or responsibilities from the public policing agencies to private companies. Despite shifts in the division of tasks and responsibilities, public policing agencies remain as a kind of *éminence grise*, a "shadow entity lurking [just] off-stage."[55] Both public policing agencies and private security companies have experienced a profound transformation in their approaches to law enforcement and crime prevention. These shifting relationships to security governance have not followed predetermined pathways, and they have varied considerably over time, space, and context.[56]

The expanded role of private security companies in the provision of protection services cannot be attributed simply to the top-down, deliberate adoption of neoliberal policies and the fixation with replacing the public distribution of goods with market discipline and commodification. To a large extent, the privatization of security in Johannesburg is the unintended consequence of the inability of public policing agencies to effectively deliver on the promise of law enforcement and crime prevention in the aftermath of the end of apartheid and the transition to parliamentary democracy. Rather than reflecting "a simple eroding of state authority or a pure form of state withdrawal," the blending of public policing and private security has resulted in a reconfigured "plural policing landscape that is characterized by both competition and collaboration."[57]

Double Paradigm Shift

Put broadly, the increasingly prominent and visible role of private security companies in crime prevention has marked a double paradigm shift.[58] The first paradigm shift involves the steady encroachment of private security companies on the once (seemingly) sacrosanct prerogatives of state-authorized public policing in the criminal justice system. In the conventional modernist paradigm of law enforcement and crime prevention, public policing agencies maintain a monopoly over the legitimate use of force and violence in the maintenance of law and order. As the institutional capacity of the public policing agencies to effectively engage in crime fighting and law enforcement has dwindled, private security companies have filled the void.[59] This lack of adequate service delivery has produced a "policing gap" that has created opportunities for private security companies to assume tasks and responsibilities that had not existed before.[60] By expanding their field of operations into the terrain of public space, private security companies have moved from a narrow focus on the protection of individual households (captured under the phrase *armed response*) to a broader stress on the maintenance of law and order in entire neighborhoods. Shifting the burden for security (whether personal or collective) from state-sponsored policing agencies to private companies has blurred the boundaries that once separated noncommodified public-service provision from profit-seeking enterprises selling security services. [61]

The second paradigm shift involves the movement from a reactive response to law enforcement toward more proactive (or preemptive) approaches aimed at stopping crime before it happens. In the conventional modernist paradigm of policing public spaces, policing agencies respond to suspected criminal behavior, reacting to what appear at face value to be transgressions of the law. This so-called preventive turn in policing has signaled a move away from reactive responses to risk management and the maintenance of law and order to the adoption instead of anticipation and deterrence as the key strategic components of crime control.[62] In Johannesburg, private security companies have increasingly adopted a model of public-space policing that involves more proactive, aggressive approaches "aimed at preventing opportunities for law-breaking."[63] More specifically, they engage in activities designed to identify potential criminals and drive them away (through intimidation or violence) or physically remove them from public spaces that border or surround the properties and persons they are hired to protect.[64] Seen in this light, a whole range of highly visible private policing strategies, ranging from mobile street patrols, the use of CCTV monitoring, targeted hot-spot surveillance, unauthorized road closures and installation of boom gates, and stop-and-frisk tactics (to name just a few), receive both legitimacy and praise because of their "preventative capabilities."[65]

A word of caution is in order. When placed in the wider sociohistorical context of law enforcement and crime prevention in Johannesburg, the conceptualization of a double paradigm shift is only partially accurate. Public policing in South Africa was never "conventional" in either the narrow or the broad sense of the term. In short, there never was a mythical golden age in which a single state-sponsored professional organization tasked with handling the policing functions of law and order was able to assert a virtual monopoly over the legitimate use of force and violence. In actuality, this modernist ideal of a stable normative order in which all-encompassing, centralized public authority was able to effectively monopolize law enforcement and crime prevention was largely symbolic.[66] In fact, under white minority rule, the maintenance of law and order was always a hybrid affair, involving overlapping public agencies and private organizations, including state authorities responsible for influx control, labor bureaus, paramilitary groups, Special Forces (elite military units), Third Force elements, and rogue vigilante groups operating outside official sanction.[67]

Risk Management and Intersecting Security Regimes

The shift from public law enforcement to private security policing has involved more than simply the replacement of one system by the other.

The security products that the private companies offer are quite different from the services that municipalities ordinarily provide. Private security companies offer different kinds of protection, target different
kinds of risk, engage in different tactics of crime deterrence, and have
different operational logics.[68] Whereas public law enforcement agencies focus primarily on the maintenance of law and order and uphold-
ing norms of propriety, private security companies direct their efforts
chiefly at minimizing risk for the clients who pay them to do so.[69]

In the field of crime prevention, policing experts have begun to think
about law enforcement in entirely new ways. Rather than conceive of
crime in terms of its biological origins in offender motivations, the inherent proclivities of individuals or groups, or causal analyses of criminality, policing experts have begun to stress its situational characteristics,
that is, those spatial and temporal aspects associated with opportunities for criminal activities.[70] In other words, policing has shifted from
order maintenance, which defines problems in terms of moral deviance
and individual culpability, to risk management, which defines problems
in terms of relative danger and exposure. Order maintenance is rooted
in punitive, deterrence-based law enforcement. In contrast, risk management starts with the premise of preventing crime before it happens.
Hence, what defines good policing is not necessarily the successful apprehension of lawbreakers but the reduction of risk.[71] Rather than focusing on the causes of crime, preventative strategies of risk management
concentrate on altering physical or social settings to reduce opportunities for criminal behavior.[72]

This shift toward risk management and away from law enforcement
has resulted in a new policing orientation, one that David Garland has
termed the "responsibilization strategy."[73] This new mode of security
governance involves public policing agencies managing crime and law
enforcement indirectly by energizing and activating private agencies, organizations, and local communities. Yet these responsibilization tactics
do not signal the off-loading of public functions or simply the privatization of crime control. On the contrary, these strategies of responsibilization have signaled the introduction of new security assemblages in
which a variety of agencies, partners, and stakeholders "interact, coop-
erate, and compete, to produce new institutions, practices and forms of
security governance."[74] Seen through the lens of neoliberal modes of ur-

ban governance, law enforcement and crime prevention are problems of risk management, whereas safety and security become a matter of individual responsibility.[75]

This proliferation of private groups involved in maintaining law and order has strongly influenced the ways in which space is imagined, organized, and managed. These shifts in security governance have raised a range of normative concerns about impartiality of provision and equity of access, along with questions regarding the responsibility, accountability, and effectiveness of policing in different spaces.[76] The partial withdrawal of public policing agencies and their replacement with private security firms and voluntary associations has produced what has been called an "extended policing family."[77] The aim of these initiatives has been to pass, or at least share, the responsibility for the maintenance of law and order in ways that move away from primary dependence on public policing agencies by embracing multiple stakeholders involved in joint crime and disorder alliances. These shifts "are embodied in the introduction of initiatives aimed at encouraging active citizenship and partnership working in the provision of policing."[78]

The shift in policing in Johannesburg reflects a changing focus in worldwide trends in crime prevention and law enforcement from apprehending criminal suspects to managing risk. Neoliberal security regimes have stressed enlisting "security stakeholders" to reduce the risk of crime not so much through conventional social welfare and educational measures but alternatively through the environmental design of physical locations in combination with the implementation of community participation (such as neighborhood watch) initiatives. The core of neoliberal security-governance regimes are risk management strategies that focus on reducing the likelihood of criminal behavior at specific places and specific times.[79]

Scholars Malcolm Feeley and Jonathan Simon have proposed that a "new penology," concerned with the regulation of disorder and the prevention of aggregate risk, has replaced the "old penology," with its focus on personal responsibility, deterrence, and punishment tailored to individual offenders.[80] Criminologists have termed this strategic shift in policing and crime policy "actuarial risk management." This new actuarial mentality draws on preventative measures (such as surveillance) and initiatives (such as "safer cities through environmental design"), works with statistical prediction and risk profiles, and seeks to engage private citizens in the management of their own security.[81]

Critics of the new penology have argued that discourses and practices of "crime control" have become increasingly comingled with entrepreneurial modes of urban governance that stress place-marketing, "quality-of-life" aesthetics, and other promotional exercises that city boosters have used to lure investment and attract visitors. The promotion of particular places with "desirable qualities" has placed management of crime and disorder squarely at the center of a spatial ordering strategy designed to "clean up" urban landscapes.[82] The core feature of this new entrepreneurial statecraft depends on the reconfiguration of crime control practices, seen through the lens of a punitive obsession with risk indicators and "dangerization."[83] This hallucinatory fixation on order maintenance and crime control works hand in hand with the punitive gaze by engaging in the targeting of suspiciousness.[84]

The Crowded Terrain of Security Governance

The stress on crime prevention is reflected not only in the emphasis on neighborhood- and community-policing efforts but also in the creation of various kinds of public-private partnerships that have brought the South African Police Service (SAPS), private security firms, and neighborhood associations together in complicated triangular relationships. In what has become typical of fortress suburbia, the SAPS has contributed to safety and security initiatives by providing the expertise for the design of crime prevention strategies. But because of their woeful lack of resources and overstretched capacities, the SAPS has largely ceded routine neighborhood patrols and armed response to private security companies.[85]

The state monopoly over law enforcement and crime prevention has dissipated in different directions: outward to private business enterprises specializing in security and protection in the commercial marketplace and downward to responsibilized consumers organized into neighborhood associations, community watch groups, and vigilant armed citizens (so-called vigilantes). This emergent triangular relationship between public law enforcement agencies, private security companies, and neighborhood associations has produced an uneasy alliance of unstable partnerships. Although these partners share a common interest in security and protection, what lurks below the surface are competing goals and different understandings about achieving these ends.[86]

Neighborhood associations, section 21 companies, business enterprises, and ward committees have sometimes become active participants in the militarization of social space. For example, Rand Merchant Bank in Sandton took the public-private partnership concept to new heights when it assumed full responsibility for maintaining the local police station free of charge after repeated requests to the public-works ministry to conduct much-needed repair work had met with little success. Similarly, in a style reminiscent of civic mobilization in the periurban townships during the turbulent 1980s, the neighborhood association in Blairgowrie organized its homeowners into street committees, which reported to five sector captains in a hierarchically structured chain of command that reached its apex at a three-person executive committee. This movement toward what has been called partnership policing—particularly a project called "Adopt a Station" whereby private companies band together to provide expertise and resources to the public police in exchange for the establishment of a local police substation in their area—marked a decisive step toward the gradual privatization of security services. In some residential suburbs, Community Policing Forums (CPFs), spearheaded by neighborhood associations, have contributed to the financing of local police budgets, including sometimes paying for the maintenance of police vehicles and providing computers and other equipment (including cell phones and photocopy paper). Many members of CPFs have volunteered to work for free in local police stations, helping with administrative tasks and other mundane duties.[87] Residents of the northeastern suburban neighborhoods of Glenhazel and Sandringham, for example, raised somewhere between $100,000 and $200,000 to establish and fund their own police station, renting a building and purchasing vehicles, furniture, and equipment. Similarly, in Rosebank, local residents collected funds to make improvements to the local police station. In Kensington, the "I Love Kensington Association" (ILKA) purchased vehicles for the Johannesburg Municipal Police Department (JMPD) and paid for the gas in order to encourage public law enforcement to conduct regular patrols for bylaw infringements. The Athol-Illovo-Inanda-Western Ridge Residents' Association (AIIWE) collected funds to purchase three vehicles, donating them to the local SAPS precinct and paying the insurance premiums. In Parkview, homeowners have sometimes paid the salaries of individual police officers. The basic cost for this private peace of mind typically ranges from R 170 to R 300 per month, and this figure amounts to a disguised tax on those who can afford it.[88]

Private security companies have steadily encroached on the prerogatives that were once the exclusive domain of public law enforcement agencies. For example, the SAPS have hired private security companies (such as Chubb Protective Services, Protea Coin, Anchor Security, Impala Security, Secuforce, and Security Wise) to guard their perimeters and to monitor the movements of staff and visitors alike, in large measure to prevent theft of weapons and pilfering of property.[89] It was revealed in 2009 that fifteen firms were hired to guard some of the more than one thousand police stations in the country. Protea Security Services and Khulani Fidelity Group Services were the two companies with the largest contracts. Critics charged that the "country's official protectors cannot even protect themselves from criminals."[90]

Private security companies have also increasingly ventured into the broad field of investigative services. Some companies have specialized in providing their expertise in criminal case building, such as forensics, fingerprint analysis, the preservation of crime scenes, examination of CCTV surveillance footage, interrogation of criminal suspects, and polygraph testing of domestic workers. Still other companies undertake intelligence gathering for wealthy households, businesses, and neighborhood associations that do not trust public law enforcement agencies to do the job.[91]

At different times and places, the SAPS has entered into a variety of cooperative arrangements with private security companies. These partnerships have ranged from informal cooperative alliances dealing with specific operational matters to formal partnerships tied together with binding agreements. The experimental pilot project unveiled in late 2008 at the Honeydew police station represented perhaps the most ambitious effort to date to forge a working alliance between the SAPS and private security companies. The Honeydew policing cluster is located in the northwest corner of the Johannesburg municipality. The sprawling area consists of a hodgepodge of settlement patterns, ranging from unpoliced open spaces (greenbelts), informal squatter settlements (including Sol Plaatjies, Matolesville, Doornkop/Thulani, Leratong, Tshepisong, Zandspruit, and Bram Fischerville), and low-income housing estates (Cosmo

City) to middle-income (Weltevreden Park) and affluent residential suburbs, gated residential communities, and business-commercial clusters.[92] Rising crime in the area—particularly the so-called trio crimes (house burglaries, business robberies, and carjackings) and the persistence of opportunistic criminality—had triggered a great deal of consternation among business owners and middle-class residents who had grown weary of the perceived inability of public law enforcement agencies to provide sufficient security.

To strengthen the fight against crime, the Honeydew SAPS (under the leadership of police-station commissioner Oswald Reddy) initiated a formal agreement with twelve private security companies designed to forge a more comprehensive alliance involving security cooperation on the ground. The brainchild of a downtown coalition of large-scale property owners called Business against Crime (BAC), this new crime-fighting partnership arose out of a Memorandum of Understanding (MOU) signed in October 2008 between the SAPS and the Security Industry Alliance (SIA), an organization that represented companies in the private security industry.[93] The idea behind this experimental program was to utilize the available resources and personnel of the participating private security companies as a supplement to the daily crime-fighting activities of the SAPS. What private security companies brought to the table was the fact that they spent much more time guarding private homes and patrolling neighborhoods. By enlisting the services of private security companies to act as the eyes and ears on the ground, the SAPS gained access to information that they could not obtain on their own. In exchange for information about suspicious-looking people and crime incidents that private security teams obtained during their routine patrols, public law enforcement agencies granted their partners enhanced policing powers. For their part, the SAPS agreed to furnish private security companies with their lists of wanted criminals and stolen vehicles operating in the precinct. The aim of this information sharing was to improve the response rate of public law enforcement agencies to crime scenes.[94] Under the terms of the agreement, private security guards were formally empowered to do official police work, which included taking charge of crime scenes at house and business robberies and carjackings if they arrived before public law enforcement officers. Private security operatives were also allowed to identify and formally arrest criminal suspects and to gather evidence admissible in court.[95]

The aim of this initiative was to enhance the overall effectiveness of public policing agencies in handling crime by improving the coordination, cooperation, and consultation with their private security partners. The key logistical component of this joint arrangement was the establishment of a specialized communications center where public policing agencies and private security companies worked together. The twelve companies (out of sixty private security firms operating in the precinct) that signed up for the project included such household names as ADT, Chubb Protective Services, Top Security, and Peaceforce. They agreed to supply radios and staff for the joint command center that operated out of the SAPS control room in Honeydew. In turn, public law enforcement agencies agreed to provide training for private security guards on how to secure crime scenes, preserve evidence, and to write detailed incident reports. The SAPS also offered instruction in radio protocol in order to facilitate direct communication between private security guards and public police. Because criminal gangs frequently listened to SAPS radio communications, information sharing through a secure network that operated independently of the official police channels was necessary. In exchange, private security companies agreed to assist public law enforcement agencies by making vehicles and trained operatives available during crime incidents.[96]

Buoyed by what appeared to be the early successes of the experimental program, high-ranking law enforcement officials unveiled ambitious plans to introduce similar initiatives in the Florida, Roodepoort, Douglasdale, and Randburg police stations.[97] Yet at the same time, skeptics raised a number of concerns about the long-term wisdom of launching such open-ended security partnerships, of mixing public law enforcement expectations with the profit-making motives of private companies. Critics such as Barbara Holtman, for example, suggested that "we should be cautious about handing power to private security companies because they are not subject to the same oversight and tight rules that control the SAPS."[98] In time, the original Honeydew crime prevention project fizzled out and was eventually disbanded after a new station commander took over and was not in favor of continuing the partnership in its original form. Ad hoc and informal cooperative arrangements between the SAPS and individual security companies have continued, but these operate outside of formal agreements.[99]

The Private Security Industry: Filling the Void

The private security industry consists of a mixture of companies that are engaged in highly differentiated activities and that have scales of operation, organizational structures, and purposes that typically bear little resemblance to one another. The public face of private security is the visible work of patrolling, guarding, personal protection, and cash in transit. At a superficial level, this work seemingly resembles conventional public policing. Yet at its root, the ultimate goal of private security policing is not to apprehend, prosecute, convict, or punish criminal offenders, and still less is it to uphold the normative superstructure that constitutes the application of criminal law. Rather, its goals revolve around the protection of private property and the management and reduction of (shared or individual) risk.[100] Within the broad field of visible private security policing, the size and scope of operations ranges from lone stationary guards to the protection of huge corporate entities that employ thousands of operatives engaged in all sorts of tasks. The multinational conglomerates have little in common with the dubious fly-by-night operations that operate on shoestring budgets, with dubious credentials and limited resources.[101]

During its formative years, the private security industry in South Africa operated much like an exclusive club with restricted membership. Entry into the industry was largely restricted at the administrative levels to those with police, military, and intelligence backgrounds. Perhaps not surprisingly, the first private security companies, which began operating in the 1980s and 1990s, were predominately owned and managed by former elite members of colonial armed forces opposed to majority rule in Rhodesia, Kenya, and Zambia. After 1994, the private security industry experienced an influx of new companies, formed primarily by retiring and cashiered members of the disbanded South African Defense Force (SADF).[102]

The private provision of protective services has progressively assumed the character of an efficiently managed modern industry. Private security companies have typically borrowed the iconic symbols of authority (distinctive uniforms, state-of-the-art weapons, badges and other insignia, accessories, and specialized vehicles) associated with public policing, and they have readily adopted the militarized language of crime prevention and law enforcement in their day-to-day work.[103] Unlike the largely reactive functions of the state law enforcement agencies, private security companies have vowed to reduce of the risk of crime through preventative action. They promise immediate armed response to called-in requests for emergency assistance. They also offer a variety of specialized services that the state-sponsored law enforcement agencies are unable or unwilling to provide in a cost-effective manner, such as proactive patrolling of neighborhood streets, premises control, static sentry duties, the monitoring of sensory devices, escorting clients to their homes, paramedic assistance, and holiday checks. Some private companies have entered the battle against crime as a paramilitary force, promising to dispatch armored vehicles and well-trained and well-armed operatives outfitted with Uzi submachine guns, military-style assault rifles, shotguns, and nine-millimeter pistols and with orders to shoot to kill unwanted intruders.[104]

The rapidly expanding role of private security services as functional surrogates for public law enforcement has gone hand in glove with new kinds of policing division of labor. Instead of focusing on crime prevention in residential neighborhoods and social congregating spaces such as shopping malls and commercial strips, public law enforcement agencies have channeled their resources into crime response, particularly into combating such high-profile criminal activities as drug trafficking, cash-and-carry heists, and violent crimes committed with illegal firearms. Private security companies, which have tapped into the vast reservoir of low-wage employees, have increasingly captured the labor-intensive security roles, such as static guard and sentry duties, patrol of residential neighborhoods, apprehension of retail crime, and the monitoring of electronic surveillance equipment. At the same time, public law enforcement has regrouped behind the supervision of security macrosystems, such as the maintenance and evaluation of crime databases, the tracking of criminal syndicates, and the prosecution and incarceration of criminal offenders. These blurred boundaries between private and public policing functions are perhaps most evident in the visible presence of private security street patrols and the virtual invisibility of public police in most exclusive residential neighborhoods. They are also evident in the growing trend of subcontracting the management of detention centers and prison facilities to private profit-making firms.[105]

Without a doubt, the growing dependence on private security is a worldwide trend. What makes the provision of private security different in Johannesburg, however, is that private security officers tend to be more heavily armed than public law enforcement agents and have assumed more core policing functions than in most other "dangerous" cities. Private policing is far more flexible and responsive than public law enforcement because it can be more readily adjusted to changing scale and scope of consumer demand.[106] The ability of private security companies to hire and fire staff and to employ individual freelancers (rent-a-cop, or piecework policing) for temporary or part-time assignments in response to market pressures is not possible in public police forces, which are required to operate under strict public-service regulations and guidelines. Private companies specializing in particular fields of security are able to acquire and use much more technically sophisticated and scientifically advanced equipment than most local law enforcement agencies can afford.[107]

Policing for Profit: The Lucrative Business of Private Security

The obsession with security has become big business. Whereas economic growth has remained more or less stagnant since the transition to parliamentary democracy, the demand for private security services has thrived. Since the 1970s, the private security industry has expanded at an astonishing rate, not just in terms of the absolute number of employees and number of companies but also in terms of net worth and revenues.[108] In the 1970s, the private security industry expanded at an astounding average rate of close to 30 percent per year. Despite a slowdown in annual rates of growth in subsequent years, private security has still been the most rapidly expanding industry in South Africa since the early 1990s.[109]

In 1990, the net worth of the private security industry was valued at R 1.2 billion ($160 million).[110] By 2006, this figure had climbed to somewhere between R 14 billion and R 18 to R 20 billion ($1.8–$2.6 billion).[111] By 2016, the amount spent on private security had ballooned to R 45 billion ($6 billion)—a third more than the government spent on public policing.[112]

Following the transition to parliamentary democracy in 1994, the private security industry became one of the largest and fastest-growing employers of unskilled and semiskilled labor in the new South Africa. Estimates of the number employed vary greatly, due in part to different systems of classification and methods of calculation. According to reliable estimates, in 1997 there were 4,437 registered security companies employing 115,331 active security officers. These numbers have skyrocketed over the years. According to figures provided by the Private Security Industry Regulatory Authority (PSIRA) in its 2010–2011 annual report, the private security industry consisted of 8,828 registered security companies (which was an 18.35 percent increase over the number of companies registered for 2009–2010) employing an estimated 411,109 active security officers, with another 1,370,000 inactive registered security officers ready for work when opportunities became available.[113] The private security industry established itself long ago as the leading supplier of entry-level jobs in a country beset with high levels of unemployment. According to estimates provided by the PSIRA, between 15,000 and 20,000 new recruits joined the private security industry each month in 2014 and 2015. This situation was so alarming that it led Frans Cronje, chief executive officer of the Institute of Race Relations, to proclaim that private companies had effectively taken over safeguarding the country.[114] According to the 2018–2019 report issued by the PSIRA, the private security industry has continued to dwarf public policing agencies: there were 2.36 million private security officers registered in South Africa in 2018 and 2019—of which close to 500,000 were employed by just over 9,000 registered and active private security companies. These figures suggest that there are close to five private security operatives for every public police officer in South Africa. Moreover, between 2001 and 2018, the number of registered and employed private security officers increased by 157 percent and the number of private security businesses grew by 65 percent. Equally astounding, during this same period the number of actively employed private security operatives was more than double the number of people working in public security services, including police officers and members of the armed forces.[115]

In all likelihood, these figures grossly underestimate the total workforce of the private security industry. First, not all companies and private security guards register with PSIRA as required by law. Second, many companies and security guards attempt to operate under the radar and unlawfully.[116] In doing these calculations, the private security industry routinely underestimates the actual number of employees because companies exclude in-house guards, private investigators, and security divisions within large corporations (for example, large-scale financial entities such as ABSA, Standard Bank, and FNB have their own internal security personnel). These employment figures do not include many unregistered personnel working for uncertified companies or self-employed individuals who make a living informally in the sector guarding cars and other property. The real numbers thus are likely much higher.[117] These numbers also exclude the well more than 200,000 in-house security guards (personnel hired to exclusively guard the premises or property of their employers). In contrast, the South African Police Service (SAPS) employed an estimated 195,000 persons in 2014, consisting of 36,304 employees in administration; 103,746 police officers engaged in visible policing; 39,748 detectives; 8,723 crime intelligence officers; and 6,331 protection and security officers. In addition, as many as 40,000 operational public police officers failed to qualify for or did not have their firearm competency certificates.[118]

All in all, in 2015, private security operatives outnumbered uniformed police officers performing policing functions by a ratio that some experts have estimated to be as high as seven to one.[119] Although relatively small-scale companies with specialized niches in the market for protection services have employed the lion's share of security personnel, large companies, such as Pretoria-based Bidvest Protea Coin Security Group (which employs an estimated 25,000 licensed security officers), Johannesburg-based Fidelity Corporate Services (which employs almost 27,000 licensed security officers), and global corporations such as Securitas, G4S, and Tyco-ADT dominate the private security industry. Owned by Tyco International, ADT has long been the largest provider of residential security in the country. In 2012, ADT claimed to have 450,000 clients in South Africa—nine times more than the next largest single company—and more than 4,000 employees in the Greater Johannesburg metropolitan region alone.[120] The private security industry has also overshadowed the South African police in logistical resources, such as the availability of armored vehicles, skills training, high-speed cars, tracking devices, and surveillance equipment as well as the quality of firearms.[121]

Despite its exponential growth and enormous size, the private security industry is a highly fragmented, precarious business characterized by cutthroat market competition, high staff turnover, and considerable customer change. Both the number of companies and types of services have fluctuated wildly. There are a number of reasons for this volatility.

The relatively low barriers to entry has meant that new companies and spinoffs from established ones form and disappear with regularity. For the most part, companies operate with low profit margins, primarily because competition is based on price for services and not quality.[122] Stiff competition has taken its toll, as some companies have disbanded and gone out of business, while others have been absorbed into larger firms. The services subsector classified under the rubric of guarding is perhaps the most volatile branch, with labor turnover of perhaps as much as 15–20 percent per month. An estimated 100,000 people leave the industry every year, and between 250 and 350 companies close every month. High turnover is mostly the result of low pay, poor working conditions, long hours, few social benefits, and the dead-end qualities of the job, with limited opportunities for upward mobility.[123]

The main branches of the industry are dominated by a handful of large companies (for example, Fidelity ADT, Securicor (South Africa), Magnum-Shield Security Services, G4S, Chubb & Supergroup, Bidvest Protea Coin Security Group, and Enforce Guarding). With more than 370,000 customers, more than 30 percent of the market share in the country, and more than 10 percent geographical coverage, Fidelity ADT ranked as the largest private security company in South Africa in 2018. Operational stations for Fidelity ADT receive around 16,000 alarm notifications in a typical day; security personnel respond to around 6,000 of these (where the large deficit is due to false alarms).[124] But there are dozens of medium-sized companies that have carved out niches for themselves in specialized fields. In addition, thousands of smaller, less-established companies provide local or regional services, particularly in the guarding sector.[125] Many unregistered, fly-by-night companies operate on a shoestring, sometimes renting weapons and sometimes illegally obtaining unlicensed firearms and ammunition from public policing agencies.[126] The most dynamic sectors of the private security industry include detection devices and building protection (closed-circuit television, security glass, and motion-detection devices), vehicle security (car alarms, antihijacking devices, and satellite tracking systems), and internal physical security and turnkey systems (security doors and biometric systems for personal identification).[127]

Perhaps most importantly, the private security industry has experienced a great deal of concentration and centralization, as larger companies have absorbed smaller ones through mergers, acquisitions, and buyouts. Over the past several decades, an unprecedented buying spree has enabled larger and more firmly capitalized companies to consolidate their market position in particular subsectors or even to branch out into new security fields. Examples of key mergers and acquisitions include the Top Security purchase of SAS (followed by the Securitas purchase of Top Security), the Securicor purchase of Gray Security, the Fidelity Guards acquisition of Khulani Springbok, the Bidvest-Magnum merger with Protea Coin, and the Sentry-Paramed merger, making the Sentry Group the largest security firm in the country. With a workforce of over 200,000 employees and an estimated 2,000 vehicles spread over 150 branches throughout South Africa, Mozambique, Lesotho, and Swaziland, the new consolidated Fidelity Services Group has established a guarding empire in southern Africa, making it one of the largest companies of its kind in the world. The Sentry-Paramed merger is typical of the shift by large armed-response companies into the provision of emergency health-care services using trained paramedics. The lack of available ambulances from public and private hospitals opened up a market opportunity that private security companies have been quick to fill.[128]

Attracted by the profit potential, many foreign security companies have made strong inroads into the lucrative security services market in South Africa. Starting in 1994, a number of large multinational corporate enterprises began to invest huge sums in the South African private security industry, buying out local firms and agglomerating them into larger entities. By 2015, the private security industry had become the largest employer in the formal private sector, more or less matching all mining operations and quarries put together. According to Costa Diavastos, president of the Security Association of SA, the investment of four large conglomerates—ADT, Chubb International, Securitas, and G4S—in private security in South Africa between 2008 and 2015 amounted to about R 4.5 billion.[129] Other foreign firms, including Tyco International (based in Exeter, New Hampshire) and Secureco (based in Singapore), have purchased local subsidiaries and injected fresh new capital into the industry, bringing with them up-to-date technologies, sophisticated hardware, and management expertise.[130]

Private security companies (some large and many small) are grouped into between six and nine recognized employers' associations that, in turn, are collectively represented by an industry-wide organization called the South African National Security Employers Association (SANSEA).

The separate associations that belong to SANSEA each cater to and represent a particular subsector within the industry. The three main subsectors are staffed guarding services (where an estimated 80–90 percent of the registered companies are located), electronic equipment and monitoring hardware, and physical security. The largest and most influential body is the Security Industry Alliance (SIA). Its core members include the biggest companies, such as Securicor, G4S, Bidvest Protea Coin Security Group, Tyco-ADT, Elvey Group, Fidelity Services Group, and Chubb Protective Services.[131] In order to counter its negative image as a loose collection of unregulated companies that put poorly trained and underprepared operatives in the field with little or no knowledge of crime prevention or law enforcement, the private security industry has introduced stricter training and entry-level educational requirements.[132] Opportunities for private security personnel to become security managers and risk analysts have created avenues for upward mobility within the industry, resulting in the improved professionalism of the leading companies.[133]

The new security economy consists of a mélange of "fear industries" that fuse private security companies with technology-hardware distributors, specialty services, and installers. Whichever market they specialize in, "the fear industries" focus on the performance of "a certain kind of alchemy—turning risk into profit."[134] A wide range of business consultants sell security solutions as remedies to danger by managing risk. Suburban residents are inundated with corporate marketing agents seeking to sell them the latest security paraphernalia.[135]

Weak Regulatory Frameworks

The steady encroachment of private security firms into arenas once reserved as the exclusive preserve for public policing agencies prompted a great deal of uneasiness and suspicion. In calling for stricter regulations, Deputy Minister of Police Fikile Mbabula proclaimed to an official gathering in 2010 that "we can't have private companies running amok in the name of fighting crime. We can't allow them to be above state organs." He reiterated the common refrain that private security companies were businesses trying to maximize profits, while public police "fight crime as part of their constitutional obligation."[136] This sentiment reflected a much deeper distrust and suspicion. High-ranking state officials have openly declared hostility toward the expansion of the private security industry. Growing concerns of a takeover by private security in South Africa triggered a parliamentary backlash, with calls to impose legal restrictions on the amount of foreign investment.[137]

State agencies such as the Private Security Industry Regulatory Agency (PSIRA) have sought to set standards and to impose a modicum of regulation on the private security industry. As a result, organizations representing the various branches of the private security industry have developed an often tense, uneasy, and contradictory relationship with state regulatory agencies. On the one hand, established companies with large market shares in highly lucrative fields of operation and with proven track records of delivering quality services have welcomed a modicum of statutory regulation of the industry because some outside oversight offers a greater measure of professionalism through shared adherence to good business standards and because it levels the playing field for fair competition. After all, strict regulatory regimes only enhance the legitimacy of established companies and prevent maverick fly-by-night firms from cutting into their market shares and undermining their reputations.[138] On the other hand, entrepreneurs in the security business have steadfastly resisted efforts to compel them to conform to labor standards, health and safety regulations, and other conditions of employment. They have also resisted efforts to force them to open their business practices to public scrutiny and to work more closely with public law enforcement agencies, especially with regard to compulsory sharing of information.[139] While the media portrayals are usually negative or cynical, the private security industry has mounted a formidable campaign to create a positive image of itself as a "professional security manager" with a proven track record of success.[140]

State regulation of the private security industry implies the adoption of "legislation accompanied by formal, direct mechanisms of control established with the explicit intention of preventing or reducing injustice, corruption, negligence, or incompetence."[141] State regulatory regimes consist of a variety of interventions, including licensing, labor conditions, and training requirements.[142] Despite concerted efforts, the private security industry has remained largely unregulated, although the Security Officers Interim Board (appointed by an amendment to the Security Officers Act in 1997) is responsible for registering all guards and maintaining minimum training standards. Critics have alleged that the Board is not only comprised of representatives largely drawn from private security companies but also funded by the industry. The Board does not have strong powers of enforcement, and, as a consequence, the private security industry has attracted many fly-by-night operators seeking to cash in on the enormous potential for making a quick profit. Cost-conscious clients want the cheapest rates for security services, thereby encouraging all sorts of disreputable companies to promise services they cannot possibly deliver.[143]

Private security operatives generally work under onerous conditions, and their assigned tasks are often tedious and dangerous. Unscrupulous companies regularly hire foreign nationals and assign them work on holidays and weekends because they know that the PSIRA does not deploy monitoring staff at those times. Companies regularly fail to comply with regulations on overtime work. The PSIRA has expressed concerns about security guards who have received no training in the use of firearms and frequently engage in excessive force when dealing with criminal suspects.[144]

As a general rule, the burgeoning private security industry has been able to avoid public scrutiny. New private security companies emerge at a much greater rate than the capacity to oversee and regulate their activities. The PSIRA has sufficient resources to monitor only about one-sixth of registered companies. All too often, private companies have paid fines for infractions but continue to operate in the same fashion that got them into trouble in the first place. Critics have routinely claimed that the public agencies responsible for registering private security guards and maintaining minimum training standards are too tightly aligned with the private security industry.[145]

PART II

THE DESIGN OF AVOIDANCE
Target Hardening in the Carceral City

Laager Neurosis and
the Architectural Design of Enclosed Places

The affluent, largely white middle classes seek above all a tranquil, controlled, and predictable environment with few surprises. They long for a flight from chance, to inhabit and negotiate safe and secure places where people like themselves, who share similar lifestyles, outlooks, and attitudes, can commingle without unwanted intrusion. The slowness and impotence of public policing agencies to meet the challenge of law enforcement in the face of entrenched crime have become truisms in the popular imagination. Class anxieties are closely linked with sociocultural identities. Because race and class were so inextricably imbricated in the social fabric of South Africa both before and after apartheid, this desire of urban middle-class residents for class separation is invariably linked with the yearning for racial exclusivity, and vice versa. With the collapse of apartheid-era rules governing the organization and use of urban space, the propertied middle classes in the new South Africa have tried to find new ways to protect their possessions, their places of residence, and the comfortable ways of life to which they have grown accustomed. Taken together, these everyday practices have transformed the spatial landscapes of the city, introducing new patterns of movement and circulation along with new habits, rituals, and gestures related to the use of social space.[1]

The fear and uncertainty associated with rising crime have gone hand in hand with the transformation of residential suburban neighborhoods into a collection of "controlled and guarded places."[2] The retreat behind walls, gates, and fences has produced an inland archipelago of fortified spaces sealed off from the surrounding spatial landscape. The borders separating safe zones from dangerous, risky ones are not fixed and immobile but flexible and mutable, shrinking and expanding in space, and ebbing and flowing over time, in a constant state of movement. This elastic geography of border making and boundary marking moves back and forth in a spatial dynamic that resembles the alternating phases of what Gramsci likened to the (defensive) war of position and the (offensive) war of maneuver. In affluent residential neighborhoods, a haphazard architecture of defense has taken shape incrementally—spontaneously at some times and deliberately at others—without a great deal of forethought. New, improvised layers of protection have been laid down over older systems of defense that failed to prevent crime. Each layer has offered hope for a final triumphal intervention against criminal incursions. Yet as quickly as the assembled forces of security have developed seemingly fail-safe systems, criminals have devised ways to circumvent them.[3]

At the end of the day, security is always porous and uncertain. The existence of unforeseen gaps and fissures in protective shields means that it is not possible to manage risk with absolute certainty. Security is inherently selective because of the impossibility of anticipating and controlling all contingencies. Practices designed to manage risk typically lead to a ghettoization of safeguards, whereby specific groups and persons are (relatively) secure only in particular locations. Seen in this way, security reflects the sum of myriad local negotiations and arrangements. The key issue, therefore, is not whether there can be protection of persons and property at all times and all places, but the nature of the concessions and compromises of risk takers.[4]

Fashioning the Suburban Fortress

This obsession with safety and security has inspired design specialists to create what can be called siege architecture.[5] The newest kinds of gated residential communities, high-rise office buildings, and apartment and condominium complexes are constructed as fortresslike enclosures that are distinguished from older, open-access building typologies in their retreat from the urban fabric. Surrounded with high perimeter walls and accessed through locked security gates, these luxury laagers have turned their backs on the surrounding streetscape. These enclosed neighborhoods and gated residential estates (or 'security villages') are exemplary expressions of crime prevention through environmental design, or what design specialists euphemistically refer to as "target hardening"—that is, "the physical strengthening of building facades or boundary walls to reduce the attractiveness or vulnerability of potential targets."[6] These cocooned places resemble islands of homogeneity and wealth set incongruously in a tempestuous sea of diversity and poverty, where the incorporation of various interdictory design features has ensured that these enclaves reinforce physical exclusivity and social isolation.[7]

Looking on crime and the fear it engenders as an affront to personal liberty, the propertied middle-class residents in Johannesburg have fortified themselves against unwelcome strangers and unwanted intruders. In the outlying suburban sprawl that spread in waves in a largely northerly arc away from the historic downtown core, the combination of physical barriers, high walls, restrictive covenants, and private security armed-response teams have transformed streets, parks, shopping centers, residential neighborhoods, and entertainment zones into security enclaves with controlled access points. The affluent residential suburbs, with their tree-lined streets, verdant parklands, and spacious homes, have been re-invented according to the stultifying logic of fortification. The newer technologies of security, image, and style have replaced the segregationist principles of racial ordering that governed the apartheid era.[8]

Although their origins can be traced to earlier decades, the serial reproduction of gated residential communities exploded beginning in the 1990s as the preferred type of residential accommodation along the peri-urban fringe of northern Johannesburg. Surrounded by securitized perimeter walls and accessible by a limited number of carefully monitored entry-exit points, these security estates represented the prototype for pseudosuburban lifestyles for rich and super-rich homeowners.[9] The insertion of these gated residential communities (consisting of anywhere from several dozen to literally hundreds of individual homes) into the existing suburban social fabric enabled real estate developers to offer up-to-date infrastructure along with a wide range of social amenities (such as signature golf courses and clubhouses, bicycle paths and nature trails, and round-the-clock security). In addition to concerns about safety and security, the driving force behind the construction of these gated residential estates was the desire for exclusivity, comfort, privacy, livability, and property investment potential.[10]

The truly over-the-top, upscale versions of these security estates have attracted the lion's share of attention in the aftermath of the transition to parliamentary democracy.[11] Yet the steady growth of middle-income townhouse-cluster developments has also become quite popular with less-affluent homebuyers wanting to emulate the sequestered lifestyles

of wealthy homeowners. Starting in the early 1990s, a "floodtide of new speculative [housing] developments" provided an almost endless variety of less expensive, vulgar imitations of high-end gated residential estates.[12] Typically arising at the far edges of the suburban frontier where land is more readily available and less expensive, townhouse clusters resemble old-fashioned row housing with the added attraction of walled perimeters and security gates. As a building typology that combines the illusion of safety and the attraction of convenience, they appeal especially to first-time middle-income homebuyers.[13]

Capsular Architecture and the Paranoid Logic of Fortification

Vernacular urbanism refers to the kinds of experimental innovations that are linked to the historically specific environments within which city building takes place, whether through historical-cultural influences, the use of materials, or local ideas. The type of vernacular urbanism that gained a foothold in the residential suburban neighborhoods of Johannesburg at the start of the twenty-first century amounts to a kind of siege architecture and the fortification aesthetic. The paranoid logic of fortification has taken on a virtual life of its own.[14]

In the affluent residential heartlands of northern Johannesburg, fear has metamorphosized into an aesthetic principle. Beginning in the 1990s if not before, residential neighborhoods have become enmeshed in an ever-expanding cycle of securitization, in which makeshift security measures are gradually (yet inexorably) superimposed on existing building typologies. Unlike the very rich, who have historically been able to securely barricade themselves whenever and wherever they wished, the intermediate propertied classes have had more to lose if they become trapped in changing urban neighborhoods besieged by depreciating property values, rising street crime, increasing congestion and noise, and deteriorating social amenities. Whereas the newer gated residential estates built from scratch have seamlessly woven security measures into their physical design motifs, self-appointed homeowners' associations in the older residential suburbs have been forced to (sometimes clumsily)

MAP 1. Northern suburbs of Johannesburg. (Data taken from OpenStreetMap.)

Map Key

≡ Enclosed Neighborhoods

■ Gated Townhouse Complexes

∴ Estate

▨ Commercial / Business
   Neighborhoods

— Highways

— Main Roads

— Roads

⊙ 0 ⊢————⊣ 1 km

Fourways

Kyalami

Paulshof

Leeuwkop

Waterfall

Sunninghill

Austin View

Petervale

Rivonia

Woodmead

Buccleuch

Ederburg

The Woodlands

Bryanston

Modderfontein
Conservation
Area

Mill Hill Ext 2

Duxberry

Gallo Manor

Kensington B

Kelvin

River Club

Morningside

St Sithians

Hurlpark

Sandown Ext

Wendywood

Alexandra

Ferndale

Parkmore

East Bank

Bordeaux

Sandown

Alexandra SP

Blairgowrie

Sandhurst

Atholl

Wynberg

Lombardy
East

Craighall

Hyde Park

Illovo

Bramley

Kew

Lyndhurst

Delta Park

Melrose

Waverley

Linden

Dunkeld

Birdhaven

Parkhurst

Greenside

Oakland

retrofit existing unsecured landscapes with new security apparatuses. This ad hoc, piecemeal approach to security has produced its share of odd, unsightly arrangements that blend somewhat incongruously with the existing built environment.[15]

The idea of *defensible space*—a term that first emerged in design circles in the United States in the early 1970s—has redefined the quality and meaning of urban living.[16] The echo of Le Corbusier's late-1920s battle cry—"We must kill the streets"—has resonated in the outlying residential neighborhoods of northern Johannesburg. The manifest trappings of security and surveillance—street barricades, security gates, armed guards, sentry posts, armed-response patrols, and closed-circuit television (CCTV) cameras—are the most ubiquitous symbols of securitization. These unattractive additions to the physical landscape are constant and repetitive reminders to frightened suburban residents that the alien worlds beyond their protective walls are hostile and dangerous places. The sharp increase in violent crime (including murder, rape, cash-in-transit heists, and bank robberies) in the year leading up to March 2018 prompted Minister of Police Cele Bkeki to declare that South Africa (with Johannesburg at the epicenter) was "close to a 'war zone.'"[17] The prevalence of the so-called trio crimes—house break-ins, armed robberies, and carjackings (sometimes accompanied by indiscriminate, gratuitous, and lethal violence)—has produced the widespread perception that danger is everywhere, with the result that suburban residents have come to feel that they are imprisoned in their own self-constructed, sequestered redoubts.[18]

Fearful homeowners have pooled their resources to hire private security companies to protect their properties and persons from the predations of criminals. Small wooden huts housing informal rent-a-cops have proliferated throughout the affluent residential neighborhoods. If a street is fairly flat and there are no major hills or depressions that might hinder visibility, then a single security guard can watch twenty to thirty private homes from a well-placed guardhouse. Armed with panic buttons to alert armed-response patrols in case of emergencies (but without

MAP 2. Gated communities, northern Johannesburg. (Data taken from OpenStreetMap. Original map appeared in Landman and Badenhorst 2012. Used with permission.)

FIGURE 1. Security sentry box. (Photo by author.)

weapons since these actually attract criminals), these stationary sentries function like human shields, the first line of defense in the war against home burglaries, carjackings, and petty theft.[19]

The high walls surrounding individual homes in the leafy residential suburbs of Johannesburg resemble carefully designed fortifications. In many neighborhoods, sidewalks have virtually disappeared, forcing pedestrian passersby—in the main, the largely invisible legions of black gardeners, maids, drivers, child-minders, guards, and housekeepers who travel to their workplaces by taxi or bus—into the streets and gutters. Social status is marked by the obtrusively broadcast promise of a rapid armed response to those who would dare trespass or intrude where they are unwelcome. Ubiquitous signs—colorfully monikered with powerful images of vicious guard dogs or menacing armed security guards—are constant reminders that the property-owning "haves" are virtually at war with the propertyless "have-nots."[20]

Northern Johannesburg has become a collection of separate suburban neighborhoods interspersed between commercial nodal points and edge cities, divided by the enduring chasm of wealth and income and superimposed on the enduring fault lines of race.[21] Suburban secessionism in Johannesburg after apartheid is a largely class-based but highly ra-

FIGURE 2. Building high perimeter walls. (Photo by author.)

cialized movement of social separation couched in the political terms of neighborhood autonomy and property rights. This drive for autonomy is articulated in a language of personal freedoms and civil liberties and leavened by fear of crime. Framed through this narrow lens, individual entitlements and class privilege become more important than social justice and the universal "right to the city."[22]

Battlefield Johannesburg: Suburban Anarchy— Initial Phase (circa 1994–2004)

> If government can't protect people, people should be free to protect themselves.
>
> —Anne Russell, chair of the East Rand Metro Association[23]

The security-driven logic of suburban enclave development has found its most visible expression in the ceaseless efforts of affluent neighborhoods to protect their property and their lifestyles by physically cutting themselves off from unwanted strangers and suspicious outsiders. If borders are little more than abstract lines denoting the imagined edges of residential neighborhoods, then security barriers give these suburban redoubts distinctive identities. Suburban residents fear contact with and contamination by the poor and the underclasses, with whom they have such ambiguous and contradictory relationships of dependency and distrust, intimacy and avoidance.[24] Neighborhood associations throughout the residential suburbs have installed elaborate surveillance-detection devices ranging from high-resolution cameras to automatic electronic gates, erected sentry-box shelters staffed twenty-four hours a day, and introduced mobile patrols by heavily armed private security armed-response teams. Suburban communities with sufficient political influence with local municipal authorities have sealed themselves off from the rest of the metropolis by enclosing entire residential neighborhoods in security fencing, channeling visitors to a few well-fortified entry points, and restricting access only to those authorized to enter.[25]

Motivated by anxieties about rising crime, concerns about property values, and unease about the perceived inability of public policing agencies to effectively provide law and order, scores of neighborhood associations in older, established residential suburbs closer to the central city sought to mimic the design features of the new master-planned, gated residential communities on the exurban fringe by closing off access roads and installing security gates. What began as a trickle in the early 1990s when a few posh suburban residential communities began to exert pressure on local municipal authorities for official permission to close off roads with security fences, boom gates, and bollards quickly turned into a flood of increasingly shrill demands to hide entire residential communities behind high fences and sentry posts, with controlled access and twenty-four hour private security patrols. At the beginning, municipal authorities dealt with each request on an ad hoc basis, but the mounting crescendo of bitter complaints about rising neighborhood crime combined with the populist rhetoric of community control forced local authorities in 1996 to formally issue a set of guidelines that regulated road closures.[26]

The first approved road closures took place in the affluent northern suburbs of Bramley, Gallo Manor, and Wendywood Village, and these were quickly followed by dozens more.[27] Energized by these early successes and unwilling to wait for the time-consuming process of obtaining official approval, many neighborhood associations simply acted unilaterally, erecting physical barricades and installing boom gates to close off streets, thereby illegally cordoning off residential neighborhoods.

FIGURE 3. Illegal road closure. (Photo by author.)

These groups even imposed variants of "pass controls" on unwanted out-siders.[28] Reliable estimates suggest that between 1996 and 2004 alone, homeowners' associations carried out more than five hundred road clo-sures in Johannesburg. These road closures, which took place outside the framework of legal statutes and without municipal authorization, were concentrated in the northern suburbs, particularly Morningside, Kew, Wendywood, Parkmore, Hurlingham, and Fourways. All in all, more than 160 kilometers of public roads throughout Johannesburg were ren-dered inaccessible to motorists as a result of illegal boom gates.[29] Unde-terred by legal niceties, neighborhood associations sought to transform these interim security measures into permanent fixtures on the subur-ban landscape. The blatant self-interest of property owners triumphed over considerations of the rule of law. As the embodiment of a kind of populist homeowners' activism, neighborhood associations took the lead in these collective acts of extralegal defiance, daring the municipal au-thorities to remove the barriers and collecting large sums of money to mount legal challenges in court.[30]

This deliberate cloistering of entire neighborhoods or whole residen-tial suburbs amounted to a kind of privatization by stealth, whereby hastily formed assemblies of property owners effectively restricted open access to public roads in flagrant violation of freedom of movement. This homeowners' revolt pitted affluent (and even not-so-affluent) suburban residents against the rule of law.[31] Local community control or self-management—what Pranap Bardhan in another context cynically referred to as "anarcho-communitarianism"—suddenly became the rallying cry for property-owning suburban residents. In what amounted to a shift from a war of position to a war of maneuver, neighborhood associations seized the initiative, imposing their own vision of postmodern laissez-faire urbanism on the affluent northern suburbs. Caught off guard and without a coherent plan or alternative blueprint, local municipal councils failed to act decisively to curb the rampant spread of self-serving parochialism, and they sought instead to placate powerful coalitions of wealthy homeowners, neighborhood associations, and real estate interests. Because they realized that to tear down unauthorized barricades would just provoke a huge outcry from enraged residents, local authorities simply refused to buck the tide and more or less turned a blind eye to illegal street closures.[32]

As the largest neighborhood enclosure of its kind at the time in the eastern metropolitan substructure, Gallo Manor and nearby Wendywood became the prototypes in the late 1990s for the subsequent headlong rush to barricade, fortify, and cordon off the residential suburban neighborhoods. Crime-weary residents of this sprawling residential zone of spacious, mock-California, ranch-style designer homes—a bottom-end faux Spanish-style hacienda cost around R 350,000 ($200,000) at that time—banded together to ring the entire residential neighborhood of some eight hundred homes with metal-spike fencing and to hire a private security company to monitor all static entry and exit points and maintain round-the-clock armed-reaction units on patrol throughout the premises. Residents erected permanent barricades to close off most of the access roads. Armed sentries stood guard at the remaining five, and only two remained open after 8:00 p.m. For the privilege of living within this self-styled, fortresslike enclosure, residents paid R 110 ($60) a month. Security cars patrolled the streets day and night in search of suspicious activity. Like early settlers establishing permanent outposts in hostile territories, the residents of Gallo Manor redefined the terms under which they lived, organizing their own security, creating their own protective boundaries, and carving out new borders along their frontiers. In launching the first successful partnership-policing project in the residential suburbs, crime-weary homeowners formed a united front against crime by drafting their domestic workers into a community forum with the local (state and private) security forces to counter housebreaking. Daily life in the cloistered laagers nurtured its own distinct vocabulary. Residents of Gallo Manor boasted about the decline of "schedule-one offences," worried aloud about "armed-response time," and kept a vigilant lookout for potential "perpetrators." Paramilitary-style security assumed a friendly, neighborly appearance, with armed sentries described as "static wardens." The private security firm Coin Security Group (headquartered in Sandton) assured homeowners that their security officers, stationary guards, and active patrol teams acquired such intimate knowledge of the neighborhoods they were contracted to protect that they were able to recognize residents on sight and to recall from memory the names of their gardeners, their domestic staff, and even their dogs.[33]

What has evolved in urban South Africa in the nearly three decades since the end of apartheid is a collective mind-set that rests on the belief that retreat within the cloistered confines of an enclosed neighborhood or "security village" provides an everyday solution to crime and an improved quality of life. For large parts of the residential suburbs of Johannesburg, cordoning off roads with security barriers and boom gates became the norm rather than the exception. These neighborhood enclosures paved the way for the privatization of such municipal services as security patrols, refuse collection, and even road maintenance. By the beginning of the twenty-first century, in the Greater Johannesburg metropolitan region alone, private security companies employed more than two hundred thousand guards, a substantial number of whom were employed to work in enclosed communities.[34] It was estimated in mid-2001 that roughly half the northern suburbs of Johannesburg had already successfully (with or without legal sanction) closed off roads to through traffic or had applications in the pipeline to erect street barricades. These suburbs included Observatory, Glenvista, Oakdene, Randburg, Sandringham, Hurlingham, Atholl, Boskruin, Oaklands, and Randpark.[35] The security panic was greatest in Johannesburg's Eastern Metropolitan Local Council, a posh suburban residential zone that included Sandton, Sandhurst, Hyde Park, Ilovo, Bryanston, and other wealthy neighborhoods. In this area alone, there were around 350 barricaded streets (most of which were closed off illegally) and around 200 totally cordoned-off

Map Key

Neighborhoods
■ Enclosed Neighborhoods

— Highways
-- Main Roads

— Roads

○ 0 ⊢——— 1 km

residential neighborhoods either completed or under review. Typically, homeowners each paid about R 300 ($160) per month to maintain these elaborate security systems, with their twenty-four-hour patrols, armed-response teams, and military-like checkpoints.[36]

Despite the steady increase in the number of illegal barricades erected in the northern suburbs, city officials procrastinated for more than four years before formulating a comprehensive road closure policy. This foot-dragging created a window of opportunity for impatient suburban residents to act on their own initiative, "taking the law into their own hands and closing off roads as and when they please."[37] While their applications for road closures languished in the city bureaucracy, frustrated and angry homeowners unilaterally erected street blockades and security checkpoints, effectively sealing off hundreds of streets and placing large sections of residential neighborhoods behind privately funded security cordons.[38] Rich and superrich property owners had learned long ago that "being forgiven is easier than getting permission: an illegal structure is often approved when a legal application made in advance is certain to be refused." This flagrant rule breaking—or what exasperated city officials called "white mischief'"—was born of a deeply entrenched sense of collective and individual entitlement and moral superiority in a country in which the cozy white rich have long constituted an insulated, powerful, and comfortable elite.[39] In order to secure their right to block off streets, affluent suburbanites established an advocacy organization, called the Combined Chairpersons Committee for Road Closures, to lobby city officials and deal with court cases on their behalf.[40]

But nowhere was the seemingly inexorable machinery of social exclusion more blatantly elitist than in the unilateral decision of wealthy homeowners of Hyde Park and Sandhurst to erect a massive seven-kilometer (four-mile) steel fence around their neighborhoods, effectively cutting off these two posh residential suburbs from the rest of the city. In an exemplary expression of security obsession taken to the extremes, this formidable barrier—appropriately nicknamed the Great Wall of Hyde Park—created at a single stroke the largest neighborhood enclosure in suburban

MAP 3. Road closures, northern suburbs. (Data taken from OpenStreetMap. Original map appeared in Landman and Badenhorst 2012. Used with permission.)

Johannesburg. At an initial cost of R 15,000 ($900) per household cou-
pled with a monthly fee of R 650 ($400), this hugely expensive megawall
closed 13 streets to traffic and sequestered about 520 trophy mansions
(some worth up to R 35 million [$20 million] apiece, with wrought-iron
gates, grand-columned entryways, and beautifully landscaped gardens)
inside the new luxury laager. In choosing to fight the war against crime
their own way, the wealthy residents literally imprisoned themselves behind insurmountable high walls, electronic surveillance, and static sentry posts and turned over authority to patrol the inner sanctum of their
new fortresslike complex to a small army of well-armed private security
guards. This exclusive neighborhood enclave was home to a veritable
Who's Who of Johannesburg high society, including Malaysian business-
man Dato Samsudin Abu Hassan, Bakos Brothers' Keith Bakos, Rebhold
Limited head Stephen Levenberg, controversial billionaire Dave King
(former head of Specialised Outsourcing), Telecel International chair
Miko Rwayitare, Dimension Data director Robert Taylor, Italtile chair
Gianni Ravazzotti, and Sandton ex-mayor Zoe Marchand. Topped with
electrified fencing to deter potential intruders, the two-meter (six-and-
a-half-foot) high metal wall was also equipped with sensor alarms connected to a central monitoring station to warn of perpetrators attempting to scale the barrier. Inside the containment perimeter, the up-to-date
security measures included surveillance cameras strategically placed all
around the site, eleven guards on shift at all times, two armed-response
vehicles on twenty-four-hour patrol, and four stationary boom gates. Although the access-control barriers were left open to accommodate rush-
hour traffic, they were closed shortly thereafter, and security guards took
it upon themselves to stop vehicles, ask for identification, and monitor by
hidden video cameras what they regarded as suspicious movement.[41]

The erection of the Hyde Park/Sandhurst barrier wall set off a rapid
chain reaction of road closures in the adjoining residential suburbs, resulting in what one exasperated city official referred to as "traffic anarchy." The distorted traffic patterns and unwanted traffic congestion provoked an angry reaction. While owners of the luxury Saxon Hotel and
Hyde Park High School joined forces with irate residents to initiate legal
action against the Sandhurst Heritage Foundation (the neighborhood association responsible for erecting the barrier wall), others took matters
into their own hands, surreptitiously dismantling huge sections of the
fence on at least five separate occasions.[42]

But enclosures have not been limited to the wealthy suburban areas of large cities. During the 1990s, petitions for neighborhood closures snowballed in cities and towns across the country. The Erkhuleni municipal council, which covers the East Rand, approved fifty applications for permission to cordon off suburban neighborhoods in the eleven towns under its jurisdiction.[43] In a comprehensive study conducted for the Centre for Scientific and Industrial Research (CSIR), Karina Landman reported that out of twenty cities and towns that indicated they had received requests for closures, 60 percent were from towns with fewer than five hundred thousand inhabitants, such as Bethlehem (with just over one hundred thousand inhabitants) and Port Shepstone (with thirty thousand inhabitants), which each received ten requests for neighborhood enclosures.[44]

Despite these Herculean efforts to create containment zones of safety, security experts and professional consultants have readily admitted that frightened residents of enclosed neighborhoods, secured estates, and gated residential communities were trapped in a paradox: installing more and more sophisticated security systems seemed to offer only a short-term, temporary solution to an explosive, ever-changing crime situation that always seemed to spiral out of control. Residents of enclosed neighborhoods can pay anywhere from R 200 to R 1,000 ($110 to $600) per month in levies. Defenders of sequestered boomtowns—whom critics have sarcastically referred to as laager activists—have insisted that incidents of serious crime decreased after road closures and other physical barriers were put in place.[45] Yet there is no reliable empirical evidence to support this claim. Available studies seem to suggest that although crime may have declined temporarily when suburban neighborhoods were enclosed, this cloistering seemed to make little difference in the long run in the overall pattern of crime rates. Enclosed neighborhoods make outsiders feel unwanted and excluded. The poor—mainly pedestrians who must make wide detours—regard enclosed streets as an inconvenient hindrance to free movement and as a kind of forced separation.[46] Although no one can legally be searched or denied access to public streets, private security companies routinely harass unwanted strangers and prevent them from entering enclosed neighborhoods. As a general rule, it is race that defines suspicion, and it is young black males who routinely attract the lion's share of attention—prompting critics to suggest that erecting barriers is a new kind of spatial apartheid.[47]

Gated residential communities and affluent suburbs were not the only collective entities that sought to close themselves off from the surrounding urban landscape.[48] In April 2001, local business leaders caused an uproar when they erected a R 450,000 ($275,000) electric security fence to barricade their industrial park from a three-thousand-strong squatter settlement at Kya Sands, north of Randburg. This electrified fence effectively trapped the squatters in a small area along the banks of the Jukskei River without any easily accessible entry or exit points. The speed at which this barrier was erected meant that cars belonging to residents of the informal settlement were stranded behind it. Exasperated by escalating burglaries of their premises, the local businesses applied to the Johannesburg council for permission to erect the fence, but they acted unilaterally before this request was approved. This high-voltage "crime-prevention cage" also did not have a shorter protective fence around it to prevent electric shocks to children and animals, as required by law. Without the intervention of the Human Rights Commission (HRC), which forced the business owners to provide a pedestrian walkway, residents of the informal squatter settlement were blocked from toilets, water, shops, and employment at the Kya Sands industrial site.[49]

While the movement to safeguard property by retreating behind barriers was taking place across the urban landscape, a historically specific kind of homeowner separatism reached its apogee in the kaleidoscopic mélange of affluent northern suburbs, stretching from Randburg in the northwest to Sandton in the northeast. The accelerated buildup of walls, barricaded streets, and other barriers transformed affluent suburban neighborhoods into cocooned enclaves that resembled something akin to walled medieval city-states. Neighborhood associations justified their decisions to close off streets, erect sentry posts, and hire armed guards on the grounds that these drastic measures were necessary to combat the rising tide of robberies, housebreakings, and carjackings. Besides installing unauthorized road closures, some neighborhood associations went even further, locking pedestrian gates at night to prevent strangers from entering neighborhoods, instructing stationary guards at boom gates to take photographs of all unknown drivers, and organizing their own voluntary nighttime street patrols.[50]

But because unauthorized boom gates and other barriers were frequently erected with little or no regard for their overall impact on vehicular circulation, they wreaked havoc on the ability of motorists to negotiate city streets. Affluent homeowners in the posh suburb of Sandhurst randomly closed off roads (including major thoroughfares) without prior notice, causing huge traffic congestion and long delays on streets between William Nicol Drive in Randburg and Rivonia Road in Sandton. In a social setting in which property rights were seen as sacrosanct and the sociocultural status of neighborhoods was intimately tied to their property values, these unilateral road closures triggered a chain reaction that rippled across the affluent northern suburbs. In response to the increase volume of vehicles diverted through their neighborhoods (which angry observers derisively dismissed as the "chicken run"), disgruntled residents in suburban areas surrounding Sandhurst, such as Inanda, Rivonia, and Hyde Park, took matters into their own hands, erecting their own street barricades to rid themselves of the unwanted burden of additional traffic.[51]

The chaos, anarchy, and uncertainty brought about by these illegal road closures provoked an angry backlash.[52] Irritated motorists lashed out at the arrogance of wealthy suburbanites who closed off access roads without prior consultation, causing considerable inconvenience by disrupting the natural flow of traffic. Emergency management services, including public police, firefighting, and medical services, complained that illegal security gates and other unexpected barriers slowed their ability to quickly respond to distress calls.[53] Critics also charged that, besides unfairly diverting traffic onto boom-free residential streets that were ill-equipped to handle the increased volume of automobiles, unauthorized road closures failed to adequately address the burning issue of neighborhood security in either an equitable or a comprehensive way.[54]

By deliberately flouting the law with their illegal road closures, wealthy homeowners in places such as Hyde Park and Sandhurst—the location of the three most expensive streets in Johannesburg—attracted a great deal of opprobrium from city officials and urban residents alike. New citizen groups and civic associations, like the Open City Forum, jumped into the fray, giving voice to irate suburbanites who opposed road closures on the grounds that the unilateral annexation of streets restricted access to public places without proper authority. In reacting to a flood of complaints lodged with the police and other local authorities, municipal leaders finally moved into action, serving court papers to Sandhurst residents who had illegally barricaded their streets. These city officials hoped to use this example as a test case to force other affluent neighborhoods to remove illegal barriers and reopen their public streets. Faced with this assault on what they regarded as the sanctity of private property, affluent members of the Sandhurst Heritage Foundation—who collectively paid an estimated R 1 million ($600,000) to build their vaunted steel wall, erect sentry posts, and hire private security patrols—adamantly refused to budge, retreating behind legal maneuvers and a wall of silence.[55]

In early 2003, the City of Johannesburg unveiled its much-anticipated policy regarding road closures. Proclaiming their intention to enforce compliance with city bylaws, municipal authorities vowed to clamp down on illegal street cordons, barricades, and boom gates. In seeking to discourage neighborhood associations from continuing to take the law into their own hands, city officials announced stiff penalties for violation of municipal regulations. In addition to establishing stringent procedures regulating the barricading of public streets, they set 17 July 2003 as the deadline for suburban neighborhood associations to apply for permission to retain the estimated 1,127 existing road closures (90 percent of which were located in the suburban arc from Randburg to Sandton) that residents had unilaterally erected without legal authorization. Homeowners' and neighborhood associations reacted angrily to what they regarded as particularly onerous application procedures, including substantial application fees, the payment of a large deposit to defray the potential cost of boom removal, and the submission of a traffic impact survey.[56]

This "battle for the streets" reached a decisive turning point in the first several days following the 17 July deadline, when the Johannesburg Roads Agency (JRA)—the city agency responsible for maintenance of streets—began to forcibly dismantle illegal barriers, including fences and walls, boom gates, and sentry boxes.[57] As surprised and embittered residents watched helplessly from the sidelines, the JRA used cutting tools and welding guns to remove close to one hundred illegal barriers in such disparate places as Randburg (in the northwest), Kensington (in the southeast), and Honeydew, Inanda, and Ferndale (in the northeast). Yet almost simultaneously, bitter suburban residents in places such as Inanda defied the prohibition against illegal road closures, feverishly erecting new barriers in the hopes of winning approval.[58] But just as quickly as the JRA began its demolition work, city officials backed away from their promise to remove five illegal road closures a day, choosing instead to rely on the courts to resolve the divisive issue. Sensing that city officials had retreated from strict enforcement of access-control regulations, neighborhood associations pushed back, gradually returning to the outlawed practices of allowing security guards to demand personal information from pedestrians, ask motorists to disclose whom they were visiting, and conduct unauthorized searches of suspicious cars.[59]

Seen from the wide-angle lens of laissez-faire urbanism, the concerted efforts of affluent homeowners to carve out sequestered enclaves represented a rational response to the threatened loss of their quaint, low-density suburban lifestyles. Homeowner politics focused squarely on the defense of the nostalgic suburban ideal of detached, single-family homes located on spacious lots with landscaped gardens and within walkable distance from schools, places of worship, and commercial shops. Yet the silent march of real estate capitalism showed no mercy for nostalgic attachments to such an antiquated vision of the romanticized past. Anxious residents of the affluent northern suburbs were faced with the seemingly inexorable forward march of rampant, large-scale overdevelopment, as high-rise office nodes have encroached on main thoroughfares, cluster housing has infilled vacant or underutilized space, and standardized mini-malls have replaced family-owned businesses.[60]

Confronted with such uncertainty, wealthy homeowners were not willing to readily surrender their security perimeters without a fight.[61] Over the next decade, road closures continued to generate acrimonious and heated debate, in which the never-ending war of words was typically conducted in the surreal language of *Alice in Wonderland*, with both camps using exaggeration and caricature to maintain the moral high ground. Trapped in the discourse of blame that accompanied debate over road closures, self-righteous protagonists unsurprisingly warned that "the alternative [to road closures] is bloody vigilantism," while angry detractors claimed that they were "elitist and racially motivated" and that at root the closures were a means to inflate property prices.[62] Nick Karvelas, head of the freedom-of-movement lobby called Open City Forum, proclaimed that the "laager activists" who endorsed road closures acted "without any respect for the rule of law and the rights of other citizens, grabbed public roads and other amenities in order to, they claim, exercise their right to security."[63] In contrast, critics suggested that Open City Forum was "no more than a publicity stunt for some bored individuals attempting to uplift their social image."[64]

Suburban residents consistently blamed "rising crime" (in their mind's eye, crime always seemed to move in an upward direction) for their almost paranoid fixation on safety and security, lashing out at the inability of public policing agencies to protect citizens and property from criminals.[65] As one irate affluent resident of Sandton declared, "Each boom, each metal fence, is an indictment of local government for its inability/ incompetence in safeguarding its ratepayers. People have the right to protect themselves from accelerating violent crime in their areas."[66] In a rather sarcastic intervention, another Sandton resident declared that it was the criminals and criminal syndicates who would be "the only beneficiaries of the [Open City] campaign."[67] On the other side, city officials more often than not interpreted unauthorized road closures that restricted access to suburban neighborhoods as a kind of self-serving (antiblack) neo-apartheid—a parochial, revanchist mentality conveniently cloaked in the high-minded, populist rhetoric of the "constitutional right to security" and "community control."[68] In its 2005 report, the South African Human Rights Commission found that unilateral road closures were in contradiction to the guarantees of basic human rights, such as the right to move freely in public spaces, as well as an expression of racial discrimination.[69] Bitter disagreements over the effectiveness of boom gates, sentry posts, and armed guards to prevent crime have frequently torn communities apart, pitting neighborhood against neighborhood and even neighbor against neighbor; the wars of words and social ostracism have occasionally slipped into more dangerous games involving petty harassment, intimidation, and threats of physical harm. The efforts of affluent suburbanites to ensure their security, to protect their property values, and to maintain their idyllic lifestyles has amounted to a war without end, with no clear winners or losers and no decisive victories or defeats.[70]

In a bitter confrontation that stretched over many years, neighborhood associations engaged in a protracted struggle involving both a war of maneuver and a war of position to defend themselves against municipal efforts to outlaw and eliminate road closures. Neighborhood associations clubbed together under the umbrella of the Combined Chairpersons Committee (CCC) to wage a legal battle with the city administration over road closures.[71] In 2010, the CCC coordinated the efforts of eighty-five road closure committees scattered across the suburban neighborhoods of northern Johannesburg, vowing to defend these groups against municipal efforts to dismantle access-restriction structures. In speaking for the Bordeaux South Residents Association in court, Rob Schwartz, chair of the CCC, argued that "the residents are tired of the bullying tactics of the city and its blatant and callous disregard for the residents' right to safety and security. The time has come for the city and its officials to be held accountable."[72] In justifying what amounted to open defiance of the law, he proclaimed, "If government agencies cannot protect the citizens, we have every right to do so ourselves."[73] In their protracted legal campaign, neighborhood associations argued in court that municipal efforts to eliminate existing road closures amounted to wasteful and fruitless spending and that, besides, public policing agencies were simply not capable—or even willing—of providing the kind of security they needed.[74]

Impatient with protracted delays in court proceedings and what they regarded as a long history of broken promises, neighborhood associations acted unilaterally to secure their residential suburbs against what they typically proclaimed was a Wild West atmosphere of crime out of control. A single example should suffice to indicate the heightened anxiety that swept across the northern suburbs. In resorting to the hyperbolic language of a "reign of terror," Elinor Bodinger, the chair of the Bordeaux South Residents Association (representing 450 separate households), declared that residents at first "put up poles ourselves to close our roads." This initial act of defiance spilled over into the collection of voluntary contributions to pay for the installation of a two-meter-high (six-and-a-half-foot-high) palisade fence (with several pedestrian gates, along a portion of Jan Smuts Avenue), the reduction of entrances (with security boom gates) from six to two, the introduction of high-tech number-plate recognition cameras monitored around-the-clock, and the hiring of what she regarded as a "deadly" private security company, under the sponsorship of Community Active Protection (CAP).[75] Faced with well-organized opposition both in the courts and on the ground, municipal officials capitulated to the relentless pressure, dropping their efforts to remove all illegal road closures, and quietly agreed not to pursue the matter further for the reason that residential neighborhoods did have legitimate security concerns.[76]

In a major concession to critics who had argued for years that the approval process for road closures was subject to endless delays, the Johannesburg Roads Agency (JDA) issued new guidelines in 2014 that aimed to streamline the seemingly onerous application procedure. The JDA agreed to allow the existing 350 to 390 road closures to remain in place, although the applications for these were never formally approved. This concession amounted to a capitulation to the relentless pressure of neighborhood associations and the power of the residential suburban lobby. But the JRA once again declared that compliance with the new policies required security guards to cease and desist from requiring visitors to register, stopping motorists at security gates, randomly searching vehicles, preventing pedestrians from entering neighborhoods, and otherwise infringing on freedom of movement.[77]

The adoption of a user-friendly application process that bypassed previous bottlenecks resulted in skyrocketing numbers of formal requests for security-access controls across the northern suburbs. In early 2017, for example, officials with the JRA reported that Region C alone received an estimated ten to twelve applications per day for security-access restrictions, primarily for the installation of boom gates.[78] Yet despite the JDA compromises, neighborhood associations continued to search for ways to surreptitiously contravene the spirit if not the letter of the law. Faced with a steady stream of fairly obvious infringements of rules governing access controls, the JRA announced in December 2016 that it would no longer tolerate illegal closures of public streets, ostensibly for security reasons. In a dramatic show of force, officials from the JRA swooped into the swanky residential suburb of Hurlingham Manor North and removed two pedestrian gates, four access-control points, and two palisade gates due to noncompliance with the city's security-access restriction policy of 2014, which guaranteed freedom of access and freedom of movement to all. Violations of existing regulations included permanently locked pedestrian gates, which were meant to be open at all times, and electronic access-control points, which were installed so as to create the impression that the residential neighborhood was privately owned and hence not accessible to all. In justifying why it had violated the law, the Hurlingham North Residents' Association (HNRA) proclaimed that it needed a facial recognition mechanism in its electronic booms after a spate of follow-home robberies.[79] In what proved to be an embarrassing legal setback, lawyers for HNRA were able to obtain a court order in less than a week that forced the JDA to restore the security gates and pay for legal costs.[80]

The gradual accumulation of unattractive makeshift security measures drastically disfigured the aesthetic qualities of residential neighborhoods, in which ominous signs promising "armed response" seem

incongruously out of place in such idyllic settings and in which high perimeter walls have rendered individual homes invisible from the road.
Suburban streets have come to resemble traffic corridors rather than
places of social congregation. The aesthetics of security-oriented landscape design communicates a message that is at odds with the suburban
ideal of walkability, open vistas, and unimpeded movement.[81]

Defending the Suburban Dreamscape: The Price of Feeling Safe

The fear of crime has driven frightened residents of middle-class neighborhoods to turn their homes into bunker-like fortresses and to enlist the
services of private security companies to provide protection. The largely
unplanned installation of such security accoutrements as CCTV surveillance cameras, watchtowers, sentry posts, boom gates, and checkpoints
has fundamentally transformed the facade of the city. The architecture
of fear has transformed residential neighborhoods, commercial shopping
complexes, and office buildings into securitized encampments. Complex
strategies of "designing out insecurity" and "designing in protection"
have come to rely on innovative technologies and spatial-design solutions that promise "safe and secure environments."[82] The sprawling metropolis—a spatially diverse territory under siege by an unending climate
of crime and violence—has metamorphosed into a vast "fearscape."[83]

Residential security in postapartheid Johannesburg—whether in fortified mansions of the superrich or the ordinary suburban-bunkered enclosure—depends on the voracious consumption of security paraphernalia. In this brave new world of fear, homeowners have become consumer
sovereigns, buying whatever security gadgetry they can afford in order
to protect themselves from the unknown. Starting in the mid-1990s, the
amount of money that homeowners begrudgingly spent on domestic security alone has steadily increased, with no end in sight. [84] Available security products and services have proliferated in rough synchronization
with the rising fear of crime. Concerned with safety, anxious homeowners want remote-controlled motorized gates at all neighborhood entryways. They want well-secured houses ensconced behind high walls
topped with metal spikes, razor wire, and high-voltage electrified fencing. They want homes outfitted with alarms and panic buttons, tamper-
proof burglar bars on all windows, and even vicious Rottweilers.[85]

Home security providers have deliberately catered to these mounting

FIGURE 4. High wall topped with electric fencing. (Photo by author.)

fears by claiming that strong safety deterrents deflect would-be thieves to nearby properties that are not as well defended. The apparent success of such promotional advertising indicates that many homeowners are willing to protect themselves to the possible detriment of their neighbors. Ironically, as housing prices rise in these defended suburbs, the surrounding pregnable neighborhoods, lacking the security shields of their wealthier neighbors, have often fallen prey to much of the crime that is pushed their way, causing a concomitant drop in property values.[86]

Private security companies with such formidable names as First Alert, Standby, Stallion, Claw, Sentry, Mantis, Peaceforce, Infantry, Sterling, First Response, Fidelity Springbok, WAR, Bad Boyz, and Everest have taken advantage of the heightened anxiety over urban crime to pro-

FIGURE 5. WAR alert armed response. (Photo by author.)

mote their security services. Without exception, every affluent suburban neighborhood or gated residential estate contracts its own private policing. Ominous signs in these neighborhoods warn of "Armed Response," "First Alert," "24-Hour Patrol," and "Zero Tolerance." Such signs are the most visible expressions of a vast private security apparatus that has supplanted virtually all routine law enforcement duties of local municipal policing agencies. This growing dependence on private guns-for-hire" marks a retreat from civic responsibility and a clear drift toward a kind of frontier vigilante mentality with its libertarian communitarian logic.[87]

The fortification of the detached single-family suburban house has mirrored the enclosure and securitization of citadel office towers, commercial buildings, and other private business establishments. The free-

FIGURE 6. Fortified gated enclosures. (Photo by author.)

dom of movement in and around these sites of social congregation depend entirely on the security technologies that protect them.[88] In their
adaptation for home use, surveillance technologies that monitor movement retain many of the traits of similar apparatuses employed in such
exemplary expressions of "mass private property" as enclosed shopping
malls, gated residential communities, and tourist entertainment sites.[89]

Monthly subscriptions to private security companies offering safety
precautions can vary greatly, depending on the quality and sophistica-
tion of the services, such as armed response and the frequency of security patrols. All in all, security packages—including of CCTV cameras, infrared sensors, and alarm systems—can cost thousands for initial
installation, upgrading and repair, and periodic service fees.[90] Frightened residents often wear panic buttons attached to chains around their
necks, carry pepper spray, and install interior security gates dividing
bedrooms from the rest of the house.[91]

Safe House: Capsular Logic

For the most part, architecture and urban design in the residential suburban neighborhoods of Johannesburg have turned away from the mod-

ernist preoccupation with the celebration of transparent and open space and toward the production of inward-looking enclosures that mitigate the anxieties engendered by danger and risk. The mundane features of architectural design have become key tactical tools in the wholesale restructuring of suburban landscapes in which retrofitted private dwellings virtually disappear behind high walls and security gates. At a time of uncertainty, the capsular logic of siege architecture has become the new design aesthetic for Johannesburg. It functions as a membrane of enclosure.[92] The search for technical fixes to combat risk offers a kind of temporary respite from fear.[93]

As extensions of human capabilities, such prosthetic devices as CCTV security cameras; high-voltage electric fencing; tall perimeter walls; re-

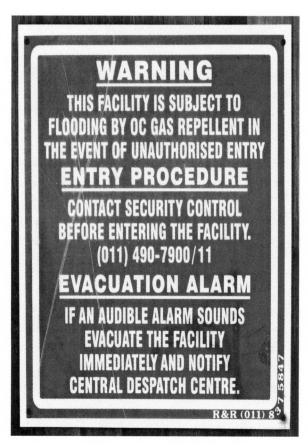

FIGURE 7. Warning sign: Poison gas. (Photo by author.)

inforced steel gates; invisible infrared motion detectors that, when activated, trip silent alarms or loud sirens (even mimicking the high-pitched
sounds of the infamous vuvulzelas); and biometric technologies such as
retinal scanning, voice recognition, and fingerprint identification systems offer technological solutions to the fear of the unknown. A considerable amount of innovation has occurred in the field of noxious gas,
thermal fog, and smoke dispensers. A company called Skunk Security,
for example, has marketed an extra-strength pepper spray alarm system (nicknamed the RobberStopper) that "attacks back," surprising unwanted intruders by filling the designated area with a highly repulsive
and irritating gas. When remotely activated from a protected place,
these security devices become offensive weapons rather than merely
static defenses in the war against criminals.[94]

In 2009, a South Africa–based company called Desert Wolf began selling versatile unmanned aerial vehicles (drones called riot control cop-
ters) outfitted with the capacity to fire pepper spray, dye marker balls,
solid plastic bullets, and blinding lasers into crowds. By 2017, Desert
Wolf had upgraded the capacity of its drone strike force to include the
delivery of stun, flash, and lethal grenades that could be fired from the
air "with pinpoint accuracy." The standard issue of elaborate sensor devices provided their remotely piloted aircraft with full night-flight capabilities and the ability to identify objects through dense smoke and other
visual impairments.[95] Concerned observers worried that it was only a
matter of time before private security companies added these flying machines to their arsenal of protection services for residential neighborhoods.[96] Taken as a whole, such powerful mechanical apparatuses seek
to blot out insecurity, the unexpected, and the dangerous.[97]

This obsession with safety and security appears in the visible traces
that permeate public space: armed-response signs, danger warnings, and
promises of zero tolerance toward criminals. This expanded capability
of prosthetic devices to detect danger and assess risk has replaced dependence on public policing agencies. As the new mechanical instruments of detection, these artificial apparatuses resemble a kind of early-
warning system on constant lookout for danger. For example, CCTV
cameras promise to expand the field of vision by penetrating those
opaque zones where danger can lurk undetected. These visual monitoring systems represent an extension and amplification of the human
eye, enhancing its capacity to see in the dark, to never become tired,

and to pan, tilt, and zoom on command. The transformation of shadows and darkness into transparent space suggests the possibility of total control—a paradigm championed by Jeremy Bentham and his visionary idea of the Panopticon.[98]

In 2018, Fidelity ADT introduced a new security-focused "smart-home" device called SecureConnect that enabled homeowners to remotely monitor their homes through live-feed CCTV cameras on their mobile phones. SecureConnect essentially transforms residences into a complete securitized "smart home," offering not only a range of security features such as alarm systems that can be armed (and disarmed) from five kilometers away and gates and garage doors that can be remotely opened or closed but also the ability to turn off other devices such as pool pumps, security lights, and even coffee machines. By linking their signal to the Fidelity ADT monitoring center, homeowners ensured the activation of armed-response patrols in the case of a breach of the security perimeter.[99]

Everyday life for middle-class residents of suburban neighborhoods pivots around two contrasting tropes.[100] The first is the idyllic dreamscape of a "normal life" fashioned around work, family, and friends—a kind of idealized, frictionless existence free from menace and danger. This yearning for a return to normalcy triggers shared feelings of nostalgia, "a longing for a home that no longer exists or never existed."[101] The second is the constant sense of foreboding, in which even the routines of daily living—a trip to the shopping mall, walking in public places, arriving home late at night—trigger anxiety. The ongoing tension between these opposing tropes has produced a kind of schizophrenic condition—on one hand, a melancholic remembrance of an imagined social world lost in time and, on the other hand, the disorientation and estrangement that come with the uncanny uneasiness caused by ever-present danger.[102]

The residential suburbs of Johannesburg have long held symbolic importance in the popular imagination of aspiring middle-class homeowners. As Johannesburg quickly grew from a frontier mining town at the end of the nineteenth century to a modern industrial metropolis during the twentieth century, middle-class residents looked longingly to the residential suburbs both as an escape from neighborhoods close to the hustle and bustle of the gritty city center and as the fulfillment of the dreamscape of spacious properties, tree-lined streets, and comfort-

able living in a faux-rustic setting.[103] From the start, the private domi-
cile—the detached single-family home—has held a special place in the
cultural imaginary of aspiring suburban homeowners.[104] Successful real
estate developers who made their fortunes in building suburbia inven-
tively combined ample bank financing, relatively inexpensive land, re-
laxed public oversight, and deliberate spatial design to construct low-
density suburban neighborhoods—albeit with varying plot sizes and
various levels of exclusivity—that would satisfy the market demand for
private homes with spacious lots.[105]

In Johannesburg, the private suburban home has always played an
oversized role as an imagined "space of sanctuary."[106] At the start, the
suburban dream house became an object of desire that has woven suc-
cessive generations of suburbanites into the interrelated narratives of upward mobility, tranquil domesticity, and spatial seclusion. For aspiring
middle-class suburban residents, home ownership represents the crown-
ing achievement of material success. The single-family dwelling provides "an affective and symbolic locus" through which the virtues of
owning your own home and the desire for the "good life" have played
out in suburban Johannesburg. The "intense cultural identification" of
personal accomplishment, happiness, and normalcy with the detached,
single-family house in the residential suburbs has invested private home
ownership with a surfeit of meaning not found anywhere else.[107]

Located in the broader terrain of neoliberal urbanism, the lurch toward expanded privatism, freedom of choice, and individual responsibility "corresponds to the position of homeowners as 'consumer sovereigns.'" The ideological defense of homeownership has long been linked
with the idea of domestic space as a haven against outside interference
and "an indivisible territorial unit that matches the needs of the household." The deeply embedded symbolic power of private property and
homeownership has gone hand in hand with the discourse of the rights
of self-defense in order to protect the sanctity of the home.[108]

As an organizational format that commodifies space, the residential
suburban subdivision functions not only as a commercial instrument
that promotes enterprise through consumption but also as a peculiar
cultural convention that reflects a whole host of values, including privacy and isolation, individuality, and personal autonomy.[109] Over the
course of the twentieth century, the suburban house acquired its iconic
meaning as a metonym for something else (domestic tranquility, sta-

ble family life, domesticity, the good life). Yet the signifying function of the contemporary suburban house is increasingly haunted by the darker underside of that suburban dream. By the end of the twentieth century, building typologies for residential accommodation underwent a profound transformation. The quintessential dream house for middle-class home buyers was the stand-alone suburban bungalow set back from tree-lined streets and surrounded by lush landscaped gardens, with a swimming pool and backyard courtyard perfect for *braais*. Arranged in neat little rows, these assemblages of spacious homes all had quaint names—Parktown, Parkview, Parkhurst, Greenside, and Hyde Park—that evoked images of verdant landscapes and quiet country lives. Starting in the 1980s, the preferred model for superwealthy residential homes became the closed security estate, which consisted in the main of a hybrid collection of separate villages comprised of look-alike McMansions set in stylized quasipastoral environments and typically linked with a signature golf course. This retreat into opulent luxury offered a convenient escape from the risk of crime, and "the home-within-the-hotel qualities" of the residential security estate became a defense against unwanted interaction with the surrounding social inequalities. Yet these "theme parks for the rich and famous" were not available for everyone.[110] Struggling middle-class homebuyers were forced by the logic of the real estate market to downsize and reconcile their suburban dreams with townhouse clusters, a distinct building typology that consisted of tightly packed, semidetached residential units set behind high perimeter walls and security gates for strictly monitoring access control. Such distinctive design features became the key security tools in these new residential housing developments.[111]

The coveted place of homeownership as a fundamental civil right or, more precisely, as a necessary foundation of individual freedom has reinforced the symbolic power of private property.[112] At a time of intensified awareness of crime and victimhood, the logic of security has driven the refiguring of the suburban dream home into an inward-looking "safe house." Yet this idyllic image of the suburban home as a site of consumer happiness and domesticated bliss has been increasingly overlaid and displaced by the idea of the (introverted and fortresslike) safe house as the source of physical security.[113]

At the height of the modernist epoch, Le Corbusier famously described the house as a "machine for living in"—a kind of immobile capsule that exemplified the principles of functional efficiency and no-frills aesthetics. Whereas rationality and order gave substance to the Corbusian vision, the fixation on security animates the idealized conception of the safe house. By designing out insecurity and building in protection, the cocooned enclosure offers a technological fix to counteract the permanent condition of uncertainty and risk. As a model of introverted space allowing residents to retreat into secure bunkers, the safe house epitomizes the capsular logic of enclosure and, as such, occupies the inward-looking space of post-public urbanism.[114]

In the apocalyptic imaginary of the criminogenic city, the idyllic life the suburban dream house promised has succumbed to deep-seated feelings of ontological insecurity. The suburban safe house exists at the intersection of domestic security and urban menace. Despite the steady accumulation of security features, the safe house is always at risk, inextricably linked to the menace and danger from which it seeks to insulate itself.[115] The serial repetition of images of suburban homes surrounded by towering walls topped with high-voltage electric fencing serves as a constant reminder that whatever exists inside the protected perimeter is that which must be protected and secured against the unknown. The safe house represents perhaps the most compelling spatial format for the assemblage of single-family dwellings that define the suburban residential fabric of the city. Whether designed into new homes or retrofitted into older ones, safety precautions that fulfill the escapist fantasies of anxious residents are of paramount importance.[116] In the visual vocabulary of postapartheid Johannesburg, the safe house is "the explicit and exact opposite of danger, violence, and disorder." With their stress on walls, gates, and barriers, inward-looking building typologies that define the suburban landscape distill and refract "a range of fears and anxieties not only about the dangers of contemporary life but also about the conditions of security that might counteract those dangers."[117]

In a metropolis that aspires to become a world-class African city, enclosed spaces and security fortification have become the dominant design motif. In the architectural imagination of securitization, stress on the separation of protected inside and menacing outside reflects the manner in which the idea of housing in the residential suburbs of Johannesburg "is increasingly refracted through the image of the safe house." As Samira Kawash has argued, the trope of a safe house does not refer to any particular architectural design or specific style as much as to

FIGURE 8. High walls and gated entry. (Photo by author.)

"an interrelated cluster of images, fantasies, ideals, and practices." As a miniaturized expression of capsular architecture, the safe house signifies the high point of what amounts to "defensible space design" or, perhaps more accurately, an "architecture of paranoia."[118]

The narrow focus on the safe house as an unfortunate but necessary antidote to danger enables home builders, real estate agents, and security providers, along with buyers and sellers, to sidestep the implications for race and class of the wholesale retreat into fortified enclaves. Over the past three decades, the so-called white flight from the inner-city ring of settled residential suburbs close to the central city has been associated with urban decay and the criminalization of a racialized urban underclass. As social commentators have suggested, the accruing socioeconomic privilege of white middle-class suburban homeowners depends on and is reinforced by the projection of chaos and criminality onto a black underclass. The schematic opposition between ontological security and imminent danger signals the interplay between innocent victims and violent perpetrators. In the continuing nightmare, the safety and comfort attributed to the suburban dream house are undermined by unwanted strangers who return in the phantasmagorical form of menacing criminals.[119] Inhabiting the dark spaces of the disorderly city, these uncanny figures of dread haunt the imaginations of frightened suburbanites. The sanitized "hygienic space" of the safe house offers protection against the unknown that lurks just outside the walls.[120]

Shifting Dangers, Elusive Threats

What distinguishes the safe house from conventional home-building practices is the way its overall spatial design "articulates and makes explicit a particular logic of enclosure"—fortification—as a necessary counterweight "to ever-present danger."[121] Defensive homeownership not only reflects the aspirations of suburban residents for safety and security but also reshapes the built environment of residential neighborhoods. The incremental retrofitting of private suburban homes into sequestered redoubts has left in its wake a discontinuous landscape of fortress-like outposts in a constant state of military-like preparedness. Bringing smart-surveillance systems into domestic space has fundamentally redefined the common understanding of home as an autonomous zone, or as Michele Rapoport has suggested, an "enclave of privacy and retreat," a "bastion of seclusion and isolation," and a "place for respite."[122] The installation of such monitoring-surveillance technologies as networked (analytics-enabled) CCTV cameras, infrared and ultrasonic detectors, photoelectric beams (which function as invisible electronic barriers akin to trip wires), silent burglar alarms, volumetric detectors, intrusion-detection devices, glass-breakage warnings, and other target-hardening crime-prevention tools in domestic settings means that residents find themselves continuously under observation.[123]

Smart security devices embedded in domestic settings are programmed to track behaviors and to identify and catalog the normal and expected versus the exceptional and unexpected. Depending on their particular functional use, they engage in processes of recognition, identification, and categorization—indispensable for triggering predetermined chains of programmed response.[124] Yet because residents voluntarily install surveillance technologies in order to monitor themselves, their family members, and their property, strategies of household security challenge conventional understandings of boundary and seclusion—the very bedrocks of the private home. To deliberately subject oneself and one's family to constant surveillance reverses the classic understanding of the disciplinary mechanisms of the anonymous panoptic gaze by shifting real power to those who are observed.[125]

Under circumstances of ontological insecurity, the problem with the safe house is that it is never truly secure. The steady accumulation of security apparatuses is accompanied by an increase in perceived danger. In the intensifying battle between homeowners and criminals, those who engage in house burglaries and carjackings have found new ways to circumvent ever-expanding security measures. Indeed, the advertising and promotional campaigns mounted by the fear industries (private security companies, businesses specializing in security paraphernalia, and the like) constantly stress the need for more and more security because prevailing systems become outmoded as criminals discover ways to circumvent them. The popular media produce a steady stream of horror stories that serve as anecdotal evidence fueling the widespread perception of an escalating "crisis in security."[126]

Capsular logic has produced a sophisticated machinery of encoded passwords, access cards, and electronically activated locks as key components of high-tech security systems. Just as the contemporary airport has become a sophisticated "surveillance machine" capable of tracking material objects and the movement of people in real time, the safe house has acquired new meaning as a sentient stronghold.[127]

High-tech security companies have become mesmerized with the technological fantasy of a perfectly controlled and sealed safe house.[128] What amounts to "a permanent feeling of insecurity" has engendered what Paul Virilio has described as the "consumption of protection."[129] Ownership of a private home is typically associated with personal identity. The marketing of smart, automated technologies for domestic use has played an increasingly important role in transforming the suburban home from a more or less neutral site of personal and familial privacy into a safe house protected from outside danger. The safe house blends the accoutrements of the smart home, in which automated domestic technologies "respond to human presence and actions and adjust themselves accordingly," with an almost paranoid fixation on safety. In promising enhanced protection, these intelligent, ambient technologies inside the home take on vital roles in shaping domestic environments by "defining physical perimeters of enclosed spaces" and thereby solidifying "the dichotomies between inside and out, private and public, safety and threat, the familiar and the strange." These automated security technologies are ubiquitous, interactive, and often invisible. They help homeowners carry out daily tasks while at the same time anticipating possible contingencies that arise from the danger outside.[130]

At the upper end of the real estate market, the latest luxury laagers designed especially for the truly superrich families are genuine bunkerlike enclosures in which the configuration of interior space resembles an elaborate security maze. These security-saturated smart houses are outfitted with what amounts to an artificial nervous system, in which electronically activated pressure pads are concealed under the floorboards, motion-sensitive monitoring devices are surreptitiously hidden in walls and entryways, and time-lapse surveillance cameras are programmed to detect the presence of unwelcome intruders and follow their movements. These and other state-of-the-art electromagnetic, optical, and acoustic sensors are linked to automated alarm systems and connected to the central command post of a private security company contracted to dispatch armed-response teams. Real estate developers typically outfit the upstairs bedrooms of these luxury residential palaces with iron "rape gates" and sometimes install high-tech, super-fortified hiding places (safe rooms) that offer an impenetrable sanctuary to which frightened residents can hastily retreat in the event of unwanted encroachment on security perimeters.[131]

From Static Defense to Proactive Offense

Deconstructing the idea of the safe house enables us to expose its underlying assumptions and internal dynamics. These fortresslike citadels are more than a single isolated building typology; they are the symbolic expressions of a whole syntax of controlled spaces linked across multiple residential suburban landscapes.[132] The logic of such prophylactic enclosures demanded new border-making practices that have replaced the almost exclusive reliance on "hard territorial boundaries" with much more flexible and mobile mechanisms "of tracking, filtration, and exclusion."[133] Wholesale dependence on static systems of visible protection, in which fixed barriers (such as outside perimeter walls, palisade fences and metal gates) and interior alarms are arranged in concentric circles, create what amount to stationary bubbles. Security experts have increasingly viewed these systems of immobile fortifications as something akin to a Maginot Line of static defense—an illusory, feel-good solution to safety that frequently breaks down when put to the test. In departing from these conventional approaches, new strategies of home defense have emphasized interlocking and integrated systems of protection that incorporate stealth and maneuverability, substituting invisible detection for visible barriers, speed for stasis, and immaterial technologies for physical obstacles. In short, home security assemblages have come to resemble less an accumulation of visible barriers and more a malleable interface between outside and inside—a mediating membrane that blends impermanent stealth technologies with permanent physical obstacles and that combines proactive public-space policing with static guarding.[134] The new language of designing in protection reflects a shift in thinking about security from an almost exclusive focus on visible barriers, defensive shields, and the engineering prowess of heavy modernity to the latticework of swarms, networks, and webs of liquid modernity. The modulating curves, folds, and layers of mobile (and invisible) security systems supplement the static (and visible) defenses of barrier walls and security gates.[135] Redesigning security systems depends on an assemblage of miniaturized portable devices—a technological fix grounded in the promise to monitor activities outside and beyond the line of sight.[136]

The construction of protective shields around individual bodies, detached single-family dwellings, and entire residential neighborhoods has produced the mythical dreamscape of suburban tranquility. The dependence of individual homeowners and residential neighborhoods on the military-like prowess of private security companies has engendered a situation that resembles what Dennis Judd in a different context has referred to as a "state of war."[137] The sophisticated security devices available to homeowners are often borrowed root and branch from state-of-the-art military technologies.[138] Private security companies have mimicked the training protocols, chains of command, and specialized equipment associated with the strategies and tactics of military operations. The language of security and militarism have blended together in the ways that managers of private security companies and heads of neighborhood associations communicate with one another.[139]

The fantasy of the safe house has come to play an oversized role in the choreographed performance of security at a time when personal safety is deemed to be at risk. The fear industries—that is, those private businesses that market and sell home security products and services—have tirelessly promoted the privatized consumption of technological fixes as solutions to the risk of criminal violence and bodily harm. In the popular imaginary of suburban living, the idea of the safe house has comingled with the idealization of the smart home, in which a host of protective paraphernalia is integrated into digital devices and electronic security systems to create a veritable force field of self-defense. The booming business in security accessories for domestic use includes a rather astonishing array of (IT) web-based electronic surveillance instruments for the home and its immediate perimeter: automated lighting and motion-detection devices, window locks and burglar bars, and remotely activated gates and remote CCTV monitoring that enable homeowners to see inside their homes from a distance. Harmonized under a single command, these integrated systems offer a "fully networked cocoon." What is on offer in the security marketplace goes well beyond a collection of hardware and software applications, where the purchase of these commodities promises "something more psychological in nature, namely, a fantasy of perfect control of the domestic environment."[140]

Both the safe house and the smart home have become emblematic of an individualized, privatized, and technology-centered response to collective anxiety. The eager and almost blind embrace of surveillance technologies and tracking systems in the smart home "puts the finishing touches on the inward-facing orientation" of what Alice Crawford has called "the wired citadel." As the biometric identification systems, CCTV cameras, thermal imaging, and infrared sensor devices accumulate in overlapping layers, the smart home becomes an electronic fortress.[141] By synthesizing outdoor perimeter security and interior detection systems (connecting every room in the house) into a single electronically monitored security shield, residents of the safe house have moved beyond the limited capacity of simply reacting to unwanted intrusions and into proactively anticipating what might happen and when.[142]

Taken to the extreme, the securitization of private living spaces that high-tech security solutions promise to ensure comes with the undermining of viable public spaces as places for mutual exchanges and chance encounters. Promoted as a do-it-yourself solution to crime, the retreat into high-security safe houses has marked a turn away from public engagement, or what political theorist Iris Marion Young has described as "civic privatism."[143] As suburban residents have "become further isolated within electronically fortified private spaces," the safe house might indeed "function to create a feedback loop of paranoia about crime." Instead of bolstering protection from risk, the dependence on the safe house has ironically contributed to an increased demand for more high-tech security applications.[144]

Security, Dwelling, Architecture

As an omnipresent apparatus of control, the Panopticon relies on its own visible presence to ensure compliance with its disciplinary power. Yet just as threats and danger have mutated in accordance with changing circumstances, strategies of security governance have also evolved. New architectures of security have begun to replace older paradigms of (visible) deterrence and (physical) containment with innovative strategies of camouflage, seduction, and deception. As Elisabetta Brighi has argued, camouflage "moves security beyond the panoptic logic of the 'gaze,' where seeing and being seen through surveillance and reconnaissance" effectively constitute the foundation for control, to a new prototype "where what becomes essential" is concealment and deception, unobtrusively assimilating surveillance techniques into the physical landscape while simultaneously remaining in plain sight. Rather than functioning as a benign background, the physical landscape itself has become a central feature of securitizing the safe house. As Brighi has also suggested, "Security deceptively disappears by blending it seamlessly into the environment through a mimetic process of dissimulation and mimicry of natural forms." The "architecture of camouflage" endows security systems with the magical powers of disappearance. Rather than acquiring their disciplinary power through their visible presence, security systems effectively become a *trompe l'oeil*—quite literally fooling the eye through elaborate masquerade and impersonation.[145]

In both nature and warfare, camouflage provides a necessary means for escaping visual detection from the probing gaze of enemies.[146] Deception and deflection enable new security systems to literally disappear from sight. Camouflage ensures that potential criminals never really know whether they are being observed. The use of the contrived architectural simulation enables the safe house to hide security technologies by means of a deliberate strategy of subterfuge and concealment. Everyday camouflage establishes a disjuncture between the appearance of safety and the reality of anxiety. The existence of these everyday forms of disguise reveals the hidden deceits of security urbanism and "the extent to which a mythical image" of untroubled insouciance is superimposed on suburban landscapes of fear. Everyday camouflage functions through deliberate means of deception, enabling the actual realities of siege architecture to blend surreptitiously into the surrounding landscape to produce the bland appearance of unremarkable ordinariness. The architecture of camouflage indicates how the outward appearance of an aesthetically pleasing landscape can actually function as a strategic intervention, that is, a means to an end as opposed to simply an object of visual contemplation—an end in itself. The aesthetics of camouflage turns transparency into its opposite. The benign facades conceal the security strategies behind banal "designer skins" of normalcy.[147] The safe house offers a powerful metaphor for the "introversion of space," whereby the primacy of safety remains hidden behind the false veneer of domestic tranquility.[148]

The focus in home security has shifted away from a singular fixation on impeding easy access using defensive systems that stress the static installation of physical barriers and has moved toward flexible arrangements with the aim of monitoring external threats using the virtual technologies of surreptitious surveillance.[149] Surveillance technologies have reduced the dependence on the physical enclosure of space by substituting the control of movement. The porous membranes of virtual walls conceal the operations of surveillance.[150]

The Technical Fix and Securitization

As Sheila Jasanoff has argued, technical innovation in security provision often follows in the footsteps of popular science fiction.[151] Science fiction writers such as William Gibson, William Burroughs, and Philip K. Dick and neo-noir films such as *Minority Report* (Stephen Spielberg), *Blade Runner* (Ridley Scott), *THX 1138* (George Lucas), and *Children of Men* (Alfonso Cuarón) provide a prescient glimpse into possible futures for surveillance and control. The anticipatory gestures of science fiction create imaginary worlds in which heightened panoptic sensibility seeks to leave nothing to pure chance.[152]

In the dreamscape of high-tech security provision, crime prevention in residential neighborhoods is more effective when sophisticated "thinking" machines replace humans. Experts in risk management contend that the human element is the weakest link in networked security systems. Such security personnel as static guards, CCTV-camera monitors, and street watchers are notoriously unreliable, since they are prone to distraction and inattention brought about by boredom.[153] Security increasingly relies on the technological fix of new imaging and sensing technologies associated with CCTV monitoring, mobile GPS and GIS systems, and software-supported biometric identification systems. Outfitted with intelligent video analytics and computer algorithms, machines—not CCTV monitors—do the actual watching. These technical innovations have become key elements in securitizing residential neighborhoods.[154]

The process of the technologization of security systems, that is, the making of technological instruments as the centerpiece of risk-aversion strategies, has reshaped the logics, rationalities, and modes of reasoning that undergird security practices. New technologies of software-supported remote sensing, automated CCTV surveillance, and the soft infrastructure of wireless microsensor networks have emerged as key infrastructural innovations that have reconfigured home security.[155] Building a safe house requires technological empowerment. Smart security requires the expertise of software developers, designers, engineers, infrastructure builders, guards, systems experts, and many others who produce protection devices. The integration of state-of-the-art technologies in a totalizing networked field of command and communication (sensing, visualization, and biometrics integrated into mobile networks) signal new and important imaginings of total control. Not surprisingly, smart security systems depend on tracking, algorithmic prediction, and massive flows of information. These elements constitute what Nigel Thrift called *qualculation*—a term used to describe how "calculation has become so ubiquitous that it has entered a new phase."[156]

Although the methods of keeping unwanted intruders off one's property have changed dramatically since the use of moats and flaming arrows during medieval times, the fundamental principles of perimeter security have remained largely the same: deterrence, detection, delay, and denial. Consumer demand for early-warning-detection and perimeter-protection systems has increased exponentially over the past two decades. Perimeter protection is the first line of defense. Hence, the ultimate security solution is a layered one consisting of three levels of protection: the outer perimeter or boundary of the property, the in-between middle zone, and, lastly, the interior spaces of the home itself. Such devices as dual-photo beam sensors create an invisible barrier that will trigger an alarm when breached. When strategically placed in concealed locations, these beam sensors establish a wall of coverage.[157]

Such automated biometric authentication systems as fingerprint-identification apparatuses, retinal-scanning devices, and face- and voice-recognition software enable frightened homeowners to recognize and verify the identities of persons seeking to enter their properties. Such new technological advances as footstep-recognition systems (in which pressure sensors are fitted below the flooring to monitor movement and can distinguish between members of the household and outside intruders) and invisible sensor devices have replaced older security systems that proved to be less than fail safe.[158]

Correspondingly, high-end software applications connected with smart phones mean that homeowners are no longer dependent on their monitoring companies to inform them of possible break-ins. The introduction of new mobile-phone technology enables homeowners in remote locations to receive real-time information on their burglar alarm status and even stream live video footage from their security cameras of any disturbance straight on to their cellular phones. Users who connect a PTZ (pan, tilt, zoom) camera to their home recording devices are able to zoom in, zoom out, and alter the direction of the camera as they view live action from a distance. The use of silent alarms enables homeowners to notify their armed-response security team in order to surprise unsuspecting burglars while they are still on the premises. Nervous homeowners can install wireless motion detection devices attached to an integrated camera system. When the sensor detects movement, it automatically activates the camera and simultaneously sends an alert to the control panel. The control panel immediately sends images and audio feeds to the central monitoring station as well as to the end user's mobile phone. Because monitoring-station staff are able to view disturbances in real time, they can verify the alarm and respond accordingly. They can also advise on whether homeowners should move their family members to another location. This up-to-date detection system is available in a pet-tolerant form, in which Target Specific Imaging™ (TSI) technology is able to distinguish between human beings and pets weighing less than eighty-five pounds.[159]

The Bunker Mentality

Proactive public-space policing blends military doctrine with urban security. This militarization of urban space involves the superimposition of hard borders on the spatial fabric of the city, carving out a vast archipelago of fortified enclaves and security zones set apart from an unknown outside that is deemed unruly and dangerous. High walls, identity checkpoints, computerized CCTV monitoring, public-space surveillance, biometric access controls, and mobile security patrols form protective shields around these safe spaces cocooned against the existential threats that lurk beyond.[160]

Put in broad terms, designing in protection and designing out insecurity are ideas that are fundamentally important to current discourses of security in risk-obsessed situations.[161] The architectural logic that informs contemporary suburban building practices places particular stress on enclosure and separation. This new urban morphology of fortified enclaves and security zones is closely linked to the evolution of the military-style technologies of low-intensity warfare. The idea of defensive urbanism captures the explicit connection between architecture and security. Whereas the architecture of circulation and mobility operates through the connective tissue of infrastructure, the architecture of fortification has reshaped urban landscapes to resemble something akin to low-intensity "battlespaces." "Modern architecture is inseparable from war," Beatriz Colomina has suggested. "It recycles the techniques and materials developed for the military."[162] The new military discourses of asymmetrical and unconventional warfare have crossed over into the governance of everyday urban life.[163] The fortress metaphor suggests a fragmented landscape that is separated by physical barriers such as walls, gates, and fences and cloaked in the indirect light of surveillance cameras. The real or imagined need for improved security translates into acceptable levels of fortification and the suffocation of the genuine public life of the surrounding streetscape.[164]

This new military urbanism consists of a combination of aggressive policing tactics, constant monitoring and surveillance, and preemptive engagement with unknown persons (in order to deter crime before it occurs)—all framed in relationship to the overall goal of supporting the comfortable lifestyles of affluent suburban residents. This obsessive securitization of everyday life has resulted in the evisceration of civil rights, the criminalization of the poor (by outlawing their tactics of survival), and the abandonment of the uniform application of the rule of law.[165]

PART III

THE FEAR INDUSTRIES
Profiting from Insecurity

Pluralizing the Provision of Security

With the end of apartheid and the transition to parliamentary democracy, the institutional and financial resources available to the SAPS were largely channeled into such crime-priority areas as high-profile burglaries of commercial establishments, international drug trafficking, carjackings, violent crimes using illegal firearms (such as bank robberies and cash-and-carry heists), and the illicit activities of criminal syndicates with global reach. For the most part, public policing had continued to operate under the conventional rules of engagement that reflected their legally sanctioned mandate: reactive law enforcement and apprehension of criminal suspects. As the SAPS have largely withdrawn their visible-policing services from affluent residential neighborhoods to concentrate on these high-profile criminal activities, private security companies have quickly filled the void, seeking to tap into a potentially lucrative market for security products. By promising quick reaction and armed response to combat crime in ways public policing agencies were unwilling or unable to, these firms have aggressively marketed their protection services—with a no-nonsense style of policing—for two types of customers: business clients in securitized office parks, enclosed shopping malls, and commercial strips, on the one hand, and relatively affluent homeowners in gated residential communities, security villages, and closed-off neighborhoods.[1]

With the militarization of their training and their operational logics, private security companies have begun to function as something akin to irregular armed forces that answer only tangentially to public authority. These firms have not only carved niches for themselves in the fields of armed response, stationary guarding services and sentry duty, vehicle tracking and recovery, the maintenance and operation of CCTV control rooms, VIP protection services, and intelligence and information gathering but also made substantial inroads into the subfields of criminal investigations (from the scene of the crime to the courtroom, forensics, and polygraph examinations.[2]

Creeping Takeover

Unlike public law enforcement agencies, private security companies do not seek to provide universal protection or blanket coverage of space but instead concentrate on minimizing disorder and preventing crime in the particular demarcated territories in which they operate under contract, such as gated residential communities, security villages, business- and city-improvement districts, and commercial shopping districts.[3] Their modus operandi revolves primarily around risk aversion, that is, minimizing the possibility of crime or disorder through the creation of literal and metaphorical barriers to keep out undesirable people who are regarded as potential threats to the security of these spaces.[4] In contrast to the liberal notion of free and unimpeded movement in public space, the approach that private security companies take in the zones they are hired to protect conforms to what Sonia Bookman and Andrew Woolford have called an "exclusionary definition of order."[5]

The primary raison d'être for private security companies is to serve the interests of their employers or their corporate clients rather than providing for a vaguely defined public interest or common good.[6] The proliferation of what has been called mass private property, such as securitized business parks, enclosed shopping malls, citadel office complexes, gated residential communities, and other fortified enclaves, has reshaped the urban landscape of Johannesburg after apartheid.[7] In a real sense, as Nan Ellin suggested, "form follows fear."[8] These post-public spaces of social congregation amount to "bubbles of security" that not only are physically separated from the surrounding cityscape but also are increasingly subjected to a style of privatized policing that differs markedly from public law enforcement in its objectives, core functions, and methods of operation.[9] While public policing has stressed apprehension of suspected lawbreakers after a criminal event has taken place, private security agencies have turned to risk-avoidance strategies designed to prevent disorder and criminal behavior before it happens.[10]

The rapid fragmentation of the metropolitan landscape into an archipelago of fortified security bubbles fundamentally reshaped spatial segregation in postapartheid Johannesburg.[11] The rapid expansion of such building typologies as enclosed shopping malls, securitized office complexes, gated residential estates, and cocooned townhouse clusters puts upward pressure on the demand for private security to protect the shared common spaces of social congregation. Such increased reliance on private security companies to protect this kind of "mass private property" has fundamentally reshaped what it means to talk of security and protection.[12]

There is a common perception in South Africa that public policing agencies are ill-trained, underresourced, overextended, and hence largely ineffective as genuine crime-fighting forces. Police officers on the ground have acquired a reputation (whether deserved or not) for incompetence, brutality, and corruption.[13] The widespread popular distrust of the public police—and the criminal justice system more broadly—is amplified by neoliberal ideologies that promote private entrepreneurial solutions to the failure of public agencies to adequately deliver safety and security and by the spread of the rhetoric of "responsibilization," which insists that individuals and local communities can best decide how to govern themselves independently of state interference.[14]

Both the rich and poor residents of Johannesburg have lost faith in the ability of state agencies to deliver basic public services, including the protection of people and property. Both groups "have taken matters into their own hands, albeit with very different means" at their disposal. Those residents who can afford to do so have more or less opted out of the consumption of virtually every public service. They buy private health care, never use public transportation—relying instead on private automobiles—enroll their children in prestigious private schools, and purchase, at exorbitant prices, the "most dazzling array of private security" services and devices on the market. In contrast, for poor residents of Johannesburg, access to basic public services has continued to fall well short of what is needed to sustain everyday life.[15] Resentment over water shortages, intermittent power outages, school closures, and predatory crime has led to service-delivery protests across the country. The inadequacy of public policing agencies to provide security from predatory crime has led poorer residents to turn to impromptu vigilante tactics to protect themselves.[16]

Criminal gangs opportunistically take advantage of circumstances in which security seems lax. For example, a spate of attacks by armed robbers targeting unwary parents dropping off and collecting their children at school led concerned residents of suburban Johannesburg to hire private security companies to guard schools. In a particularly telling example, a team of robbers, using a blue Jeep Grand Cherokee and a white BMW X5 with at least two sets of false license plates, struck at least five times in a matter of weeks outside schools in northern Johannesburg, stealing expensive jewelry from mothers in broad daylight and in front of dozens of passersby.[17] Criminal gangs sometimes follow unsuspecting motorists home after trips to shopping malls, attacking them when they pause to open their driveway gates. In October 2006, burglars assaulted and robbed eighty-two-year old Nadine Gordimer, the world-famous South African novelist, locking her in a storeroom and taking cash and jewelry from her Parktown home. There have been frequent cases in which thieves have tortured or killed their victims with hot irons, knives, and boiling water in order to get what they wanted—even when their victims have not provoked them by refusing them anything.[18]

Shoot-outs between private security operatives and suspected criminals take place with frightening regularity.[19] Confrontations between private security armed-response teams and criminal gangs sometimes lead to terrible consequences for innocent passersby. For example, in 2008, twelve-year-old Emily Williams was shot and killed by a stray bullet during a shoot-out between armed robbers and private security operatives in Fairmont.[20] The frequency with which armed civilians have chased after and engaged in shoot-outs with would-be assailants has prompted some observers to claim that the streets of Johannesburg resemble the lawless Wild West.[21]

The move toward proactive private policing of public space has fundamentally reshaped the relationship between public law enforcement and private security. Private security companies have steadily encroached on the once sacrosanct prerogatives of public law enforcement and apprehension of suspected criminals. As Julie Berg has argued, private policing of public space has meant that private security companies have pushed the limits of their legal authority "further and further by drawing in the police at later and later stages of the arrest process, such as delivering suspects at the doorstep of police stations, sometimes filling in the relevant paperwork on behalf of the police and providing video footage as evidence of the transgression."[22] On occasion, residential associations have hired private security companies to monitor the prosecution of suspected criminals as they enter the criminal justice system, keeping a watchful eye on dockets so that they do not "disappear," attending court sessions, supplying evidence such as CCTV video footage, and gathering eyewitness testimonies.[23] By going well beyond their mandate to reduce crime in residential neighborhoods with which they have signed contracts, private security companies have simultaneously enhanced their own reputations and legitimacy as crime-fighting forces and reinforced the widely held view that public law enforcement agencies are incompetent and that the criminal justice system is incapable of prosecuting criminals.[24]

Armed-response units working with private security companies are better trained in the use of firearms, better prepared to engage with criminal gangs, and more committed to their work than are public police officers. Their systems of communication and intelligence gathering on the ground exceed those of public policing agencies. They are outfitted with arsenals of highly efficient weaponry, they operate with military-like efficiency in high-powered vehicles, and they never hesitate to use lethal force.[25]

The Evolving Policing Division of Labor

Beginning in the early 1990s, middle-class residents in the suburban neighborhoods of northern Johannesburg began to fortify their homes in response to the perceived threat of increasing crime. The installation of fortified entrance gates, reinforced-steel window bars, electric fencing, and high perimeter walls topped with metal spikes or razor wire became commonplace for frightened homeowners. Countless numbers of private security companies—including many well-established firms with international reputations and dozens of other local homegrown firms—entered the market, offering such protection services as the installation of security gates, electric fencing, and panic buttons along with the guarantee of immediate armed response to deter unwanted intruders.[26]

This turn toward securitization of individual homes marked the beginning of a rapidly growing residential market for private security services. Driven by racially tinted anxieties about crime and class concerns about property values, affluent residents responded to the perceived threats to their personal safety in largely individualistic ways. Depending on what they were willing to pay for the security services on offer, homeowners entered into separate contracts with the private security company of their choice. The security services that these companies provided were largely defensive and reactive in nature. Companies stationed fully equipped armed-response vehicles in neighborhoods in which they had secured a large number of contracts with individual homeowners. The armed-response teams (usually consisting of a single private security operative per car) remained stationary in their vehicles, waiting to be summoned by emergency calls triggered by the activation of an alarm or when a paying client pressed a panic button.[27]

By the late 1990s, homeowners in affluent suburban neighborhoods began to establish voluntary associations as a way to collectively address their concerns about rising crime and the threat to their property values. Exasperated with the perceived inability or unwillingness of public policing agencies to provide security, these neighborhood associations began to close roads off with heavy metal gates and to erect boom gates to control access to their neighborhoods. Some neighborhood associations applied to the municipal authorities for permission to erect boom gates, but for the most part, these road closures took place unilaterally and without official authorization.[28] This defiance of municipal statutes led to long and highly contentious battles between the neighborhood associations and local authorities over the legality and legitimacy of road closures.[29]

Faced with extended court challenges to existing legislation and with irate homeowners relentless in their criticism of the incompetence of public policing agencies to provide some semblance of safety and security, municipal authorities backed down. The successful efforts of residential associations to barricade roads and close off suburban neighborhoods marked the beginning of an important shift in the organization of private security. The steady expansion of such securitized building typologies as gated residential communities, enclosed townhouse clusters, upscale shopping malls, fortified office complexes, and other closed-off spaces coincided with the implementation of new kinds of collective security arrangements in which private security companies were hired to guard entryways and exits, to regularly patrol the outside perimeter walls, and to monitor CCTV cameras.[30] Whereas older residential suburbs were originally built in accordance with an open-plan, easy-access model, neighborhood associations later sought to emulate the kinds of shared protective services that had become commonplace in newer, enclosed enclaves that had emerged as the dominant prototype for residential accommodation. In what might be seen as the opening wedge of collective security, neighborhood associations began to collect dues from members to share in the cost of barricading streets, erecting boom gates, and hiring static private security guards to monitor entry-exit points. For the first time, neighborhood associations and private companies entered into security agreements that involved not just reactive armed response for individual homeowners but a shared communal commitment to crime prevention.[31]

This overdetermined convergence of collective consumption of security packages with the advent of proactive crime prevention strategies marked a crucial turning point in the private marketplace for risk management products. By the mid-2000s, neighborhood associations were increasingly realizing the power of collective consumption, and they began to demand better, more effective performance from private security companies. Like all voluntary organizations, neighborhood associations faced the problem of free riding, in which homeowners were able to take advantage of the benefits of collective consumption whether or not they paid for these services.[32] To cover the costs of such an expanded repertoire of private security services, neighborhood associations undertook concerted campaigns aimed at expanding their paid membership as a way of ensuring a steady cash flow.[33] Whereas individual homeowners dealt with private security companies from a relatively disadvantaged vantage point, neighborhood associations—as collective agents—were in a far stronger marketplace bargaining position to demand better, more effective, and more comprehensive services from private security companies and to negotiate advantageous terms with these service providers.[34]

As one might imagine, private security companies promising rapid armed response were often thinly spread over vast geographical areas because they had signed contracts with individual homeowners in widely dispersed residential suburbs. Fierce competition between the early arrivals—especially established global security companies such as ADT, Chubb Protective Services, and Fidelity Services Group—over market share meant that these profit-seeking firms found themselves in the unenviable position of trying to reduce overall costs by minimizing services.[35] Less established but more aggressive private security companies with roots in South Africa seized the opportunity to create a niche in the market for protection services, offering a new proactive model of policing designed not to respond to crimes in progress or crimes that had already happened but to proactively anticipate criminal activities before they could take place. These private companies, particularly Core Tactical, 24/7 Security Services, CSS Tactical, 7 Arrows Security, and Beagle Watch, aggressively pursued a marketing strategy aimed at supplementing separate contracts with individual homeowners with collective security agreements with neighborhood associations. In exchange for hefty monthly fees, private security companies promised not just armed response but a commitment to implement more far-reaching and sophisticated crime prevention strategies based on managing risk. The core of this approach to crime prevention involved rolling out a greater number of dedicated armed-response vehicles in particular neighborhoods where trained operatives engaged in highly visible, round-the-clock mobile patrols with the goal of confronting all suspicious persons who ventured into the public spaces of suburban residential neighborhoods.[36]

By effectively using their collective purchasing power, neighborhood associations were able to gain greater control over the spatial management and governance of their residential suburbs and commercial zones.[37] As a general rule, the adoption of crime prevention strategies such as access control and the monitoring of security gates, mobile patrols, and CCTV command centers was largely limited to enclosed enclaves such as gated residential estates, high-rise apartment complexes, security villages, and securitized townhouse clusters. Yet at this point, residential associations in older suburban neighborhoods began to demand the introduction of proactive security services that focused on crime prevention through mobile patrols of such public places as streets, commercial districts, parks, and vacant areas.[38]

In certain respects, proactive public-space security companies have come to resemble private armies, somewhat akin to mercenary brigades inserted into residential neighborhoods as an alien occupying force. As the opening wedge of the criminal justice system, public policing agencies focus first and foremost on effective law enforcement and the apprehension of criminal suspects. This approach to crime prevention is largely reactive. In contrast, proactive private security companies concentrate on preemptive crime deterrence through identification of risk, containment of danger, and displacement of perceived threats. [39] At the end of the day, these competing logics of security governance have remained at loggerheads.[40]

Community Active Protection (CAP) and Public Space Policing

Stories of origins are often illuminating. Not only do they typically suggest the start of a causal chain of events that seems to lead inexorably along a predetermined teleological pathway, but they also dispense with the messiness of polygenesis. The formation of the first Community Active Protection (CAP) in Glenhazel—what Chief Rabbi Warren Goldstein called "the story of miracles and wonder"—is one such tale.[41]

In response to growing fears that contact crimes (that is, those involving physical assault and bodily injuries) had reached unprecedented levels throughout the city, key leaders of various Jewish community organizations in Johannesburg came together to devise new security initiatives for residential neighborhoods at the northeast edge of the suburban belt in which many Jewish people lived, attended schools, and worshipped at synagogues.[42] The original security plan for the Greater Glenhazel area called for neighborhood associations to form section 21 (not-for-profit) companies that could then apply to the city for official permission to establish Residential Improvement Districts (RIDS).[43] As a regulatory platform that authorized a distinctive kind of spatial governance, RIDs were modeled after the City Improvement Districts (CIDs) that had spread like wildfire over the downtown core of Johannesburg starting in the late 1990s. The formation of RIDs would have enabled neighborhood associations (operating as section 21 companies) to mandate the collection of compulsory additional payments on existing rates and services bills from all homeowners within a legally sanctioned geographical area.[44]

Spearheaded by Chief Rabbi Goldstein among others, the neighborhood association in Glenhazel became the first residential suburb outside the downtown core to approach the city with a request to create a residential CID.[45] Approval for the creation of a CID required at least a 51 percent buy-in on the part of ratepayers.[46] In seeking to emulate the successful implementation of a RID called *Legae La Rona* (Our Place) in the Johannesburg inner city, the CAP leadership began an aggressive advertising campaign at least as early as 2006 that was designed to convince homeowners and business owners to join the effort. In their appeal to the city administration to acquire this legal status, the residential association in Glenhazel argued that the suburban neighborhoods in question were overwhelmingly Orthodox Jewish and that worshippers there needed special protection when walking to temple services on Saturdays.[47]

After much rancorous debate, the efforts to establish a several residential CIDs in the Greater Glenhazel area came to a standstill. The
main point of contention revolved around the question of mandated levies that would have compelled all property owners to contribute to CAP
private security services whether or not they wished to do so. Some residents claimed that these additional levies were instituted without any
consultation. They complained that many of the meetings were held in
synagogues and Jewish schools, thereby excluding those who were not
Jewish.[48] Faced with a shortfall of funds, the founders of the CAP security plan successfully appealed to wealthy Jewish business owners for
anonymous donations. This influx of capital was sufficient to get the initiative off the ground.[49]

In lieu of creating their own residential CIDs at some time in the future, neighborhood associations in Glenhazel and Waverley took the initiative to employ private security companies to protect them, raising
the funds among themselves to pay at rates well above the usual fees
for proactive services. Largely undertaken at the inspiration of Warren
Goldstein, chief rabbi of Johannesburg, and Bradley Sifris, national vice
president of a Jewish self-protection organization called the Community
Security Organization (CSO), the Glenhazel Active Protection (GAP) security initiative was launched in 2005 following the outbreak of a series
of home invasions and violent assaults. Formed as a not-for-profit company, GAP not only hired private security companies to undertake active patrolling of residential streets but also established a twenty-four-
hour call center that residents were encouraged to contact in case of a
crime emergency.[50] To get the security project underway, the start-up
unit in Glenhazel constructed a comprehensive database that included
the names, addresses, and phone numbers of occupants of all households in the neighborhood. This initial step was following by training
for more than four hundred domestic employees in how to spot suspicious activities and in the protocols for reporting these activities to the
call center.[51]

From the start, what distinguished the GAP proactive policing initiative from existing neighborhood security programs was the pronounced
and formidable display of preparedness. By dressing in military-style tactical gear, driving high-speed black vehicles with colorful insignia, and
arming themselves with semiautomatic rifles and shotguns, private security operatives combined both the requisite equipment (vehicles and

weaponry) and iconic symbolism (uniforms and badges) that gave them the semblance of legitimate authority. Their physical appearance and demeanor enabled them to establish and display an almost unquestioned "authoritative presence."[52] GAP boasted that their security personnel who patrolled neighborhood streets in high-performance vehicles (called Tactical Response Units) were highly trained with special skills that they acquired because of their extensive military or police backgrounds.[53]

Community Active Protection (CAP): "Reassurance Policing or Vigilantism by Proxy?"[54]

From the start, GAP organizers claimed great success in reducing crime by as much as a staggering 80 percent in the residential neighborhoods in which they first introduced mobile proactive patrolling. These initial proclamations of success triggered a great deal of interest from nearby neighborhood associations, who took steps to replicate this model in their areas.[55] Rebranded Community Active Protection (CAP) the following year, this novel approach to proactive crime fighting quickly spread to surrounding residential suburbs. CAP programs included those in Savoy and Waverley (SWAP); Melrose Birdhaven; Sydenham; Morningside; Houghton; Greater Rouxville, Senderwood, and Linksfield; Gresswold/Balfour Park; Sandringham; Saxonwold; Sandown-Strathavon (SCAP); Greater Oaklands Orchards; Houghton; Highlands-North; Victory Park; and Emmarentia-Greenside. Almost overnight, the CAP experiment with aggressive private policing spawned the serial replication of cloned offspring consisting of a "collection of proactive, multifaceted, integrated and community-run security schemes" radiating outward from their core constituencies in Greater Glenhazel. According to their own promotional materials, CAP leaders proclaimed that their "dynamic and innovative [approach to] fighting crime yielded resounding success across all areas incorporated into the scheme, reducing crime [in its zones of protection] by a staggering 80–90 percent."[56]

As a distinctive kind of paramilitary private security force, the CAP model became entrenched as the leading edge of what came to be known as proactive public-space policing.[57] The underlying rationale behind the development of this new brand of privately organized, public-space policing was the startling revelation, uncovered in a CSO intelligence assessment surveying crime victims in Glenhazel, that the weakest link in the crime prevention chain was not the ineffective security efforts focused on transforming private homes into minifortresses and guarding mass private property (shopping malls, office buildings, and entertainment zones) but the shadowy in-between spaces outside of existing security perimeters. The private security industry that had begun to evolve in the late apartheid period concentrated on fortifying homes and offices with high walls, electrified fencing, remote sensing devices, and armed-response services, but "almost all predatory crimes were initiated in public space: in people's driveways, at stop streets and traffic lights, on sidewalks."[58] What the CSO discovered was that neighborhood residents were most vulnerable to robberies and assaults during their journeys along the unprotected corridors connecting one securitized enclave to another. What was needed, then, was a shift in focus to policing of the unguarded conduits—the public spaces (such as streets, parks, and sidewalks) that are essential locations for the normal conduct of everyday life.[59]

The private security companies that CAP employed "bore all the hallmarks of the military backgrounds" of their owners and managers.[60] With combat experience in either the Israeli Defense Force or the apartheid-era South African Defense Force (SADF), these owners and managers looked on crime fighting as tantamount to engaging in a low-intensity war in which their fields of operations were residential neighborhoods under attack by wily criminal gangs. The first generation of tactical officers who were employed to police the streets was recruited from available pools of out-of-work soldiers of fortune, such as Portuguese-speaking Angolan mercenaries from the formidable 32 "Buffalo" Battalion, an infamous counterinsurgency unit that was known for its brutality and that fought on the side of the SADF in the Angolan civil war.[61] These tactical officers adopted a modus operandi that was deliberately aggressive and intimidating. They drove oversized 4x4 vehicles painted black, and they openly brandished a formidable array of weapons, including pump-action shotguns and assault rifles. CAP security personnel trained local residents to look out for suspicious-looking people and vehicles and report this information to a twenty-four-hour hotline.[62]

What overdetermined the creation of the CAP initiatives in Glenhazel, Waverley, and Sandringham was the disproportionate number of Orthodox Jewish residents living in those neighborhoods and the high concentration of synagogues, yeshivas, and Orthodox Jewish schools.[63]

With a Jewish population that was estimated at 90 percent, Greater Glenhazel (which includes Glenhazel, Percelia, Talboton, Fairmount, Glensan, Fairvale, Sunningdale, Silvamonte, and parts of Highlands North, Sandringham, and Lyndhurst) is the recognized hub of Orthodox Jewish life in Johannesburg. By the second decade of the twenty-first century, the Jewish population had shrunk by about 40 percent from its peak in the late 1980s.[64] The estimated fifty thousand Jewish people who have remained in Johannesburg tend to live in insular communities and to identity with some variant of Zionist ideology. Despite very few reported incidents of blatant anti-Semitism, Zionist organizations in Johannesburg have remained fearful and vigilant. In 1993, the Jewish Board of Deputies of South Africa took steps to form an organization, named the Community Security Organization (CSO), committed to safeguarding the Jewish presence in South Africa. The CSO was loosely modeled on the British-based Community Security Trust in the United Kingdom, which for several generations has focused on guarding Jewish religious and cultural installations, "documenting incidents of anti-Semitism, and working closely with British security agencies." Since its inception, the CSO has not deviated from its self-declared mission of protecting and "securing Jewish life and the Jewish way of life." Besides intelligence gathering, the primary activities for CSO members have consisted of providing armed security guards to protect synagogues, Jewish schools, key Jewish installations, and cultural events.[65]

The CSO has long exemplified the fixation with external threats. From the start, the CSO drew on a long tradition of military pilgrimages to Israel. The first chief executive of the CSO, Mark Notelovitz, acquired the rank of colonel in the Israeli Defense Force before he returned to his native South Africa to lead the organization. Ideologically speaking, the CSO emerged out of a militant orientation that the historian Yuri Slezkine has called "muscular Zionism," a "tradition cultivated by the incipient Zionist movement of the early twentieth century."[66] By tapping into a deep ideological current of collective self-interest, the CSO presented itself as the legitimate protector of the Jewish way of life in Johannesburg.[67]

In Johannesburg alone, there are over fifty Orthodox congregations linked with burial societies, schools, day-care facilities, and retail businesses.[68] In their assessment of the overall threat to Jewish communities in South Africa, the leaders of the CSO concluded that the Jewish people faced an existential threat not from mass public violence or high-profile acts of anti-Semitism but from the slow hemorrhage of "serial predatory crimes" that would undermine the resolve of Jewish people to remain in the country. The threat was existential because without adequate protection that could provide peace of mind and a sense of safety and security, Jewish people would emigrate en masse, leaving behind only those without the financial means to leave, thus corroding Jewish life and its cultural presence in Johannesburg.[69]

The Moral Ambivalence of Buying Private Security

As Marcel Mauss suggested a long time ago, relations of exchange cannot be easily reduced to instrumental, utility-maximizing processes alone. They are also central to the production and maintenance of particular social relations of reciprocity and mutual obligation.[70] Nonutilitarian monetary transactions often coexist and overlap with market-based relations of commodity exchange. In all sorts of ways, monetary negotiations are often invested with ethical and normative considerations, producing webs of significance that extend well beyond the supposedly detached impartiality of marketplace bargaining.[71]

The provision of private security is not simply a "[commercial] industry supplying services and products to its customers" in the competitive marketplace but also a set of institutional arrangements that both "exercise power and regulate conduct."[72] In this sense, the buying and selling of security services constitute a civic-minded "practice of governance" that cannot be unambiguously reduced to the logic of commodity exchange alone. Monetary transactions between private companies providing security services and neighborhood associations "elicit affective [that is, emotional] investments and moral claims" that are shaped not only by impersonal market forces but also by the discourses of fear, belonging, mutual obligation, and a sense of community.[73] To the extent that security constitutes a social good realized through its collective consumption, the practice of exchanging money for safety suffers from a legitimacy deficit, pitting narrow self-interest and individualism against the public interest and the general welfare.[74] As some have argued, the need and desire for security "retains a social value which prompts unease and discomfort about its commercial exchange—not least at the prospect of individual security being dependent on one's personal wealth."[75]

For "organized Jewry" (a term used by Jonny Steinberg and Monique Marks) in Johannesburg, the turn toward private security provision produced a paradox—a dilemma "expressed in the simultaneous desire to protect one's own and to reach out to others." For Steinberg and Marks, "Security triggers feelings of extreme discomfort when it is traded for money or when it is hoarded by an exclusive group."[76] Bringing collective security under the umbrella of commodity exchange appeared "to lift a drawbridge between Jewish and other lives," thereby potentially undermining "trust, reciprocity and goodwill with all sorts of people who are neither their neighbors nor fellow Jews" and putting at risk "these relationships and thus making participation in common life more difficult."[77]

Monetary transactions between neighborhood associations and private security providers have unfolded within particular regimes of power. Whether disguised as donations or "contributions," payments for collective security services are integrally connected with preconceived notions of what it means to belong to the Jewish community of Johannesburg and with the rights and duties associated with this status. The moral ambivalence of buying and selling security in the competitive marketplace brings into sharp relief legitimation claims that justify the acquisition of protection services in terms that stress obligation, collective responsibility, and reciprocity rather than commodity exchange and the cash nexus.[78]

Extending the Reach of Private Security Governance

The CAP initiatives blend paid professional staff—including legal experts, data analysts, information technology experts, and investigative personnel who manage the key logistical and financial operations of the organization through the centralized Incident Command and Control Centre (ICCC)—with the legions of unpaid volunteers (including call operators and CCTV monitors) who coordinate the day-to-day activities of the separate CAP initiatives in the residential neighborhoods.[79] The CAP approach to public-space policing has involved extending the geographical reach of security surveillance into what were considered unpoliced or underpoliced areas.[80] The establishment of a twenty-four-hour-a-day ICCC created a "single point of contact for all residents" in the residential neighborhoods under the protection of a CAP initiative. The installation of CCTV cameras provided those persons monitoring screens at the ICCC headquarters with the capacity to track the movements of suspicious vehicles and persons. CAP management encouraged alert residents in their areas to report suspicious activities, including "any two or more males walking or driving together."[81]

From a security operational point of view, the ICCC functions as a centralized administrative and logistics command center, a clearinghouse through which to channel all information and active-response activities, including the coordination of medical and security responses. It is the nerve center that effectively holds together a far-reaching security unit through its monopoly over information gathering, storage, and retrieval on the one hand and its control over centralized coordination of activities on the other. Staffed with a team of trained response personnel, the ICCC operates as a kind of invisible hand involved in the rapid deployment of Tactical Response Units (TRUs), the around-the-clock monitoring of strategically placed wireless CCTV cameras and the investigation of incidents in real time from an unobtrusive vantage point.[82]

The activities of the ICCC are separated into two divisions: control and operations. The state-of-the-art control room functions as the central clearinghouse from which to monitor all incoming calls and dispatch all units in the field. Because they have real-time access to the central data repository, operators in the control room are able to verify information almost immediately. Since they are handpicked from CAP areas, they bring a "wealth of local, area-specific knowledge." On average, operatives answer calls to the control room in under 3.6 seconds, and the average response time to a call is under 3 minutes 5 seconds.[83]

Another key element of the proactive security shield is the neighborhood Blockwatch system, in which resident volunteers—two persons per car for two-hour shifts—drive around the streets of their neighborhoods in unmarked personal vehicles every night of the week and report suspicious activities. The Blockwatch patrollers are in constant radio contact with the ICCC and operate with strict instructions to gather information about irregular behavior, pass it along to the control center, and never intervene in a situation. Tactical response teams, consisting of two armed security officers per vehicle, patrol the streets twenty-four

CAP Incident Command and Control Centre (ICCC) Administrative Structure

FIGURE 9. CAP ICCC administrative structure. (Based on Goldstein 2011.)

hours a day. As a supplement to regular patrols, the ICCC also has at its disposal a specialized and highly trained group, called the Central Intervention Unit (CIU), that can be deployed into recognized hot spots in the CAP tactical areas (and beyond) to prevent crime.[84]

Overlaying layers of surveillance, both electronic and human, supplement these tactical response teams. In addition to wireless CCTV cameras placed at strategic locations, undercover spotter teams patrol the streets, searching for unusual activities. The more dangerous business of actually confronting whatever threats emerge is left to the highly trained tactical officers, "most of whom have been handpicked from previous positions in the military and police services." By saturating the streets with boots on the ground, CAPs provide a blanket of security protection in neighborhoods under its watch.[85]

One key innovative feature that the CAP model offers residents in the neighborhoods where they patrol is the establishment of spotter points, or filter points, located at key street junctions. These spotter points consist of designated locations (usually street corners) where two static security guards in small enclosures remain in direct around-the-clock radio communication with mobile TRUs. The purpose of these spotter points, which are usually situated in areas with low traffic volumes, is to create a convenient means for residents who fear they are being followed by suspicious persons to drive past, alerting the security guards by texting, blowing their horns, or flashing their vehicle lights. This signal triggers a response from the TRUs to investigate immediately. As an extra

FIGURE 10. CoreTac tactical safe-zone poster. (Photo by author.)

safety precaution, since drivers frequently do not notice if suspicious vehicles are following them, CAP has advised all residents to always drive through the filter points (seven safe zones in Glenhazel alone), especially when returning home from a shopping center, from school, or from any other outing. The CAP personnel who monitor these filter points are always on the lookout for suspicious vehicles.[86]

In addition, some CAP initiatives have launched an eyes-on-the-street program enlisting domestic workers and other household staff in the battle against criminality, "training them how to stay on the lookout for crime and rewarding them financially if they [successfully] spot or report criminal activities."[87] This effort mirrors similar Domestic Watch programs (most notably the one initiated by Penny Steyn) in which household staff are trained as low-level lookouts, watching the premises of their employers.[88]

In its promotional materials, CAP has proclaimed that it is "an innovative, multi-faceted anti-crime initiative designed to proactively combat crime, utilizing a mix of early identification, counter-observation, surveillance and static and mobile armed patrols."[89] The aim of various CAP initiatives is to provide a deterrent to crime, thereby contributing to the reduction of criminal incidents (or occurrences) in the neighborhoods in which they operate. According to Mandy Yachad, technical advisor to the Greater Oaklands Orchards CAP, the security approach "is about being physically present and making undesirables feel uncomfortable and unwelcome. Making sure they have no peace of mind operating in a public space."[90] This policing mentalité, which Julie Berg has called "a form of reassurance policing," fills a gap left by the inability of public policing agencies to effectively combat crime in the residential suburban neighborhoods.[91]

The aim behind these wide-ranging CAP initiatives is to create an impregnable security zone in which serious crime is reduced to a minimum. The means to accomplish this goal involve the creation of a broad security nexus that emulates a military-style organizational structure, with a centralized command-and-control headquarters where departments are arranged in a functional hierarchy, outfitted with the operational capabilities designed to respond to any security emergency and with access to high-quality information that greatly exceeds that which is available to public police agencies. In the dreamscape of CAP management teams, this model resembles "a highly trained, technologically sophisticated police department [outfitted] with a corps of well-educated police responding obediently to the policies, orders, and directives of a central administrative command."[92]

In 2009, the ICCC created its own legal department to track court cases of criminal suspects apprehended by CAP operatives and handed over to the SAPS.[93] This initiative aims to counteract widespread skepticism about the effectiveness of the criminal justice system by ensuring that suspected criminals "stand trial in court and receive the sentences they deserve." The CAP legal team "follows up each arrest made, the details of the incident, the case number, in which jail the suspect is being held, when the suspect appears in court and the outcome of the case." In seeking to ensure that the ends of justice are served, the CAP legal department "identifies procedural and other irregularities, thereby maintaining case integrity and ensuring convictions."[94]

As part of its commitment to criminal investigations, the Tactical Debriefing Department is responsible for gathering detailed "information on every contact crime or attempted contact crime." After an incident has taken place, CAP immediately dispatches debriefers to the scene "to interview the victims in order to gather as much information as possible." The primary function of the debriefing department is to identify current trends and patterns in criminal activity.[95] Finally, the SAPS liaison team works closely with the public law enforcement agencies with regard not only to information sharing but also to planning joint operations (such as roadblocks, raids on suspected criminal hideouts, forcible evictions of hijacked buildings, and the like).[96]

Moreover, the central CAP organization offers a variety of supplementary security products for sale. One such service promises to conduct a complete screening for prospective domestic staff, contractors, or security guards, including fingerprinting, a polygraph test, careful review of references from previous employers, and thorough criminal background checks. CAPs also offer to provide electronic keypads for security gates and mobile panic kits that substitute for existing alarm systems.[97] The ICCC generates considerable income from the marketing of these security products and from fees for its overall administration of its security operations, which include legal services that follow active criminal cases through the courts. Although the various CAP security initiatives rolled out in over fifty residential neighborhoods are registered as section 21 (not-for-profit) companies, some experts in the security field have suggested that ICCC central headquarters has operated at least in part as a private, profit-making commercial enterprise.[98]

The ICCC has engaged in knowledge production through its intelligence-gathering capabilities, which far exceed those the SAPS has at its disposal.[99] In short, the classification, compilation, and analysis of data lies at the center of the CAP strategy of risk management. The risk assessment models that the ICCC has adopted resemble what Mike Levi and David Wall (following Roger Clarke and others) have called "dataveillance," or "the proactive surveillance of what effectively become suspect populations, using new technologies to identify 'risky groups'" and suspicious persons.[100]

At the end of the day, the CAP security plan marked a paradigm-shifting moment in the private provision of protective services.[101] This new approach to security governance has involved restructuring practices of boundary marking and border making.[102] What has distinguished the CAP initiative is the willingness of its tactical response units to resort to coercive tactics as the predominant mode of security governance.[103] The CAP model engages in "border control practices" that authorize private security agents to act outside the law in "anomalous zones" (where public space becomes a kind of terra incognita) in which they claim the legitimacy and power of the law, but are not constrained by it.[104]

Yet it was almost inevitable that this aggressive approach to proactive policing would occasionally produce excess. In late 2007, after a security officer from Core Tactical shot and wounded a fellow operative in a case of mistaken identity, the aggressive policing tactics of CAP came under a mounting degree of public scrutiny.[105] Some critics warned of the danger of the "Colombiasation" of Johannesburg, with "'islands' of secure and invariably rich neighborhoods in a 'sea' of criminality and poverty."[106]

At the end of 2015, CAP and the CSO formally separated their activities and went their separate ways. Until that time, they were closely aligned, with shared office space and the same emergency call center with an identical phone number. On the one hand, since its inception, CAP had grown by leaps and bounds into a large communal security organization with a paid professional staff supplemented by volunteers from affiliated neighborhood associations. By the end of 2010, the CAP initiative had become operational in fifteen areas and had brought at least 150,000 residents under its protection. By 2019, the number of operational areas had more than doubled. By expanding into such noncontiguous areas as Bryanston, Lombardy, Cyrildene-Observatory, and Victory Park along with the contiguous areas of Sandown-Strathavon, Morningside, and West Road South, the CAP initiative has extended its functional field of operations into more than twenty zones consisting of more than fifty separate residential suburban neighborhoods in which the number of residents under CAP protection clearly exceeded 300,000 persons.[107] In contrast, the CSO remained committed to its original aim of focusing on "the security and medical needs of the Jewish community, communal facilities and the orderly and safe continuation of Jewish life."[108]

Preventative Security: Proactive Policing and the Cleansing of Public Space

The CAP experiment with proactive public-space policing was grounded in an entirely different approach to risk management and security provision. In residential communities with deeply entrenched fears of violent crimes, particularly home invasions and hijackings, anxious middle-class homeowners welcomed private security companies because of their promise of rapid armed response and their zero tolerance approach

CAP Operating Neighborhoods

Bramley
Bryanston Riverclub North
Craighall & Craighall Park
Cyrildene Observatory
Emmarentia Greenside
Glenhazel
Greater Glenhazel
Greater Oaklands
Orchards
Gresswold
Highlands North

Houghton
Melrose Birdhaven
Morningside Middle Rd
Norwood
Parkwood
Sandhurst
Sandown Strathavon
Savoy Waverley
Saxonwold
Senderwood Linksfield
Victory Park
West Road South
Westcliff

GAP Operating Neighborhoods

Rouxville
Raedene Estate
Talboton
Fairmont
Percelia Estate
Highlands North
Dunhill
Glensan

Fairmount Ridge
Glenhazel
Fairvale
Glenkay
Sandringham
Silvamonte
Sunningdale
Lyndhurst

Map Key

CAP

GAP

Neighborhoods

— Highways
— Main Roads
— Roads

⊙ 0   1 km

to crime. The CAP model has evolved into an exemplary expression of highly visible, proactive public-space policing. The aggressive style and intimidating presence of CAP tactical response teams anticipated what quickly unfolded in many residential suburban neighborhoods under the banner of proactive public-space policing.[109]

In the conventional (liberal-modernist) understanding of public space, the wide array of shared sites of social congregation, including parks, playgrounds, squares, streetscapes, sidewalks, and other communal gathering places, function as open and accessible areas inviting social mingling and chance encounters.[110] As the spatial expression of the democratic public sphere in which open dialogue and social interaction predominate, public space is the privileged site of social interaction where difference and diversity collide in what Iris Marion Young has called "side-by-side particularity."[111] Yet this idealized image of public space as unproblematically open to all comes face-to-face with everyday realities on the ground. Despite the rhetoric of openness, access to public space does not always conform to an idealized norm of civility and tolerance. As Doreen Massey has argued, the regulation of public space takes place in multiple—sometimes subtle and sometimes forceful—ways that uphold and reflect conflicting, and sometimes exclusionary, social practices.[112] Public space is "always already" inundated with (dis)orderly lines of exclusion.[113]

What has been called proactive public-space policing involves control over access and use of virtually all shared sites of social congregation, including not only exemplary expressions of mass private property such as shopping malls, gated residential estates, hotel lobbies, commercial strips, and sports-entertainment venues but also public streets, parks, playgrounds, and city-owned land. The aim of proactive public-space policing is to monitor these sites, minimizing the risk of harm by creating orderly and predictable interactions and leaving nothing to chance.[114]

Proactive public-space policing did not emerge fully formed and all at once, like Minerva from the head of Jupiter. Rather, it has evolved in fits and starts, spread unevenly over space and time. To meet the demands for this emerging market for preventative security, private security companies began around 2004 or 2005 to introduce new operating

MAP 4. Geographical distribution of suburban areas under contract with community and beagle watch. (Data taken from OpenStreetMap.)

procedures designed to reduce the risk of crime in residential neighborhoods. Instead of remaining a reactive force responding to lawbreaking
already underway, private security companies began to aggressively patrol neighborhood streets in search of suspicious characters who might
be inclined to participate in criminal activities. The animating logic
behind proactive public-space policing is that there is a distinction between, on the one hand, legitimate users of social congregating space—
that is, law-abiding citizens exercising their rights—and, on the other
hand, unwanted trespassers who fall into the category of potential criminals.[115] In everyday encounters with ordinary people, private security
companies have pushed the limits or exceeded the boundaries of legality. In using tactics that restrict the freedom of movement of ordinary
people going about their daily business, private security companies have
engaged in practices that conjure up collective memories of apartheid
principles of influx control.[116]

The adoption of a new image of no-nonsense policing and the pro-
curement of state-of-the-art weaponry has dovetailed with new operating procedures in the field. Rather than simply responding to emergency calls, the tactical response units have begun to actively patrol the
residential neighborhoods they were hired to protect, looking for suspicious people and out-of-the-ordinary activities. Tactical officers stop vehicles and question their occupants about where they are going and with
whom they intend to meet. On occasion, they inquire whether they can
search the vehicle and personal possessions of occupants. Private security operatives regard any refusal to comply with this request as tantamount to suspicious behavior, thereby justifying forcing occupants out
of their vehicles and detaining them while calling for the assistance of
SAPS officers. Private security tactical response teams routinely patrol
uninhabited open spaces such as riverbeds, public parks, and vacant lots,
driving away informal squatters and burning down their meager dwellings. At the behest of retail-shop owners along commercial avenues,
these security teams harass uninvited street traders and confiscate their
goods, chase away the homeless, and intimidate anyone considered to be
a potential thief.[117]

The targets of these new strategies of spatial governmentality are unwanted users of public space in residential neighborhoods and the commercial streets associated with them.[118] Private security armed-response
teams follow a strict protocol of engagement: they are instructed to in-

vestigate all unusual activities and to stop and question suspicious persons. Both public policing agencies and private security companies engage in blatant racial profiling. Whether on foot or in a vehicle, two or more black men traveling through a securitized residential neighborhood invariably draw the attention of private security tactical teams.[119] In the language of both public and private policing agencies, two or more black males together are almost universally referred to as Bravos—a quasimilitary term that identifies black men (in a racialized criminal imaginary) as inherently suspicious and threatening.[120]

Private security companies have become the main instruments of policing the public spaces of upscale residential neighborhoods. The adoption of new techniques of spatial governance often involves gratuitous force and violence directed against unemployed and underemployed black men. The intimidation and harassment of the urban poor amounts to a carceral continuum in which prisonlike confinement is extended into the everyday public spaces of the city.[121]

Reconfiguring Territory: The Hypersecurity of Public-Space Policing

Territory exemplifies bounded space.[122] In a real sense, then, territory is entangled with questions of sovereignty, jurisdiction, and authority, where its production involves measuring, mapping, and surveying terrain.[123] As Michel Foucault has suggested, "Territory is no doubt a geographical notion, but it's first of all a juridico-political one: the area controlled by a certain kind of power."[124] Seen in this light, the production of territory (or, territorialization) involves the imposition of new technologies of power, in which distinct modes of regulation—or what Faranak Miraftab has called "'zonification' strategies"—are grafted onto bounded space. [125]

The reorganization of space and the management of movement are the key features of proactive public-space policing. At root, this kind of policing involves carving out carefully monitored demarcated territory, or what Zoltán Glück in another context has called "the production of security space."[126] Proactive public-space policing reshapes the frontier borderlands—with their ambiguities and indeterminacies—into a clearly demarcated territory, or a space inscribed with new forms of power. The grounded territorial practices or technologies of proactive public-space policing produce and rework landscapes of power through

territorialization. This production of territory involves bringing neighborhood streets, parks, and social gathering places under the control of
private security teams via the paramilitarization of public space, where
the underlying logic of security blurs the boundaries between policing
and military warfare.[127]

The reciprocal relationship between the practices of security and the
production of territory undermines the conventional notion of public
space as a porous and permeable platform, or conduit, for unhindered
movement.[128] Proactive public-space policing involves the transformation of fluid neighborhood spaces into demarcated territory. The imbrication of territory, spatial governance, and the logic of security has
reshaped urban environments. Proactive public-space policing establishes uneven typologies of spatial regulation, leading to a patchwork
of urban spaces in which "bubbles" or "corridors" of security are interspersed with areas without ostensible protection.[129] By effectively closing off their neighborhoods and authorizing the aggressive monitoring of streets, residents' associations have effectively cobbled together
market-based alliances with private security companies to create "parallel" spaces that are outside the public domain and are governed by a
wide array of competing and incommensurate rules and regulations.[130]

The production of territory involves the intersections of legality, governance, and space. As such, territorialization is always an ongoing, contested process that combines an uneasy mixture of persuasion and intimidation. By turning a blind eye to what private security companies
actually do in the conduct of their business, public policing agencies
have effectively approved the deregulation of the governance regimes
overseeing security in public space. Private security companies exert a
particular kind of extralegal authority over neighborhood territory, beholden neither to public policing agencies nor to the letter of the law.[131]

The shifting spatial performance of private policing is most evident in
everyday practices on the ground.[132] At the microphysical level, the goal
of security management under the mandate of proactive public-space
policing is to inhibit the movement of unwanted persons through a combination of static checkpoints, CCTV surveillance, and mobile patrols.
Proactive private security companies mark their territory by means
of the visible display of placards and metal signs affixed to walls. As a
kind of performance art, these ostentatious manifestations of power an-
nounce their presence via the promise of armed response and other dire

warnings, such as "Beware: You Are Entering a Crime-Free Zone."[133] Monitoring and restricting movement of people is a form of governmentality. Yet governmentality is not simply a managerial system for channeling movement in space but also a form of rule in which the primary relationship of the governing apparatuses to residential neighborhood associations is one of providing physical protection of persons and their possessions. At the end of the day, static checkpoints and borderlines are fabricated constructions that achieve the aura of authenticity and legitimacy through the everyday rituals of power. In short, the performance of sovereignty enables private security companies to claim legitimacy that, at root, derives from their capacity to use force and intimidation to separate rightful users of neighborhood public space from those who are considered out of place and without legitimate claims of belonging.[134]

The fortified lines that define the borders of enclosed spaces are the antithesis of those indeterminate frontier spaces that are never fixed in place. In contrast to the geographical symmetry of static places, frontier zones consist of elastic and irregular geographies of movement and flow where distinctions between inside and outside are not easily marked. Subjected to continuously shifting pressures of expansion and contraction, the borderless domain of the frontier opens outward onto tenuous and ill-defined patterns of interaction, engagement, and confrontation.[135] The aim of proactive public-space policing is to close off frontier zones by eliminating the gaps and filling in the cracks.[136]

Pro-active policing does not simply manage and fortify public space through aggressive tactics; it also reconfigures sites of social congregation by establishing new social-spatial orders of inclusion and exclusion.[137] The primary mode of governance for proactive public-space policing is displacement, that is, the removal and expulsion—through a combination of intimidation, force, and violence—of "undesirable persons" from places where they are not wanted. These practices of territorialization effectively push unwelcome others outside the boundaries that mark the territory of private security companies.[138] These territorialized strategies of displacement relegate the unwanted persons to a limbo status outside the law, almost totally at the mercy of private security teams.[139] When successful, this strategy yields a perforated, patchwork urban landscape, with secured corridors connecting homeowners with schools, commercial shopping locations, and places of worship, entertainment, and leisure.[140]

5

Unaccountable Policing

In the classic Weberian conception of sovereignty, public policing agencies maintain at least the semblance of a state-sponsored monopoly on legitimate violence. Under these circumstances, security governance produces flat homogeneous space in which—at least in theory—the rule of law has universal application and the rights of citizenship guarantee equal protection. In contrast, the proliferation of multiple security regimes has partitioned urban landscapes into multiple mini-sovereignties that employ a range of overlapping but sometimes conflicting tactics to manage those residents who use and occupy space.[1] Yet the absence of a single, all-encompassing sovereign power has exposed urban space to a kind of fluidity and contingency that "allows for the suspension of the normative universe of the rule of law."[2] Put another way, the complex intersection of security, legality, and governance has reconfigured urban landscapes into a variegated assemblage of territorialized containers (or what Keith Hayward has called "container spaces"), each of which is governed by different sets of rules and regulations. In these containers, petty sovereigns wield "the power to render unilateral decisions," subject to no law and accountable to no one but themselves.[3]

The provision of security has "moved from centralized, hierarchical, command-and-control models of public policing, to decentralized, non-hierarchical," polycentric, network-oriented approaches, in which key decision making and on-the-ground operational practices evolve through "collaborations, partnerships and interdependencies."[4] As a hybrid assemblage of heterogeneous policing practices, security governance has become fluid, fragmented, and dispersed across territory.[5] The provision of security has become much more multilateral, horizontal, rhizomatic, extensive, nodal, and transversal. It is organizationally fragmented and hybridized and is weblike in form.[6]

The multiplication of decentered modes of spatial governance and pluralized policing practices has produced a highly uneven territorial patchwork of security zones that resemble what Lucia Zedner has referred to, in metaphorical terms, as "quilts," "bubbles," "corridors," "webs," "mosaics," "networks," or "nodes."[7] Because spaces of security are so "folded, twisted, stretched, and entangled," it is difficult if not impossible to talk of ordered hierarchies and strict divisions of policing.[8] The proliferation of multiple modes of "governing territory through zonal controls" has produced a spatially flexible policing terrain, thereby fundamentally reshaping the power dynamics of the provision, delivery, and regulation of policing services.[9]

In Johannesburg, the security regimes cobbled together through the intersection of public policing agencies, private security companies, and neighborhood associations have produced and reinforced an armature of spatial coding instruments that separates orderly, desirable people and activities from disorderly, undesirable ones. Claims of neutrality mask normative, if not largely latent, conceptions of who belongs and who does not. Sorting along vectors of class and power provides a powerful organizing logic. By creating and enforcing spatial borders, private security operatives sort individuals within residential neighborhoods into binary categories of those who have a legitimate right to be there and those who constitute illegitimate trespassers.[10]

The shift toward the exclusionary politics of law and order policing has exposed the counterfeit idealism of genuine public space and, correlatively, reflects the emergence and consolidation of new forms of regulating the poor who inhabit the city.[11] Popular perceptions of undesirable or disorderly cityscapes are often likened to aggressive panhandling, vagrancy, loitering, drug dealing, irksome conduct, and sleeping in the rough.[12] A host of social-sorting and filtering mechanisms tied to zoning codes, aggressive policing practices, and regimes of private property enact a vision of urban form that reflects and spatially enforces core normative liberal identities associated with safe and comfortable spaces, defined by pleasurable encounters in an aesthetically pleasing environment.[13]

Security Zones: Manufacturing the Spaces of Exception

Exceptionality "refers to the conditions in which law is not enacted as a set of rules but precisely as an exception to those rules."[14] The logic of exceptionalism creates zones of extralegal indeterminacy and extrajuridical power. Under circumstances in which perceived danger shapes popular perceptions of risk, there is no return to a state of (liberal-democratic) normalcy. Regimes of exception become the norm.[15]

The spaces of exception appear most clearly at the borderlands—the territorial frontier that marks the threshold separating perceived danger from the promise of protection. Private security companies often depict public parks, streetscapes, and driveways as Hobbesian places of anarchy where anything can happen. These indeterminate spaces constitute "environments of insecurity" or "outlaw territories" that call into motion strategies of "counterinsurgency."[16] The borders that define the edges of residential neighborhoods in Johannesburg constitute a permanent state of exception, where the suspension of the rule of law on the basis of a perceived threat gives way to the extralegal discretionary powers of the administrative guardians of borders who arbitrarily decide between authorized users of social space and unauthorized intruders.[17] In this sense, bordering practices, rather than border lines per se, constitute the main mechanisms for the governance of mobility through the enforcement of social sorting.[18]

In Johannesburg, the performance of security manifests itself in such border-making processes as the multiplication of building typologies that physically separate themselves from their immediate surroundings, in the placement of a network of cameras and other mechanical detection devices, in the installation of sentry posts and checkpoints, and in mobile policing patrols.[19] As both symbolic markers and physically demarcated spaces, the borders that encircle residential neighborhoods act to animate an "imagined and territorialized community."[20] The routine performance of bordering transforms what is a legal right—mobility—into something abnormal or deviant.[21] When challenges to the legitimacy of the security zone arise, those who perform the tasks of securitization exert their authority through the tactics of unilateral stop and frisk, intimidation, and physical force. The rule of exception, therefore, appears at the margins—at borderland locations where the authority of public policing approaches its vanishing point and the full force of private security comes into play. The anxiety generated by the discourse of crime has enabled private security companies to consolidate wide discretionary power in ways that allow them to act unilaterally and almost without restraint.[22]

The logic of security rests on the distinction between those who can be governed through liberal standards (through the rule of law, with its powers of persuasion and normative appeals to the common good) and those who must be controlled by illiberal means through extralegal co-ercion and force.[23] Proactive public-space policing operates on the prem-ise that space is overcrowded with the wrong people. Private security companies engage in the elaborate social construction of unknown per-sons as intrinsically suspicious, and hence they constitute potentially dangerous threats to persons and property. In the calculation of risk, un-known persons such as itinerant job seekers, informal traders, wander-ing youths, and homeless vagabonds share the characterization as suspi-cious Others, not needed and hence not wanted.[24]

Hard and Soft Infrastructures of Security

The logic of security effectively blurs the line between combating crime and engaging in low-intensity warfare.[25] Seen from this perspective, crime can never be defeated (that is, eliminated) but only contained or displaced. The logic of security "presupposes that the danger is already inside." Potential criminals are everywhere. Just as private spaces are under threat from unwanted intrusion, public spaces are also not safe. If the conventional approaches to law enforcement and crime prevention are rooted in a "presumed-innocent-until-proven-guilty" paradigm, then the logic of security "engages with the temporarily ill-defined and spa-tially ambiguous 'conflict,'" pitting legitimate crime fighters against po-tential criminals in ways that seek to preempt criminal occurrences.[26]

Streets, sidewalks, and parking facilities are vital yet vulnerable spa-tial nodes in everyday movement in the city. Such public spaces are sites of constant motion, but movement through such physical environments is overlaid with anxiety and fear.[27] Mobility represents an imminent threat to security, because it is not subjected to careful monitoring and social sorting.[28]

Security management revolves around the control of flows of peo-ple by means of configuring and reconfiguring space. This reordering of space amounts to building safer cities through environmental design, where the installation of walls, gates, and barriers is able to channel the movement of people in desired directions. Contested public spaces be-come saturated with stationary surveillance technologies, mobile patrolling, and ever-vigilant eyes on the street.[29] Such microlevel assemblages as CCTV monitoring, saturation patrols, and search-and-seizure tactics resemble counterinsurgency operations. These microlevel tactical interventions are directed at "(re-)producing the macro-level distinction who belongs and who does not."[30]

Proactive public-space policing has effectively redefined sidewalks, driveways, streets, parks, and other social gathering places as quasi-hostile environments. These are ambiguous spaces in which danger lurks. Hence, they become zones of legal indeterminacy, in which the rule of law is flexible and subject to arbitrary interpretation.[31]

At root, the concept of defensive space refers to siege architecture and target hardening, where such security assemblages as road closures, boom gates, and other physical barriers produce fortified enclaves. If defensive space constitutes the war of position, then proactive order-maintenance policing resembles the war of maneuver, with its mix of mobile tactics and stress on preemptive deterrence. The application of counterinsurgency doctrines to crime fighting has completely altered the terrain of law enforcement and crime prevention. New modes of security management are aimed at the "pre-emptive identification, targeting, and tracking of illegitimate flows" of persons who are unknown and hence suspicious.[32] As David Bewley-Taylor has argued, concept wars are protracted armed conflicts waged against an elusive and abstract concept, such as drugs, terrorism, or even crime, rather than against a recognizable and concrete enemy. Concept wars are typically open-ended and highly mutable. According to Bewley-Taylor, "The absence of an enemy that can offer unconditional surrender, has the potential to produce perpetual conflict" with no end in sight.[33]

The rhetoric of crime fighting in Johannesburg bears an uncanny resemblance to a concept war, or what Allan Feldman has called "securocratic wars of public safety." Rather than focusing on territorial conquest per se or the military defeat of a recognizable enemy, securocratic wars of public safety aim at mobilizing sufficient force to counteract what is regarded as "territorial contamination and transgression."[34] Proactive public-space policing discursively constructs suspicious persons as threats to the democratic-liberal order and hence as targets of illiberal modes of security governance.[35] By operating within the seemingly neutral discourses of reasonableness and responsibility, the architects of proactive public-space policing have been able to articulate an uplifting vision of the public interest and the common good in a language of civility that "mystifies the roots" of these rehabilitated neighborhood streets within a narrow vision of upscale, sanitized spaces that serve the parochial needs of the propertied middle-class residents.[36]

If urban landscapes can be understood as assemblages of different mobilities, where different modes of portability experience varying degrees of facilitation and interruption, then power and control over movement can significantly shape everyday life in the city.[37] In effect, private security companies have become "machines for processing and controlling mobility through space."[38] They have taken over the "production of stratified mobilities in urban environments."[39]

In the rational calculation of deciding who belongs and who does not, private security companies—acting at the behest of neighborhood associations—distinguish between known persons with an ascribed right to be there and suspicious persons who pose a threat because of their potential to engage in criminal behavior. The construction of this kind of bifurcated normative order rests on the presumption that public spaces are inherently risky and dangerous because of the presence of unknown persons who are suspicious by definition.[40]

Proactive public-space policing is rooted in the legitimating rhetoric that crime constitutes an emergency requiring the suspension of civil liberties, legal rights, and basic freedoms. Those who justify extralegal measures claim that the exigencies of fighting crime demand exceptional measures. After all, criminals are lawless and operate outside the sphere of expected norms of decency and propriety. In this way of thinking, it is impossible to fight ruthless criminals without extraordinary measures and extralegal powers. Under a liberal constitutional order, this idea that an emergency situation of factual danger—in this instance, the inability of public policing agencies to prevent crime—validates the temporary lifting of the rule of law has existed in various guises (for example, martial law, the state of siege, and the state of exception) since the nineteenth century, if not before.[41]

Yet the emergency powers that private security companies have claimed for themselves under the banner of protective services are not really categorically distinct from the broader repertoire of public policing practices. Whatever differences exist are a matter of degree and not of kind.[42] Strict demarcations between the rule of law (normalcy) and its suspension in the name of emergency are almost always untenable. Distinctions between normalcy and emergency are "made difficult, if not impossible" in the actual practice of policing. In the everyday life of order maintenance, as Oren Gross has argued, "the exception is hardly an exception at all." With the merging of the exception with the rule, the fire wall safeguarding and protecting legal rights, individual freedoms, and civil liberties has broken down.[43] The inauguration of this blurred zone of spatial governance is visible to those who wish to see it but invisible to those who chose to ignore it.[44]

The Practice of Private Policing: The Performance of Authority and the Appearance of Legitimacy

As demands for personal security and risk management have grown exponentially in an artificially nurtured environment of fear, so too has the private security industry continued to expand and become increasingly malleable, offering a growing array of protection services and tapping into specialized niche markets. As the security services industry has blended into the social fabric of urban life and become increasingly interdependent with public policing mandates, oversight agencies have experienced difficulties differentiating the activities of various players on the ground and thus holding them accountable in accordance with their various mandates.[45]

For the most part, private security companies acquire their powers to act as policing agents from the laws of contract and of property. Unlike the public policing agencies whose powers are grounded in official statutes that regulate the use of physical (and lethal) force in the maintenance of law and order, the powers of private security personnel derive principally from their delegated status as legal agents of owners and managers of private property.[46] Because private security police enjoy this legal status as delegated agents of the property owners who employ them, they are able to exercise the more extensive powers the law extends to property owners over and above those of ordinary citizens.[47] Under the terms of the Criminal Procedure Act 51 of 1977, private security personnel possess wide discretionary powers to arrest persons without a warrant on suspicion of committing a criminal offense, to break open premises in order to carry out the arrest, and to use force—even deadly force—should the person offer resistance. In addition, by virtue of their acquired legal status as agents of property owners, they have the authority to banish trespassers and deny entry to private premises, to detain and interrogate criminal suspects and search their personal property, and to use lethal force to protect the property of their employers.[48]

Private security operatives, including static sentry guards and armed-reaction teams, enjoy the same legal powers as any other private citizen; for example, they can make a citizen's arrest in limited circumstances. This discretionary authority contains a great deal of room to stretch and bend what is legally permissible, and the criminal justice system has generally interpreted actions of this sort in a flexible way. Like ordinary citizens, private security personnel are empowered to detain, without a warrant, anyone who is reasonably believed to have committed pretty much any criminal offense and who is fleeing anyone who reasonably appears to be authorized to make an arrest.[49] Yet the toolbox for private security operatives contains fewer formal legal powers than the range of options to arrest and detain (even the use of physical force) available to public law enforcement officers.[50] Unless they obtain permission from public police officers to act at their behest or are granted some limited official status, private security operatives do not have the special statutory coercive powers that empower their public counterparts to arrest and detain criminal suspects, to use physical force, and to discharge weapons in the line of duty.[51]

But just as public policing agencies have a plentiful supply of tools that they can use without fear of legal repercussions, so too do private security operatives have a plethora of instruments at their disposal. These instruments "are less overtly coercive in securing public compliance with their demands, but often no less effective in getting the job of policing done." Private security companies operate with a range of physical, personal, and symbolic instruments that supplement what they are legally empowered to do.[52] Besides the discretionary powers that enable private security operatives to maneuver within the rule of law, they also draw on their symbolic status, which is achieved through their intimidating demeanor and their official appearance.[53] In the performance of their duties, private security operatives strive to obtain the acquiescence and consent of frightened urban residents. As Thomas Scott and Marlys McPherson pointed out a long time ago, "public misunderstanding of the law" gives private security agents a distinct advantage in the field because urban residents often do not fully comprehend their own rights.[54] Wearing military-like uniforms, driving menacing-looking ve-

FIGURE 11.   CSS wanted poster. (Photo by author.)

hicles, and openly brandishing weapons enables private security agents to assume the appearance of legitimate authority. In a particularly brazen display of bravado, proactive private security companies have begun to issue their own wanted posters prominently displaying grainy photographs of suspected criminals in public places.[55]

Cultivating this aura of legality and legitimacy is part theatric performance (visibility) and part sleight of hand (masquerade). This pretense of officially sanctioned authority has effectively masked the sometimes indiscriminate use of physical force that is not sanctioned under the rule of law and that has remained hidden beneath layers of faux legitimacy.[56]

Private security policing is a form of regulation that oscillates between a rational mode of order maintenance and a "magical mode of being" that seems to offer the protection that public policing agencies are unable to provide.[57] In both conversations with key figures in neighborhood associations and in various advertising brochures, private security companies present themselves as the only capable force standing between (respectable) order and (criminal) chaos.[58]

The Marriage of Convenience: Private Security Companies and Residential Neighborhood Associations

For the most part, private security companies that are engaged in local crime-control services under contract with individual homeowners or neighborhood associations are far and away the most hyperactive wing of the protection industries. Private security officers are the most visible and most effective agents of security governance in the suburban residential neighborhoods of Johannesburg. They have replaced the coercive powers of public policing agencies with their own brand of crime prevention and protection services. They have become the first line of defense against criminality, and through their practices they have insinuated themselves into the social fabric of everyday life.[59]

Private companies that have adopted a proactive public-space policing approach have acquired their much-deserved reputation as uncompromising crime fighters because they practice a particularly punitive and aggressive approach to policing work, including armed mobile patrolling and rapid response to even the most minor offenses.[60] The proactive strategies of public-space policing found their source of inspiration primarily in the zero-tolerance model of spatial governance that Mayor Rudolph Giuliani adopted in the 1990s in New York City.[61] Private security companies have in essence become a kind of low-intensity, paramilitary war machine deployed by neighborhood associations to control territory and establish their feigned legitimacy. Private security officers who work for legally licensed companies operate with a great deal of latitude and impunity in carrying out their duties and responsibilities in the field.[62] They create spatial order by denying entry or expelling suspicious or undesirable persons from places where they are not wanted. The idea of proactive public-space policing is certainly not new, but the way that private security companies have implemented it in Johannesburg differs markedly from that of other localities and situations.[63]

Working hand in glove as willing partners in a crime prevention alliance, neighborhood associations and private security companies have taken the lead in expanding the theater of operations for security governance. Operational managers for private security companies have convinced neighborhood associations that active patrolling—both visible and assertive, aggressive and unrelenting—can prevent crime before it occurs through the constant monitoring of unknown vehicles and suspicious persons whom they consider to be potential criminals. Put specifically, preventative security measures have worked on the underlying premise that aggressive tactics directed at unwanted people are justified because in the long run, following suspicious persons, stopping them, and even physically escorting them out of neighborhoods act as powerful deterrents to crime.[64]

Neighborhood associations and private security companies have negotiated contracts for proactive policing that consists of round-the-clock mobile patrolling in such public spaces as suburban streets, parks and other open spaces, and commercial districts. In order to obtain more services, neighborhood associations have sometimes sweetened the pot, paying for armed-response vehicles, weapons, and uniforms and giving them to private companies free of charge in exchange for the promise of more active and regular patrolling. For their part, private security companies have asked that neighborhood associations endorse them when they have sought to challenge their competitors in the lucrative market for armed-response contracts with individual households.[65]

The visible signs of no-nonsense policing present an aura of legality and legitimacy. With company names like W.A.R., Fearless, Special Armed Services, ShockEm Security, Bad Boyz, Peaceforce, Impact Force Protection Services, Freedom Fighters Security, Razor Spike, and Mamba Strike Force, private security companies give the distinct impression that they are tough on crime. Private security tactical teams openly display weapons, including canisters of pepper spray and nightsticks but particularly semiautomatic rifles, pistols, and shotguns. They operate out of sleek, high-speed vehicles built for maneuverability. These vehicles are often painted black, with company logos in bold letters, and outfitted with bulletproof paneling and windows, powerful night-lights, and steel bumpers. Companies have introduced their own insignia and distinctive uniforms, including matching black trousers and shirts, steel-plated body armor (including bulletproof vests), badges, company logos, and heavy boots. The intention is to present a fearsome

FIGURE 12. Collage of security company logos. (Photo by author.)

image of tough, disciplined soldiers who are prepared to do whatever it takes to prevent crime from occurring in the residential neighborhoods under their protection.[66] The visible display of weapons and black, ninja-like uniforms—the ostensible "facade of power"—has provided a convenient masquerade that has enabled private security officers to intimidate and harass unwanted persons at their own discretion and without legal sanction.[67]

To operationalize this approach to preventative security, private security companies have rebranded their images, upgraded their equipment, reinvigorated their skills training, and rethought their standard
operating procedures.[68] Seeking to shed the conventional language of
"armed response" and its links to old-style reactive policing approaches,
proactive companies have instead rebranded their security teams under
the rubric of tactical officers, strike forces, and special tactical units. Instead of operating with a single person in each vehicle (which has been
the standard practice for older companies such as ADT), proactive companies outfit their vehicles with two officers—one called the driver and
the other the shooter. This tactical shift in staffing has enabled these
companies to be much more active in the field of operations—the driver
maneuvers the vehicle, leaving the unencumbered shooter free to engage in firefights with suspected criminals. Private security officers use
a range of firearms—including holstered handguns, semiautomatic pistols, high-caliber assault rifles, and pump-action shotguns—and either
carry them on their person or store them in their vehicles. These advanced military-grade firearms provide a much more effective lethal arsenal than those at the disposal of the public policing agencies.[69]

Standard high-speed tactical vehicles have an entire range of equipment that can be of assistance in quickly entering properties and in apprehending suspected criminals: pepper spray, handcuffs, batons, lad-
ders for scaling walls, bolt cutters, fire extinguishers, jumper cables,
flashlights, heavy carpet (for placing over electric fencing), binoculars,
rubber mats, sledgehammers, and crowbars.[70] Well-trained teams of tactical officers operate with military precision, maintaining proper inter-
vals, establishing fields of fire that offer tactical advantage, and keeping
weapons always at the ready.[71]

For the most part, owners and managers of proactive private security companies bring years of military or public policing experience to
their work. At least in the formative years, instructors (who were able
to obtain South African ID booklets) were recruited from counterinsurgency units such as Koevoet and the 32 "Buffalo" Battalion that operated
under the command of the apartheid-era South African Defense Force
(SADF) in Namibia and Angola, respectively. Many private security operatives have moved back and forth between working for military contractors in Iraq and Afghanistan and for transoceanic shipping companies dealing with Somali pirates. These military-policing backgrounds
have meant that these private companies bring certain operational skills

FIGURE 13. Tactical response team in the field of operations. (Photo by author.)

and the clear mind-set that crime fighting is functionally equivalent to low-intensity war. [72]

As a general rule, the best-prepared private security companies have required mandatory military or paramilitary training in urban warfare for their security teams. All instructors have combat experience in military units. These training exercises include using assault rifles and high-caliber pistols properly, practicing shooting regularly at authorized firing ranges, keeping equipment in working order, mastering high-speed vehicle pursuit, maintaining proper physical fitness, and learning operational field tactics, enhanced close-combat skills, and first-aid assistance and emergency scenarios. Private security companies often rely on special-operations teams with SWAT experience for dangerous operations and maintain dog units to locate criminal suspects. Besides their standard patrol vehicles, all proactive private security companies have specialized tactical units (with strike force capabilities) at their disposal. Highly trained, more experienced, and heavily armed teams driving faster, armor-plated vehicles act as a force multiplier when called on to respond to any and all emergency situations, such as a home invasion in progress, the pursuit of carjackers, or active shoot-outs with suspected criminals.[73]

In their skills-training exercises, weapons experts working for private security companies routinely use CCTV surveillance footage of real events to instill in their tactical officers proper operating procedures when they come under fire from armed criminal gangs. It is not uncommon for organized criminal gangs—sometimes operating with close to fifteen members with three high-speed getaway vehicles—to have received military training themselves, perhaps with a foreign army. It is for this reason that leaders of security operations for neighborhood associations frequently become involved in the hiring of tactical officers, adamantly insisting that these guns for hire have military combat experience.[74]

Private security armed-response teams are heavily armed and typically indoctrinated in the old style of harsh policing. Like many public law enforcement officers, they believe that arresting suspects and prosecuting individual cases have become unduly cumbersome and time-consuming. Instead of turning suspects over to the criminal justice system, private security operatives often administer their own form of punishment on the spot, sometimes physically assaulting lawbreakers, even those only suspected of criminal intent.[75] They use physical force (or the threat of it) to extract information from intimidated criminal suspects. In carrying out what they regard as their mandate, private security companies frequently blur the line of legality by engaging in unlawful searches of persons and seizures of personal possessions. Private security teams have confiscated the meager goods of informal traders in order to drive them off the streets. They have also conducted lightning raids in the open spaces close to residential neighborhoods, tearing down and burning makeshift shacks. The exercise of this kind of indiscriminate violence is largely hidden from view and typically goes unreported. Thus, no one is held accountable.[76]

As a general rule, public policing agencies have condoned and encouraged the harsh treatment of suspected criminals, and they themselves often engage in mistreatment of those in detention. It is also the case that respectable urban residents and leaders of neighborhood associations tacitly approve of abusive tactics, in part because they would rather not know what really happens when private security operatives confront unwanted visitors in their residential suburbs.[77] Despite formal constitutional guarantees for an entire repertoire of legal rights and protected civil liberties, both the public police and private security operatives practice a perverse kind of racial profiling, targeting young black men (almost universally referred to as Bravo Mikes) who appear poor and unemployed as their principal objects of attention.[78]

By the second decade of the twenty-first century, what were once considered experimental innovations in security governance quickly became commonplace. These included such crime prevention measures as ensuring that private security guards at the boom gates have radio contact with armed-response vehicles, providing every household in the residential suburbs with an on-site panic button linked to their security companies, maintaining open SMS contact between private security control rooms and individual residents, and replacing security guards frequently (because of the fear of insider crime). Many private security companies have even implemented their own version of covert operations where they enlist their own undercover operatives to impersonate gardeners, domestic workers, or maintenance staff with the ostensible purpose of keeping an ear to the ground for criminal activities or suspicious visitors.[79] For the most part, established private security companies have come to rely on a coterie of confidential informants (such as maintenance workers and even informal car guards in neighborhood shopping areas) to provide them with information on loiterers, drug dealers, and petty thieves who have come into the area. They routinely reward domestic staff and street traders when they provide tips about suspicious activities, paying bonuses for information leading to the arrest and conviction of criminal suspects.[80] Volunteer security teams (sometimes grouped under Blockwatch initiatives) attached to neighborhood associations work closely with private security companies, providing information gathered from regular patrols of their residential suburbs. [81]

Private security assemblages consist of the aggregation of technologies, techniques, and special operations involving skilled personnel with expert knowledge.[82] The range of services that private security companies have put on offer has grown in tandem with the breadth and diversity of the technologies and techniques they employ in order to provide protection. In their operations, private security companies have gradually encroached on the terrain that was once the exclusive preserve of public law enforcement agencies. For the most part, proactive public-space companies have created their own CCTV surveillance systems for monitoring public streets and have established data-gathering capabilities (equal or better than those of the local SAPS precincts) linked with central command-and-control centers.[83]

The Grey Zone: Targeted Governance and the Discretionary Use of Force

In a climate of insecurity, proactive public-space policing promotes the clampdown on, or securitization of, insecure territories by the strengthening of targeted governance.[84] These strategies of targeted governance mirror the shift in policing and security governance from a logic of discipline and punishment to one of risk management. Targeted governance operates along several axes of preventative policing, most notably the information-mediated identification of problem spaces, problem populations, and specific activities defined as risky and dangerous.[85] This approach adopts new social control techniques that focus on the management of territory through psychological intimidation and physical exclusion rather than stress crime prevention through law enforcement.[86]

In the conduct of their duties, private security operatives function as the agents of exception, the petty sovereigns who, as Judith Butler has said, are "delegated with power to render unilateral decisions," are operating with discretionary authority that "they do not inaugurate or fully control," and are "accountable to no law and without any legitimate authority."[87] In the maintenance of law and order, the exercise of discretion is a vital feature of everyday policing and security governance. Both public police agencies and private security operatives occupy a fuliginous liminal space between lawmakers and law enforcers: these agents of security have extensive leeway to choose what to police or not to police.[88] As Walter Benjamin proposed some time ago, policing practices amount to a suspension of the validity of the law rather than to a simple and unambiguous enforcement of legal norms. In an insightful and powerful intervention called "Critique of Violence," Benjamin suggested that contrary to conventional democratic-liberal principles, it is entirely untrue that the ends of police violence are always identical or even connected to those of universal law.[89] Put in another way, the enactment of policing violence to preserve the law is actually not distinguishable from law-making. By assuming the powers to decide who is recognized by the law and who is not, policing agents act on their own accord to "enact sovereign power." That is, by commanding the capacity "to make exceptions to the law," they "create the legal ends themselves."[90] In short, wherever legal protections are discontinued and withdrawn from the domain of their usual jurisdiction, extralegal authority fills the void, assuming the capability to "institute and enforce law of its own making."[91]

Proactive public-space policing operates in the liminal space of perpetual suspension of legal rights. In what Miriam Ticktin has called the "space of juridical indeterminacy," the discretionary leeway that private policing agents use in the conduct of everyday "order maintenance" exemplifies how the law operates with the logic of exception.[92] What is important is that private security policing "happens in the name of law and order, not whether or not it is law."[93] Crucially, the rules governing legitimate arrest are so vague; they are defined in such a way that private security officers can act as sovereign agents—that is, the officers alone have the power to determine what behaviors constitute the legitimate use of space and which do not, since this determination is primarily a matter of subjective judgment.[94]

As a general rule, scholarly writing on legal and extralegal policing has focused on the boundaries separating the legitimate use of authorized force from the illegitimate and unsanctioned use of violence.[95] In Johannesburg after apartheid, the separation between the legitimate and illegitimate use of force amounts to nothing more than a fluid zone, an opaque territory largely hidden from view. It is here where overreach and selective enforcement have become the norm rather than the exception. The vagueness in the legal statutes allows for a great deal of discretion and latitude on the ground. Although private security officers have little legal authority to stop and detain suspicious persons not suspected of actually committing a crime, they operate with a great deal of impunity in not only detaining persons they consider suspicious but also searching them. These aggressive policing techniques are tactical tools in an arsenal of domination, intended to create a hostile environment that is uninhabitable by the urban poor.[96]

From the safety of their cars or from behind café windows, middle-class suburban residents are often subjected to the daily spectacle of private security teams harassing people in the streets. Adopting for all intents and purposes the abstract tropes of postlinearity and chaos theory, private security agents typically engage in swarming tactics, dispatching multiple armed-response teams in reaction to even the most minor infractions or suspicious activities. This elaborate choreography of aggression and intimidation is designed to give the impression of unchallenged sovereignty and omnipotence.[97] These visible displays of order-maintenance policing—what Julie Berg has called "a form of reassurance policing"—fill a gap left by the inability of public policing agencies to effectively combat crime in the residential suburban neighborhoods.[98]

It almost goes without saying that such policing is racially inflected. In conducting their everyday operations, private security tactical teams often engage in stop-and-search procedures, confronting and questioning young black men either on foot or in a vehicle.[99] According to South African law, private security companies are legally allowed to stop people under only two conditions: (1) there is reason to believe that the person either has just committed or is about to commit a serious criminal offense; or (2) the person consents to the stop and search. Private security operatives in the field routinely engage in pretext stops, where the presence of suspicious-looking young black men provides a convenient excuse to stop, confront, and intimidate anyone they choose. Armed-response teams in the field often interpret the refusal of a person to consent to being searched as tantamount to admission that a crime is either about to be committed or has been committed, thereby justifying detaining persons against their will, opening of the trunks of their cars, and rummaging through their pockets.[100]

Private security officers routinely resort to physical force and violence both to extract information from persons caught committing a crime and to convince potential criminals to stay out of a particular neighborhood.[101] The main modus operandi that private security teams employ is intimidation—stopping vehicles, harassing occupants, and threatening unknown passersby. On occasion, private security tactical response teams have pushed the limits of legal propriety, photographing workers at construction sites and demanding to see their identification booklets to check their South African citizenship. Even when members of neighborhood associations know that the boundaries of what is legally permissible have been blurred or ignored, they generally turn a blind eye, preferring not to inquire too deeply into the precise methods that private security companies use to drive unwanted persons out of their neighborhoods. With few exceptions, members of neighborhood associations strongly believe that aggressive tactics are the primary reason why criminal activities in their neighborhoods either have declined or are not as terrible as it otherwise might be.[102]

Private security teams routinely do not hesitate to engage in wild shoot-outs with suspected criminals. As one managing director of a private security company bragged, "Every suspect you shoot is no longer on the streets."[103] For example, in what was described as a "mini-war" in a suburban neighborhood in early 2017, two operatives working for Ren-

Track, a private tracking company, exchanged heavy gunfire with two carjackers armed with AK-47 assault rifles. The suspects were cornered in the driveway to a house, and during the firefight, one was killed and the other severely wounded.[104] Examples like this one could be multiplied many times over. It is also not unusual for armed civilians to chase suspected criminals and to engage in wild firefights with pistols and rifles. Events involving indiscriminate shooting where unlucky bystanders are caught in the cross fire have become commonplace in public gathering places.[105]

The Delicate Balance between Visible and Invisible Policing

As a general rule, the private policing of public space involves a delicate balance between selective visibility and invisibility in the approach to crime prevention and risk management.[106] Signs advertising the presence of particular armed-response companies and marking boundaries between one residential neighborhood and the next are ubiquitous. The most hyperactive private security companies practice high-visibility policing, in which the facade of legitimate authority consists of an open display of weapons, a no-nonsense demeanor, and the physical appearance of active-duty combat soldiers. The adoption of visible policing has dovetailed with zero-tolerance approaches to crime prevention, or a style of security governance consistent with the principle that clamping down on petty quality-of-life incivilities and petty crimes can effectively eliminate the kinds of environments in which more serious crimes are allowed to incubate and fester.[107]

In Glenhazel and Waverley, for example, the private security companies linked with the Community Active Protection (CAP) initiative have engaged in a kind of stage-managed (Goffman-like) dramaturgical performance: tactical officers careen around the public streets in black-colored armored vehicles, make a point of brandishing high-powered rifles, and dress in military-style uniforms. This carefully orchestrated display of weapons, uniforms, badges, insignia, cameras, and other accoutrements of high symbolic value communicate messages of bravado and evoke responses from onlookers, ranging from helping to assuage the anxieties of law-abiding residents to instilling fear among lawless youth. Private security companies affiliated with the CAP initiative have constructed watchtowers in the main public park, where tactical officers

armed with high-powered rifles stand guard over suburban residents using the facilities.[108]

Careful branding has enabled relatively small companies like NYPD
to distinguish themselves from their competitors and hence to carve out
niche markets for specialized protection services. According to Greg
Margolis, managing director, NYPD used BMW vehicles "because they
look sleek and are fast." Whereas the industry norm is three vehicles for
400 clients, NYPD claimed to have one vehicle per 150 clients. The crème
de la crème are 4x4 SWAT vehicles, operated by two heavily armed security guards outfitted with an assortment of lethal weapons. The company operates primarily in Parkhurst, Emmarentia, Greenside, Westcliff, and Parktown North. In order to establish its bona fides, NYPD
deliberately plagiarized from the New York City Police Department the
stylized blue uniforms and lettering on the sides of its 4x4 vehicles. "We
wanted to get the feel and look of the [New York City] police department," Margolis explained, because "it instills fear in criminals."[109]

As a general rule, private security companies—or what George Rigakos has called the "new parapolice of late modernity"—have taken on
the task of "making 'dangerous' populations 'known.'" This creation
of knowable subjects is accomplished through processes of constant observation and interpretation and the creation of digital, virtual hyper-
panoptic systems aimed at making both their own security employees
and the suspicious populations they monitor transparent and accountable. This "parapolice machine" and the risk management practices it
supports appear as packaged security commodities marketed to a nervous citizenry.[110]

In contrast, a great deal of the policing work that private security
companies undertake occurs in the shadowy world of masquerade and
deception. This shield of invisibility enables private security operatives
to engage in tactics they would like to conceal from public scrutiny:
harshly interrogating criminal suspects, physically mistreating detainees, assaulting defenseless job seekers and homeless vagabonds, and paying members of one criminal gang to inform on the activities of others.
Managers of private security companies use opaque language to suggest
that what they do to protect residential neighborhoods may be beyond
the terrain of strict legality. Their extralegal tactics are often revealed
through gesture and innuendo rather than through explicit admission.[111] Without a doubt, private security companies engage in activi-

ties that bend the law and, as such, constitute infringements of constitutionally guaranteed civil liberties and human rights. Yet these violations
rarely if ever come to the surface.[112]

In their promotional work, private security companies have proven
to be remarkably adept at creating realistic scenarios for crime narratives, variations of the truth that add layers of meaning to perceived
threats and risk. After all, anxious customers in search of security are
motivated as much by structures of feeling and by what they want to believe as by statistical facts. Private security companies cultivate and reinforce both individual and collective fears in order to sell their expensive
security products.[113]

One principal goal of proactive public-space policing carried out by
private security companies is to make incongruous, out-of-place persons
and their unsightly activities simply disappear. Perhaps not so surprisingly, much of this work of coercion takes place in plain sight. In Johannesburg and other cities, law-abiding citizens have attached themselves
to socially constructed norms of middle-class aesthetic propriety, where
impoverished job seekers, aimless youth, itinerant street traders, and
beggars are lumped together with potential criminals. Private security
officers employ a range of interdictory tactics designed to displace unwanted persons whose troubling behaviors and appearance signal disorder, rendering them invisible by banishing them from places where
they do not belong through a combination of intimidation and physical
force.[114]

Such strategies of proactive public-space policing invariably target disadvantaged and vulnerable persons through the use of punitive policing
measures that rarely match the supposed threat that these people pose.[115]
For the most part, proactive public-space policing has less to do with personal safety and the threat of crime and more to do with expurgating
unsightly persons and their transgressive antisocial behaviors and, in so
doing, improving the aesthetic appeal of public spaces.[116] These revanchist measures are legitimated through the discursive tropes of crime
and fear.[117]

Visibility is the handmaiden of power relations: it demands attention,
it announces the rules of the game, and it upholds hegemonic control.[118]
In contrast, invisibility obscures power relations; it stifles debate, con-
ceals truths, and deflects attention. The stress that hyperactive private
security companies put on visible performativity and open displays of

FIGURE 14. CCTV camera mounted on wall. (Photo by author.)

bravado is equally matched by their fixation on invisible policing.[119] Un-like the raison d'être behind public policing, private security compa-nies are primarily concerned with developing strategies aimed at pre-venting *opportunities* for crime to occur over and above apprehending criminal suspects and reacting to *actual* lawbreaking.[120] This emphasis on preventive policing has meant that private security companies have placed an inordinate focus on information gathering and data analysis in order to assess risk by identifying and anticipating opportunities for breaches of the law.[121] The collection and evaluation of information are not ancillary or secondary activities but core features of risk manage-ment strategies.[122]

In so many ways, CCTV surveillance camera systems epitomize the balance between visibility and invisibility. Mounted on tall poles, out-side front gates, and along perimeter walls, CCTV cameras are a ubiq-uitous presence in residential suburban neighborhoods. These "off-site monitoring" devices also include "smart booms," which require driv-ers of vehicles to push a button for the boom gate to lift. Pausing at the boom gate enables cameras to acquire a visual image of the driver, the make, the model, and the registration number of the vehicle. These me-chanical devices make visible what might otherwise remain cloaked in secrecy. By transforming vision into a collective enterprise, CCTV cameras effectively socialize visuality. In addressing the "stubbornness of invisibility" and attempting "to roll back the unseen," CCTV cameras seek to make known what is unknown.[123] In this sense, CCTV surveillance technologies epitomize the urban uncanny—material representations of an uncomfortable sense of dread.[124]

With their CCTV monitoring screens, private security control rooms operate as command-and-control centers for a far-flung network of material objects and people directed at bringing to light, through identification, classification, and recording for future use, all manner of suspicious activities. CCTV surveillance systems consist of a hybrid assemblage of computer hardware, electronic devices, analytics (algorithms) software, state-of-the-art cameras, flat-screen monitors, real-time streaming of digitalized images, and ever-watchful observers to provide round-the-clock visual surveillance, thereby creating the illusion of effective vigilance.[125]

The Secret World of Intelligence Gathering

The evolving modalities of security provision have put tremendous pressure on private security companies to develop expertise in areas conventionally regarded as the exclusive preserve of public policing agencies. Besides providing a variety of security services for their paying clients, private security companies engage in the production, storage, and dissemination of information. As intelligence brokers, private security companies are in a powerful position to share, exchange, sell, or withhold information.[126] Careful and systematic information gathering has given private security companies a distinct advantage over public policing agencies whose capabilities for collecting and analyzing data lag behind. In any intelligence network, the aim is not to monopolize and withhold all information but to disseminate it selectively to achieve such desired outcomes as the commercial marketing of their services, the maintenance of influence over clients, and the realization of profits.[127] In this sense, security intelligence is a quintessential club good, made available to group members but not to outsiders.[128] When shared with clients, security intelligence serves as an index—or a symbolic representation—of the more abstract notion of the security services that are produced or consumed under the terms of a contractual obligation.[129] Private security companies package information in statistical compilations and ar-range categories in ways designed to bring comfort to their always anxious clients.[130]

As part of their overall strategy of expanding their services, a number of private security companies focus a great deal of attention on intelligence gathering. They have begun to construct and maintain their own databases consisting of accurate crime statistics (including frequencies, trends, and types of criminal activities) for the residential neighborhoods in which they have contracts. By analyzing this mass of information, private security companies are able to pinpoint crime hot spots, identify criminal patterns, monitor the types of vehicles and weapons that criminal gangs use, study the tactics of these groups, and seek to anticipate where they might strike next. Private security companies often enlist the support of a network of paid informers to supply a steady stream of intelligence on known criminal syndicates, sometimes recruiting gang members to inform on their rivals and paying underworld figures for information. They frequently pay undercover informants to infiltrate criminal syndicates, to hang around known gathering places for criminals, and to frequent *shabeens* (nightclubs) where known criminals spend their leisure time. Private security managers claim that they pay rewards for information that leads to arrests and convictions.[131] The accumulation and interpretation of these sorts of data have ensured that private security companies are better informed and hence better prepared than the public law enforcement agencies to combat crime in residential neighborhoods where they have contracts.[132]

For the most part, private security companies maintain and operate a command-and control center that processes incoming "calls from residents and dispatches tactical units" to investigate reports of suspicious activities. They maintain extensive databases of information collected from residents, from interrogation of criminal suspects, from victims of crime, from their patrols, and from police records.[133] They regularly collect and store license registration numbers not only for legitimate residents but also for suspicious vehicles. They routinely gather biometric and social-network data for the identification of potential criminals. At the very least, the biometric data consists of collections of photographs of people, including domestic workers, informal security guards, construction workers employed at building sites in residential neighborhoods, suspicious persons who have been previously stopped and searched, and those whose images have been captured on CCTV surveillance cameras. The social-network data includes information on known visitors to residential neighborhoods, such as the types of vehicles they drive, their license registration numbers, who their friends are, and where they go. This information is stored in computerized databases and in CCTV surveillance footage. Private security companies also conduct follow-up interviews with victims of such crimes as house burglaries, carjackings, and street robberies to create profiles outlining the modus operandi of criminal gangs.[134]

A key element in proactive public-space policing is the identification of crime targets and at-risk sites. From their own data gathering, private security companies have learned that armed break-ins of private residences often come in waves and during vacation periods (especially December) when homeowners would be more likely to be away. Using information gathered from paid informants about planned house break-ins or carjacking operations, private security armed-response units have sometimes engaged in staged ambushes, outfitted with heavy weapons and dressed in camouflage gear. With instructions to shoot to kill, they lie in wait for criminals to approach their intended targets. Some private security companies prefer to use anonymous spotters along major traffic routes to trace the movements of criminal gangs as they proceed in high-speed getaway cars from their hideaways to their destinations. In most instances, private security tactical teams inform the public police of their intentions and request the presence of a SAPS officer in order to obtain official sanction for firing weapons.[135]

Some private security companies have successfully lured top criminal investigators from public police services in order to bolster their own detective and forensic capabilities. For example, in one well-known instance, the private security company CSS Tactical hired former SAPS top cop Major General Bushie Engelbrecht and Brigadier Piet Byleveld (the longest-serving murder and robbery investigator in the SAPS) as members of their executive team. Besides their long-standing contacts with undercover informants in the townships, the two men brought their expertise and years of experience as specialists in criminal investigations and special corporate projects.[136]

For the most part, private security companies that are engaged in proactive public-space policing bring together a range of operational procedures and tactics to ensure that the neighborhood streets and other open-access spaces are safe. In the typical case, private companies divide the policing of residential neighborhoods into proactive patrolling of public space and armed response (first responders) for domestic alarm signals. Although there is some variation in the actual procedures they use (whether CCTV monitoring or static guards at boom gates), private security personnel monitor entry and exit points into residential areas by channeling all visitors through designated area-access-control points. This strategy of establishing only a few choke points gives private security officers an easy way of recording vehicle registration and telephone numbers from all visitors. These efforts at establishing sociospatial control over territory involve rules and practices—what Steve Herbert has called a "normative order"—that both constrain and enable the behavior of private security armed-response teams.[137]

Because private security companies conduct data-gathering activities largely under a cloak of secrecy and maintain a monopoly over intelligence gathering, neighborhood associations must rely on trust. Managers of private security companies go out of their way to cultivate the confidence of leaders of neighborhood associations. In the fierce rivalry for private protection contracts with these associations, private security companies often make exaggerated claims about their successes while at the same time criticizing their competitors. If crime rates decline in suburban neighborhoods, the trust that neighborhood associations put in private security companies easily metamorphoses into an attitude somewhat akin to blind faith.[138]

Critics often draw an analogy between private security companies and organized criminal enterprises by suggesting that both tend "to stimulate the very dangers against which protection is then required."[139] As profit-making enterprises, private security companies operate in a highly competitive marketplace that depends on "the continuation of the very crime and insecurity [they promise] to fight."[140] Even though leaders of residential associations often suspect private security companies of wrongdoing, they typically turn a blind eye when faced with the alternative of having no protection at all.[141] Yet because of this visceral distrust, residents have not simply transferred their dependence on (and their allegiance to) public law enforcement to private security companies. Instead, the approach of suburban residents to everyday policing typically "straddles these two spheres," thereby constantly disrupting any simplified dichotomy between public and private security provision.[142]

Flexibility and Inflexibility

Private security companies have effectively established a monopoly over the legitimate use of force and violence in the residential suburbs in which they have legally sanctioned contracts with neighborhood associations. In their provision of various security services, they have shown themselves to be quite flexible, operating along a continuum of coercive practices in accordance with their contracts and the expectations of their clients.[143] Conversely, however, private security companies appear quite inflexible in their tactical approaches to crime prevention. The prevailing mentality of security governance has placed inordinate stress on an order maintenance approach to crime prevention rather than on a customer service or social service perspective.[144] As a general rule, proactive public-space policing has relied on stop-and-frisk tactics when dealing with unknown persons entering residential neighborhoods. Private security companies regard aggression and intimidation when confronting suspicious persons as necessary in order to fulfill their goal of deterring crime.[145]

Yet by uniformly adopting these tactics, these hyperactive private companies have adopted a combative approach to unknown persons deemed suspicious from which it is difficult to de-escalate. Once private security tactical teams have decided that someone has no legitimate reason to be in the neighborhood, they seek to physically escort the unwanted person out of the area.[146] If any suspicious person objects and refuses to leave, security operatives revert to a series of intimidation tactics that can easily escalate to physical force and violence: closely following the movements of the suspicious person, alerting public law enforcement officers, taking photographs without permission, and engaging in tough talk. Taken together, the aim of these carefully choreographed tactics is to increase pressure on unwanted persons to make it as uncomfortable as possible for them to remain where they are not wanted.[147]

There is plenty of circumstantial evidence—provided by informal interviews, anecdotes, hearsay, court testimonies, journalist accounts, personal observations, and the like—that private security personnel do not shy away from roughing up young black men who inadvertently stray into areas in which they are not wanted. While they are rarely if ever reprimanded, private security guards routinely beat suspected criminals before turning them over to public law enforcement personnel. These extrajuridical practices constitute a kind of shadow policing beyond public scrutiny and outside legal norms. Private security companies look upon the public streets of the city as war zones. Their goal is to outfox, outmuscle, and outgun criminal gangs. Shoot-outs with suspected criminals are regular occurrences.[148]

Cooperation and Competition

One strong current in the scholarly literature on systems of networked security governance has placed a great deal of emphasis on a cooperative division of labor and shared responsibilities between public policing and private security—captured with the slogan "public-private partnerships." In the contemporary pluralized landscape of security provision, partnership-policing arrangements "are often the norm, rather than the exception."[149] Public police officers and private security operatives have developed a wide range of informal and ad hoc relationships, due in large measure to their everyday contact on the job. What drives these multifaceted relationships are primarily utilitarian concerns with accomplishing their goal of fighting crime. These functional relationships amount to what Bruce Baker has called "negotiated tactical alliances."[150] At times, private security personnel supplement and assist the public police. But under other circumstances they compete with public law enforcement agencies. Both private security companies and public policing organizations share information about crime trends and particular incidents in residential neighborhoods. They participate as more or less equal partners in Community Policing Forum (CPF) meetings held at local SAPS precinct headquarters. Yet in seeking to expand the market for their repertoire of services, private security companies inevitably encroach on the domain of public law enforcement agencies. In everyday conversations with heads of neighborhood associations, private security officials typically ridicule the efficiency and preparedness of public policing agencies, sharing stories about the lack of commitment and dedication of the SAPS and Johannesburg Municipal Police Department (JMPD) and about their inadequate training and preparedness to handle criminal situations.[151]

In day-to-day field operations, private security operatives and public police on the ground share information and resources. Operatives at command centers for private security companies listen to police radio frequencies, monitoring crimes in progress and vehicle pursuits in real time. Whether or not they are called on to join, private security tactical teams respond to calls announcing crimes in progress or engage in the hot pursuit of stolen vehicles. When they apprehend criminal suspects, private security operatives call in the SAPS and turn over the detainees, thereby ensuring that SAPS personnel get the official credit as arresting officers. These ad hoc interactions have produced a modicum of mutual respect and trust.[152]

Yet collaboration and cooperation often occur in tandem with competition and deceit.[153] Both public police officials and private security operatives routinely supply certain information to each other. Yet at the same time, they often withhold everything they know. Private security companies keep detailed records of crime trends by every conceivable measure. By tracking statistical patterns and monitoring the modus operandi of criminal gangs (through paid informants), they are able to identify crime hot spots, detect criminal routines, and forecast the spatial-temporal coordinates of the likelihood of future incidents. Since intelligence gathering is a key feature of the services that private security companies offer residential neighborhoods, they are extremely reluctant to share it with public policing agencies.[154]

The SAPS and JMPD have welcomed the supportive role of private security companies as a force multiplier in carrying out high-level operations, especially when they are particularly dangerous or require a massive show of force.[155] The SAPS and JMPD sometimes call on private security companies to provide resources—vehicles, tactical teams, and heavy weapons—for joint missions. They often work together to carry out large-scale clampdowns on illegal activities (such as building hijackings and street trading); to assist with evictions from condemned buildings; to conduct water and electricity cutoffs; to set up roadblocks in stop-and-search operations to check for illicit drugs and weapons, stolen vehicles, unlicensed drivers, and safety violations; to conduct large sweeps of greenbelts to clear out unauthorized squatters; and to break up strikes and demonstrations. After locating safe houses for criminal syndicates in places such as Alexandra and Diepsloot, some private security companies have organized special-ops teams (with white operatives disguising themselves in black face paint) to execute raids in the townships in search of stolen property such as vehicles and weapons. The SAPS and JMPD are always in charge of strategic operations, even when private security companies are responsible for intelligence gathering.[156] Along with leaders of neighborhood associations, private security companies sometimes offer gifts of radio transmitters and computers to the local SAPS stations in the areas in which they work. These largely ad hoc interactions between public policing agencies and private security companies continue because they are mutually beneficial to both parties.[157]

Yet sometimes the undue stress on the formal and institutional ties that bind public policing and private security together in new hybrid alliances has meant that the enduring underlying tensions that have accompanied these new types of cooperative security arrangements have been overlooked. Personal relationships more than institutional connections have shaped the types of partnering that have evolved over time. The relationships between public policing agencies and private security companies are highly complex rather than idyllic and seamlessly interwoven. These relationships have careened between cooperation and competition and between mutual dependence and deep distrust. At the end of the day, private security companies are in the protective services business to make a profit. Expanding their market share depends on the inability of public policing agencies to provide adequate security for residential neighborhoods.[158]

On balance, high-ranking police begrudgingly acknowledge that the presence of private security companies—especially in carrying out constant patrols in residential neighborhoods and in guarding such mass private property sites as gated residential estates, shopping malls, and tourist-entertainment venues—has contributed to the reduction of crime and thus assisted public police agencies in maintaining law and order.[159] When private security companies focus their attention on particular residential neighborhoods, public policing agencies are able to reallocate their scarce resources to other areas. As a general rule, the SAPS commanders hold joint weekly meetings at local precinct offices, where representatives of neighborhood associations, private security companies, and the JMPD come together to share information about criminal activities and to coordinate activities.[160] But participants in these meetings are not always completely forthcoming, as both public police officials and private security managers are often cautious about sharing information.[161] On the one side, public policing agencies often express serious concerns that unscrupulous private security companies may be involved in their own criminal enterprises and may sell information to criminal syndicates regarding planned raids and law enforcement operations. On the other, private security companies boast to their neighborhood clients that their information-gathering capabilities far exceed those of the public law enforcement agencies. Disclosing too much information to the public police would threaten their competitive edge in the marketplace for private security.[162]

Private security companies have lobbied public policing agencies to grant their operatives the status of police reservist or at least allow unpaid volunteers enlisted to assist public law enforcement to ride along in private security tactical response vehicles on patrol. Reservist status effectively grants private security officers much wider discretion in the use of lethal force. Public law enforcement agencies have pushed back, arguing that allowing private security operatives to become police reservists would create an untenable situation because the operatives would then use their newly acquired status as public police to lure new private customers. Private security personnel doubling as police reservists would have divided loyalties, whether serving as law enforcement officers or catering to the interests of their paying clients.[163]

Neighborhood associations purchase security services as a collectively consumed commodity, but the eventual benefits are not spread evenly across member households. As a packaged commodity, security services are a diffuse good that is difficult if not impossible to measure in strictly business terms "as a return on investment."[164] For this reason, private companies must engage in a deliberate strategy of convincing their often skeptical clients that their security services are actually worth the high cost to individual residential households. The standard rhetorical strategy is to stress before-and-after figures chronicling rates of crime reduction after private security came on board in a particular residential neighborhood. Because statistical formulations rely on subjective interpretations of how to classify crime incidents, private security companies have plenty of discretion via clever measurement techniques to make claims that are impossible to validate. Thus, leaders of neighborhood associations have remained suspicious of the accuracy of the claims that private security companies provide.[165]

Put broadly, the relationship between neighborhood associations and private security companies rests on a curious blend of interpersonal trust and blind faith. Managers of private security companies have become adept at marketing their security services—exaggerating their successes by publicizing high-profile arrests and downplaying their failures by shifting the blame elsewhere. Like snake-oil salesmen and used-car dealers, these managers make bold promises that they are genuinely unsure they can keep, stressing how their secret surefire solutions to crime prevention are state of the art and cutting edge and how the strategies and tactics of their competitors have proven to be ineffective.[166]

In their public pronouncements, public policing agencies, private security companies, and neighborhood associations talk approvingly of their harmonious and symbiotic relationship as one in which they are partners against crime. Yet the tensions that occasionally spill over into open conflict expose the deceit of appearances. What may seem to signal genuine mutual respect and admiration can mask a certain amount of suspicion and distrust mixed with duplicity and opportunism. In practice, relations between public law enforcement agencies and private security companies are characterized by a great deal of strain, which derives fundamentally from their incompatible aims. As integral partners in the municipal administration, the SAPS and the JMPD are charged with maintaining public order and the protection of urban residents through law enforcement and the apprehension of criminal suspects. Public policing agencies measure their success at keeping reported crime lower than expectations, at arresting criminal suspects, and at prosecuting crimes via the criminal justice system. In contrast, private security companies are profit-making enterprises engaged in the business of protecting the properties of their paying clients and minimizing their risks of bodily harm. These companies are able to maintain their existing client base and attract new customers under circumstances in which insecurity and fear of crime remain high. The dependency that individual homeowners and neighborhood associations develop on the private provision of security services derives from the widespread perception that without the protective shield of proactive armed response and visible public-space policing, crime rates could easily spiral out of control. Private companies look at the delivery of security services as a means to manage risk for their paying clients, not as a strategy for overall crime reduction.[167] Managers of private security companies perversely boast that by successfully displacing crime from residential neighborhoods in which they operate, they increase their opportunities for securing new clients in surrounding residential suburbs where the criminals have migrated.[168]

As a general rule, private security companies have an ambivalent relationship with public law enforcement agencies. As a consequence, these private firms have deliberately engaged in what appear to be contradictory practices.[169] On the one hand, private security companies have sought to gain legitimacy by aligning with the idealized image of an efficient "security provider" and mimicking the outward appearance and demeanor of public law enforcement agencies. By wearing standardized uniforms, staffing their management ranks with ex–police officers, and driving official-looking patrol vehicles (all totemic emblems suggesting "symbolic stateness"), private security companies create the impression that they fulfill the dual roles of law enforcement and crime prevention.[170] The symbolic borrowing of the stylistic accoutrements of public policing—standardized uniforms, badges, and weapons and menacing body language—allows private security providers to imitate the authority of public policing agencies and hence to fabricate what Adam White has described as a "general impression of stateness."[171] Private security companies have used all means at their disposal to cultivate a self-serving image of themselves as an elite paramilitary force, steeped in an ethos of "technological professionalism" and hence adopting a "degree of symbolic state-like legitimacy."[172] These efforts "to secure legitimacy by association" enable private security companies to gloss over their profit-seeking motives and instead present themselves "as state-deputized institutions functioning in accordance with the state guaranteed public good."[173]

On the other hand, private security companies have sought to disassociate themselves from public policing agencies, which have a reputation for being hopelessly corrupt, inefficient, and averse to work. At the same time, public law enforcement agencies routinely accuse private security companies of unfairly criticizing them and providing false information about the competence of their officers. This ambivalent attitude of private security companies toward public policing agencies has helped to foster suspicion and a lack of trust between the two at the highest levels of both organizations. Consequently, collaboration between them is limited to somewhat circumscribed areas of common concern that are mutually beneficial.[174]

As a general rule, private security companies encourage the already widely held perception that the public police are ill-prepared, unde-requipped, and untrustworthy when it comes to protecting middle-class residential neighborhoods. This lack of trust in the capabilities of public policing agencies has manifested itself in a number of ways. Some neighborhood associations in residential suburbs have paid private security companies to conduct criminal investigations into such high-profile crimes as unsolved home invasions or carjackings. In addition, a number of neighborhood associations have hired private security companies to shadow state prosecuting authorities through the criminal justice system, following court cases to ensure that dockets do not go missing and that criminals get punished.[175]

On balance, the relationship between the public policing agencies and the private security companies is often tense and competitive. There is plenty of circumstantial evidence suggesting that private security companies exaggerate crime threats, sensationalize their role in crime prevention, and manufacture false information in order to expand their market share in residential neighborhoods. Public policing agencies strongly suspect that private security companies stage illegal home burglaries to sow fear and thus increase their client base. But private security companies also accuse public policing agencies of incompetence and corruption. Middle- and high-ranking public police officials accuse private security companies of withholding information and refusing to share crime intelligence while at the same time demanding to have privileged access to official police records, including the national database on information about stolen vehicles. Both public policing agencies and private security companies have expressed concerns that the untrustworthy, unscrupulous persons on the "other side" willingly engage in illegal activities to serve their own self-interests.[176]

To a certain extent, high-ranking officials in both the SAPS and the JMPD consider the expanding role of the private security industry as an overall threat to their mandate and prerogatives as public policing agencies. With higher wages and better resources, the private security industry has increasingly lured high-ranking personnel away from public policing agencies and the military, especially in crucial fields such as skills training, intelligence gathering, logistics, and business management. It is not uncommon for high-ranking police officials to leave public service in order to create their own private security firms.[177] Rising concerns about the growth of private companies as a powerful social force with tentacles in all sorts of markets prompted lawmakers to call for stricter standards governing operating procedures and to introduce legislation placing limitations on the extent of foreign ownership in the private security industry.[178]

Private companies offer security services that range from static guards to mobile armed-response tactical teams and from personalized training in evasive driving and pistol shooting to the installation of CCTV towers in residential neighborhoods. They have thus greatly expanded the commodities they sell and the markets they have created.[179] Without doubt, the private security industry has blended into the social fabric of everyday life to such an extent that it is virtually impossible to imagine negotiating urban space outside its protective shield. The ubiquity of private security services on the market has meant that public oversight agencies have experienced considerably difficulty in differentiating between legitimate business enterprises that provide worthy products and illegitimate ones that deceive or even cheat their customers.[180]

6

Responsibilizing Citizenship

The preventive turn in crime control policies that emerged in the last decades of the twentieth century came into existence as a response to the growing dissatisfaction with the capacity of welfare-rehabilitative and penal-punitive models of criminal justice to adequately deal with public safety.[1] Scholars and policy makers alike described these innovations in situational crime prevention as an "epistemological break" with the failed policies of the modernist era,[2] "a major shift in paradigm,"[3] and "a long-overdue recognition that the levers and causes of crime lie far from the traditional reach of the criminal justice system."[4] This new way of thinking about "crime and its prevention" not only "challenge[d] many of the modernist assumptions about professional expertise, specialization, paternalism and monopoly" but also established a framework that encouraged stronger and more active civic participation in community safety partnerships.[5] The core ideas behind the new logic of security governance involve the adoption of more proactive strategies of risk management, that is, the embrace of novel ways of thinking about how to reduce crime by anticipating where and under what circumstances criminal activities are more likely (or less likely) to occur and hence forestalling that which has not yet happened and may never happen.[6] This new approach to risk management rests on the presumption that "instead of pursuing, prosecuting, and punishing" suspected criminals after the fact, the real aim of crime prevention is "to reduce the supply of criminal events by minimizing criminal opportunities, enhancing situational controls, and channeling conduct away from criminogenic situations."[7]

"Preventative policing partnerships" have become a defining characteristic of crime prevention strategies.[8] In response to the increasing loss of faith in the effectiveness of public law enforcement agencies and the criminal justice system to effectively combat crime, homeowners in residential neighborhoods in Johannesburg have experimented with various kinds of self-activated crime-prevention strategies. A key feature of this new direction in security governance has involved the appeal to local community organizations to become active agents in their own protection—the eyes and ears on the ground working to buttress an overburdened and understaffed public police force. The primary aim of various interlaced networks of partnership-policing experiments is "to foster crime prevention and to enhance community safety, primarily through the cultivation of community involvement and the dissemination of crime prevention ideas and practices."[9] This turn toward community involvement, particularly to the enlisting of volunteer (self-activated) organizations as "partners against crime," has opened up a "bewildering array of communitarian and technical fixes," which made their appearance as antidotes to rising threats of crime and disorder.[10]

Yet despite the good intentions attached to them, the terms *partnership* and *community* are neither neutral ideas nor ones with stable and fixed definitions. Rather, their meanings are "discursively constructed and contested through political rhetoric," policy implementation, regulatory frameworks, and local "grassroots practice."[11] The sometimes strange organizational formations that have emerged under the umbrella of such hybrid concoctions as partnership policing and community policing partnerships make it difficult to pinpoint precisely what they actually mean.[12]

"Community" as Empty Signifier

Proponents of local control and self-governance often invoke the idea of community as the setting within which responsibilized citizens actively take charge of their own security. The widespread (and somewhat indiscriminate) use of the term *community* endows it with an exalted status in the political discourse of civic communitarianism.[13] Those who endorse strategies of active citizenship in localized self-governance celebrate the normative ideal of what Jonathan Davies has called heterophily, or the idea that successful community policing can nurture shared values, affective trust, and a sense of belonging among otherwise atomized, disconnected, and diverse suburban homeowners.[14]

As a general rule, the idea of community is so familiar and commonplace that it is quite easy to take what it means for granted. More often than not, community is regarded as a repository of such positive (and normative) values and cherished ideals as trust, tolerance, and cooperation. But on closer inspection, what is meant by community is not so readily apparent. The idea of community functions more like a loose folk term—with "warm associations," as Steve Herbert has suggested—than like a precise analytic concept.[15]

Because of its multiple meanings, the notion of *community* is inherently problematic. It can be used to refer to an aggregation of congruous group identities and the imagining of common affinities or as a means for categorizing difference. In short, community can signify both diversity and exclusivity, on the one hand, and homogenous clusters based on class, ethnicity, or shared culture, on the other. This intrinsic ambiguity endows community with a dual nature: while it embraces group homogeneity, it also rejects internal difference in order to preserve purity.[16] Communities are social constructions whose meanings are derived from the sociocultural circumstances within which they originate.[17]

The polyvalence of the notion of community exposes its almost infinitely malleable qualities as a "floating signifier" without a fixed reference point. It carries "a multiplicity of significations," capable of alignment with a wide spectrum of understandings of everyday life in the city. In the conventional wisdom, ideas such as community suggest an intrinsic "vibrancy, coherence, continuity, and stability" rooted in the civic virtues of sharing and reciprocity. This communitarian ethos conjures up an imaginary associational life in which "everyone can relate in a civil and urbane fashion to everyone else." But as David Harvey has pointed out, there is a "darker side" to this romanticized image of communitarianism. From the very early phases of large-scale urbanization linked to the expansion of industrial production, policy makers looked upon the spirit of community as an antidote to threats of social disorder, class conflict, and revolutionary violence. The retreat behind the mantra of "community" generally brings to mind uplifting images of responsible citizens engaging in self-governance. Yet community also functions as "one of the key sites of social control and surveillance," relying on various mechanisms of social exclusion to maintain internal cohesiveness. More often than not, well-established communities define their own self-interests against those of others (in what might be called a defensive politics of difference) and construct filtering mechanisms that establish rules of inclusion and exclusion.[18]

Enlisting Community in Johannesburg:
Self-Help Policing and Risk Management

The idea of active citizenship and community involvement has become increasingly prominent during the past three decades of policy debates concerned with the shifting terrains of urban governance.[19] In Johannesburg, municipal city officials connected with law enforcement and crime prevention initiatives have gone out of their way to extol the virtues of community involvement and active citizen participation as bedrock principles for ensuring local safety and security.[20] The mantra of "creating safer communities" has been crucial in the shift toward the promotion of stricter policing policies that promise to be tough on crime. In Johannesburg, the policies and practices of community-based safety and crime control initiatives have coincided with a new localism in which residential associations—particularly in middle-class neighborhoods of the northern suburbs—have taken matters into their own hands, hiring private security companies to patrol their streets, blocking off access with permanent barriers, and erecting boom gates to monitor entry and exit. By asserting their collective rights as law-abiding citizens to protect themselves and their property from criminals, residents of suburban neighborhoods have established themselves as a formidable social force.[21] This rhetoric of the sovereign subject responsible for his or her own safety has dovetailed with the popular perception that only a well-armed citizenry can offer protection against criminality.[22]

The idea of the self-governing community is one of the defining features of the shift toward neoliberal modes of urban governance. As a "discursive resource of almost limitless potential," the idea of community—as "a theatre of governance, identity, rule and performance"—stretches far and wide over a variety of terrains. [23] The appeal of a "self-governing community" works precisely because it offers an alternative model of decentralized local control that does not rely exclusively on the public provision of services. Local self-governance and empowerment are predicated on the retreat of the state administration from the affairs of local communities.[24]

By appealing to municipal authorities to devolve responsibility for safety to the neighborhood level, residential associations are able to establish semiautonomous zones of local control. As exemplary expressions of self-governing communities, neighborhood associations epitomize new modalities of networked power that exist outside the penetrating eye of public law enforcement agencies. Voluntary self-governance schemes, such as community policing forums and neighborhood watch programs, fit neatly into the paradigm of neoliberal governmentality. Community policing represents one particular form of participatory activism and civic engagement. Under circumstances in which suburban residents have become increasingly apprehensive about crime and have lost faith in the capabilities of municipal law enforcement agencies to protect them, they have warmly embraced the idea of local participation in security governance. The idea behind community policing is the belief that urban residents ought to take a proactive role in organizing their own security.[25] Community policing offers residential associations a wide range of options for providing their own protection against crime, including hiring private security companies, establishing community policing forms tied to local SAPS precinct stations, and creating neighborhood watch programs.[26]

Community policing initiatives reflect state-sponsored efforts to mobilize neighborhood associations to engage in what Patrick O'Malley and Darren Palmer have called "the governance of security 'at-a-distance.'"[27] Ironically, state-sponsored community policing initiatives have dovetailed with the expanded delivery of private security services. Once mobilized under the umbrella of state encouragement, residential associations with sufficient financial power have sought greater control over their own safety "by purchasing largely repressive and coercive policing services directly from the private security industry."[28] The drift toward paramilitary approaches to private security policing reflects an ongoing crisis of legitimacy in which public policing agencies have largely lost the trust of local communities.[29] At face value, the devolution of security matters to neighborhood associations seems to applaud the noble aims of decentralized self-governance. Yet what is often overlooked is the inherently plural, unstable, and contradictory nature of local security projects—or what Adam Edwards and Gordon Hughes have called "public safety regimes."[30] As a general rule, the practice of local crime prevention oscillates between the polar extremes of, on the one hand, community safety projects that operate within the sanctions of the law and, on the other hand, more exclusionary zero-tolerance, extralegal enforcement-oriented strategies of crime prevention that criminalize the poor.[31]

One principle aim behind community policing initiatives has been to generate greater participation and active leadership from neighborhood associations in promoting quality-of-life concerns, that is, not just tackling those grievous social harms conventionally classified as crimes but also proactively working toward the elimination of incivilities and antisocial nuisances that contribute to the deterioration of social congregating places.[32] As an intended long-term outcome, community safety is often linked to the communitarian ambition of replacing fragile, atomized, fearful, and insecure communities with neighborhood associations confident enough and sufficiently mobilized to take responsibility for their own safety.[33]

Social Exclusion "from Above" and from Below

One striking paradox of urban marginality is that poor people are both invisible and yet closely observed.[34] As Ralph Ellison recounted a long time ago in *Invisible Man*, black men negotiate city streets as anonymous beings, never seen but always unwanted.[35] In Johannesburg, itinerant job seekers, beggars, newspaper sellers, child-minders, gardeners, idle youth, curbside traders, and informal car guards are a ubiquitous presence on the public streets. But despite their physical presence, they are typically ignored or regarded as nuisances by middle-class residents, who go merrily about their daily lives of working, shopping, doing errands, and keeping appointments. For those marginalized people who fall outside the mainstream of urban life, however, the assertion of their visibility is the sine qua non for the realization of whatever meager opportunities exist for them to earn an income. Destitute people must be seen in order to draw the attention of better-off residents who may offer work or a handout.

Despite their existential condition of invisibility, marginalized residents of the city are constantly subjected to different kinds of observation. The mechanical gaze of CCTV cameras, the vigilance of security guards, and the eyes and ears of neighborhood watch groups transform the invisible poor into visible objects of scrutiny.[36] This engagement with the production of legibility revolves around making the unknowable somehow knowable. Unknown persons are, by definition, not to be trusted. The ghostly presence of the urban poor is filtered through the lens of suspicion. Heightened anxiety about danger and crime "creates suspects out of the urban poor."[37]

As a social construct, "the criminal suspect" is a relational category, brought to life by the wariness of public policing agencies, private security teams, neighborhood watch groups, suburban residents, and the law itself directed at criminalizing the urban poor. For the forces of law and order, suspected criminals are "a clearly definable social group," consisting primarily of idle youth, jobless men, and untrustworthy household staff.[38]

In order to gain the cooperation of an alert citizenry and to institute responsible modes of policing in line with the transition to parliamentary democracy, municipal authorities in Johannesburg initiated a host of new programs designed to promote law enforcement and crime prevention. During the late 1990s and early 2000s, strategies in the so-called war against crime underwent a profound restructuring. By 2002, security analysts estimated that about 50 percent of urban residents relied on neighborhood watch organizations or community-based self-protection groups for their security. In response to these changing circumstances, public police officials actively sought to harness the energy of these privately organized anticrime initiatives as a way of enlisting the assistance of local communities in crime-prevention efforts while at the same time curbing the violent excesses of extralegal vigilantism. Far from acting as outsiders passively looking on, public law enforcement agencies turned their attention to localized community policing as the war against crime shifted from an emphasis on apprehension and prosecution of criminal suspects to a stress on crime prevention. The rising fear of crime triggered a groundswell of local community interest and participation, ranging from the establishment of neighborhood watch programs and the hiring of private security protection to collecting money to fund local police stations.[39]

The steady expansion of neighborhood watch programs reflected the shift toward communities taking collective responsibility for the production of their own safety and security. The scale of these local programs ranged from monitoring a few houses to whole streets and from a particular area to an entire residential suburb. Neighborhood watch initiatives have exemplified the spirit of defensible space, an idea popularized by Oscar Newman in the 1970s as a means of preventing crime.[40] The logistics of social organization has varied from loosely coordinated ad hoc efforts at the grassroots level to tightly integrated networks of overlapping security regimes orchestrated from above.[41]

By definition, neighborhood watch initiatives depend on the cooperation of an alert citizenry. Residents must act as the eyes on the street, mobilized to notice everything out of the ordinary, keeping a lookout for and immediately reporting suspicious behavior and the presence of unwanted strangers.[42] One key element of neighborhood watch programs consists of the organization of nighttime patrols, during which volunteers drive around their own neighborhoods in their own vehicles. In the typical case, those working each shift bring along a kit bag that contains a logbook, pepper spray, and a clipboard. Volunteers look for suspicious vehicles, and they record the registration numbers, the make and model, and any distinguishing marks. In constant cell-phone contact with private security companies and the local SAPS substation, these patrollers amount to a kind of first-line defense in the war on crime. Aided and abetted by public law enforcement agencies, the neighborhood watch mentality often results in discriminatory practices directed at the urban poor and in routine targeting of the most vulnerable.[43]

The principal aim of community policing initiatives has been to create stronger links of trust and mutual respect between distrustful suburban residents and public law enforcement agencies. For example, following the end of apartheid and the transition to parliamentary democracy, state officials introduced Community Policing Forums (CPFs) as mandatory structures attached to each precinct police station. The purpose of the CPFs was to create a platform for joint security projects not only to supplement the efforts of public law enforcement agencies unable to stem the upsurge of crime but also to bridge the gap between public policing agencies and ordinary citizens.[44]

Since the mid-1990s, the proliferation of local community-policing initiatives has transformed the middle-class suburban landscape of Johannesburg.[45] The line between what neighborhood associations are entitled to do and what they should leave to conventional law enforcement agencies has become blurred. The increase in the number of neighborhood watch–type organizations in affluent residential suburbs has been mirrored by the expansion of community- and street-policing structures in depressed neighborhoods and in the townships along with the rapid spread of vigilante groups operating outside the law. Under the guise of democratic (and inclusionary) policing, localized community control has become, in practical terms, an effective mechanism of social exclusion of the poorest of the poor. The seemingly divergent approaches to law enforcement and crime reduction—community participation (soft policing) versus zero tolerance (hard policing)—have reinforced one another. Despite their gestures toward social justice and social inclusion, neighborhood associations in middle-class residential suburbs have typically used the rhetoric of zero tolerance to justify and legitimate exclusionary practices directed against itinerant job seekers, curbside traders, and aimless youth. Even in depressed inner-city neighborhoods (such as Hillbrow, Berea, and Joubert Park) close to the central city, the expanded use of street patrolling has opened up space for informal rough justice and vigilantism. With its neutral-sounding get-tough-on-crime rhetoric, the zero tolerance approach has promoted quick-fix solutions and hence has justified sweeping the poor off the streets. By promoting zero tolerance approaches to crime in the name of public order, municipal policing strategies have paradoxically condoned if not encouraged two extreme forms of social ordering in affluent residential suburbs: (1) legal discrimination through the use of bylaws and restrictive covenants (in gated residential communities, for example) to effectively criminalize poverty by outlawing those activities that the poor rely on for their daily survival; and (2) the use of intimidation, harassment, and even extralegal force and illegitimate violence (vigilantism) to keep unwanted poor people out where they are not wanted.[46]

The Model of Polycentric Policing: Community Security Governance through Partnerships

Although they are governed by different logic and employ different technologies, conventional disciplinary strategies of social control and new modes of spatial management actually complement one another.[47] Municipal authorities have largely embraced the archetype of private entrepreneurialism as the paradigmatic model on which to frame the provision of security services. In the emergent enterprise culture of neoliberalism, the idea of community assumes new meaning as a relational network of active agents, autonomous actors, and self-interested stakeholders who enter into partnership-policing arrangements with law enforcement agencies to ensure their own safety as independent sovereign consumers. As municipalities seek to govern more while spending less, local authorities have adopted strategies that rely on the active engagement of individual citizens in collective vigilance over guarded spaces. In

the neoliberal approach to risk management, mobilized citizens participate in their own self-governance, whether by lending support to community policing initiatives, joining neighborhood watch groups, or voluntarily subjecting themselves to the scrutiny of metal-detector devices,
electronic surveillance, and other kinds of anonymous monitoring.[48]

Initiatives calling for active community participation as partners
against crime involve the deliberate diffusion of responsibility for the delivery of crime control, the reduction of disorder, and the promotion of
safer neighborhoods.[49] Security initiatives that stress local self-governance
extol the virtues of community involvement, popular participation, and
active citizenship. Yet such bland, noncontroversial pronouncements often overlook how community safety initiatives are always and at once
"sites of contradiction, ambiguity and ambivalence."[50]

By definition, building cohesive, safe communities means excluding
those who are regarded as different and those do not conform to acceptable behaviors. Under the rubric of public safety, community policing
initiatives actually create territorial geographies by defining and maintaining "the shifting boundaries between deviance and belonging, order
and disorder."[51] This exercise of territoriality amounts to a kind of spatial policing—or a method of sociospatial control.[52]

The narrative construction of community policing partnerships veers
between two extremes. At one end, in the liberal democratic imagination, security partnerships represent a new mode of popular participation in local governance—one that "gives a voice to pluralism and diversity and restores public faith" in the political order and cements the
consent of the governed.[53] Framed as part of the long-term shift from
public provision of social services to localized self-help initiatives, community safety efforts are often rhetorically linked to the romanticized
"communitarian ambition of replacing fragile, atomized, fearful and
insecure communities" with those sufficiently emboldened and "confident enough to take responsibility for their own safety."[54] Whatever the
name—problem-solving policing, trust policing, relationship-based policing, community policing, or partnership policing—local safety partnerships share the common vision of reducing crime through building
trust and mutual respect. In contrast, dystopian accounts stress punitive deterrence, discriminatory targeting of unwanted others, and criminalization of the poor as inherent features of community policing partnerships. Those who adopt this perspective imagine community safety

initiatives as a collection of largely "repressive, 'revanchist' policing practices aimed at retaking public space" from the undeserving and disrespectful occupiers of space and returning it to the deserving, respectful residents.[55] This particular approach to public safety typically falls under the rubric of order maintenance (or "broken windows") policing and often acquires the code name zero tolerance to distinguish it from soft policing.[56]

The cornerstone of proactive community policing efforts in Johannesburg are the security initiatives attached to neighborhood associations. Because proactive, public-space private security is so exceptionally expensive for less-than-affluent households, some neighborhood associations have tried to devise their own self-protection schemes by cobbling together overlapping initiatives. The neighborhood association called the "I Love Kensington Association" (ILKA), for example, spearheaded a multifaceted security scheme to reduce crime in their suburban neighborhood. As part of its organizational effort, ILKA created a number of bite-sized subcommittees that sponsored their own street-level policing. Some of these street committees hired stationary guards to monitor the public streetscape from sentry boxes. The steady accretion of security measures placed a substantial financial burden on residential homeowners. In addition to paying for stationary guards under the auspices of "street committees" and hiring armed-response units to protect their individual households, residential homeowners—as dues-paying members of the ILKA—were compelled to contribute to the collective costs of contracting with still another private security company to provide protection services for the entire neighborhood, including conducting regular mobile patrols of the public streets.[57]

The ILKA also initiated the Kensington Sector Security Forum (KSSF) as part of the local Community Policing Forum (CPF) that was attached to the Kensington SAPS station. As part of their joint security initiative, KSSF-CPF has sponsored volunteer street patrollers who wear bulletproof vests and carry firearms. ILKA took further steps to take charge of security, creating a household-level database that enabled them to do everything from monitoring elderly persons living alone to keeping informed about abandoned buildings, watching them for unauthorized entry and unauthorized squatting. By working closely with the Johannesburg Municipal Police Department (JMPD), ILKA aggressively pursued bylaw infringements, such as vagrancy, illegal dumping, street begging, and curbside trading. Taken together, these overlapping and intersecting layers of security created a rather byzantine system that was confusing in both organizational terms and financial responsibilities.[58]

In a similar vein, the security initiatives undertaken in the upscale residential suburb of Melville are complex and convoluted. The Melville Residents' Association includes the Melville Security Initiative (MSI), which consists of a board of residents who manage the monthly contributions paid by individual households and, in turn, use these funds to hire private contractors and service providers. Established in 2009, the MSI not only contracted with the proactive public-space security company CSS Tactical (now operated under the umbrella of Beagle Watch) to conduct regular mobile patrols of the suburban streets but also encouraged street committees (consisting of anywhere from twelve to forty households) to hire static security guards to watch for and report suspicious vehicles or unknown persons wandering through the suburban streetscape.[59]

In a separate initiative, the Melville Residents' Association and the SAPS police station in nearby Brixton jointly launched the Community Policing Forum (CPF) for Melville. The Melville Sector Crime Forum (MSCF) functions as the communications channel funneling information, feedback, and advice between the neighborhood association and the local SAPS station. A team that included the SAPS, CSS Tactical (now Beagle Watch), and the MSCF oversaw the initial placement (undertaken by a company called Fibrehoods) of seventy-six CCTV cameras strategically placed at key intersections to monitor vehicular traffic and pedestrian movement throughout the suburban streets. The MSI paid for the installation of about half of the CCTV cameras, while Fibrehoods donated or sponsored the remainder. A company named Red Surveillance monitors the cameras (aided with a state-of-the art License Plate Recognition System linked with the SAPS national database), and Beagle Watch responds to incidents on the ground. This hybrid combination of surveillance technologies, private security patrols, and static guards has produced an elaborate patchwork quilt of protection for residents and patrons of commercial venues alike.[60]

On occasion, anger and resentment about criminality has boiled over into a kind of self-actualized middle-class vigilante action. Following a spate of armed robberies in 2009 in the adjoining Melville Koppies Nature Reserve, the Melville Koppies Volunteer Management Committee

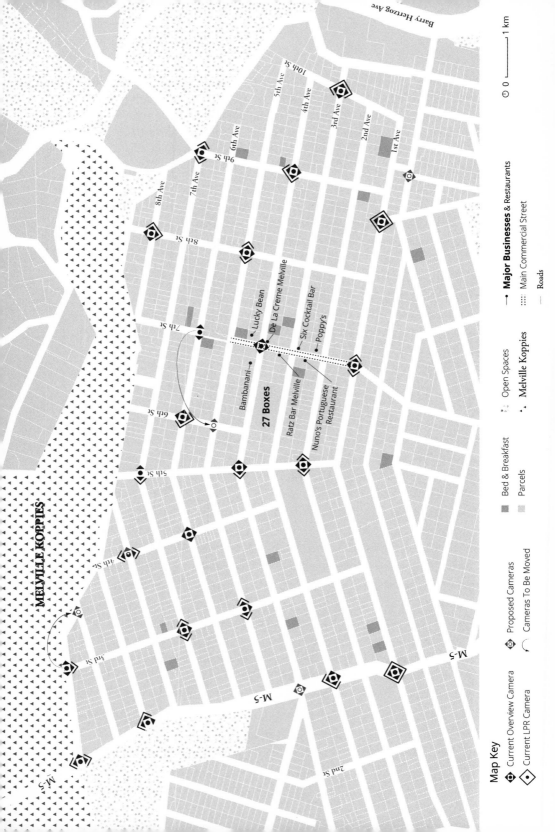

Map Key

Current Overview Camera

Current LPR Camera

Proposed Cameras

Cameras To Be Moved

Bed & Breakfast

Parcels

Open Spaces

Melville Koppies

Major Businesses & Restaurants

Main Commercial Street

Roads

0 ——— 1 km

MELVILLE KOPPIES

Barry Herzog Ave

10th St

5th Ave

4th Ave

3rd Ave

2nd Ave

1st Ave

6th Ave

7th Ave

8th Ave

9th St

8th St

7th St

6th St

5th St

4th St

3rd St

2nd St

M-5

27 Boxes

Bambanani

Lucky Bean

De La Creme Melville

Six Cocktail Bar

Poppy's

Ratz Bar Melville

Nuno's Portuguese Restaurant

and the MSCF organized, on their own initiative, private surveillance teams armed with binoculars to lay in wait for suspected criminals. Eventually, two young men were apprehended with the assistance of a SAPS helicopter. These young men were charged with eighteen counts of aggravated robbery and received prison sentences of forty-five years and thirty-five years.[61]

Sovereign Subjects: Alert Citizens and Engaged Communities

Community policing initiatives have appeared under many different guises: citizen automobile and foot patrols, neighborhood watch groups, training sessions for domestic staff, networked telecommunications and crime alerts (via social media outlets), and advisory councils, local newsletters, crime-prevention publications and presentations, protective escort services for at-risk populations, and volunteer monitors around schools, outdoor parks, playgrounds, and other public places. Because of the widespread popular support of neighborhood associations, volunteer policing has acquired a newly-minted legitimacy virtually overnight. Actively encouraged by public law enforcement agencies and enthusiastically embraced by a responsibilized citizenry, various self-organized policing initiatives are no longer considered to be a kind of extralegal vigilantism. Because these voluntary security activities are largely uncoordinated outside their local contexts, it is difficult to estimate how extensive they have become. But as the provision of security has become a responsibility explicitly shared between conventional public law enforcement agencies and urban residents, volunteer policing has spread throughout the urban landscape.[62]

The strategy of community policing is premised on the belief that conventional public law enforcement agencies lack the capacity to successfully prevent crime without the active and willing participation of urban residents. New strategies of security governance have shifted the burden of law enforcement onto a vigilant citizenry, individuals who are expected to take responsibility for and participate in their own protec-

MAP 5. Placement of Melville security cameras: Phase one and phase two. (Data taken from OpenStreetMap and the chief surveyor-general, Gauteng cadastral.)

tion. This transformation in policing has involved the reorientation of local communities (and particularly suburban neighborhoods) from operating as passive consumers of public police protection to operating as active coproducers of safe and secure environments.[63]

In the language of neoliberal governance, the term *responsibilization* refers to the transformation of collective responsibilities into private duties: individuals and private organizations are "increasingly sanctioned to perform duties that previously fell under the purview" of public authorities. As Jennifer Carlson has argued, those private citizens who more actively and prudentially participate in their own governance "represent a particular kind of 'responsibilized' subject." What she has called the "sovereign subject" signals the emergence of a specific political rationality—one marked by the capacity (and even the desire) of individuals to perform sovereign functions that state agencies have typically monopolized, particularly "the exercise of lethal and legitimate violence," in the name of self-defense.[64] The devolution of the state monopoly over the use of legitimate violence authorizes citizens "to assume responsibility for their own self-protection," which in part consists of voluntary engagement with private groups authorized to provide protection services outside the umbrella of public law enforcement.[65] This recasting of the meaning of citizenship enlists law-abiding citizens as active participants in the pursuit of those "deemed dangerous or deviant" and justifies this enlarged role by reference to "prescriptive norm[s] grounded in the right to security."[66] As Christine Hentschel has suggested, the ubiquitous search for *security* has been transformed into a skill-intensive technique of the self—detached from the greater common good yet placed at the core of *self-actualizing citizenship* practices.[67]

The prevailing master narrative of neoliberal governance suggests that responsibilization is a totalizing, exclusivist, and top-down strategic intervention that creates a hierarchical form of social control by governing at a distance.[68] Set within the legitimizing rhetoric of limited government and the minimal state, the devolution of security functions to "responsible" citizens and their collective agencies has marked the demise of what Les Johnston and Clifford Shearing have called "the professional police hegemony" and the emergence of multilateralized regimes of security governance.[69] This concept of multilateralized security governance means that diverse networks of commercial enterprises, voluntary associations, community groups, individual citizens, state-sponsored regulatory agencies, and public policing agencies are incorporated into multiple security regimes. The kinds of cooperation and team-play that have produced various collaborative partnership arrangements have resulted in complex networks of security assemblages rather than in a single state-policing agency responsible for law enforcement and crime prevention.[70]

In the absence of a formal legal discourse about human rights that includes a basic commitment to freedom of movement, active citizen groups can formulate their own solutions to security provision that mimic an idealized version of public policing. While these proposals for grassroots security interventions are seductive, community policing initiatives run the risk of animating a narrowly conceived NIMBY philosophy, in which an overzealous responsibilized citizenry takes it upon themselves to extend their security zones to the public spaces of residential neighborhoods. Models of community-managed policing can easily mask "deep injustices and violations of [human] rights" on the grounds of maintaining middle-class aesthetic standards. Equally important, the framing of rights through a willingness (and ability) to pay effectively elevates the marketplace bargaining power of neighborhood associations to an exalted place of privilege through the acquisition of special entitlements. Within the rhetoric of neoliberal governance, this willingness-to-pay discourse subsumes the right to the city to the logic of the marketplace. In reverting to a culture of legality, affluent residential associations "are able to use existing laws or frame new laws to their advantage in denying the poor any right" to move freely in their neighborhoods.[71]

The strategic importance of community involvement, popular participation, and active citizenship in the preventative turn in policing cannot be regarded simply as the direct outcome (or by-product) of privatization or market liberalization. Although the clarion call of neoliberal policy initiatives at the end of the twentieth century provided a vital and convenient sociopolitical background, partnership-policing schemes also developed their own distinctive political dynamics and historically specific raison d'être.[72] Acknowledging the multiple ways in which an alert citizenry—through a plethora of voluntary associations and private initiatives—is enlisted into the fight against crime enables one to "resist the temptation to launch an overbearing critique" of security governance rooted in one-sided, simplistic notions of neoliberalism.[73] Local mobilizations around safety and security cannot be attributed simply to the replacement of public policing agencies with private for-profit companies. All sorts of public-private partnerships have developed problem-solving initiatives for localities struggling with high rates of crime. Defining security governance exclusively in terms of neoliberal modes of urban governance signals a kind of abstract reification, which overlooks—in the quest for an underlying essence and an overarching teleology—the complex intersection of space and power. Methods of crime control have become so fragmented and heterogeneous that they defy any singular logic. Policing thus consists of a wide array of institutional mechanisms for managing crime and disorder, involving private agents and public agencies in various relations and interconnections with each other. The relationships between public administration, market competition, and voluntary initiatives are complex, involving a great deal of overlap, conflict, and confusion.[74]

In strictly neoclassical economic terms, the conventional analysis of private security rests on the assumption that "the trade in protective goods and services can and should be understood using the standard economic view of markets." Seen in this light, "markets for security commodities are a space of free and voluntary exchange that allocates good and services efficiently" in accordance with individual preferences and ability to pay. Yet, strictly speaking, the buying and selling of security services does not conform to the expectations of an unencumbered free market and rational economic calculation but instead spills over into the realm of sentiment and belief. A plethora of "inconvenient facts . . . shape and constrain the kinds of security purchases individuals and organizations are willing to make, and how they think and feel about the sale of various protective products."[75] The distribution of private security services is not solely the outcome of personal preference and consensual exchange between buyer and seller. Private security services fall into that murky terrain of what Margaret Jane Radin has called "contested commodities," namely, those goods for which "the place and limits of market exchange in their production and distribution" are subject to dispute.[76] Dispositions, structures of feeling, fear and anxiety, and personal values influence market-supplied kinds of protection services. Put in analytic terms, the straightforward assimilation (or reduction) of private security service provision in "a typical market exchange where a solvent buyer meets an enterprising seller does not reflect the more complex nature" of the relationship. There is an element of moral economy to hiring private policing that sometimes gets lost in the haste to reduce transactional exchange to the narrow framework of neoliberal privatization of security services.[77]

In Johannesburg, neighborhood associations purchase private security services as club goods, that is, as bulk commodities for collective consumption. The free-rider problem—in which individual households steadfastly refuse to pay their share of the collective expense—clouds, and hence undermines, idealized understanding of free-market exchange. Further, the market exchange of protective services does not follow from full disclosure of factually accurate information about crime and danger but from structures of feeling, belief, and fear. Private security companies collect data about crime rates and patterns and then disclose the information only in small doses in order to enhance their share in the marketplace for private security services. What motivates individual homeowners and neighborhood associations to purchase private security services is the uneasy paranoia that accompanies the fear of becoming a victim of crime. In a world in which useful information about criminal patterns is hoarded and concealed, private security companies prey on this pervasive sense of personal risk and danger. It is thus not possible to reduce the buying and selling of private security services merely to "instrumental calculation of how resources can most efficiently be deployed to [reduce risk and] ensure protection." Security markets are not simply "places to which individuals and organizations are free to turn to satisfy their demands for protection." Seen from another angle of vision, the buying and selling of protection services are "morally charged and contested practices of governance" that shape conduct, producing ways of seeing and experiencing the social world. Commodified security services thus constitute a form of private power whose "scale, distribution," and social practices contribute to the reproduction of social relations and social inequalities.[78]

Neighborhood associations have increasingly played a more proactive role in managing risk, using the leverage of marketplace competition to, on the one hand, demand expanded services from their publicspace security providers and to, on the other hand, pressure nonpaying residents to contribute to collectively consumed security services. Many neighborhood associations have sought to transform themselves into professional organizations that resemble business enterprises. Following the lead of the Parkhurst Residents and Business Owners Association

(PRABOA), the Craigpark Residents' Association (CRA), which serves the residents of Craighall, Craighall Park, and Dunkeld West, partnered with a private company (Dimension Data) to offer a scheme that would provide considerably faster fiber-optic internet service—with cable television, video on demand, and telephone options—for its 2,500 households. Through its partnership with the private security company CSS Tactical, CRA directly linked this fibre-to-the-home (FTTH) scheme to its neighborhood security initiative. By strategically placing high-definition closed circuit television (CCTV) surveillance cameras at entry and exit roads as well as at intersections and traffic circles throughout Craighall and Craighall Park, CSS Tactical was able to monitor suspicious activities and to tap into the national vehicle identification database (ENAT) in real time. In exchange for its efforts to enlist more members in the FTTH program, CRA garnered 25 percent of the profits.[79]

Domestic Servants: The New Foot Soldiers in the War on Crime

In dozens of suburban neighborhoods as widely dispersed as Parktown North, Parkview, Parkhurst, Dunkeld West, Hurlingham, Greenside, and Emmarentia, affluent property owners have turned to new tactics that involve their paid employees in the fight against crime. At the urging of local neighborhood associations, frightened homeowners have enrolled their domestic workers (gardeners, child-minders, and house cleaners) in extensive crime-prevention training programs and self-defense courses sponsored by local police stations or by organizations such as Domestic Workers Watch.[80] Under the supervision of public policing agencies, domestic workers are trained to be the eyes and ears of suburban neighborhoods, an informal army mobilized to protect their "Madams and Masters." In marshaling household staff to protect the property of their employers, neighborhood associations and public policing agencies have jointly organized monthly meetings to train household employees not to trust strangers walking in the street or knocking at the door, whether they are well-heeled salespersons or street beggars.[81] These meetings include not only instructions on how to identify potential criminals and how domestic workers should react when they observe a crime in progress but also lessons in "fighting off attackers with rolled-up magazines, broomsticks, chairs, and even keys." After completion of this basic training course, these "no-nonsense nannies"—as one enthusiastic observer put it—are enlisted in neighborhood crime-prevention efforts, serving as unofficial "look-outs," or the "extra eyes and ears of the police service."[82]

The program called Domestic Workers Watch has exemplified the kind of bottom-up monitoring that Mark Andrejevic has labeled "lateral surveillance," or what might be deemed insider, horizontal vigilance of familiar surroundings. Whereas the all-seeing gaze of the Panopticon is rooted in a hierarchical, top-down form of centralized monitoring, lateral surveillance amounts to a bottom-up strategy that engages responsible citizens in a do-it-yourself monitoring of what is within range of their gaze.[83] Rather than simply displacing top-down forms of outside monitoring, these horizontal practices "emulate and amplify" other kinds of surveillance, "fostering the internalization" and individuation of regimes of security governance and their deployment into the private realm. Lateral surveillance provides a means for offloading some of the responsibilities of security management onto neighborhood residents themselves. This do-it-yourself monitoring amounts to a kind of shadow-state security apparatus.[84]

"Community is not simply the territory within which crime is to be controlled," Nikolas Rose has argued. "It is itself a means of [security governance]."[85] In a postliberal age in which every unknown person who ventures into neighborhood territory is considered a potential criminal suspect, homeowners and their domestic staff are encouraged "to become spies." Cooperative efforts in not only tracking out-of-the-ordinary activities but also gathering routine information are key components of neighborhood watch initiatives. By enlisting household staff to monitor suspicious activities at the microscale of the street, Domestic Workers Watch amounts to an invitation to paid employees to actively participate in lateral surveillance in the name of neighborhood security.[86]

Leaders of neighborhood associations and private security companies have provided plenty of anecdotal evidence to suggest that thieves seeking to gain entry into homes often impersonate employees from legitimate private companies or municipal agencies, claiming to have come in order to repair, service, or install something. There are instances in which burglars dressed as public police officers were able to gain entry into solidly locked homes.[87] On the other side of the equation, private security companies have repeatedly warned that domestic workers are a potentially weak link in crime prevention. After an unexplained house break-in occurs, private security companies insist that their clients enable them to subject their domestic workers to a polygraph test in order to detect "inside involvement." Managers of private security companies have argued vehemently that a large percentage of home invasions take place because criminal gangs make use of information that domestic staff—whether inadvertently or deliberately—divulge about the type of security systems in use and where valuables are stored.[88] There is plenty of circumstantial evidence to suggest that ambulant spotters working for criminal gangs mark targets—piles of rocks, assembled soda cans, sticks implanted in the ground, and so on—to identify private homes with compromised security systems.[89] Both private security operatives and volunteers associated with neighborhood security initiatives have insisted that informal car guards who operate outside restaurants and commercial shops at night are notoriously unreliable characters, sometimes working hand in glove with thieves who break into parked vehicles.[90]

The Downside of Community Policing Initiatives

The mobilization of such local organizations of self-governance as neighborhood watch groups to perform tasks once the privileged preserve of public law enforcement is tantamount to building what amount to parallel shadow-state institutions.[91] The security initiatives that neighborhood associations have undertaken exemplify the devolution of municipal authority in the conjoined realms of law enforcement and crime prevention. These undertakings presume that communities and responsible citizens are both willing and able to engage in local self-governance. To a considerable extent, the success of community policing and security initiatives rests on the self-sacrifice, dedication, and enthusiasm of volunteers and individual coordinators. Put broadly, advocates for community policing suggest that if localized security initiatives are successful, then "neighborhoods are more cohesive, in better control of their internal dynamics," and better able to mobilize the assistance of public policing agencies.[92] As an abstract ideal, the vision of community policing rests on the somewhat shaky assumption that participants can be transformed from a disconnected collection of self-serving, atomized individuals into "a public-spirited collectivity, capable of acting together in the common interest."[93]

At the end of the day, neighborhood associations amount to loose and sometimes fragile confederations of homeowners united by their feelings of vulnerability and their desire for security in the face of their heightened anxieties about crime. Volunteer policing schemes have unfolded unevenly across the residential landscape of Johannesburg, and the free-rider problem is an ongoing source of tension and resentment that undermines the spirit of community self-governance.[94] While some individuals who manage security initiatives for neighborhood associations receive modest financial compensation for their time-consuming efforts, most participants are unpaid volunteers whose self-sacrifice has contributed to keeping these projects afloat.[95] The percentages vary considerably, but often less than half the households in a residential neighborhood voluntarily contribute funds to pay for the collective protection services of private security companies. Self-sacrificing participants in voluntary security initiatives often become frustrated with what they regard as the indifference and free-riding of others. This resentment easily turns into withdrawal and inactivity.[96]

The Microphysics of Power: Vigilantism and Exclusionary Practices at the Local Level

> It is not that we do not feel for homeless people. We are prepared to help. But this [nearby] veld also poses a security threat to businesses and it appears that criminals come from the area.
> —Jeremy Hinds, anxious resident of suburban Kelvin[97]

The urban landscape of Johannesburg consists of a complex array of property regimes, particularly such post-public spaces as enclosed shopping malls, mixed-use private commercial developments masquerading as community villages, and pseudopublic spaces where owners and managers highly supervise access, appropriate dress, and acceptable behavior. In many respects, these regulated and sanitized places have replaced the ideal imaginary of public parks and village high streets as sites for social congregation and chance encounter. These post-public spaces sit incongruously with abandoned and disowned places that are often put to adaptive reuse by desperate people in search of shelter. These in-between places include parks, playgrounds, hillsides, drainpipes, and linear corridors along streams and rail lines. Many of these out-of-the-way locations have become contested sites, pitting affluent residential homeowners against homeless squatters, informal traders, and runaway street kids.[98]

The shift toward pluralized modes of security governance has gone hand in hand with the devolution of policing authority to neighborhood associations. New community-based policing strategies have incorporated neighborhood associations and responsibilized citizens into security governance. At first glance, the encouragement of local communities to participate in the production of their own security seems to suggest a kind of democratic empowerment and participatory governance. Yet entrusting local communities with organizing their own self-protection has a darker side. Questions of complicity and moral responsibility are indeed complex. The caring rhetoric of looking out for the survivalist needs of the urban poor can paradoxically become part of a general effort to normalize banishment and displacement.[99]

New community-based policing strategies that target homeless squatters, idle loiterers, and other urban outcasts typically emphasize spatial dispersal of potential troublemakers to other areas rather than simply seeking to arrest and prosecute lawbreakers. Under circumstances in which the criminal justice system functions only haphazardly and criminality seems to be somewhat immune to conventional law enforcement, popular endorsement of and support for constitutionally guaranteed protections and safeguards of legal rights have lost much of their appeal. Various kinds of impromptu street justice fill the void, where extralegal vigilantism becomes a substitute for the rule of law.[100] Small black-owned companies such as Mapogo a Mathamaga, for example, have only a tenuous grip on market share for providing security services in the residential suburbs. But by promising "to fight crime the African way," they have developed a reputation for no-nonsense policing, largely in the poorer peri-urban communities surrounding Johannesburg. In their advertising appeal, Mapogo a Mathamaga claims that "people who are found in possession of our customer's goods do not have the luxury of long-lasting court cases and being found innocent on a technical point. They will immediately be dealt with in a traditional way." In suggesting the use of force and violence against homeless people, Mapogo a Mathamaga asserts that "vagrant removal is done in the normal African manner."[101]

Stories of concerned citizens residing in affluent suburban neighborhoods who have mobilized to clear in-between spaces of unwanted

FIGURE 15. MAPOGO A MATHAMAGA poster. (Photo by author.)

squatters, homeless people, or informal traders could be repeated almost endlessly. A few examples should suffice. These instances offer a concrete picture of the kinds of "invisible violence" to which the urban poor are regularly subjected. According to Nancy Scheper-Hughes, these kinds of "structural violence" refer "to the ease with which humans are capable of reducing the socially vulnerable . . . into expendable non-persons." Deemed necessary for the maintenance of social order and respectable propriety, this structural violence is linked with "the invisible 'social machinery' of inequality and oppression that reproduces social relations of exclusion and marginalization via ideologies, stigmas, and dangerous discourses."[102] These "pathologies of power"—to borrow a phrase from Paul Farmer—"produce paralysis and powerlessness among vulnerable [people] who are forced into complicity with the very social forces that are poised, whether intentional or not," to banish them from where they are not wanted.[103]

By August 2000, anxious middle-class residents of Kelvin, a posh suburban section of Sandton, had reached their collective limit with what they perceived as the homeless problem. Kelvin, which was one of the first residential tract developments to acquire official permission to close off roads, is an enclosed suburban redoubt, patrolled by twenty-four-

FIGURE 16. Sign warning about guard dogs at the ready. (Photo by author.)

hour security, where individual houses are linked by electronic panic buttons to a central command. A spate of armed robberies at a shopping center located at the entrance to Kelvin triggered a moral panic about safety and security. Residents targeted homeless squatters who had built shacks on vacant land near the entrance to the suburban neighborhood, identifying them as the source of their fears and blaming them (without evidence) for the robberies. Residents claimed that the informal settlement constituted a health hazard because squatters used the site as an illegal dumping ground for refuse, as an open toilet, and as an unauthorized shebeen (liquor outlet) from which itinerant traders sold alcohol out of their cars. They further contended that homeless people built their shelters in the underbrush, cut down trees to make fires at night, and discarded trash everywhere. Fearing that the informal encampment devalued their properties, irate homeowners insisted that the Sandton town council cede jurisdiction over the vacant land to them so that they could clean it, fence it, and expel the homeless.[104]

In the gentrifying neighborhood of Parkhurst, Verity Park is a popular meeting area for local residents. Half a city block in size, the park itself forms part of the greater recreation center that consists of tennis courts, a *pétanque* piste, a community clinic, a swimming pool, a library, and a recreation hall. In 2007, local residents formed a community organization to solicit voluntary contributions to pay for the maintenance of the park. Not all residents contributed, but everyone was welcome to use the park. The routines of social interaction and chance encounter at the park helped to create a sense of local community.

The presence of homeless people in Verity Park provoked a strong reaction among some local residents. In 2012, the neighborhood association pressured the local city councillor to call on law enforcement agencies to respond to what residents considered a nuisance. In a joint operation, the SAPS and a private security company arrested eleven people. According to the eyewitness report of an academic researcher, some of the local residents who frequently used the park were very vocal in their disapproval of the homeless people. After the forcible removal of the homeless from the park, residents made no mention of them. "Not one person that I spoke to referred to the police raid or the arrests," René Hoenderdos proclaimed. "It was almost as if the homeless people did not exist and that the whole incident never occurred."[105]

Urban Informatics and the Engaged Citizenry

The widespread use of information and communications technologies has fundamentally altered how ordinary middle-class residents have learned to manage their own security. Expanded capacities for information processing have become embedded in the urban physical environment. As Mike Crang and Stephen Graham have argued, "The informational landscape is both a repository of data and also increasingly communicates and processes information." Strategically placed sensors, transponders, and processors are able to activate devices in ways that have altered how urban residents view security. The ambient intelligence built into sensing machines has reshaped the surrounding environment, transforming it into an active agent that has a part in organizing daily lives and is no longer just a passive backdrop.[106]

The increasing ubiquity of digital technologies, internet services, and social media in the everyday lives of ordinary middle-class residents has allowed for a seamless transition from the visible and to the invisible infrastructures of security.[107] Road closures, enclosed building typologies, high walls, and security gates constitute the material embodiments of visible security (so-called target hardening). In contrast, surreptitious

CCTV monitoring, remote sensing, and interpersonal networks via cell phones and SMS texting constitute a largely unnoticed and invisible shield of protection. For example, a popular cell-phone app enables users to monitor movements of suspected criminals or suspicious persons. Linked with a live channel, the mobile app works like a two-way radio. Anyone can download the app and register. In order to ensure that criminals cannot infiltrate the network, users cannot achieve trusted status until they pass a background check. Volunteers staff the sponsored control room, responding to emergency distress calls.[108] Taken as a whole, these information and communication technologies have created an entirely novel environment that has fundamentally altered the terrain within which risk management takes place.[109]

Exclusionary Effects of Privatizing Space

Existential uncertainty—or what Zygmut Bauman has called "liquid fear"—consists of the "diffuse, scattered, unclear, unattached, unanchored, free-floating" anxieties that have "no address" and "supersede rationality in influencing human action."[1] In Johannesburg, fear has become a way of life. By animating suspicion, it produces wariness of strangers and erodes social trust. Fear thrives on ambiguity and the unknown. It undermines social mixing and destabilizes possibilities for a genuine public culture. Fear has mutated into a kind of permanent state of emergency that ordinary urban residents in Johannesburg (largely unconsciously) accept as normal and habitual—a naturalized condition governing the routines of everyday life. The "constant state of alertness," or "low-intensity panic," as Linda Green has suggested elsewhere and in another context, "remains in the shadow of waking consciousness."[2]

Fear of the unknown and the unexpected induces ordinary urban residents to take seemingly extraordinary steps in order to minimize risk. In seeking to offset perceived threats to personal safety, urban residents have retreated into the capsular world of enclave spaces.[3] The accoutrements of security are blended into the physical fabric of everyday life. Concrete manifestations of societal fears are everywhere, with the ubiquitous presence of security cameras, private police patrols, ominous signs promising armed response, electric fencing, high walls, and security gates.

The pervasive atmosphere of existential uncertainty has created a vacuum in which fear and suspicion are able to thrive and metastasize. The very malleability of the discursive significations enables collective fear to retain its grip over frightened urban residents. The fixation on insecurity and danger has given rise to what Lars Svendson has referred to as "a way of looking at the world," or a pervasive culture that has insinuated itself in everyday life.[4] Ambiguity and apprehension are precisely what allow large-scale fears to appear as collective representations. The power of risk and danger is what gives rumors and gossip their credibility.

The urban landscape is saturated with images of fear and foreboding, creating a kind of permanent unease and disorientation. As a kind of free-floating signifier, fear is a powerful discursive force that influences the ways in which suburban residents retrofit their private homes into fortified safe houses, relate to all unknown persons as inherently suspicious, and gingerly navigate the in-between spaces between one enclosed enclave and another.[5]

Uncertainty is the driving force behind the success of the fear industries—that is, those business enterprises wishing to market and sell protection services as a way of managing risk. Seeking to profit from a heightened sense of threat and danger, the fear industries not only play on existing anxieties but create new ones that did not exist before. Promising to minimize risk and reduce threats, private companies competing for market share parade security services and products before anxious consumers, hoping to profit from expanding sales of the latest gadgetry or supposedly fail-safe electronic devices. By engaging in an orchestrated charade in which they offer antidotes to fear and panaceas for uncertainty, the fear industries create their own demand. As objects of wish fulfillment, security solutions become both intelligible, by possessing a kind of "naturalized authority" that seems to speak for itself, and compelling, "the stuff of fantasy and desire."[6]

In the end, the first casualties of this pervasive culture of fear are genuine tolerance of difference and openness to chance encounters. Fear of the unknown Other goes hand in hand with racial profiling. Race becomes a visible marker—a signaling device indicating a putative essence that takes on a life of its own as a register of both white privilege and black disadvantage.[7] The constant sense of foreboding and danger have become inscribed in the collective imagination of ordinary urban residents, where unemployed and marginally employed black men become objects of fear. Safe and secure environments remain elusive and transitory.[8]

Unmaking State Security Apparatuses

Born out of turbulent times that culminated in a negotiated settlement to end white minority rule, the new South Africa has lived a complicated double life: at once a liberal parliamentary democracy and, at the same time, a fragile social order characterized by profound socioeconomic inequalities, criminal violence, and lawlessness. The movement toward democratic consolidation ushered in with the historic April 2014 elections was not accompanied by diminishing violence and disorder but by their displacement and dispersal. Under white minority rule, violence and coercion revolved around challenging or defending state power. In recent decades, the terrain of lawlessness has become more diffuse and decentralized, where criminality, insecurity, and disorder have spread unevenly over the social landscape. The great strides taken toward the entrenchment of parliamentary democracy have yielded an inclusionary multiparty (electoral) system grounded in the rule of law. Yet the ineffectiveness in curbing criminal violence, the widespread allegations of police corruption, and the sometimes arbitrary and indiscriminate use of lethal force has undermined the legitimacy of state law enforcement agencies and the criminal justice system. State-sanctioned violence, the militarization of public security, extralegal policing, criminality, lawlessness, and vigilantism "have all posed serious threats" to the legitimacy of the democratic order "and the rule of law."[9]

In the new South Africa, the disjuncture between the miracle narrative of liberal democracy (with its free and fair elections, discourses of constitutional rights, and flourishing civil society) and the grounded realities of entrenched inequalities, persistent poverty, and limited opportunities for upward mobility amounts to a paradox.[10] What is perhaps ironic is that in South Africa, where democratic institutions are robust and individual rights are enshrined in constitutional guarantees, popular trust in the effectiveness of public law enforcement and crime prevention has failed to live up to expectations. The persistence of pervasive criminal violence and lawlessness have both produced and reinforced deep-seated feelings of insecurity that cut across race and class lines.

In Johannesburg, the social worlds of criminal violence, lawlessness, and disorder cannot be disconnected from the draconian policing tactics designed to combat them. Paradoxically, the liberal values enshrined in the constitutional order have disappeared amid the illiberal policing practices on the ground. In a real way, violence begets violence, triggering an escalating spiral of disorder that amounts to a permanent state of insecurity. This security crisis cannot be detached from enduring inequalities that are so blatantly visible in the social construction of the life-worlds inhabited by the affluent and in those social circumstances under which the urban poor are condemned to marginality. The dark, shadowy side of parliamentary democracy, constitutionalism, and the rule of law is that the maintenance of social order does not simply represent a benign activity (as liberal democratic theory would have it) in which law enforcement and the criminal justice system are exclusively directed at protecting a rights-bearing, law-abiding "citizenry from the threat of criminal disorder."[11] Taken together, public law enforcement and private security operate not just to prevent crime but to protect private property and, more broadly, to uphold the structural inequalities embedded in everyday life.[12]

Hybrid Security Governance and the Limits of State Sovereignty

The unbundling of security governance practices has fundamentally altered the policing division of labor. The private provision of security services has steadily encroached on the terrain once occupied exclusively by public law enforcement agencies. The retreat of public policing from law enforcement and crime prevention has resulted in a kind of shared sovereignty over territory. In providing protection services aimed at guarding and monitoring mass private property (such as gated residential communities, residential neighborhoods, city improvement districts, enclosed shopping malls, and themed entertainment zones), private security companies have come to operate as a kind of de facto state security apparatus. The emergence of hybrid modes of security governance has meant that public law enforcement agencies hold only irregular sway over the territories under their nominal jurisdiction and have lost their grip on the functions they once held almost exclusively.[13]

Yet despite the turn toward the privatization of security services, public policing agencies have maintained a functional bureaucratic administrative apparatus, an effective legal system, and a clear monopoly over the legitimate use of violence in some fields of law enforcement and criminal justice. But the strong functional presence of public policing agencies in the state-sanctioned maintenance of law and order has become blurred at the edges, where the legitimate use of coercive force all too often gives way to the arbitrary exercise of extralegal violence. There are fields of operation in which public policing agencies have maintained a significant degree of territorial penetration but a lesser degree of logistical presence, with little or no legitimacy. The routine deployment of public policing agencies to clear downtown streets of unauthorized street vendors, to evict unauthorized squatters from derelict buildings, to put down popular protests organized around poor service delivery, and to disperse frequent demonstrations in poor urban slums and neighborhoods provides ample evidence of the organizational capacity of public policing agencies to bring force to bear in the maintenance of law and order. [14] Yet it is here where the outward display of physical force is matched by the virtual absence of legitimacy. What these strategic interventions represent are not so much the expression of Weberian kinds of all-seeing, panopticon control and regulation but rather a "qualitatively different kind of state governmentality," one rooted in the capacity "to repeatedly precipitate localized 'states of exception'" through massive displays of physical force and violence that "symbolically demonstrate the arbitrary power" of the public policing agencies. Put in another way, the establishment of these states of exception through periodic raids and occasional patrols has become the principle mode of governance through which public policing agencies assert their sovereignty over territory. Rather than seeking to establish (in the Weberian mold) an exclusive monopoly over the legitimate use of force and violence, public policing agencies work in an operational field of fragmented, partial sovereignties in which the arbitrary use of routinized extralegal force has become a substitute for the quest for legitimacy.[15]

Epilogue

Into the Night
Co-authored with Alex Wafer

Ethnographic fieldwork is a distinctive mode of inquiry that privileges firsthand experience by offering a way to penetrate realms of everyday life that are not easily discernible using the formal procedural rules of measurement and classification favored by positivist-oriented social science disciplines.[1] As such, ethnography is a particular approach to knowledge production that provides the kind of up-close-and-personal vantage point from which to observe social practices and relationships that often unsettle conventional ways of knowing.[2] With its attention to the experience of the everyday, ethnography offers a particularly useful perspective from which to probe the ordinary, the mundane, and the quotidian. And in so doing, it provides a valuable way of knowing the city.[3]

As a general rule, ethnographic fieldwork entails rigorous preparation and careful attention to detail in the conduct of research. At the same time, it allows for serendipitous happenstance and accidental discoveries that are often overlooked in large-scale generalizations. Serendipity is a key element in the discovery of the often invisible (and often secret) life-worlds of the city. Stumbling onto unexpected connections and patterns enables us to challenge and overturn conventional understandings of social processes, thereby opening up new ways of knowing. It is often these "inconvenient facts" that compel us to explore alternative explanations that deviate from what we might have expected to find.[4]

"Traveling ethnography" is a genre of fieldwork that brings together multisited observations of ordinary people in their everyday (natural) settings. When conducting what Margarethe Kusenbach has referred to as "go-alongs," field-workers accompany individual informants on their everyday excursions. As an approach that goes far beyond conventional in-situ observation techniques and interviewing practices, go-alongs provide certain advantages when it comes to uncovering the role of place in everyday lived experience.[5] What sets the go-along as a qualitative research technique apart from such conventional ethnographic approaches as participant observation and interviewing of key informants "is its potential to access some of the transcendent and reflexive aspects of lived experience" as they come into being in their actual situations. Observing people in their natural settings enables us to observe events as they actually take place and relationships as they actually exist on the ground.[6]

Partnership Policing

The Community Policing Forums (CPFs) in the Johannesburg inner city began because of legislation enacted in 1995. In the first decade after the transition to parliamentary democracy, the South African Police Service (SAPS) experimented with new approaches to sector policing and problem-oriented policing methods designed to improve police conduct and institute professionalism in the conduct of its duties. These experiments with local bottom-up involvement in policing represented an effort to rebuild community trust in public law enforcement agencies that had long been associated with state-sponsored repression and violence before the transition to parliamentary democracy. The establishment of CPFs attached to SAPS substations marked the start of active partnerships between public policing agencies and local communities. Despite the 1995 legislation, the CPFs did not really get off the ground until around 2006.[7]

Traveling on several occasions with volunteer members of the CPFs on nighttime patrols in the high-crime inner-city precincts of Hillbrow, Berea, and Joubert Park offers a particularly advantageous lens through which to observe partnership policing and the labyrinthine operations of the parallel shadow state.[8] The institutional support that public policing agencies have transferred to CPFs has empowered these voluntary associations to claim legitimacy and to act with a great deal of self-declared authority. Volunteer members of CPFs frequently refer to themselves as police auxiliaries, emboldened to search people at random, to intimidate, and to arrest with impunity. And yet like conventional public policing agencies, their capacities to maintain law and order are partial, relying on moments of collective display of force rather than on real infrastructures of logistical and social support.

Above all else, the formation of CPFs represents the establishment of new technologies for governing at a distance—in which public policing agencies rely on surrogate forces to engage in law-and-order activities at their behest, while they retreat into the background. This mode of indirect governance enables public policing agencies to not only claim they are working through partnerships with local communities but also distance themselves from the sometimes extralegal practices that such forms of surrogate policing imply.

Despite popular perceptions that the inner-city neighborhoods lack a public security presence, they are saturated with policing agencies. At any given moment, the Hillbrow SAPS deploys about five hundred members and reservists outfitted with over a hundred vehicles to carry out their duties across its fifteen-square-kilometer precinct. The SAPS disproportionately concentrates its resources in the zones where the CPF street patrollers operate, that is, the main public spaces. These SAPS officers are complemented by hundreds of Johannesburg Municipal Police Department (JMPD) officers, a variety of private security teams engaged in many different operations, stationary sentries watching particularly buildings, and assorted numbers of informal car guards. Taken together, this assemblage of security personnel engaged in all sorts of activities that combined "to create a dense, multilayered, and highly visible policing presence."[9]

What distinguishes the volunteers from the CPF is that they are the only security group that patrols on foot, concentrating on such public spaces as streets and sidewalks, parks, markets, and the in-between places separating buildings. Despite its noticeable disadvantages, patrolling on foot offers more opportunities for generating large numbers of arrests. An ambulatory group has more ways of cornering suspected criminals than do police officers operating from vehicles and is better equipped to chase down potential lawbreakers in high-rise, high-density neighborhoods, such as Hillbrow, Berea, and Joubert Park. The effectiveness of this strategy, in part, centers on the fact that the street patrollers are civilians and not members of the public police force. Unlike the public police, the street patrollers can blend into their surroundings, using the element of surprise to apprehend suspected criminals. Because they are not beholden to hierarchical police decision-making and rules of engagement, they are able to patrol the hot spots that the public police assiduously avoid. Yet perhaps most importantly, residents of the inner city tend to categorically reject the legitimacy of the public police, seeing them as an occupying force that indiscriminately uses coercion and violence and is prone to corruption and favoritism. Hence, inner-city dwellers support the CPF volunteers as members of the community.

Public policing agencies work hand in glove with local CPFs. SAPS officers and CPF leaders look on various kinds of private security as alternative sources of stability outside of public policing agencies, even though private companies such as the infamous Bad Boyz have a reputation for heavy-handed tactics. The CPF leadership has identified small-business owners, managers of securitized apartment blocks, and private security companies as the main sources of stability and order in neighborhoods where overcrowding, unauthorized squatting, and crime are rampant. The main goal of CPF patrols is to demonstrate a visible presence on the streets, to indicate that community members care about safety, and to establish rapport with local business owners.

Life-Worlds of the Urban Poor

Outside observers typically characterize the Johannesburg inner city in such homogenizing terms as dangerous and crime-ridden. They refer to these gritty neighborhoods as notorious no-go areas, in which residents are seen almost exclusively through the dystopian lens of desperate poverty. The inner city is indeed largely a place of precarious living, in which desperation and high levels of unemployment are facts of everyday life. But what these broad generalizations miss is the degree of unevenness in these neighborhoods, where exploitation coexists with cooperation and pockets of tranquility are interspersed with high-crime zones. Property investors have purchased dilapidated buildings, neglected and abandoned by their rightful owners, and transformed them into securitized rent factories. Small shopkeepers vigilantly guard their wares, selling to a clientele in need of household goods. All sorts of informal businesses have produced functioning markets that exist outside of state regulation and control.[10] Informality provides a means of income generation for tens of thousands of the urban poor.[11]

Even after night falls, street life is vibrant, active, and buzzing. Residents of the inner city consist of diverse groups of individuals: foreign immigrants, job seekers wanting accommodation closer to places of work, young mothers, itinerant youth, street hawkers, runaway children, casual laborers, and car guards. Informal street traders at fixed market stalls sell everything from fruit and vegetables to shoes and clothing.

Small storefront shops—sometimes owned and managed by Pakistani, Somali, or Ethiopian clerks—specialize in inexpensive household items. Loud music blasts from bars and nightclubs, where bouncers with metal pipes guard the doors, surveilling the clientele. Many of these places double as low-level sites of prostitution and drug-dealing. The frequency of unauthorized squatting and the lack of formal tenancy contracts create a sense of impermanence and fluidity, although many of the people with whom we talked had lived in the inner-city neighborhoods for a decade or more.[12]

As a general rule, community safety initiatives straddle the blurry fault lines between state-authorized crime control measures within the boundaries of the law and extralegal informal practices that sometimes resemble vigilantism. Governance of crime involves a combination of fear and vigilance, on the one hand, and determination and expectation, on the other. Wary residents must always be watchful, expecting the unexpected. Small shopkeepers are especially vulnerable, because shoplifting and petty theft are commonplace. Those caught trying to steal are dealt with on the spot: thieves are beaten almost without mercy. On occasion, CPF volunteers play the role of mediators and protectors, preventing the victims of crime from exacting a kind of rough justice disproportionate to the offense.

Playing at Policing: The Performance of Security

We arrived early at the Hillbrow Police Station (located on Esilen Road, at the western edge of the inner city) on a Friday, just as afternoon was turning into evening. We lingered in the parking lot, waiting to meet our contact person. The shift was changing, and the place was abuzz with activity. We mingled with small groups of people clustered near the entrance to the building, with police officers rushing out of the building on their way home, and with those sauntering into the station, getting ready for the night's work. Residents of nearby buildings wandered past, seemingly oblivious to what was happening. Tall apartment towers cast ever-longer geometric shadows across the bustling streets. The energy was palpable.

Once a reluctantly handsome midcentury concrete pavilion, the Hillbrow Police Station seems to have lost its battle with time. Once a despised symbol of the apartheid system, the building has yet to ac-

quire a new meaning. Effaced by decades of brutalist utilitarian additions and more recently erected fortifications around the entire perimeter, the sprawling complex offers a kind of unremarkable shabbiness that
matches the drabness of the surrounding streetscape at the heart of the
inner city.[13]

After a long wait, we were greeted by Moses Molefe (not his real
name), the leader of the CPF, who was expecting us. He explained that he
had organized CPF patrols of the inner city every Thursday, Friday, and
Saturday night for at least the past ten years. As the late afternoon shadows gradually enveloped the streets in darkness, the last small groups of
people milling around seemed, as though by some inexorable osmosis,
to congeal into one. A team of about fifteen CPF volunteers had formed.
Even though we were outsiders and observers, we never felt unwelcome.
Maybe we provided witness to the selfless dedication and bravery of this
little band of volunteers, who genuinely believe they make a difference
in protecting ordinary people going about their nightly routines. Maybe
we were just a curious distraction at the end of a long week.

After chatting with Moses for a few minutes, we followed the small
group as it filed casually but purposefully into the police station precinct
with a clear sense of reverence. After moving across an old gracious ter-
razzo atrium at the entryway, down a dimly lit corridor, and through a
small, innocuous doorway, we stepped into a cavernous room that was
double-volume in height, perhaps sixty feet in length, and forty feet in
width. Flattened out by bright florescent lights, the room smelled of
the stale air. The only furniture in the obviously disused room was an
old wooden desk surrounded by several dilapidated office chairs in a far
corner. The SAPS precinct commander allowed the CPF volunteers, almost as an afterthought, to use the community hall as a gathering place.
Members of the CPF trickled into the room, arriving one or two at a
time. After about a half hour, around twenty-five people had gathered,
including Moses, a single plainclothes police officer, around ten women,
and a mixed group of men ranging in age from early twenties to mid-
fifties. Suddenly, as if out of nowhere, a SAPS captain appeared, the senior police officer in charge of coordinating the CPF volunteers. The
plainclothes police officer distributed brightly colored vests (yellow and
green with reflective strips) to all volunteers. We were asked to sign in
"for duty" The captain called us to order, commanding us to line up in
two columns in a sort of military-style formation. He issued a pro forma

warning about the dangers of the inner city, the need to stick closely together, and the importance of watching for stragglers. He told us that the goal was to provide security for innocent people in the streets by looking for troublemakers, potential thieves, and drug dealers. Our goal was to protect and serve. He finished his informal speech by telling the assembled volunteers to watch out for the "professors," to make sure the two of us got home "in one piece." He then turned the meeting over to Moses, who led the group in a prayer in isiZulu, an appeal to a Higher Authority meant to calm us and prepare us for the night patrol.

Membership in the CPF consists entirely of volunteers. The numbers for the night patrols range between about fifteen and twenty-five, depending on the time of year and day of the week and weather conditions. Every night patrol has a different route through the inner city, designed to keep criminals off guard and to surprise the unsuspecting. Night patrols target hot spots—that is, street corners, darkened alleys, and open parks where criminal activities are rampant.

On the Edge of the Void

Our group headed out of the building and into the now-dark streets. Almost immediately, the three or four volunteers in the lead confronted a man urinating. The man was an off-duty police officer. The volunteers chastised him, loudly telling him that he was a disgrace and was setting a bad example for ordinary people. Across the street from the police station, an older woman sat on the curb with several other women gathered around to her. She had broken her ankle by tripping on a pothole, and she was awaiting an ambulance. At least a half an hour later, the volunteers in the lead crossed the path of the ambulance coming to fetch the injured woman. The volunteers verbally assaulted the ambulance crew, criticizing them for coming so late when the woman was suffering.

The experienced woman volunteer in charge of the itinerary carried a map with our precise route. Following her lead, we headed south, toward the railroad lines and the darkened streets around Park Station, the main transit depot in the Johannesburg central city. During the day, this area bustles with informal traders who line the curbside selling foodstuffs, dry goods, and clothing. With the informal traders gone, the streets looked unkempt and dirty, filled with discarded trash.

Despite the fact that it was about three hours after dark, the streets were crowded with people: older men on their way to any one of dozens of tall apartment blocks, traders packing up their pavement stalls, young women and men walking or loitering on street corners, and young children—some tugging at their mothers hands and others just on their own. From their dress and manner, it was clear that these were ordinary working-class people, some with low-paying jobs, some with temporary work, and others between jobs or out of work. The class mixture was fairly homogeneous.

We quickly turned east, moving toward Joubert Park, the largest open green space in the inner city. The single plainclothes policer (James) with us opened the locked gate. After our group entered the park, he locked the gate behind us. Three of the women volunteers wandered away from the group, heading for the bushes, where they could relieve themselves in private. Some men in the group did not bother with such decorum. Moses told us that in the past the park was a notorious place for armed robberies and assaults. A few years earlier, a member of the CPF on patrol had been stabbed to death in a botched robbery. Moses said that thieves often posed as homeless squatters, waiting for unsuspecting victims. We did not see any hangers-on sleeping in the park. As we reached the other side and exited, James closed and locked the gate behind us.

As we moved further away from the police station in an easterly direction, we avoided the busy streets, choosing first to patrol the quiet areas. From the bottom end of Quartz (a street well-known for its down-and-out street prostitutes), three blocks east and a block north of the police station, we proceeded northward up the hill in the direction of the Highpoint Shopping Centre on Pretorius Street. The mercurial private security company called Bad Boyz has its inner-city headquarters in the El Capitan Building, at the corner of Womarans and Quartz Streets. The headquarters consists of a few offices, a CCTV control room on the bottom floor, and Spartan residences for perhaps as many as fifty private security operatives. A week earlier, we had tried to talk with Hendrick DeClerk, the owner of Bad Boyz, but without success. Bad Boyz has virtually monopolized the private security business in the inner city, combining static guarding of residential buildings and business storefronts with armed-response patrols in high-speed vehicles. The inner city is dotted with high-rise residential buildings and apartment complexes outfitted with floor-to-ceiling steel gates where fingerprint iden-

FIGURE 17. Bad Boyz security vehicle. (Photo by author.)

tification technology provides access for authorized residents only. Bad Boyz provides private security for two main clients in the inner city— the Ikaya Precinct and the *Legae La Rona*, a securitized residential complex of around fourteen apartment buildings cut off from the surrounding streetscape with a tall perimeter fence and armed sentries in elevated watchtowers.

The Highpoint Shopping Centre is the geographical focal point of Hillbrow. By day, this busy area consists of a frantic and seemingly chaotic choreography of people and cars and noises. At night, a more subdued but lively night market attracts curbside traders who sell everything from barbequed meat to clothing. Trading stalls spread out in several directions: east and west along Pretorius and across the shopping plaza to Kotze Street. This area constitutes the commercial heart of Hillbrow.

Many of the traders in the night market were pleased to greet the CPF volunteers. Some informal traders whom we recognized from previous work in the area joked with us about joining the patrol. Group cohesion broke down a bit as volunteers spread out, chatting with friends and acquaintances. On the whole, despite the effort that went into the preparation and the dedication of the participants, it seemed clear that the group of volunteers dressed in their luminescent vests was making very little impression as a serious security force on the people gathered in the streets.

As we reached Pretorius Street, conversations died down. The area was much more dangerous than the quiet streets we had left behind. Almost as if by some unspoken agreement, the patrol gathered itself together again. We turned left along the surprisingly busy thoroughfare, where the noise and light and movement suddenly became intense. The mood in the group changed. At this point in the journey, we had somehow broken into two tight groups: the small unit in front acted as the wedge in the crime prevention patrol, while the group behind us assumed the role of a protection detail as it weaved through shop entrances, chatting with store clerks. Illegal weapons and drugs were the main problems, the group leader told us. We were informed that there was a police car somewhere behind us, ready to provide backup in case of trouble.

Active Patrolling and Private Vigilance

After about an hour, the pattern of the patrol became clear. CPF volunteers fanned out along both sides of streets, approaching groups of people (usually young men) standing at street corners or gathered around informal trading stalls. The volunteers announced their presence, stating that they were there to protect the community from criminals.

Seemingly at random, CPF patrollers confronted men and women on the street, demanding to search their pockets, their handbags, and their possessions for weapons (handguns and knives) and drugs. Faced with a fait accompli, an overwhelming number of somewhat startled persons complied, raising their hands or leaning open-legged against an available wall. Several volunteers would search the person, starting with the shirt pockets, trousers, and crotch areas and ending with the ankles and shoes. Volunteers treated any hesitation or refusal to submit to search as a sign that the person who had been confronted had something to hide. CPF patrollers surrounded the hesitant persons and proceeded to search them—using whatever force was necessary. Several other volunteers would stand guard, waiting to see if anyone in the crowd broke and ran—a clear indication that the person was a suspicious character. When suspects ran off, the volunteers sprinted after them in hot pursuit,

FIGURE 18. Stop and frisk. (Photo by author.)

cornering and then frisking the suspect. If someone did not comply with the initial request, several volunteers would surround the suspicious person, grabbing his or her hands and occasionally bringing him or her down to the pavement roughly. One young woman volunteer seemed particularly adept at this tactic, often placing either her knee or her boot on a suspect's head while others searched his or her pockets.

The presence of a single plainclothes police officer—even driving in a patrol vehicle several blocks away—provides the formal legal justification for the stop and frisk and the search and seizure of suspected criminals. Whatever legal protections for ordinary people exist, these rights undergo a rather dramatic transformation at night. From the start, it is clear that respect for civil liberties quickly disappear in the exhilarating rush to apprehend suspected criminals. CPF volunteers typically announced to those about to be searched that they should lean up against the wall with their legs spread. Women patrollers frequently confronted other women on the street and demanded to search their handbags and parcels. One member of the team—a short, stocky, middle-aged woman—demanded to see the identity documents of a young man on the street. When he failed to produce them, she shoved him, pushed him to the wall, slapped him, and then punched him in the face. Community policing initiatives have framed their approach to lawlessness and criminality through the lens of penal populism. Community policing patrols have deliberately borrowed the language of punitive discipline as the justification for their almost indiscriminate use of force and violence as a legitimate means to inflict vengeful retribution on criminals.[14]

At the corner of Banket Street, we came across two SAPS vans parked at odd angles outside an apartment block. We watched as several SPS officers rushed over to the young men standing near the open doorway to the dilapidated building. The young men fled in panic up the stairs with two uniformed police officers and several CPF patrollers in hot pursuit. Following them, we charged up a grim flight of stairs to the third floor. When we encountered no one, we returned to the street. The uniformed police officers were wrestling several young men into the back of the SAPS van and shouting instructions to grab a few more young men standing nearby. Using flashlights and sticks, police and patrollers probed the dark recesses of the broken-down stairwell, looking for drugs and weapons. The searchers discovered numerous small plastic bags filled with various substances. The CPF patrol leader excitedly told us that these packets contained marijuana, heroin, and cocaine. The confiscated drugs were passed from person to person, ending with a SAPS officer who promised to deposit them at the police station—maybe. The drug bust was over just as quickly as it had begun. Like hundreds of other crumbling buildings without water and electricity, the ruined apartment block was home to unauthorized squatters, who in exchange for access to extremely overcrowded flats paid exorbitant sums of cash to hijackers who controlled the premises by force. Impromptu drug houses like this are sprinkled all over the inner city.

As we left Pretorius Street and moved onto less-traveled side streets, we were enveloped in darkness, making it impossible to identify much of anything. The lone police officer who accompanied us on this part of the journey shouted to the group—who had clustered in tight knots—to spread out. In military training terminology, this practice of patrolling is known as maintaining the interval. If organized gangs were watching us, they would not be able to tell how few we were. Small numbers put us at risk for those who might be tempted to try to rob us or shoot at us. What added to the anxiety was that the police officer wearing a bulletproof vest, while we were not. As the night sounds faded and gradually turned into an eerie silence, we became acutely aware of the rhythmic cadence of our collective walking. In the absence of any other illumination, the light of the moon caused the apartment towers that lined the streets to cast ghostly brown shadows. When we reached Fife Avenue, veteran volunteers became visibly nervous. The darkened streetscape appeared surreal and menacing. Moses said that this area, from Soper Road to Olivia, was very dangerous, that we were not going to venture any closer to where we might encounter trouble, and that we needed to move along quickly.

Violating our prearranged instructions, the CPF patrollers gradually separated into small clusters. The SAPS police vehicle was nowhere in sight. By day, this part of the inner city is filled with people, including street traders and their customers as well as men and women on their way to and from work. But at night, the streetscape assumes an entirely different character: rival gangs of drug dealers linked to organized crime carve up the territory and stake claims to discrete street corners. Our presence did not go unnoticed, but it was cautiously tolerated. We walked south on Catherine and then turned east at Primrose Terrace, skirting Pullingerkop Park on our right. This scruffy terrain does not really constitute so much a park as the narrow crest of the hill before it slopes steeply down towards the inner city: hence the name of the neighborhood, Hillbrow.

We headed north to Pullingerkop Park, a five-block thin stretch of open space lined at the southern end with the few remaining groups of informal traders packing up their wares and heading home. Pullingerkop Park is a site notorious for open-air drug dealing, with middle-class buyers coming from other parts of Johannesburg to purchase marijuana and cocaine. Homeless wanderers with nowhere else to go mingle with drug addicts and teenage runaways huddled for warmth around fifty-gallon drums heaped full of burning wood and trash. The volunteers in the CPF patrol seemed more intent on chasing away the drug users than on confiscating drugs from the dealers.

At this point, the police officer in the SAPS vehicle that had followed the CPF night patrol from the start asked whether we would like to join him and another member of the CPF group on an active-duty excursion through the inner city. We climbed into the back seat and off we went at high speed. What surprised us was the number of SAPS vehicles on the streets of Hillbrow, Berea, and Joubert Park at night. Our plainclothes driver seemed to take a rather haphazard approach to patrolling, driving randomly around the streets, seemingly without purpose. Whenever he saw several SAPS vehicles pulled over at the curb, we stopped to lend assistance or just talk and joke. The dispatcher from a faraway SAPS office kept up a steady stream of announcements about police actions, responding to armed robberies in progress or to calls from a frantic woman claiming she had been beaten by a boyfriend.

On our excursions through the inner city, we observed several roadblocks in action, where the SAPS and the JMPD jointly stopped and inspected all vehicles on the road. These checkpoints are places where the application of the law is constantly negotiated and modified on the spot. At night in the inner city, the rule of law is ephemeral. When we observed drivers who were being questioned for broken headlights or operating a vehicle without proper license plates, it became obvious that it is not the legal statutes themselves that determine the legitimacy and power of the law but those operating in the name of municipal authority (or those operating at the behest of public authority) who decide at their own discretion what is a violation and what is not.

We assisted in the arrest of three men for disorderly conduct outside a bar. The crowd was noisy and restless, and a little angry. The culprits were handcuffed and pushed into a police van. At another point, we stopped a man driving the wrong way on a one-way street. The policer jumped out of the SAPS vehicle and approached the other car warily. After joking with the visibly drunk driver, the SAPS officer let him drive off with nothing more than a warning.

We then stopped a white four-door passenger vehicle. Again, the SAPS officer approached the car cautiously, asking the driver to produce identification and to exit the vehicle. The SAPS officer confiscated vehicle registration papers and personal documents (including a passport) from the rather disappointed middle-aged driver. It turned out he carried a passport identifying him as a citizen of Nigeria. The SAPS officer told the man to drive his car to the Hillbrow police station, park it, and join us in the back seat of the police vehicle. The Nigerian man complied willingly. The CPF colleague with us in the SAPS vehicle confronted this "criminal suspect," claiming that he had "arrested" him weeks earlier for drug dealing. Our CPF colleague said that our Nigerian passenger was a known midlevel drug dealer whose job in the criminal syndicate was to supply runners on the street with drugs, monitor their behavior, and collect the proceeds.

The mood was jovial, as accusations of wrongdoing were matched by counterclaims of innocence. The SAPS officer instructed the Nigerian man to call his "brother," and we would meet him on the street in front of an apartment complex several blocks away. The brother approached the car, and with the window down pressed something into the Nigerian's hand. Although the light was dim, it was clear that the brother had passed along a handful of money. After exchanging pleasantries, we drove back to the Hillbrow police station. The SAPS officer accompanied the Nigerian man to his car and returned his papers to him. As the Nigerian man drove off, our CPF colleague announced with a great deal of anguish that police from the top to the bottom took bribes, and he greatly disapproved. Needless to say, despite our presence, the SAPS officer did little to hide his complicity.[15]

Counterspaces and Alternative Stories

The CPF patrollers returned to the Hillbrow police station around midnight. Volunteers were eager to get home, yet they still had to negotiate the same streets where the patrols had visited hours earlier. We returned our luminescent uniforms and prepared to leave. We watched our fellow volunteers as they tentatively ventured into the neighborhood, walking in small groups, no longer a collective and without the protection of SAPS vehicles following behind.

It soon became readily apparent that, until this moment, we had just been skirting the rough edges of the nocturnal economies of the inner city. During the crucial early-evening hours, the CPF patrols maintain some kind of visible policing presence. But there are other, more opaque and sinister nocturnal worlds that the CPF patrols do not normally penetrate. As the two of us left the building and thanked Moses for his guidance, several SAPS officers tentatively approached us, asking if we would like to see the real nightlife of Hillbrow. We agreed, and off we went with two active-duty police officers in a SAPS vehicle.

Police officers working in precincts close to where all manner of vice prevails must make some kind of uncomfortable peace with these circumstances. Our journey into the demimonde felt like a montage of stylish Hollywood crime dramas with its roots in film noir. The darkened streets, washed drab yellow-brown by the dull city lights, smelled of dust and sewage and anxiety. The night sounds formed a languid torpor suspended in a nervous and capricious potentiality.

We stopped by several nondescript nightclubs at the low end of the stripper-prostitution market. Our SAPS escorts approached these disreputable places with police lights flashing, only to be greeted by bouncers and security guards whom they obviously knew. Managers retreated into the clubs only to return with cans of Red Bull and other stimulant drinks since the SAPS officers were on all-night duty. It became clear that the SAPS officers on the ground depend on this motley crew of unsavory characters as part of an extended assemblage that becomes responsible for order maintenance in the inner city at night.

After driving around aimlessly for what seemed like hours, we arrived at the Summit Club, an infamous private club on Pretoria Street. For decades, this place served as the barometer for the public image of Hillbrow as the gathering place for bohemian good-for-nothing idlers captivated by the hedonistic lifestyles of the times. In the 1960s, it was an elite members-only club, with an indoor swimming pool and the site of the first discotheque in Johannesburg. In the 1980s, the Summit Club became the epicenter of an urban cultural quasi resistance to the straight-laced conservatism of apartheid, hosting risqué parties at which black and white South Africans socialized in violation of the race laws. Nowadays, it is a byword for reprobate licentiousness: a high-end strip club that doubles as a brothel.

We were ushered inside the multistory building by our SAPS chaperones, who were on a first-name basis with the club manager and the crowd of bouncers at the door. We walked in without paying the cover charge and were immediately offered free drinks and a private booth. With the exception of only a few white and Asian women, all of the hundred or more dancers, hostesses, and waitresses were black women. The blaring music and the flashing lights seemed to conspire against the weight of sadness that permeated every pore of the place. The SAPS officers said they would retrieve us in a half hour when they finished their patrol. No doubt we were becoming inconvenient, tiresome, or both. Perhaps the novelty of entertaining us had worn off. After several hours, we began to believe they had forgotten us. But eventually they returned for us and transported us back to the Hillbrow Police Station, where we retrieved our car.

Fragments of Alterity

The spatial logics of the inner city mirror, albeit in exacerbated form, those asymmetrical relations of power that permeate the city more broadly.[16] Despite the embedded presence of crime and danger mixed with desultory law enforcement, there are "alternative ways of using, organizing, experiencing, and coexisting in space" that offer potential counternarratives that cut against the grain of the dominant dystopian narratives of place.[17] These "fragments of possibility" can be found in surprising places. Hillbrow Radio is an exemplar of such a "counter-space"—a heterotopic site that stands against the prevailing ethos of precarity and uncertainty.[18] The radio station occupies the top floor of a squat, innocuous 1980s low rise on the corner of Claim and Van Der Merwe, overlooking a vacant lot that serves as parking space for the nearby Summit Club.

The radio station is an oasis of tranquility with an upbeat vibe. The main room is not a vast space—perhaps thirty feet wide and a hundred feet long. The low ceiling coupled with the florescent tube lighting gave the place a kind of claustrophobic feeling. Several young people in their twenties and thirties were lounging on a couple of couches that looked like the worn display models from a 1990s discount furniture store. A couple of young children were running about with high energy.

We were warmly welcomed. Someone claiming to be the producer insisted that we go on the air with their late-night host. To be clear, Hillbrow Radio is not a large commercial radio station. In fact, the station does not broadcast on a known frequency but only streams live over the internet. This place seemed to be Hillbrow at its best: certainly unbeautiful and unpretentious, but optimistic and ambitious—a celebration of Hillbrow as a welcoming place of endurance and even opportunity. Despite its bleak surroundings, Hillbrow Radio offers a sense of community to the dozen or so staff members and their friends.

The radio host did actually interview us for at least half an hour. He asked us to explain what we were doing in the middle of the inner city so late at night and to give our impressions of Hillbrow. We muddled through, not knowing if anyone was even listening. By the end, we realized that we were part of a very different rhythm of the inner city than that of the conventional narratives of anxiety and fear.

CPF Volunteers

The CPF volunteers are all residents of the inner city. Yet for the most part, the volunteers consist of an unlikely mixture: some older residents who seemed to have been participating in CPF patrols for many years and some younger participants, who were disproportionately women. With the exception of a few veteran patrollers, there seemed to be a high degree of turnover and inconsistent participation. Most of the volunteers were either between jobs or not regularly employed. It seemed evident than an unemployed older man of Pakistani descent participated in CPF patrols because he had been robbed and his shop destroyed by vandals. Women, who constitute the majority of volunteers, seemed particularly empowered by the experience of working together to provide security for inner-city residents. We observed that the women appeared to be much more willing than others to use physical force to intimidate and subdue passersby who did not comply with their demand to submit to a full body search.

The CPF does not pay salaries or even stipends, but many participants made it clear that they regarded their volunteer work as a possible steppingstone to permanent employment. With a great deal of pride, CPF leaders suggested that many volunteer patrollers had acquired entry-level jobs with the SAPS, JMPD, or private security companies operating in the inner city. Still others found work as building managers in the inner city.

It is clear that the CPF nighttime patrols actually achieve very little in the way of combating lawlessness in the inner city. Even large patrols were too small and the neighborhoods too vast for volunteer crime fighters to make any real difference. In the minds of senior SAPS officers in charge of the CPFs, the volunteer patrols play an important role in building trust between actively engaged citizens and local police stations. Active engagement with the CPF patrols seemed to give volunteers a degree of personal fulfillment and a sense of self-empowerment. Without exception, volunteers took pride in their efforts and were con-

vinced that their participation made a difference in keeping their neighborhoods safer.

Surrogate Policing

CPF patrolling represents a kind of performance infused with tactical
displays of bravado and commitment. In short, playing at policing has a
great deal of symbolic value but does very little to reduce crime.[19] There
is a distinct banality embedded in the whole process—the ad hoc organization, the inconsistent numbers of CPF patrollers (depending on who
decides to participate), and the selection of routes. The enthusiasm for
our presence as outsiders seemed to suggest a kind of vindication for
the efforts of the CPF patrollers. Perhaps the motivation in part behind
the patrols is less about security as such and more about a personalized
sense of duty in the face of insecurity.

While the law in the modern liberal state apparatus considers all citizens to be in possession of equal rights, decisions on the ground about
the application of the law are constantly made in arbitrary and whimsical
ways. As a mode of governance, surrogate policing substitutes extralegal
discretion for the legally constituted authority of state law enforcement
agencies. Discretionary powers—unwritten and unspoken—operate at
the intersection of codified legal statutes and their application. Public policing agencies welcome working with CPF groups such as the one in
Hillbrow because it allows them to maintain a feigned innocence. The
presence of SAPS officers effectively deputizes CPF members, enabling
them to search and frisk random passersby, to enter buildings, and to
sometimes physically assault those they find in possession of weapons or
drugs. SAPS officers know that CPF members engage in infringements
of conventional civil liberties. This kind of surrogate policing blends
with extralegal vigilante activities in which public police agencies can le-
gitimately claim they did not engage directly.

Notes

PREFACE

1. Italo Calvino, *Invisible Cities* (London: Farber & Farber, 1972), 37.

2. Anthony Giddens has developed this idea of the "ontological insecurity" of modern life. See Anthony Giddens, *The Consequences of Modernity* (Cambridge, UK: Polity Press, 1990). See also Teresa Dirsuweit, "Between Ontological Security and the Right Difference: Road Closures, Communitarianism and Urban Ethics in Johannesburg, South Africa," *Autrepart* 2 (2007): 53–71.

3. By way of comparison, see Carl Smith, *Urban Disorder and the Shape of Belief: The Great Chicago Fire, the Haymarket Bomb, and the Model Town of Pullman* (Chicago: University of Chicago Press, 1995), 11. 15, 34–35; and Richard Williams, *The Anxious City* (New York: Routledge, 2004), 1–24.

4. Mike Davis, "Fortress Los Angeles: The Militarization of Urban Space," in *Variations on a Theme Park: The New American City and the End of Public Space*, ed. Michael Sorkin (New York: Hill and Wang, 1992), 154, 155.

5. Nan Ellin, "Shelter from the Storm or Form Follows Fear and Vice Versa," in *Architecture of Fear*, ed. Nan Ellin (New York: Princeton Architectural Press, 1997), 13–45.

6. This idea is taken from Janet Roitman, *Fiscal Disobedience: An Anthropology of Economic Regulation in Central Africa* (Princeton, NJ: Princeton University Press, 2005), 7–8.

7. See, among others, Julie Berg, "Seeing Like Private Security: Evolving Mentalities of Public Space Protection in South Africa," *Criminology & Criminal Justice* 10, no. 3 (2010): 287–301; Michael Kempa et al., "Reflections on the Evolving Concept of 'Private Policing,'" *European Journal on Criminal Policy and Research* 7, no. 2 (1999): 197–223; and Claire Bénit-Gbaffou, Laurent Fourchard, and Alex Wafer, "Local Politics and the Circulation of Community Security Initiatives in Johannesburg," *International Journal of Urban and Regional Research* 36, no. 5 (2012): 936–57.

8. Krista Mahr, "High South African Crime Rates and Low Faith in Police Boost Private Security in Gauteng," *Financial Times*, 12 May 2017; and Staff Writer, "The Biggest Types of Private Security Businesses in South Africa," *Business Tech*, 16 November 2017; and Karinda Jagmohan and Kwanda Njoli, "Citizens Spend R160bn on SAPS, Private Security," *Weekend Argus*, 16 September 2018.

9. See Mfaniseni Fana Sihlongonyane, "The Rhetorical Devices for Marketing and Branding Johannesburg as a City: A Critical Review," *Environment & Planning A* 47, no. 10 (2015): 2134–52. See also George Marcus and Angela Rivas Gamboa, "Contemporary Cities with Colonial Pasts and Global Futures: Some Aspects of the Relations between Governance, Order, and Decent, Secure Life," in *Postcolonial Urbanism: Southeast Asian Cities and Global Processes*, ed. Ryan Bishop, John Phillips, and Wei-Wei Yeo (New York: Routledge, 2003), 227–42 (esp. 228).

10. Robert Park, "The City: Suggestions for Investigation of Human Behavior in the Urban Environment," in *The City: Suggestions for Investigation of Human Behavior in*

the Urban Environment, ed. Robert Park, Ernest Burgess, and Roderick McKenzie (Chicago: University of Chicago Press, 1925), 1.

11. These ideas are adapted from Achille Mbembe and Sarah Nuttall, "Writing the World from an African Metropolis," *Public Culture* 16, no. 3 (2004): 347–72; Kevin Lynch, *The Image of the City* (Cambridge, MA: Harvard University Press, 1960), 1–5; Steve Pile, *Real Cities: Modernity, Space and the Phantasmagoria of City Life* (Thousand Oaks, CA: Sage, 2005), 15–16, 47–51, 57–61; and James Donald, *Imagining the Modern City* (Minneapolis: University of Minnesota Press, 1999), ix–xiii, 1–27. While positivist-realist approaches to studying urbanism remain powerful in scholarly circles, there are emergent voices (Ananya Roy, Achille Mbembe, Filip DeBoeck, AbdouMaliq Simone, Jennifer Robinson, Garth Myers, and Matthew Gandy, to name only a few) that have carved out new terrain for research and writing.

12. See Walter Benjamin, *The Arcades Project*, trans. Howard Eiland and Kevin McLaughlin (Cambridge, MA: Belkap Press, 1999).

13. For a valuable survey of the "ocularcentric" point of view, see Martin Jay, *Downcast Eyes: The Degeneration of Vision in Twentieth Century French Thought* (Berkeley: University of California Press, 1993).

14. For the treatment of some of these ideas, see Graeme Gilloch, *Myth and Metropolis: Walter Benjamin and the City* (London: Polity Press, 1996); Iain Borden et al., "Things, Flows, Filters, Tactics," in *The Unknown City: Contesting Architecture and Social Space*, ed. Iain Borden et al. (Cambridge, MA: MIT Press, 2001), 2–28; and Timon Beyes and Chris Steyeart, "Strangely Familiar: The Uncanny and Unsiting Organizational Analysis," *Organizational Studies* 34, no. 10 (2013): 1445–65.

15. Grady Clay, *Close-Up: How to Read the American City* (Chicago: University of Chicago Press, 1973), 29, 23.

16. Donald, *Imagining the Modern City*, 8–11. For a wider discussion, see Sharon Zukin, "Space and Symbols in an Age of Decline," in *Re-presenting the City*, ed. Anthony King (New York: Macmillan, 1996), 43–59.

17. See Pile, *Real Cities*, 21, 35, and 131–39.

18. W. I. Thomas and D. S. Thomas, *The Child in America: Behavior Problems and Programs* New York: Knopf, 1928), 571–72.

19. See, for example, Louise White, *Speaking with Vampires: Rumor and History in Colonial Africa* (Berkeley: University of California Press, 2000), 30–43.

20. See Farah Mendlesohn, *Rhetorics of Fantasy* (Middletown, CT: Wesleyan University Press, 2008), for a discussion of different kinds of fantasy.

21. See Kevin Robins, "Prisoners of the City: Whatever Could a Postmodern City Be?," in *Space and Place: Theories of Identity and Location*, ed. Erica Carter, James Donald, and Judith Squires (London: Laurence & Wishart, 1993), 303–30 (esp. 318, 326).

22. Dieter Ingenschay and Joan Ramon Resina, preface to *After-Images of the City*, ed. Joan Ramon Resina and Dieter Ingenschay (London: Cornell University Press, 2003), xi–xvii.

23. See Anthony Vidler, *The Architectural Uncanny: Essays in the Modern Unhomely* (Cambridge, MA: MIT Press, 1992), 3–4, 12–13.

24. Raphael Samuel, "Reading the Signs," *History Workshop* 32 (1991): 89.

25. For the source of these ideas, see Victor Bergin, *Some Cities* (Berkeley: University of California Press, 1996), 175.

26. Jonathan Raban, *Soft City: A Documentary Exploration of Metropolitan Life* (London: Picador, 1974), 9–10.

27. Samuel, "Reading the Signs," 88, 90, 92.

28. See Samuel, "Reading the Signs," 105.

29. See Anna Kligmann, *Brandscapes: Architecture in the Experience Economy* (Cambridge, MA: MIT Press, 2007), 3, 6, 16–17, 83–84.

30. Raban, *Soft City*, 4, 9, 10.

31. See Martin J. Murray, *City of Extremes: The Spatial Politics of Johannesburg* (Durham, NC: Duke University Press, 2011), 213–44.

32. See Teresa Caldeira, *City of Walls: Crime, Segregation, and Citizenship in São Paulo* (Berkeley: University of California Press, 2000), 4–5.

33. Caldeira, *City of Walls*, 4, 16.

34. See Martin J. Murray, "The City in Fragments: Kaleidoscopic Johannesburg after *Apartheid*," in *The Spaces of the Modern City: Imaginaries, Politics, and Everyday Life*, ed. Gyan Prakash and Kevin Kruse (Princeton, NJ: Princeton University Press, 2008), 144–78.

35. See Martin J. Murray, "City of Layers: The Making and Shaping of Affluent Johannesburg after *Apartheid*," in *Urban Governance in Post-Apartheid Cities*, ed. Marie Huchzermeyer and Christoph Haferburg (Stuttgart: Schweizerbart, 2014), 179–96.

36. Michel Foucault, *Discipline and Punish: The Birth of the Prison*, trans. Alan Sheridan (New York: Vintage, 1991), 26.

37. Christine Hentschel, *Security in the Bubble: Navigating Crime in Urban South Africa* (Minneapolis: University of Minnesota press, 2015), 3.

38. See Smith, *Urban Disorder and the Shape of Belief*, 10, 11, 12.

39. For the source of some of these ideas, see Roger Keil, "The Urban Future Revisited: Politics and Restructuring in Los Angeles after Fordism," *Strategies* 3 (1990): 105–29 (esp. 105–6).

40. See Lynch, *Image of the City*, 1–32. See also M. Christine Boyer, "Twice Told Stories: The Double Erasure of Times Square," in *Unknown City*, ed. Borden et al., 30–52.

41. Michel de Certeau, *The Practice of Everyday Life*, trans. Steven Rendall (Berkeley: University of California Press, 1984), 92–93, 101.

42. These ideas are derived from a reading of Rob Shields, "Visualicity," *Visual Culture in Britain* 5, no. 1 (2004): 23–36 (esp. 23–25).

43. See Pile, *Real Cities*, 20–21, 26–28, and 59–61.

44. Steve Pile, "The Un(known) City . . . or, an Urban Geography of What Lies Buried Below the Surface," in *Unknown City*, ed. Borden et al., 262–78 (esp. 264).

45. Pile, "Un(known) City," 262–78, esp. 269.

46. Vidler, *Architectural Uncanny*, 3–4, 7–11.

47. Pile, "Un(known) City," 269.

48. See Matthew Farish, "Cities in Shade: Urban Geography and the Uses of *Noir*," *Environment and Planning D* 23, no. 1 (2005): 95–118 (esp. 111).

49. This idea of the urban uncanny is taken from Anthony Vidler. He associates the

uncanny with "the contrast between a secure and homely interior and the fearful invasion of an alien presence" (p. 3). "The uncanny," Vidler suggests, is "sinister, disturbing, suspect, strange; it would be better characterized as 'dread' than terror, deriving
its force from its very inexplicability, its sense of lurking unease, rather than from any
clearly defined source of fear—an uncomfortable sense of haunting rather than a persistent apparition" (p. 23). See Vidler, *Architectural Uncanny*, 3–5, 22–25.

50. Colin McFarlane, "Assemblage and Critical Urbanism," *City* 15, no. 2 (2011):
204–24.

51. For the source of this idea, see Stephen Collier, "Topologies of Power: Foucault's
Analysis of Political Government beyond 'Governmentality,'" *Theory, Culture & Society*
26, no. 6 (2009): 78–108 (esp. 78).

52. See Laura Podalsky, *Specular City: Transforming Culture, Consumption, and Space
in Buenos Aires, 1955–1973* (Philadelphia: Temple University Press, 2004), 26.

53. See Jani Scandura, *Down in the Dumps: Place, Modernity, American Depression*
(Durham, NC: Duke University Press, 2008), 8–9.

54. See Lee Ann Fujii, "Five Stories of Accidental Ethnography: Turning Unplanned
Moments in the Field into Data," *Qualitative Research* 15, no. 4 (2015): 525–39; and Susan
Murray, "A Spy, a Shill, a Go-Between, or a Sociologist: Unveiling the 'Observer' in Par-
ticipant Observer," *Qualitative Sociology* 3, no. 3 (2003): 377–95 (esp. 379).

55. See Keller Easterling, *Enduring Innocence: Global Architecture and Its Political Masquerades* (Cambridge, MA: MIT Press, 2005), 11–12.

INTRODUCTION

1. Helen Epstein, "The Mystery of AIDS in South Africa," *New York Review of Books*
(20 July 2000), 50.

2. For a review of the different literatures on moral panics, see Arnold Hunt,
"'Moral Panic' and Moral Language in the Media," *British Journal of Sociology* 48, no. 4
(1997): 629–48.

3. See Erich Goode and Nachman Ben-Yehuda, *Moral Panics: The Social Construction
of Deviance* (Cambridge, MA: Blackwell, 1994), 124–43.

4. See Omar Bartov, "Defining Enemies, Making Victims: Germans, Jews, and the
Holocaust," *American Historical Review* 103, no. 3 (1998): 771–816 (esp. 773–74).

5. See Albert Fu and Martin J. Murray, "Cinema and the Edgy City: Johannesburg,
Carjacking, and the Postmetropolis," *African Identities* 5, no. 2 (2007): 279–89; Leon de
Kock, "From the Subject of Evil to the Evil Subject: 'Cultural Difference' in Postapartheid South African Crime Fiction," *Safundi* 16, no. 1 (2015): 28–50; Lindiwe Dovey, "Redeeming Features: From *Tsotsi* (1980) to *Tsotsi* (2006)," *Journal of African Cultural Studies* 19, no. 2 (2007): 143–64; and Rosalind Morris, "Style, *Tsotsi*-Style and *Tsotsitaal*: The
Histories, Politics and Aesthetics of a South African Figure," *Social Text* 28, no. 2 (2010):
85–112.

6. See Achille Mbembe, "Aesthetics of Superfluity," *Public Culture* 16, no. 3 (2004):
373–405 (esp. 380–81, 383).

7. Wilf Nussey, "After Apartheid, Hope and Decay," *Guardian Weekly* (London),
19 November 1995; and Jean Comaroff and John Comaroff, "Alien-Nation: Zombies, Im-

migrants, and Millennial Capitalism," *The South Atlantic Quarterly* 101, no. 4 (2002): 779–805. See also Setha Low and Neil Smith, eds., *The Politics of Public Space* (New York: Routledge, 2006).

8. For the "sanitation syndrome," see Maynard Swanson, "Sanitation Syndrome: Bubonic Plague and Urban Native Policy in the Cape Colony, 1900–1909," *Journal of African History* 18, no. 3 (1977): 387–410.

9. Martin J. Murray, "Alien Strangers in Our Midst: The Dreaded Foreign Invasion and 'Fortress South Africa,'" *Canadian Journal of African Studies* 37, nos. 2–3 (2003): 440–66; and Jean Comaroff and John Comaroff, "Criminal Obsessions, after Foucault: Postcoloniality, Policing, and the Metaphysics of Disorder," *Critical Inquiry* 30, no, 4 (2004): 800–824.

10. Lindsay Bremner, "Bounded Spaces: Demographic Anxieties in Post-Apartheid Johannesburg," *Social Identities* 10, no. 4 (2004): 455–68 (esp. 457–58).

11. These ideas are taken almost verbatim from Joel Modiri, "The Colour of Law, Power and Knowledge: Introducing Critical Race Theory in (Post-) Apartheid South Africa," *South African Journal on Human Rights* 28 (2012): 405–36 (esp. 424).

12. Modiri, "Colour of Law," 408.

13. Modiri, 405, 406.

14. Modiri, 435.

15. Modiri, 416.

16. Modiri, 407, 412.

17. See Jean Comaroff and John Comaroff, *The Truth about Crime: Sovereignty, Knowledge, Social Order* (Chicago: University of Chicago Press, 2016), xiii, 5.

18. Comaroff and Comaroff, "Criminal Obsessions, after Foucault," 800–801.

19. See Carl Smith, *Urban Disorder and the Shape of Belief: The Great Chicago Fire, the Haymarket Bomb, and the Model Town of Pullman* (Chicago: University of Chicago Press, 1995), 10–11.

20. M. Christine Boyer, *The City of Collective Memory: Its Historical Imagery and Architectural Entertainments* (Cambridge, MA: MIT Press, 1996), 19.

21. Jean Comaroff and John Comaroff, "Figuring Crime: Quantifacts and the Production of the Un/Real," *Public Culture* 18, no. 1 (2006): 209–46; Chandre Gould, Johan Burger, and Gareth Newham, "The SAPS Crime Statistics: What They Tell Us—and What They Don't," *South African Crime Quarterly* 42 (2014): 3–12; and Gail Super, "The Spectacle of Crime in the 'New' South Africa: A Historical Perspective (1976–2004)," *British Journal of Criminology* 50, no. 2 (2010): 165–84.

22. See, for example, Roger Tijerino, "Civil Spaces: A Critical Perspective of Defensible Space," *Journal of Architectural and Planning Research* 15, no. 4 (1998): 321–37.

23. Martin J. Murray, *City of Extremes: The Spatial Politics of Johannesburg* (Durham, NC: Duke University Press, 2011), 210, 213–44.

24. Paul Virilio, *City of Panic*, trans. Julie Rose (New York: Berg, 2005), 68, 70–71; and Lieven de Cauter, *The Capsular Civilization: On the City in the Age of Fear* (Rotterdam: NAi, 2004), 65–66, 85–87.

25. See Arjun Appadurai, *Modernity at Large: Cultural Dimensions of Globalization* (Minneapolis: University of Minnesota Press, 1996), 33.

26. See Christine Hentschel, *Security in the Bubble: Navigating Crime in Urban South Africa* (Minneapolis: University of Minnesota Press, 2015), 1.

27. Andy Clarno and Martin J. Murray, "Policing in Johannesburg after Apartheid," *Social Dynamics* 39, no. 2 (2013): 210–27.

28. Svetlana Boym, *The Future of Nostalgia* (New York: Basic Books, 2001), 8.

29. From dozens of interviews with representatives of security initiatives attached to neighborhood associations, what is unquestionably clear to me is that residential homeowners see no realistic alternative to fortifying their homes in ways that mimic what their neighbors have done. See Andy Clarno, Rescaling White Space in Post-*Apartheid* Johannesburg," *Antipode* 45, no. 5 (2013): 1190–1212.

30. Philip Harrison and Alan Mabin, "Security and Space: Managing the Contradictions of Access Restriction in Johannesburg," *Environment & Planning B* 33, no. 1 (2006): 3–20; and Claire Benít-Gbaffou, "Unbundled Security Services and Urban Fragmentation in Post-*Apartheid* Johannesburg," *Geoforum* 39, no. 6 (2008): 1933–50. See also interviews with Josie Adler and Chris Zenferna, 11 June 2012; Cecile Loedolf, 7 July 2008; Gareth Newman, 11 July 2011; and John Penberthy, 19 June 2003.

31. Nicolas Dieltiens, "The Making of the Criminal Subject in Democratic South Africa" (master's thesis, University of the Witwatersrand, 2011), 2.

32. Mark Salter, "When the Exception Becomes the Rule: Borders, Sovereignty, and Citizenship," *Citizenship Studies* 12, no. 4 (2008): 365–80.

33. Asa Boholm, "Situated Risk: An Introduction," *Ethnos: Journal of Anthropology* 68, no. 2 (2003): 157–58.

34. Jock Young, *The Vertigo of Late Modernity* (Thousand Oaks, CA: Sage, 2007).

35. Clarno and Murray, "Policing in Johannesburg," 210–27.

36. For a theoretical exposition of the notion of the stranger, see Vince Marotta, "The Stranger and Social Theory," *Thesis Eleven* 62 (2000): 121–34.

37. John Rundell, "Imagining Cities, Others: Strangers, Contingency and Fear," *Thesis Eleven* 121, no. 1 (2014): 10.

38. See Mike Davis, *City of Quartz: Excavating the Future of Los Angeles* (New York: Vintage, 1992), 227, 229, 239, 244.

39. See Michel de Certeau, *The Practice of Everyday Life*, trans. Steven Rendall (Berkeley: University of California Press, 1984), 115–22.

40. Steve Pile, "The Un(known) City . . . or, an Urban Geography of What Lies Buried Below the Surface," in *The Unknown City: Contesting Architecture and Social Space*, ed. Iain Borden et al. (Cambridge, MA: MIT Press, 2001), 262–79 (esp. 269).

41. Robert Warren, "Situating the City and September 11th: Military Urban Doctrine, 'Pop-Up' Armies and Spatial Chess," *International Journal of Urban and Regional Research* 26, no. 3 (2002): 614–19; Jon Coaffee, "Urban Renaissance in the Age of Terrorism: *Revanchism*, Automated Social Control or the End of Reflection?," *International Journal of Urban and Regional Research* 29, no. 2 (2005): 447–54; Stephen Graham, "The Urban 'Battlespace,'" *Theory, Culture & Society* 26, nos. 7–8 (2009): 278–88; and Stephen Graham, "When Life Itself Is War: On the Urbanization of Military and Security Doctrine," *International Journal of Urban and Regional Research* 36, no. 1 (2012): 136–55.

42. See Tessa Diphoorn, *Twilight Policing: Private Security and Violence in Urban South Africa* (Berkeley: University of California Press, 2016), 6–23.

43. Adi Ophir, Michal Givoni, and Sari Hanafi, introduction to "The Power of Inclusive Exclusion," in *The Power of Inclusive Exclusion: Anatomy of Israeli Rule in the Occupied Palestinian Territories*, eds. Adi Ophir, Michal Givoni, and Sari Hanafi (New York: Zone Books, 2009), 15–30.

44. I would like to acknowledge Christine Hentschel as the source of these ideas. See Hentschel, *Security in the Bubble*, 2.

45. See De Cauter, *Capsular Civilization*, 78–81.

46. See, for example, Adam Ramadan and Sara Fregonese, "Hybrid Sovereignty and the State of Exception in the Palestinian Refugee Campus in Lebanon," *Annals of the American Association of Geographers* 107, no. 4 (2017): 949–63 (esp. 950–51, 953).

47. For the source of some of these ideas, see Sara Fregonese, "Beyond the Weak State: Hybrid Sovereignties in Beirut," *Environment and Planning D* 30, no. 4 (2012): 655–74.

48. Les Johnston, "From 'Pluralization' to 'the Police Extended Family'": Discourses on the Governance of Community Policing in Britain. *International Journal of the Sociology of Law* 31, no. 3 (2003): 185–204.

49. Michael Kempa, Philip Stenning, and Jennifer Wood, "Policing Communal Spaces: A Reconfiguration of the 'Mass Private Property' Hypothesis," *British Journal of Criminology* 44, no. 4 (2004): 562–81.

50. Tim Newburn, "The Commodification of Policing: Security Networks in the Late Modern City," *Urban Studies* 38, nos. 5–6 (2001): 829–48 (esp. 833).

51. See Anthony Minnaar, "Private–Public Partnerships: Private Security, Crime Prevention and Policing in South Africa," *Acta Criminologica: Southern African Journal of Criminology* 18, no. 1 (2005): 85–114; and interview with Anthony Minnaar, 6 July 2011.

52. Lindsay Bremner, "Closure, Simulation, and 'Making Do' in the Contemporary Johannesburg Landscape," in *Under Siege: Four African Cities. Freetown, Johannesburg, Kinshasa, Lagos. Documenta 11_Platform 4*, ed. Okwui Enwezor et al. (Ostfildern-Ruit, DE: Hatje Catnz, 2002), 153–72.

53. See, among others, AbdouMaliq Simone, "Straddling the Divides: Remaking Associational Life in the Informal City," *International Journal of Urban and Regional Research* 25, no. 1 (2001): 102–17.

54. See de Certeau, *The Practice of Everyday Life*, 91–110.

55. Henri Lefebvre, *The Production of Space*, trans. Donald Nicholson-Smith (Oxford, UK: Blackwell, 1991), 16–18.

56. For a useful comparison, see James Donald, "This, Here, Now: Imagining the Modern City," in *Imagining Cities: Scripts, Signs, Memory*, eds. Sallie Westwood and John Williams (London: Routledge, 1997), 181–201.

CHAPTER 1

1. The ideas for this and the following paragraphs are taken from Drew Forrest, "Reasons for Alarmist Fantasies Abound," *Business Day*, 29 May 1998.

2. Rather than interpret moral panics as irrational and superstitious responses to perceived external stimuli, I treat them as active interventions that shape the moral order. Just like production, trade, or migration, they connect places and people and forge spatial links between groups and regions.

3. This idea is borrowed from George Rudé, introduction to *The Great Fear of 1789:*

Rural Panic in Revolutionary France, by Georges Lefebvre, ix–xvi, esp. xiii (Princeton, NJ: Princeton University Press, 1982).

4. See Drew Forrest, "Reasons for Alarmist Fantasies Abound," *Business Day*, 29 May 1998; and Wilf Nussey, "After Apartheid, Hope and Decay," *Guardian Weekly* (London), 19 November 1995.

5. For a wider discussion of these issues, see Gabrielle Spiegel, "History, Historicism, and the Social Logic of the Text in the Middle Ages," *Speculum* 65, no. 1 (1990): 59–86 (esp. 62); Jay Smith, "No More Language Games," *American Historical Review* 102, no. 5 (1997): 1413–40 (esp. 1415–17); and David Mayfield and Susan Thorne, "Social History and Its Discontents: Gareth Stedman Jones and the Politics of Language," *Social History* 17, no. 2 (1992): 165–88 (esp. 187, 188).

6. These ideas are borrowed almost verbatim from Pradeep Jeganathan, "Checkpoint: Anthropology, Identity, and the State," in *Anthropology in the Margins of the State*, ed. Veena Das and Deborah Poole (Santa Fe, NM: School of American Research Press, 2004), 67–80 (esp. 70).

7. This framework is derived from Aijaz Ahmad, *In Theory: Classes, Nations, Literature* (New York: Verso, 1992), 182–83.

8. See Smith, "No More Language Games," 1416, 1417.

9. See Spiegel, "History, Historicism, and the Social Logic," 62.

10. See Smith, "No More Language Games," 1439–40.

11. Sean Hier, "Conceptualizing Moral Panic through a Moral Economy of Harm," *Critical Sociology* 28, no. 3 (2002): 311–34.

12. See Sean Hier, "Thinking beyond Moral Panic: Risk, Responsibility, and the Politics of Moralization," *Theoretical Criminology* 12, no. 2 (2008): 173–90.

13. For the source of some of these ideas (sometimes taken almost verbatim) in this and the following paragraphs, see Marshall Gregory, "Fictions, Facts, and the Fact(s) of (in) Fictions," *Modern Language Studies* 28, nos. 3–4 (1998): 3–40 (esp. 3, 26, 30–31); and Carl Smith, *Urban Disorder and the Shape of Belief: The Great Chicago Fire, the Haymarket Bomb, and the Model Town of Pullman* (Chicago: University of Chicago Press, 1995), 1–16.

14. For the source of some of these ideas, see Gregory, "Fictions, Facts, and the Fact(s)," 3–40; and Smith, *Urban Disorder and the Shape of Belief*, 11–12.

15. See, for example, Brenda Cooper, *Magical Realism in West African Fiction: Seeing with a Third Eye* (London and New York: Routledge, 1998).

16. The literature is extensive, but see, for example, Liam Kennedy, "Alien Nation: White Male Paranoia and Imperial Culture in the United States," *Journal of American Studies* 30, no. 1 (1996): 87–100; Chris Waters, "'Dark Strangers' in Our Midst: Discourses of Race and Nation in Britain, 1947–1963," *Journal of British Studies* 36, no. 2 (1997): 207–38.

17. See Lindsay Bremner, "Bounded Spaces: Demographic Anxieties in Post-Apartheid Johannesburg," *Social Identities* 10, 4 (2004), 455–68.

18. See Nevzat Soguk, *States and Strangers: Refugees and Displacements* (Minneapolis: University of Minnesota Press, 1998); and Elana Gomel, "Aliens among Us: Fascism and Narrativity," *Journal of Narrative Theory* 30, no. 1 (2000): 127–62.

19. See Stanley Cohen, *Folk Devils and Moral Panics* (New York: Routledge, 2011); and

Erich Goode and Nachman Ben-Yehuda, "Moral Panics: Culture, Politics, and Social Construction," *Annual Review of Sociology* 20 (1994): 149–71.

20. See Eric Hobsbawm, "Introduction: Inventing Traditions," in *The Invention of Tradition*, ed. Eric Hobsbawm and Terence Ranger (Cambridge and New York: Cambridge University Press, 1983), 1–14 (esp. 2, 4, 7).

21. Sara Ahmed, "Affective Economies," *Social Text* 22, no. 2 (2004): 123, 126.

22. For a useful comparative analysis, see Susan Ruddick, *Young and Homeless in Hollywood: Mapping Social Identities* (New York and London: Routledge, 1996), 51–66.

23. See Ian Baucom, *Out of Place: Englishness, Empire and the Locations of Identity* (Princeton, NJ: Princeton University Press, 1999).

24. See Jean Comaroff and John Comaroff, "Criminal Justice, Cultural Justice: The Limits of Liberalism and the Pragmatics of Difference in the New South Africa," *American Ethnologist* 31, no. 2 (2004): 188–204.

25. The film *District 9*, which focused on a sensationalized alien invasion, epitomizes this current of fictional representations of fear of the Other. See Michael Valdez Moses et al., "*District 9*: A Roundtable," *Sarafundi: The Journal of South African and American Studies* 11, nos. 1–2 (2010): 155–75; Adéle Nel, "The Repugnant Appeal of the Abject: Cityscape and Cinematic Corporality in *District 9*," *Critical Arts* 26, no. 4 (2012): 547–69; and Aghogho Akpome, "'Zones of Indistinction' and Visions of Post-Reconciliation South Africa in *District 9*," *Sarafundi: The Journal of South African and American Studies* 18, no. 1 (2017): 85–97.

26. Beatriz Jaguaribe, "Cities without Maps: Favelas and the Aesthetics of Realism," in *Urban Imaginaries: Locating the Modern City*, ed. Alev Çinar and Thomas Bender (Minneapolis: University of Minnesota Press, 2007), 100–120 (esp. 102–3).

27. Danielle Burger Allen, "Race, Crime and Social Exclusion: A Qualitative Study of White Women's Fear of Crime in Johannesburg," *Urban Forum* 13, no. 3 (2002): 53–79.

28. See Jaguaribe, "Cities without Maps," 103–4.

29. See Achille Mbembe and Sarah Nuttall, "Writing the World from an African Metropolis," *Public Culture* 16, no. 3 (2004): 347–71.

30. The ideas for this paragraph are borrowed from Loren Kruger, "Filming the Edgy City: Cinematic Narrative and Urban Form in Postapartheid Johannesburg," *Research in African Literatures* 37, no. 2 (2006): 141–63 (esp. 141).

31. De Certeau, *The Practice of Everyday Life*, 115–30.

32. See Jane Rendell, "'Bazaar Beauties' or 'Pleasure Is Our Pursuit': A Spatial Story of Exchange," in *The Unknown City: Contesting Architecture and Social Space*, ed. Iain Borden et al. (London: MIT Press, 2001), 105.

33. For comparative purposes, see Mary Douglas, *Purity and Danger: An Analysis of the Concepts of Pollution and Taboo* (London: Routledge and Kegan Paul, 1966); and Liisa Malkki, *Purity and Exile: Violence, Memory, and National Cosmology among Hutu Refugees in Tanzania* (Chicago: University of Chicago Press, 1995).

34. See Leo Marx, "The American Ideology of Space," in *Denatured Visions: Landscape and Culture in the Twentieth Century*, ed. Stuart Wrede and William Howard Adams (New York: the Museum of Modern Art, 1991), 62–78 (esp. 63).

35. Roland Barthes, *Mythologies* (New York: Hill and Wang, 1972), 143–44.

36. See Samira Kawash, "The Homeless Body," *Public Culture* 10, no. 2 (1998): 319–40 (esp. 320–21, 322–23).

37. Kawash, "The Homeless Body," 322–23.

38. See Rosalyn Deutsche, *Evictions: Art and Spatial Politics* (Cambridge, MA: MIT Press, 1996), 275–76.

39. Although I have modified its meaning, I have borrowed this idea from Nancy Scheper-Hughes, *Death without Weeping: The Violence of Everyday Life in Brazil* (Berkeley: University of California Press, 1992), 220, 224, 230.

40. For the source of this idea, see Gail Hershatter, *Dangerous Pleasures: Prostitution and Modernity in Twentieth-Century Shanghai* (Berkeley: University of California Press, 1997), 34–35.

41. See Henri Lefebvre, *The Production of Space*, trans. Donald Nicholson-Smith (Oxford: Blackwell, 1991), 203.

42. Some of the ideas expressed here are derived from E. Valentine Daniel, "Tea Talk: Violent Measures in the Discursive Practices of Sri Lanka's Estate Tamils," *Comparative Studies in Society and History* 35, no. 3 (1993): 568–600.

43. For the use of the term *crime talk*, see Richard Sparks, Evi Girling, and Ian Loader, "Fear and Everyday Urban Lives," *Urban Studies* 38, nos. 5–6 (2001): 885–98 (esp. 887). See also Teresa Caldeira, *City of Walls: Crime, Segregation, and Citizenship in São Paulo* (Berkeley: University of California Press, 2000), 2, 14, 17–101.

44. See Donna Haraway, *Primate Visions: Gender, Race, and Nature in the World of Modern Science* (New York: Routledge, 1989), 8–9.

45. These ideas are derived from a critical reading of Arnand Yang, "'A Conversation of Rumors': The Language of Popular *Mentalités* in Late Nineteenth-Century Colonial India," *Journal of Social History* 20, no. 3 (1987): 485–505 (esp. 485–86).

46. See Barry Glassner, *The Culture of Fear* (New York: Basic Books, 1999), 3.

47. For comparative purposes, see Smith, *Urban Disorder and the Shape of Belief*, pp. 147–74 in particular.

48. Yiannis Gabriel, "The Narrative Veil: Truth and Untruths in Storytelling," in *Myths, Stories and Organizations: Premodern Narratives for Our Times* (Oxford, UK: Oxford University Press, 2004), 21–22, 24, 25.

49. See Yang, "A Conversation of Rumors," 485–86.

50. Gabriel, "Narrative Veil," 21–25.

51. Jean Comaroff and John Comaroff, "Figuring Crime: Quantifacts and the Production of the Un/Real," *Public Culture* 18, no. 1 (2006): 233–34.

52. See Pierre Bourdieu, *The Logic of Practice*, trans. Richard Nice (Cambridge, UK: Cambridge University Press, 1990).

53. See Michel Foucault, *Discipline and Punish: The Birth of the Prison*, trans. Alan Sheridan (New York: Vintage, 1991), 149.

54. See Chris Wickham, "Gossip and Resistance among the Medieval Peasantry," *Past & Present* 160 (1998): 3–24.

55. Jean Comaroff and John Comaroff, "Policing Culture, Cultural Policing: Law and Social Order in Postcolonial South Africa," *Law and Social Inquiry* 29, no. 3 (2004): 513–46. For a wider discussion, see Louise White, "Vampire Priests of Central Africa:

African Debates about Labor and Religion in Colonial Northern Zambia," *Comparative Studies in Society and History* 35, no. 4 (1993): 746–47.

56. Jean Comaroff and John Comaroff, "Naturing the Nation: Aliens, Apocalypse and the Postcolonial State," *Journal of Southern African Studies* 27, no. 3 (2001): 627–51. See also Caldeira, *City of Walls*, 19–20.

57. A. S. K. Joommal, "Crime Decrease Claims Are Myths Designed to Lull the Public," *The Star*, 28 February 1998.

58. Jean and John Comaroff refer to crime statistics as exemplars of "quantifacts," that is, "statistical representations that make the world 'factual.'" See "Figuring Crime," 209–10.

59. See, for example, James Scott, *Seeing Like a State: How Certain Schemes to Improve the Human Condition Have Failed* (New Haven, CT: Yale University Press, 1998).

60. See Anthony Altbeker, "Puzzling Statistics: Is South Africa Really the World's Crime Capital?" *SA Crime Quarterly* 11 (2005): 1–8.

61. Anonymous, "City Fears Fuel Security Boom," *Cape Argus*, 24 May 2001. See Comaroff and Comaroff, "Figuring Crime," 214–15.

62. Anonymous, "Crime in South Africa: It Won't Go Away," *Economist*, 1 October 2009; Aislinn Laing, "Crime Is Never Far Away from You in Johannesburg," *The Telegraph* (London), 11 July 2015; Graeme Hosken, "Fear Rules Joburg, but Cape Town Is Murder Capital," *Sunday Times*, 29 June 2016; Anonymous, "South Africa 'a Country at War' as Murder Rate Soars to Nearly 49 a Day," *The Guardian* (London), 29 September 2015; and Aphiwe Ngalo and Hlumela Dyantyi, "Murder, Attempted Murder and Robbery the Three Biggest Headaches for SAPS," *Daily Maverick*, 29 September 2018.

63. It is also true that some crimes are overreported, particularly when successfully lying about being the victim of criminal wrongdoing can yield financial gain. This is especially the case with false reporting to insurance companies in making claims about stolen property. See Sesona Ngqakamba, "Joburg Man Gets Six Months for False Reporting of a Hyjacking," *News 24*, 20 June 2018.

64. Anonymous, "If You Get Mugged, Don't Bother Reporting It," *The Star*, 2 May 1998. See also Farouk Araie, "Crime Out of Control," *Saturday Star*, 27 March 2017.

65. The literature on this topic is extensive. See, for example, Euan Conley, "South Africa: A Really Attractive White-Collar Crime Venue for Criminals," *Global Investigations Review*, 13 October 2016; and Steven Gruzd, "White-Collar Crime Thrives When Ethics Aren't Enforced," *South African Jewish Report*, 15 March 2018.

66. Under any and all circumstances, how information is collected, what counts as evidence, and how categories shift over time make crime statistics (and quantitative data in general) notoriously unreliable. See Comaroff and Comaroff, "Criminal Obsessions, after Foucault," 800–801.

67. Comaroff and Comaroff, "Criminal Obsessions, after Foucault," 800–801.

68. See Judy Coffin, "Artisans of the Sidewalk," *Radical History Review* 26 (1982): 89–101.

69. Comaroff and Comaroff, "Figuring Crime," 228–30.

70. Anonymous, "Mufamadi Explains Crime-Count Disparity," *The Star*, 6 March 1998; and Anonymous, "Press, Opposition Challenge Crime Statistics," *BBC Worldwide*

Monitoring, 7 February 2001; Anonymous, "Government Use of Crime Statistics Undermines Credibility," *Business Day*, 10 February 1998; and Mark Shaw and Antoinette Louw, "Government Risks Undermining the Credibility of Crime Statistics by Using Them for Its Own Ends," *Business Day*, 2 October 1998.

71. See Stephen Mulholland, "Crime Is a Problem for the Whole Country, Mr Mbeki," *The Star*, 13 June 1999. In order to draw attention to the seriousness of house burglaries, the popular media revealed that even the minister of safety and security Sydney Mufamadi was not immune to crime. Ten of the thirty homes on his street in the Sandton suburb of Bryanston were targeted by criminals in the space of several months (Anonymous, "Crime Comes Calling," *Cape Argus*, 26 May 1999).

72. Teresa Dirsuweit, "Johannesburg: Fearful City?," *Urban Forum* 13, no. 3 (2002): 3–19; and Comaroff and Comaroff, "Figuring Crime," 209–46.

73. Nikolas Rose, "Governing Cities, Governing Citizenship," in *Democracy, Citizenship and the Global City*, ed. Engin Isin (New York: Routledge, 2000), 101, 102.

74. See Peter Wollen, "*Blade Runner*: 'Ridleyville' and Los Angeles," in *The Hieroglyphics of Space: Reading and Experiencing the Modern Metropolis*, ed. Neil Leach (New York: Routledge, 2002), 236–43.

75. W. I. Thomas and D. S. Thomas, *The Child in America: Behavior Problems and Programs* (New York: Knopf, 1928), 571–72.

76. David Harvey, *Spaces of Hope* (Berkeley: University of California Press, 2000), 157.

77. For the source of this idea, see Erin Graff Zivin, *The Wandering Signifier: Rhetoric of Jewishness in the Latin American Imaginary* (Durham, NC: Duke University Press 2008).

78. Evi Girling, Ian Loader, and Richard Sparks, "A Telling Tale: A Case of Vigilantism and Its Aftermath in an English Town," *British Journal of Sociology* 49, no. 3 (1998): 474–75.

79. Comaroff and Comaroff, "Figuring Crime," 221.

80. Mary Douglas, *Risk and Blame: Essays in Cultural Theory* (London: Routledge, 1992), 29–30.

81. See, for example, Patrick Lenta, "'Everyday Abnormality': Crime and In/security in Ivan Vladislavić's Portrait with Keys," *The Journal of Commonwealth Literature* 44, no. 1 (2009): 117–33.

82. See Douglas, *Purity and Danger*, 1–3, 8–9.

83. See Caldeira, *City of Walls*, 137.

84. Lindsay Bremner, "Crime and the Emerging Landscape of Post-Apartheid Johannesburg," in *Blank___: Architecture, Apartheid and After*, ed. Hilton Judin and Ivan Vladislavić (Rotterdam: NAi, 1998), 48–63.

85. For the source of this idea, see Haraway, *Primate Visions*, 289.

86. See Timothy Gilfoyle, "Prostitutes in History: From Parables of Pornography to Metaphors of Modernity," *American Historical Review* 104, no. 1 (1999): 117–41 (esp. 129).

87. See David Pinder, "Subverting Cartography: The Situationists and Maps of the City," *Environment and Planning A* 28, no. 3 (1996): 405–27 (esp. 405, 419, 421). See also Pierre Bourdieu, *Outline of a Theory of Practice* (New York: Cambridge University Press, 1977), 105.

88. See Pinder, "Subverting Cartography," 422–23.

CHAPTER 2

1. Bongani Madondo, "Send Task Force to Save Hillbrow!" *City Press*, 20 April 1997.

2. Mercedes Hinton, The State on the Streets: Police and Politics in Argentina and Brazil (Boulder, CO: Lynne Rienner, 2006).

3. See, for example, Andrew Faull, "Need or Greed? Corruption and Integrity Management in a Gauteng Police Station," *SA Crime Quarterly* 28 (2009): 11–19.

4. See Maria Loś, "Post-Communist Fear of Crime and the Commercialization of Security," *Theoretical Criminology* 6, no. 2 (2002): 168.

5. Rebecca Harrison, "Witness: Pizza and Machetes: Living with Crime in Johannesburg," *Reuters*, 19 April 2007.

6. Gail Super, "The Spectacle of Crime in the 'New' South Africa: A Historical Perspective (1976–2004)," *British Journal of Criminology* 50, 2 (2010): 176. See also Gail Super, *Governing through Crime in South Africa: The Politics of Race and Class in Neoliberalizing Regimes*, new ed. (New York: Routledge, 2016), 133–42.

7. Anthony Altbeker, *A Country at War with Itself: South Africa's Crisis of Crime* (Cape Town: Jonathan Ball, 2007); Mark Shaw, *Towards Safer Cities: The South African Debate on Options for Urban Safety*, monograph series, no. 11 (Pretoria: Institute for Security Studies, 1997), 1–25; Suren Pillay, "Crime, Community and the Governance of Violence in Post-Apartheid South Africa," *Politikon* 35, no. 2 (2008): 141–58; and Jean Comaroff and John Comaroff, "Figuring Crime: Quantifacts and the Production of the Un/Real," *Public Culture* 18, 1 (2006): 209–46.

8. Loś, "Post-Communist Fear of Crime," 178.

9. Claire Bénit-Gbaffou, "Unbundled Security Services and Urban Fragmentation in Post-Apartheid Johannesburg," *Geoforum* 39, no. 6 (2008): 1933–50; and Thomas Blom Hansen, "Performers of Sovereignty: On the Privatization of Security in Urban South Africa," *Critique of Anthropology* 26, no. 3 (2006): 279–95.

10. Anthony Minnaar and Duxita Mistry, "Outsourcing and the South African Police Service," in *Private Muscle: Outsourcing the Provision of Criminal Justice Services*, ed. Martin Schönteich et al., monograph series, no. 93 (Pretoria: Institute for Security Studies, 2004), 38–54.

11. Claire Bénit-Gbaffou, "Community Policing and Disputed Norms for Local Social Control in Post-Apartheid Johannesburg," *Journal of Southern African Studies* 34, no. 1 (2008): 93–109; Sabelo Gumedze, "The Private Security Sector in Africa: The 21st Century's Major Cause for Concern?," occasional paper no. 133 (Pretoria: Institute for Security Studies, 2007), 1–20; Lars Buur and Steffen Jensen, "Vigilantism and the Policing of Everyday Life in South Africa," *African Studies* 63, no. 2 (2004): 139–52; and Gail Super, "Volatile Sovereignty: Governing Crime through the Community in Khayelitsha," *Law and Society Review* 50, no. 2 (2016): 450–83.

12. Martin Schönteich, *Unshackling the Crime Fighters: Increasing Private Security Involvement in South Africa's Criminal Justice System* (Johannesburg: South African Institute of Race Relations, 1999); Jenny Irish, *Policing for Profit: The Future of South Africa's Private Security Industry*, monograph 39 (Pretoria: Institute for Security Studies, 1999), 1–27; Mark Napier, et al., *Environmental Design for Safer Communities* (Pretoria: Council for Scientific and Industrial Research, 1998). See also Scott Calvert, "In Johannesburg Suburbs, an Obsession with Security," *Baltimore Sun*, 22 May 2005.

13. Bénit-Gbaffou, "Unbundled Security Services," 1933–50.

14. Ian Loader, "Plural Policing and Democratic Governance," *Social & Legal Studies* 9, no. 3 (2000): 323.

15. Benoit Dupont, "Private Security Regimes: Conceptualizing the Forces that Shape the Private Delivery of Security," *Theoretical Criminology* 18, no. 3 (2014): 263.

16. Interviews with Carl Chemaly, Steve Lenahan, and Andre Viljoen, 11 June 2012; Vickie Drinkwater, 2 February 2016; Ryan Roseveare and Glenn du Toit, 2 July 2014; and David de Lima and Andre Viljeon, 28 June 2012.

17. Dupont, "Private Security Regimes," 265.

18. Clifford Shearing and Philip Stenning, "Private Security: Implications for Social Control," *Social Problems* 30, no. 5 (1983): 493–506 (esp. 501). See also Clifford Shearing and Philip Stenning, "Modern Private Security: Its Growth and Implications," *Crime & Justice* 3 (1981): 193–245.

19. See Trevor Jones and Tim Newburn, "The Transformation of Policing? Understanding Trends in Policing Systems," *British Journal of Criminology* 42, no. 1 (2002): 129–46.

20. Much of the scholarly literature on the transformation of policing has implicitly or otherwise presumed the existence of a mythical golden age in which a single state-sponsored professional organization tasked with managing the policing functions of regulation and surveillance was able to assert a virtual monopoly over the legitimate use of force and violence. In reality, this modernist projection of organizing the social world around a holistic, cohesive notion of normative order and of maintaining law and order through an all-encompassing, centralized public authority was largely a symbolic one. See Tim Newburn, "The Commodification of Policing: Security Networks in the Late Modern City," *Urban Studies* 38, nos. 5–6 (2001): 829–48 (esp. 829–30); Robert Reiner, "Policing a Postmodern Society," *Modern Law Review* 55, no. 5 (1992): 761–78; and David Garland, "The Limits of the Sovereign State: Strategies of Crime Control in Contemporary Society," *British Journal of Criminology* 36, no. 4 (1996): 445–71.

21. Bénit-Gbaffou, "Unbundled Security Services," 1934.

22. See Ian Loader, "Private Security and the Demand for Protection in Contemporary Britain," *Policing and Society* 7 (1997): 143–62 (esp. 147); David Bayley and Clifford Shearing, "The Future of Policing," *Law and Society Review* 30, no. 3 (1996): 585–606; Les Johnston, *Policing Britain: Risk, Security, and Governance* (Harlow: Longman, 2000); and Les Johnston, *The Rebirth of Private Policing* (New York: Routledge, 1992).

23. Ian Loader, "Consumer Culture and the Commodification of Policing and Security," *Sociology* 33, no. 2 (1999): 373–92; and Lucia Zedner, "Too Much Security?," *International Journal of the Sociology of Law* 31, no. 3 (2003): 155–84 (esp. 156–57).

24. See Clifford Shearing, "Policing: Relationships between Its Public and Private Forms," in *Alternative Policing Styles: Cross-Cultural Perspectives*, ed. Mark Findlay and Uglješa Zvekić (Cambridge, MA: Kluwer Law and Taxation Publishers, 1993), 203–28; and Eugene McLaughlin and Karim Murji, "The Postmodern Condition of the Police," *Liverpool Law Review* 21 (1999): 217–40; and Willem De Lint, "A Post-Modern Turn in Policing: Policing as Pastiche?," *International Journal of the Sociology of Law* 27 (1999): 127–52.

25. Anthony Minnaar, "Private–Public Partnerships: Private Security, Crime Prevention and Policing in South Africa," *Acta Criminologica: Southern African Journal of*

Criminology 18, no. 1 (2005): 85–114. See also interview with Anthony Minnaar, 6 July 2011. For the debate about the extent to which policing has undergone a fundamental restructuring over the past thirty years, see, for example, Les Johnston and Clifford Shearing, *Governing Security: Explorations in Policing and Justice* (London: Routledge, 2003); Bayley and Shearing, "The Future of Policing"; and Jones and Newburn, "Transformation of Policing?"

26. Phillip Stenning, "Powers and Accountability of Private Police," *European Journal on Criminal Policy and Research* 8, no. 3 (2000): 328.

27. Newburn, "Commodification of Policing," 830. See also Ian Loader and Neil Walker, *Civilizing Security* (Cambridge, UK: Cambridge University Press, 2007), 3.

28. David Garland, *The Culture of Control: Crime and Social Order in Contemporary Society* (Oxford, UK: Oxford University Press, 2001); and Marina Caparini, "Applying a Security Governance Perspective to the Privatisation of Security," in *Private Actors and Security Governance*, ed. Alan Bryden and Marina Caparini (Münster: LIT Verlag, 2006), 263–82.

29. Adam Crawford and Stuart Lister, "Additional Security Patrols in Residential Areas: Notes from the Marketplace," *Policing & Society* 16, no. 2 (2006): 164–88 (esp. 164–65).

30. Crawford and Lister, "Additional Security Patrols," 171. See also Shearing and Stenning, "Modern Private Security," 193–245.

31. Les Johnston, "Privatization and the Police Function: From 'New Police' to 'New Policing,'" in *Beyond Law and Order: Criminal Justice Policy and Politics in the 1990s*, ed. Robert Reiner and Malcolm Cross (Basingstoke, UK: Macmillan, 1991), 18–40; and Les Johnston, "Policing Diversity: The Impact of the Public-Private Complex in Policing," in *Core Issues in Policing*, ed. Frank Leisham, Barry Loveday and Stephen Savage (London: Longman, 1996), 54–70.

32. See Jennifer Wood and Clifford Shearing, *Imagining Security* (New York: Routledge, 2007); and Mark Button, *Doing Security: Critical Reflections and an Agenda for Change* (New York: Palgrave Macmillan, 2008).

33. See Jones and Newburn, "Transformation of Policing?," 129–30. See also J. W. E. Sheptycki, "Policing Postmodernism and Transnationalization," *British Journal of Criminology* 38, no. 3 (1998): 485–503; and Kate Meagher, "The Strength of Weak States? Non-State Security Forces and Hybrid Governance in Africa," *Development and Change* 43, no. 5 (2012): 1073–1101.

34. See Patrick O'Malley and Darren Palmer, "Post-Keynesian Policing," *Economy & Society* 25, no. 2 (1996): 137–55; Adam Crawford and Stuart Lister, *The Extended Policing Family: Visible Patrols in Residential Areas*, Centre for Criminal Justice Studies, University of Leeds (York: Joseph Roundtree Foundation, 2004); Trevor Jones and Tim Newburn, eds., *Plural Policing: A Comparative Perspective* (New York: Routledge, 2006); Les Johnston, "From 'Pluralisation' to 'the Police Extended Family': Discourses on the Governance of Community Policing in Britain," *International Journal of the Sociology of Law* 31, no. 3 (2003): 185–204; Phillip Stenning, "Governance and Accountability in a Plural Policing Environment: The Story So Far," *Policing* 3, no. 1 (2009): 22–33; Tim Newburn and Robert Reiner, "Policing and the Police," in *The Oxford Handbook of Criminology*, ed. Mike Maguire, Rod Morgan, and Robert Reiner (Oxford, UK: Clarendon Press, 1997), 910–52; Dominique Boels and Antoinette Verhage, "Plural Policing: A State-of-

the-Art Review," *Policing: An International Journal of Police Strategies & Management* 39, no. 1 (2016), 2–18; Loader, "Plural Policing and Democratic Governance," 323–45; and Eugene McLaughlin and Karim Murji, "The End of Public Policing? Police Reform and the 'New Managerialism,'" in *Contemporary Issues in Criminology*, ed. Leslie Noaks, Michael Levi, and Mike Maguire (Cardiff: University of Wales Press, 1995), 110–27.

35. See Lucia Zedner, "Liquid Security: Managing the Market for Crime Control," *Criminology & Criminal Justice* 6, no. 3 (2006): 267–88; Eugene McLaughlin and Karim Murji, "Lost Connections and New Directions: Neo-liberalism, New Public Managerialism, and the 'Modernization' of the British Police," in *Crime, Risk, and Justice: The Politics of Crime Control in Liberal Democracies*, ed. Kevin Stenson and Robert Sullivan (Cullompton, UK: Willan, 2001), 104–21.

36. Lucia Zedner, for example, has argued—and correctly in my view—that "the symbolic monopoly on policing asserted by the modern criminal justice state may just be a historical blip in a longer-term pattern of multiple policing providers and markets in security." See "Policing before and after the Police," *British Journal of Criminology* 46, no. 1 (2006): 78. See also Adam Crawford, "Plural Policing in the UK: Policing beyond the Police," in *Handbook of Policing*, 2nd ed., ed. Tim Newburn (New York: Routledge, 2008), 147–81.

37. Adam Crawford, ed., "The Governance of Crime and Insecurity in an Anxious Age: The Trans-European and the Local," in *Crime and Insecurity* (Cullompton, UK: Willan, 2002), 27–28. See also Lucia Zedner, "The Pursuit of Security," in *Crime, Risk, and Insecurity*, ed. Tim Hope and Richard Sparks (London: Routledge, 2000), 200–214.

38. Garland, *Culture of Control*, 17.

39. Mark Button, "Private Security and the Policing of Quasi-Public Space," *International Journal of the Sociology of Law* 31, no. 3 (2003): 227–37; Jones and Newburn, "Transformation of Policing?"; Minnaar, "Private–Public Partnerships," 85–114; Michael Kempa et al., "Reflections on the Evolving Concept of 'Private Policing,'" *European Journal on Criminal Policy and Research* 7, no. 2 (1999): 197–223.

40. Adam Crawford, "Policing and Security as 'Club Goods': The New Enclosures?," in *Democracy, Society, and the Governance of Security*, ed. Jennifer Wood and Benoît Dupont (Cambridge, UK: Cambridge University Press, 2006), 111.

41. Crawford and Lister, "Additional Security Patrols," 168–70.

42. For the origins of this idea, see Loader, "Commodification of Policing and Security," 384.

43. Loader, "Commodification of Policing and Security," 384.

44. Garland, "Limits of the Sovereign State," 448–52. See also Nick Tilly, "Privatizing Crime Control," *The Annals of the American Academy of Political and Social Science* 679, no. 1 (2018): 55–71.

45. See Joshua Freilich and Graeme Newman, "Regulating Crime: The New Criminology of Crime Control," *The Annals of the American Academy of Political and Social Science* 679, no. 1 (2018): 8–18; and Joshua Freilich and Graeme Newman, "Transforming Piecemeal Social Engineering into Grand Crime Prevention Policy: Toward a New Criminology of Social Control," *Journal of Criminal Law & Criminology* 105, no. 1 (2016): 203–32.

46. Les Johnston, "Private Policing in Context," *European Journal on Criminal Policy and Research* 7, no. 2 (1999): 175–96; Les Johnston, "Crime, Fear and Civil Policing," *Urban Studies* 38, nos. 5–6 (2001): 959–76; Newburn, "Commodification of Policing"; Markus Kienscherf, "Security Assemblages and Spaces of Exception: The Production of (Para-) Militarized Spaces in the U.S. War on Drugs," *Radical Criminology* 1, no. 1 (2012): 19–35; Zedner, "Liquid Security," 267–88; Clifford Shearing, "Nodal Governance," *Police Quarterly* 8, no. 1 (2005): 57–63; Jarrett Blaustein, "The Space Between: Negotiating the Contours of Nodal Security Governance through 'Safer Communities' in Bosnia-Herzegovina," *Policing & Society* 24, no. 1 (2014): 44–62; and Rita Abrahamsen and Michael Williams, *Security Beyond the State: Private Security in International Politics* (Cambridge, UK: Cambridge University Press, 2011), 3, 11.

47. Richard Ericson, "The Division of Expert Knowledge in Policing and Security," *British Journal of Sociology* 45, no. 2 (1994): 149–75; Richard Ericson, *Crime in an Insecure World* (Cambridge, UK: Polity Press, 2007); Boas Shamir and Eyal Ben-Ar, "Challenges of Military Leadership in Changing Armies," *JPMS: Journal of Political and Military Sociology* 28, no. 1 (2000): 43–59; Jean-Paul Brodeur, *The Policing Web* (Oxford, UK: Oxford University Press, 2010); Adam Crawford and Stuart Lister, "The Patchwork Shape of Reassurance Policing in England and Wales: Integrated Local Security Quilts or Frayed, Fragmented and Fragile Tangled Webs?," *Policing: An International Journal of Police Strategies & Management* 27, no. 3 (2004): 413–30; Tessa Diphoorn, "Twilight Policing: Private Security Practices in South Africa," *British Journal of Criminology* 56, no. 2 (2016): 313–31; and Bruce Baker, *Multi-Choice Policing in Africa* (Uppsala, SE: Nordiska Afrikainstitutet, 2008).

48. Johnston, "Crime, Fear and Civil Policing," 973; Johnston, "Private Policing in Context," 175–96; and Newburn, "Commodification of Policing."

49. Kempa et al., "Evolving Concept of 'Private Policing,'" 199. See also Clifford Shearing and Jennifer Wood (in collaboration with John Cartwright and Madeleine Jenneker), "Nodal Governance, Denizenship & Communal Space: Challenging the Westphalian Ideal," in *Limits to Liberation after Apartheid: Citizenship, Governance & Culture*, ed. Steven Robins (Athens: Ohio University Press, 2005), 97–112.

50. Adam Crawford, "Joined-Up but Fragmented: Contradiction, Ambiguity, and Ambivalence at the Heart of New Labour's 'Third Way,'" in *Crime, Disorder and Community Safety: A New Agenda?*, ed. Roger Matthews and John Pitts(London: Routledge, 2001), 54–80 (esp. 60).

51. Kempa et al., "Evolving Concept of 'Private Policing,'" 199.

52. Richard Yarwood, "The Geographies of Policing," *Progress in Human Geography* 31, no. 4 (2007): 447–65 (esp. 448). See also Susan Smith, "Police Accountability and Local Democracy," *Area* 18, no. 2 (1986): 99–107; and Steve Herbert, "The Normative Ordering of Police Territoriality: Making and Marking Space with the Los Angeles Police Department," *Annals of the Association of American Geographers* 86, no. 3 (1996): 567–82.

53. See Rita Abrahamsen and Michael Williams, "Securing the City: Private Security Companies and Non-State Authority in Global Governance," *International Relations* 21, no. 2 (2007): 237–53; Rita Abrahamsen and Michael Williams, "Security Privatization and Global Security Assemblages," *Brown Journal of World Affairs* 18, no. 1 (2011):

153–62; Irish, *Policing for Profit*, 1–27; and Rutger Claassen, "The Marketization of Security Services," *Public Reason* 3, no. 2 (2011): 124–45.

54. See Lucia Zedner, "The Concept of Security: An Agenda for Comparative Analysis," *Legal Studies* 23, no. 1 (2003): 153–73 (esp. 161–62).

55. Adam Crawford, "Networked Governance and the Post-Regulatory State: Steering, Rowing, and Anchoring the Provision of Policing and Security," *Theoretical Criminology* 10, no. 4 (2006): 458.

56. Zedner, "Liquid Security," 269; and Clifford Shearing and Jennifer Wood, "Nodal Governance, Democracy, and the 'New Denizens,'" *Journal of Law and Society* 30, no. 3 (2003): 400–419.

57. Tessa Diphoorn and Helene Maria Kyed, "Entanglements of Private Security and Community Policing in South Africa and Swaziland," *African Affairs* 115/461 (2016): 711; and Bruce Baker, "Living with Non-State Policing in South Africa: The Issues and Dilemmas," *Journal of Modern African Studies* 40, no. 1 (2002): 29–53.

58. For the source of this idea, see Andy Clarno and Martin J. Murray, "Policing in Johannesburg after Apartheid," *Social Dynamics* 39, no. 2 (2013): 210–27.

59. See, for example, Julie Berg, "Challenges to a Formal Private Security–SAPS Partnership: Lessons from the Western Cape," *Society in Transition* 35, no. 1 (2004): 105–24; Mark Button, "Policing of Quasi-Public Space"; and Michael Kempa, Phillip Stenning, and Jennifer Wood, "Policing Communal Spaces: A Reconfiguration of the 'Mass Private Property' Hypothesis," *British Journal of Criminology* 44, no. 4 (2004): 562–81.

60. Dominique Wisler and Ihekwoaba Onwudiwe, "Community Policing in Comparison," *Police Quarterly* 11, no. 4 (2008): 427–446 (esp. 433); Martin Schönteich, "Fighting Crime with Private Muscle: The Private Sector and Crime Prevention," *African Security Review* 8, no. 5 (1999): 65–75; Martin Schönteich, Anthony Minnaar, Duxita Misty, and K. C. Goyer, eds., *Private Muscle: The Provision of Criminal Justice Services*, monograph series, no. 93 (Pretoria: Institute for Security Studies, 2004); and Minnaar, "Private–Public Partnerships," 111–12.

61. Julie Berg, "Seeing Like Private Security: Evolving Mentalities of Public Space Protection in South Africa," *Criminology & Criminal Justice* 10, no. 3 (2010): 287–301 (esp. 295). See Monique Marks, Jennifer Wood, and Clifford Shearing, "A Thin or Thick Blue Line? Exploring Alternative Models for Community Policing and the Police Role in South Africa," in *Community Policing and Peacekeeping*, ed. Peter Grabosky (New York: CRC Press, 2009): 153–68.

62. David Kennedy, *Deterrence and Crime Prevention: Reconsidering the Prospect of Sanction* (London: Routledge, 2008).

63. Berg, "Seeing Like Private Security," 288.

64. Clarno and Murray, "Policing in Johannesburg after Apartheid."

65. Ian Cook and Mary Whowell, "Visibility and the Policing of Public Space," *Geography Compass* 5, no. 8 (2011): 612.

66. Newburn, "Commodification of Policing," 829–30; Robert Reiner, "Policing a Postmodern Society," *Modern Law Review* 55, no. 5 (1992): 761–78; and Garland, "Limits of the Sovereign State."

67. Clarno and Murray, "Policing in Johannesburg after Apartheid."

68. Zedner, "Liquid Security," 269–70.

69. George Rigakos, *The New Parapolice: Risk Markets and Commodified Social Control* (Toronto: University of Toronto Press, 2002); and Richard Ericson and Kevin Haggerty, *Policing the Risk Society* (Toronto: University of Toronto Press, 1997).

70. Adam Crawford, *Crime Prevention and Community Safety: Politics, Policies and Practices* (Harlow, UK: Addison Wesley Longman, 1998), 72. See also Zedner, "Concept of Security," 153–75; and Adam Edwards and Gordon Hughes, "The Preventive Turn and the Promotion of Safer Communities in England and Wales: Political Inventiveness and Governmental Instabilities," in *Crime Prevention Policies in Comparative Perspective*, ed. Adam Crawford (London: Willan, 2009), 62–85.

71. Patrick O'Malley, "Risk and Responsibility," in *Foucault and Political Reason: Liberalism, Neo-liberalism, and Rationalities of Government*, ed. Nikolas Rose, Thomas Osborne, and Andrew Barry (Chicago: University of Chicago Press, 1996), 189–207.

72. Malcolm Feeley and Jonathan Simon, "Actuarial Justice: The Emerging New Criminal Law," in *The Futures of Criminology*, ed. David Nelken (London: Sage, 1994), 173–201; Nancy Reichman, "Managing Crime Risks: Towards an Insurance Based Model of Social Control," *Research in Law and Social Control* 8 (1986): 151–72; and Patrick O'Malley, "Policing Crime Risks in the Neo-Liberal Era," in *Crime, Risk and Justice*, ed. Kevin Stenson and Robert Sullivan (Cullompton, UK: Willan Publishing, 2001), 89–103.

73. Garland, "Limits of the Sovereign State," 445–71.

74. Jelle van Buuren, *Security as a Commodity: The Ethical Dilemmas of Private Security Services*, INEX Policy Brief, paper 6 (Oslo: International Peace Research Institute, 2010), 1.

75. Anne-Marie Singh, *Policing and Crime Control in Post-Apartheid South Africa* (Burlington, VT: Ashgate, 2008), 46; Patrick O'Malley, "Risk, Power and Crime Prevention," *Economy & Society* 21, no. 3 (1992): 252–75; and O'Malley, "Risk and Responsibility.

76. Yarwood, "Geographies of Policing," p. 448; and James Sheptycki, "Book Review: A. Crawford, S. Lister, S. Blackburn and J. Burnett, *Plural Policing: The Mixed Economy of Visible Patrols in England and Wales*," *Social Legal Studies* 17, no. 1 (2008): 147.

77. Adam Crawford, Stuart Lister, Sarah Blackburn, and Jonathan Burnett, *Plural Policing: the Mixed Economy of Visible Patrols in England and Wales* (Bristol: Policy Press, 2005).

78. See Yarwood, "Geographies of Policing," p. 448. See also Adam Crawford, *The Local Governance of Crime: Appeals to Community and Partnerships* (London: Clarendon Press, 1997); Adam Crawford, "The Pattern of Policing in the UK: Policing beyond the Police," in *Handbook of Policing*, ed. Tim Newburn (Cullompton, UK: Willan, 2003), 136–69; Peter Goris and Reece Walters, "Locally-Orientated Crime Prevention and the 'Partnership Approach,'" *Policing* 22, no. 4 (1999): 633–45; and Gordon Hughes, Eugene McLaughlin, and John Muncie, *Crime Prevention and Community Safety: New Directions* (London: Sage, 2001).

79. Bénit-Gbaffou, "Community Policing and Disputed Norms," 93–95.

80. Malcolm Feeley and Jonathan Simon, "The New Penology: Notes on the Emerging Strategy of Corrections and Its Implications," *Criminology* 30, no. 4 (1992): 449–74; Feeley and Simon, "Actuarial Justice," 173–201; and Malcolm Feeley and Jonathan Si-

mon, "The Form and the Limits of the New Penology," in *Punishment and Social Control*, enlarged 2nd ed., ed. Thomas G. Blomberg and Stanley Cohen (New York: Aldine de Gruyter, 2003), 75–94.

81. O'Malley, "Risk and Responsibility," 196.

82. Roy Coleman and Joe Sim, "Contemporary Statecraft and the 'Punitive Obsession': A Critique of the New Penology Thesis," in *The New Punitiveness: Trends, Theories, Perspectives*, ed. John Pratt et al. (Cullompton, UK: Willan, 2005), 105.

83. Michalis Lianos and Mary Douglas, "Dangerization and the End of Deviance: the Institutional Environment," in *Criminology and Social Theory*, ed. David Garland and Richard Sparks (Oxford, UK: Oxford University Press, 2000), 103–26 (esp. 103–4).

84. Coleman and Sim, "Contemporary Statecraft," 107.

85. Berg, "Seeing Like Private Security," 287–301. Interviews with Nazira Cachalia, 30 May 2006, and 24 June 2011; J. M. Tau, 25 June 2012; Wayne Minnaar, 9 July 2014; and Major M. S. Mohlanga, 8 February 2016.

86. Ian Loader and Neil Walker, "Policing as a Public Good: Reconstituting the Connections between Policing and the State," *Theoretical Criminology* 5, no. 1 (2001): 9–35 (esp. 10).

87. Interviews with Brigadier P. P. Billings, 4 July 2014; Tony Botes, 25 June 2014; Wendy Vorster-Robertson, 4 July 2014; Stewart Rider, 15 June 2012; and Anthony Modena, 4 July 2014.

88. Staff Reporter, "South African Jews to Fund Johannesburg Police Station," *Jewish Telegraphic Agency*, 21 April 1997; Ferial Haffajee, "Suburbs Search for Better Private Security Service," *Financial Mail*, 8 September 2000; Sarah Oppler, "Partnership Policing Creates a United Front against Crime," *The Star*, 15 March 1997; and Sibonelo Radebe, "'Orphan' Police Station Has Guardian," *Business Day*, 2 June 1999. See interviews with Eve Jammy, 4 July 2014; Lornette Joseph, 10 July 2014; Jonathan Hackner and Elton Hill, 20 June 2012; and Lionel Stein, 1 July 2014.

89. In 2004, the SAPS was spending R 3.8 million a month, or R 45 million a year, to pay private security companies to guard their facilities. About twenty different companies were contracted to provide security at a total of 145 police premises countrywide. These include police stations, police headquarters in Pretoria (at R 186,637 a month), VIP protection offices in Pretoria and Cape Town, the Commercial Crime Unit in Johannesburg, several training colleges, and even a shooting range in Graaff-Reinet. Companies included Chubb Protective Services, Protea Security, Anchor Security, Impala Security, Secuforce, Security Wise, and Coin Security. See Angela Quintal, "Police 'Buying Protection' from Private Firms," *The Star*, 8 December 2004.

90. Carlen DuPlessis, "Private Security Costs Cops 121m Rands," *The Star*, 14 March 2009.

91. See Andy Clarno, *Neoliberal Apartheid: Palestine/Israel and South Africa after 1994* (Chicago: University of Chicago Press, 2017), 143–44. See interviews with Jenny Reid, 11 July 2014; Gareth Newman, 11 July 2011; Andrew Seldon, 13 June 2012; and focus group with Hi-Tech Security Solutions, 13 June 2012.

92. In 2008, the Honeydew police station was faced with the second-highest house

robbery rate and the seventh-highest business robbery rate in the entire country. See Annalise Kempner, "Private Security Alignment Initiative," *Servamus* 102, no. 1 (2009): 28–32 (esp. 28).

93. Sekgololo Angel Mabudusha, "The Policing of Illegal Squatting in the Green-belts within Weltevereden Park Area," (master's thesis, University of South Africa, May 2010), 32–33. See Kempen, "Private Security Alignment Initiative," 28.

94. Olaotse John Kole, "Partnership Policing between the South African Police Service and Private Security Industry in Reducing Crime in South Africa," (Ph.D. diss., University of South Africa, June 2015), 3, 88.

95. Thandi Skade, "Security Guards 'Won't Have Police Powers,'" *The Star*, 30 October 2008.

96. See Kempen, "Private Security Alignment Initiative," 39).

97. Karen van Rooyen, "Private Guards Get More Powers to Police the Suburbs," *Sunday Times*, 26 October 2008; and Tessa Diphoorn, *Twilight Policing: Private Security and Violence in Urban South Africa* (Berkeley: University of California Press, 2016), 130.

98. Xolani Mbanjwa, "Experts in Limbo about New Anti-Crime Plan," *The Star*, 31 October 2008. See also interviews with Barbara Holtman, 28 June 2011; and Margaret Gichanga, 10 July 2014.

99. Email correspondence with Major-General O. D. Reddy, 14 August 2017; and Margaret Gichanga, 15 August 2015.

100. Zedner, "Liquid Security," 269–70.

101. Zedner. See also Trevor Jones and Tim Newburn, *Private Security and Public Policing* (Oxford, UK: Clarendon, 1998), 80–82.

102. Evadne Grant, "Private Policing," in *Acta Juridica*, ed. Thomas Bennett, Derry Devine, Dale Hutchison, Solly Leeman, and Dirk Van Zyl Smit (Cape Town: Juta, 1989); and Mark Shaw, *Crime and Policing in Post-Apartheid South Africa: Transforming under Fire* (Bloomington: Indiana University Press, 2002), 22–28. During the early 1980s, the state security apparatus under *apartheid* created a number of private security firms to act as fronts for the illegal trade in weapons, ivory, diamonds, and other precious stones. See Singh, *Policing and Crime Control*, 43.

103. See Mark Shaw, "Crime in Transition," in *Policing the Transition: Further Issues in South Africa's Crime Debate*, ed. by Mark Shaw et. al., monograph series, no. 12 (Pretoria: Institute for Security Studies, 1997), 7–27; and Sarah Oppler, "Partners against Crime," in *Policing the Transition: Further Issues in South Africa's Crime Debate*, ed. Mark Shaw et. al., monograph series, no. 12 (Pretoria: Institute for Security Studies, 1997), 7–27, 50–65, respectively. See also Shaw, *Crime and Policing in Post-Apartheid South Africa*, 102–18; and Gumedze, "The Private Security Sector in Africa," 1–20. See also Ryan Carrier, "Dissolving Boundaries: Private Security and Policing in South Africa," *African Security Review* 8, no. 6 (1999): 37–43.

104. Shaw, "Crime in Transition," 7–28; and Staff Reporter, "The Guardian Angel of Soweto," *Star Business Report*, 23 May 1999.

105. The outsourcing of detention and prison functions is an important story that requires further exposure and analysis. See Bongani Hans, "Privatizing Prison 'Was

a Huge Mistake,'" *Business Day*, 6 November 2013; Wyndham Hartley, "Ndebele Acknowledges Failure of Private Prisons," *Business Day*, 6 November 2013; and Ilse de Lange, "Inmate Set for R200K Private Prison Payout," *The Citizen*, 19 May 2016.

106. Kris Pillay, "Repositioning the Private Security Industry in South Africa in the 21st Century," *Acta Criminologica* 14, no. 3 (2001): 66–74; and Julie Berg, "Private Policing in South Africa: The Cape Town City Improvement District—Pluralisation in Practice," *Society in Transition* 35, no. 2 (2004): 228.

107. Gill Moodie, "Crime Wave Robs Some, Pays Others," *Sunday Times*, 22 July 2001.

108. Julie Berg and Jean-Pierre Nouveau, "Towards a Third Phrase of Regulation: Re-Imagining Private Security in South Africa," *SA Crime Quarterly* 38 (2011): 23–32 (esp. 23–24); and Abrahamsen and Williams, *Security beyond the State*, p. 21.

109. Anthony Minnaar, "Oversight and Monitoring of Non-State/Private Policing: The Private Security Practitioners in South Africa," in *Private Security in Africa: Manifestations, Challenges, and Regulations*, ed. Sabelo Gumedze, Institute for Security Studies, monograph series, no. 139 (Pretoria: Institute for Security Studies, 2007): 128–49; and Minnaar, "Private–Public Partnerships," 85–114. See also Shaw, *Crime and Policing in Post-Apartheid South Africa*, 102–18; Irish, *Policing for Profit*, 13–15; and Schönteich, *Unshackling the Crime Fighters*, 18–25.

110. Irish, *Policing for Profit*, 2–4; Shaw, "Crime in Transition," 20.

111. Raenette Taljaard, "Private and Public Security in South Africa," in *The Private Security Sector in Africa*, ed. Sabelo Gumedze, monograph series, no. 146 (Pretoria: Institute for Security Studies, July 2008), 69–106 (esp. 72–73). See D. Albert, "New Security Company Identifies Niche Market," *Security Focus* 22, no. 1 (2004): 56; and T. Reynolds, "South Africa's Security Business Is Booming," *Pretoria News*, 24 July 2004; Minnaar, "Private–Public Partnerships," 104–6; Minnaar, "Oversight and Monitoring," 128–49; Anthony Minnaar, "Crime Prevention, Partnership Policing and the Growth of Private Security: The South African Experience," in *Policing in Central and Eastern Europe: Dilemmas of Contemporary Criminal Justice*, ed. Gorazd Mesko, Milan Pagon, and Bojan Dobovsek (Maribor, SI: University of Maribor, 2004), 1–25.

112. See Shaun Swingler, "South Africa's R40bn Private Security Industry under Threat," *Daily Maverick*, 14 May 2017; Janine Stephen, "Private Security: Blending in to Protect the Well-Heeled," *Business Day*, 20 September 2017; and Conrad van Rooyen, "South Africa's Security Industry Boom," *Hi Tech Security Solutions Magazine*, October 2017.

113. Private Security Industry Regulatory Authority, *Annual Report 2010/2011* (Centurion, ZA: Private Security Industry Regulatory Authority, 2011). See also Ministry of Police, "South Africa Has World's Largest Private Security Industry; Needs Regulation—Mthethwa," *Defence Web*, 30 October 2012, available at https://www.defenceweb.co.za/industry/industry-industry/south-africa-has-worlds-largest-private-security-industry-needs-regulation-mthethwa.

114. Frans Cronje, *FastFacts: They All Lived Together in a Crooked Little House* (Johannesburg: Institute of Race Relations and Centre for Risk Analysis, issue 289, no. 9, Sep-

tember 2015); and Amanda Watson, "South Africa's Choice: Private Security or Vigilantism," *The Citizen*, 24 September 2015.

115. Nivashni Nair, "First Food, Then Private Security," *The Times*, 20 July 2015; and News24 Wire, "Private Security Officers in SA Outnumber Police and Army," *Business Tech*, 23 September 2015, available at http://businesstech.co.za/news/general/99248 /private-security-officers-outnumber-sa-police-and-army-combined/. See also Ahmed Areff, "More Private Security than Police and Army Combined," *News24*, 23 September 2015, available at http://www.news24.com/SouthAfrica/News/More-private-security -than-police-army-combined-SAIRR-20150923; and Staff Writer, "Private Security vs. Police Officer Numbers in South Africa," *Business Tech*, 12 June 2018; Staff Writer, "This Is How Much Private Security Guards Now Earn in South Africa," *Business Tech*, 15 October 2018.

116. Ministry of Police, "World's Largest Private Security Industry."

117. Natalie Jaynes, "Flying below the Radar: The Armed Private Security Sector in South Africa" (Criminal Justice Initiative, occasional paper no. 11, Open Society Foundation for South Africa, Pinelands, ZA, 2012), 1–43.

118. Staff Writer, "40,000 SA Police Do Not Have Firearm Competency Certificates," *Business Tech*, 11 September 2015, available at http://businesstech.co.za/news /general/98135/40000-sa-police-do-not-have-firearm-competency-certificates/. See South African Police Service, *Annual Report 2010/2011* (Pretoria, ZA: Government Printing Office, 2011). For earlier figures, see Minnaar, "Private–Public Partnerships," 102–6; and Johan Burger, "Crime Combating in Perspective: A Strategic Approach to Policing and the Prevention of Crime in South Africa," *Acta Criminologica* 19, no. 2 (2006): 105–18.

119. Berg, "Private Policing in South Africa," 224–50; Berg, "Challenges to a Formal Private Security–SAPS Partnership," 105–24; Irish, *Policing for Profit*, 10–11; and Michael Kempa and Clifford Shearing, "Microscopic and Macroscopic Responses to Inequalities in the Governance of Security: Respective Experiments in South Africa and Northern Ireland," *Transformation* 29, no. 2 (2002): 25–54.

120. Mike Cohen, "Crime-Busting G4S Faces South Africa Private Security Curbs," *Bloomberg News*, 7 April 2014, available at http://www.bloomberg.com/news/articles /2014-04-06/crime-busting-g4s-at-risk-as-south-africa-curbs-private-security. See Clarno, *Neoliberal Apartheid*, 130; and interviews with Tiaan Joubert, and Johan Van Ben Berg, 26 June 2012.

121. Information in this paragraph is derived from the following sources: Taljaard, "Private and Public Security in South Africa," 72–73; Irish, *Policing for Profit*, 1–21; Schönteich, *Unshackling the Crime Fighters*, 22–24; Shaw, *Crime and Policing in Post-Apartheid South Africa*, 102–5; and Jaynes, "Flying below the Radar," 1–43. See also interviews with Earl Stoles, 20 June 2012; and Nazira Cachalia, 30 May 2006, and 24 June 2011.

122. Zedner, "Liquid Security," 269–71; and Jones and Newburn, *Private Security and Public Policing*, 80–82.

123. Julie Berg, "The Private Security Industry in South Africa: A Review of Applicable Legislation," *South African Journal of Criminal Justice* 16, no. 2 (2003): 178–96; Julie Berg, *The Accountability of South Africa's Private Security Industry: Mechanisms of Control*

and Challenges to Effective Oversight (Cape Town: Criminal Justice Initiative of the Open Society Foundation for South Africa, 2007), 7–10; and Berg and Nouveau, "Towards a Third Phrase of Regulation," 23–32.

124. Staff Writer, "Robbery, Hijacking and Break-In Crime Trends in South Africa in 2018," *Business Tech*, 25 February 2018.

125. Minnaar, "Private–Public Partnerships." See Roy Macfarlane, "The Private Sector Security Industry in South Africa," *African Defence Review* 19 (1994): 25–29; Haffajee, "Suburbs Search"; and Staff Reporter, "The Fight against Crime Has a New Face," *Sunday Independent*, 4 May 2002.

126. Alex Eliseev, "Cop Held over Guns for Guards," *The Star*, 4 December 2009.

127. Sabelo Gumedze, "Regulating the Private Security Sector in South Africa," *Social Justice* 34, nos. 3–4 [109–110] (2007): 195–207; and Rita Abrahamsen and Michael Williams, "Privatization, Globalization, and the Politics of Protection in South Africa," in *The Politics of Protection: Sites of Insecurity and Political Agency*, ed. Jef Huysmans, Andrew Dobson, and Raia Prokhovnik (New York: Routledge, 2006), 34–47. See interviews with Jack Edery, 19 June 2012, and 1 July 2014; Justin Hydes, 19 June 2012; Tiaan Joubert, 26 June 2012; and Frederic Lancelin, 19 June 2012.

128. Gill Moodie, "Crime Wave Robs Some, Pays Others," *Sunday Times*, 22 July 2001; Irish, *Policing for Profit*, 11–14; and Staff Reporter, "Small Security Firms Endangered," *Star Business Report*, 23 May 1999.

129. Dewald van Rensburg, "Private Security Amendment Bill 'the Enemy of SA Economy,'" *City Press*, 11 October 2015; and Geoff Burt and Eric Muller, *Foreign Ownership Bans and Private Security: Protectionism or Security Sector Governance?* (Kitchener, CA: Centre for Security Governance, July 2016).

130. For early inroads by multinational companies, see R. W. Johnson and Irina Filatova, "Analysis: Foreign Investors Threatened," *United Press International*, 6 October 2001; James Lamont, "Concern at S. Africa Security Sector Plan," *Financial Times* (London), 4 October 2001; Staff Reporter, "Calm Needed in Security Storm," *Business Day*, 8 October 2001; Staff Reporter, "Foreign Investor Ban Bid Dropped," *Business Day*, 11 October 2001; Staff Reporter, "An Industry Hijacked," *The Economist* (6 October 2001); and Henri Cauvin, "Homegrown Guards," *New York Times*, 9 October 2001.

131. Shaw, *Towards Safer Cities*, 1–25; Shaw, "Crime in Transition," 7–27; Shaw, "Crime, Police and Public in Transitional Societies," 1–24; Shaw, *Crime and Policing in Post-Apartheid South Africa*, 102–5; and Taljaard, "Private and Public Security in South Africa," 75–76. See also interviews with Ingo Mutinelli, 1 July 2014; and Jack Edery, 19 June 2012, and 1 July 2014.

132. Ken Livingstone and Jerry Hart, "The Wrong Arm of the Law? Public Images of Private Security," *Policing and Society* 13, no. 2 (2003): 159–70 (esp. 162).

133. Minnaar, "Private–Public Partnerships," 97–98.

134. Caitlin Zaloom, "The Productive Life of Risk," *Cultural Anthropology* 19, no. 3 (2004): 365.

135. Interviews with Andrew Seldon, 13 June 2012; Jack Edery, 19 June 2012, and 1 July 2014; Patrick Frimat, 19 June 2012; Justin Hydes, 19 June 2012; and Tiaan Joubert, 26 June 2012.

136. Mfundekelwa Mkhulisi, "We Must Rein in Security Firms," *Sowetan*, 2 September 2010.

137. Van Rensburg, "Private Security Amendment Bill"; and Burt and Muller, "Foreign Ownership Bans and Private Security."

138. Singh, *Policing and Crime Control*, 44–45; and Tessa Diphoorn, "Surveillance of the Surveillers: Regulation of the Private Security Industry in South Africa and Kenya," *African Studies Review* 59, no. 2 (2016): 161–82. See also interviews with Johan Van Ben Berg, 26 June 2012; Tiaan Joubert, 26 June 2012, and Margaret Gichanga, 10 July 2014.

139. Berg, "Private Security Industry in South Africa," 178–96; and Singh, *Policing and Crime Control*, 40–45, 55–60. See also interview with Margaret Gichanga, 10 July 2014.

140. Livingstone and Hart, "Wrong Arm of the Law?," 162.

141. Daniel O'Connor et al., "Seeing Private Security Like a State," *Criminology and Criminal Justice* 8, no. 2 (2008): 203–4.

142. Interviews with Margaret Gichanga, 10 July 2014; Jenny Reid, 11 July 2014; and Tony Botes, 25 June 2014.

143. See Berg, "South Africa's Private Security Industry," 7–8; Berg, "Private Security Industry in South Africa," 178–96; and interview with Margaret Gichanga, 10 July 2014.

144. Clarno, *Neoliberal Apartheid*, 152–55. See interviews with Margaret Gichanga, 10 July 2014; and Tony Botes, 25 June 2014.

145. Interviews with Margaret Gichanga, 10 July 2014; and Tony Botes, 25 June 2014.

CHAPTER 3

1. Karina Landman, "Man the Barricades! Gated Communities in South Africa," *Crime & Conflict* 21 (Spring 2000): 24–26; Karina Landman, "Privatizing Public Space in Post-Apartheid South African Cities through Neighborhood Enclosures," *GeoJournal* 66, nos. 1–22 (2006): 133–246; and Karina Landman and Martin Schönteich, "Urban Fortresses: Gated Communities as a Reaction to Crime," *African Security Review* 11, no. 4 (2002): 71–285.

2. For this phrase, see Nan Ellin, "Fear and City Building," *The Hedgehog Review* 5, no. 3 (2003): 52.

3. Lindsay Bremner, "Crime and the Emerging Landscape of Post-*Apartheid* Johannesburg," in *Blank___: Architecture, Apartheid, and After*, ed. Hilton Judin and Ivan Vadislavić (Rotterdam: NAi, 1998), 48–264 (esp. 59–260); and Lindsay Bremner, "Remaking Johannesburg," in *Future City*, ed. Stephen Read, Jürgen Rosemann, and Job van Eldijk (London: Spon, 2005), 32–47 (esp. 45).

4. See, for example, Alice Hills, "The Unavoidable Ghettoization of Security in Iraq," *Security Dialogue* 41, no. 3 (2010): 301–21 (esp. 301).

5. For a broad discussion, see Taner Oc and Steven Tiesdell, "Urban Design Approaches to Safer City Centres: The Fortress, the Panoptic, the Regulatory, and the Animated," in *Landscapes of Defense*, ed. John Gold and George Revill (Harlow, UK: Pearson Educational Press, 2000), 188–208; Eugene McLaughlin, "Walled Cities: Surveillance,

Regulation and Segregation," in *Unruly Cities?*, ed. Steve Pile, Christopher Brook, and Gerry Mooney (London: Routledge, 2000), 96–136.

6. See Karina Landman, "Serious about Safety" (paper presented at Urban Planning & Environment Symposium, Pretoria, ZA, 5–9 April 1999), 5, available at https://researchspace.csir.co.za/dspace/bitstream/handle/10204/2824/Landman2_1999.pdf ?sequence=1&isAllowed=y.

7. Nan Ellin, "Shelter from the Storm or Form Follows Fear and Vice Versa," in *Architecture of Fear*, ed. Nan Ellin (New York: Princeton Architectural Press, 1997), 13–45 (esp. 33–37).

8. Bremner, "Crime and the Emerging Landscape," 59–60, 62; Ian Fife, "Storming the Barricades," *Financial Mail*, 28 July 2000; and Mark Shaw and Antoinette Louw, *Environmental Design for Safer Communities: Preventing Crime in South Africa's Cities and Towns*, monograph series, no. 24 (Midrand, ZA: Institute for Security Studies, 1998).

9. André Czeglédy, "Villas of the Highveld: A Cultural Perspective on Johannesburg and Its "Northern Suburbs," in *Emerging Johannesburg: Perspectives on the Post-Apartheid City*, ed. Richard Tomlinson et al. (New York, Routledge, 2003), 21–42; and Derek Hook and Michelle Vrdoljak, "Gated Communities, Heterotopia and a 'Rights' of Privilege: A 'Heterotopology' of the South African Security-Park," *Geoforum* 33, no. 2 (2002): 195–219.

10. Ulrich Jürgens and Martin Gnad, "Gated Communities in South Africa: Experiences from Johannesburg," *Environment and Planning B* 29, no. 3 (2002): 337–53; Ulrich Jürgens, Martin Gnad, and Jürgen Bahr, "New Forms of Class and Racial Segregation: Ghettos or Ethnic Enclaves?," in Tomlinson et al., *Emerging Johannesburg*, 56–70; Karina Landman, "Gated Minds, Gated Places: The Impact and Meaning of Hard Boundaries in South Africa," in *Gated Communities: Social Sustainability in Contemporary and Historical Gated Developments*, ed. Samer Bagaeen and Ola Uduku (London: Earthscan, 2010), 49–62; and Alan Mabin, "Suburbanisation, Segregation, and Government of Territorial Transformations," *Transformation: Critical Perspectives on Southern Africa* 57 (2005): 41–63 (esp. 50).

11. See Jürgens and Gnad, "Gated Communities," 337–53; Hook and Vrdoljak, "Gated Communities," 195–219; Czeglédy, "Villas of the Highveld," 21–42; and Karina Landman, "Gated Communities in South Africa: Tensions between the Planning Ideal and Practice," *Town and Regional Planning* 61 (2012): 1–9.

12. Clive Chipkin, *Johannesburg Transition: Architecture & Society from 1950* (Johannesburg: STE Publishers, 2008), 354. See also Alexandra Parker, "The Effects of Walls in the Suburbs of Johannesburg" (master's thesis, faculty of Engineering and the Built Environment, University of the Witwatersrand, Johannesburg, 2008).

13. Martin J. Murray, *City of Extremes: The Spatial Politics of Johannesburg* (Durham, NC: Duke University Press, 2011), 314–19; and Alison Todes, Dylan Weakley, and Philip Harrison, "Densifying Johannesburg: Context, Policy and Diversity," *Journal of Housing and the Built Environment* 33, no. 2 (2018): 281–99.

14. These sentences are taken almost verbatim from Martin J. Murray, "City of Layers: The Making and Shaping of Affluent Johannesburg after *Apartheid*," in *Urban Governance in Post-Apartheid Cities*, ed. Marie Huchzermeyer and Christoph Haferburg (Stutt-

gart: Schweizerbart, 2014), 179–96 (esp. 188). See also Alan Lipman and Howard Harris, "Fortress Johannesburg," *Environment and Planning B* 26, no. 5 (1999): 727–40.

15. Bremner, "Crime and the Emerging Landscape," 59–60, 61–62; Derek Hook and Michele Vrdoljak, "Fear and Loathing in Northern Johannesburg: The Security Park as Heterotopia," *Psychology in Society* 27 (2001): 61–83; and Richard Ballard, "Bunkers for the Psyche: How Gated Communities Have Allowed the Privatisation of *Apartheid* in Democratic South Africa" (Dark Roast Occasional Paper Series, no. 24, Isandla Institute, Cape Town, 2005, http:/www.isandla.org.za.

16. See Oscar Newman, *Defensible Space: Crime Prevention through Urban Design* (New York: Macmillan, 1972), 1–25; and Oscar Newman, *Creating Defensible Space* (Washington, DC: Department of Housing and Urban Development, 1996).

17. Citizen Reporter, "57 South Africans Murdered a Day—Crime Statistics," *The Citizen*, 11 September 2018; Nomahlubi Jordaan, "Three of Joburg's Police Districts Record Increase in Murders," *Sunday Times*, 8 May 2018; and Nico Gous, "US, Canada, Britain Warn about Travelling to South Africa after Crime Stats Release," *Sowetan*, 14 September 2018.

18. See Staff Reporter, "Crime Stats Figures Released," *The Citizen*, 19 September 2014; Corné Eloff, "Understanding Trio Robbery Crimes through Spatial Analysis," *PositionIT* (November/December 2010): 48–49; and Karina Landman, "Reconsidering Crime and Urban Fortification in South Africa," in *The Urban Fabric of Crime and Fear*, ed. Vania Ceccato (New York: Springer, 2012), 239–66.

19. Nicki Padayachee, "The Price of Feeling Safe in the Suburbs," *Sunday Times*, 9 April 2000. See also Paul T. Clark, "Security Assemblages: Enclaving, Private Security, and New Materialism in Suburban Johannesburg" (master's thesis, University of the Witwatersrand, Johannesburg, 2016), 50–79; and Karina Landman, "Gated Neighbourhoods in South Africa: An Appropriate Urban Design Approach?," *Urban Design International* 13 (2008): 227–40.

20. For the ideas in this paragraph, see Dennis Judd, "The Rise of the New Walled Cities," in *Spatial Practices: Critical Explorations in Social/Spatial Theory*, ed. Helen Liggett and David Perry (Thousand Oaks, CA: Sage, 1995), 144–66 (esp. 161); and Lipman and Harris, "Fortress Johannesburg," 732–33.

21. See Murray, "City of Layers," 179–96.

22. Karina Landman, "Exploring the Impact of Gated Communities on Social and Spatial Justice and Its Relation to Restorative Justice and Peace-Building in South Africa," *Acta Juridica* 7 (2007): 134–55.

23. Anne Russell, chair of the East Rand Metro Association, quoted in Sabelo Ndlangisa, "Booming Battle Looms over Bid to Seal off Suburbs," *Sunday Times*, 2 September 2001.

24. Karina Landman, *An Overview of Enclosed Neighbourhoods in South Africa* (Pretoria: CSIR, 2000), 9–18. For comparative purposes, see Teresa Caldeira, "Fortified Enclaves: The New Urban Segregation," *Public Culture* 8 (1996): 303–28 (esp. 311).

25. Landman, "Privatizing Public Space," 133–46; and Trudi Smit, Karina Landman, and Christoffel Venter, "The Impact of Crime and Neighbourhood Enclosures on Travel Behaviour and Transport Patterns in South Africa," in *Safety and Security in Tran-*

sit Environments: Crime Prevention and Security Management, ed. Vania Ceccato and Andrew Newton (New York: Palgrave Macmillan, 2015), 234–50.

26. Claire Bénit-Gbaffou, "Policing Johannesburg Wealthy Neighborhoods: The Uncertain 'Partnerships' between Police, Communities and Private Security Companies," *Trialog* 89 (2006): 21–26; and Anna Cox and Chimaimba Banda, "Bang Go Those Booms if Joburg Gets Its Way," *The Star*, 31 March 2003.

27. C. Jacobs, "Locking Out the Criminals," *Sunday Times*, 10 May 1998.

28. Anna Cox, "More Suburbs Want Fences and Booms," *The Star*, 23 March 1998; and Landman, *An Overview of Enclosed Neighbourhoods*, 9–18. For example, in affluent neighborhoods such as Sandringham, enumerators working for Census 2001 complained about their difficulty gaining access to the "walled suburb": having to negotiate their way past boom gates and then having to contend with high walls, electric fences, intercom systems, and suspicious residents. See Staff Reporter, "Count Us Out! Walls Keep the Rich Safe from Census," *Sunday Times*, 14 October 2001.

29. Yolanda Mufweba, "The Boom Comes Down on Illegal Road Closures," *The Star*, 11 July 2003.

30. Landman, "Privatizing Public Space," 133–46; Landman, "Gated Neighbourhoods in South Africa," 227–40; Philip Harrison and Alan Mabin, "Security and Space: Managing the Contradictions of Access Restriction in Johannesburg," *Environment and Planning B* 33, no. 1 (2006): 3–20; Teresa Dirsuweit and Alex Wafer, "Scale, Governance, and the Maintenance of Privileged Control: The Case of Road Closures in Johannesburg's Northern Suburbs," *Urban Forum* 17, no. 4 (2006): 327–52.

31. See Pranap Bardhan, *The Role of Governance in Economic Development* (Paris: OECD Development Center, 1997), 45.

32. For the source of this information, see Jonny Steinberg, "Fortress Sandton Contributes Zero to the Rule of Law," *Business Day*, 6 July 1998; and Gary Collins, "Back to the *Laager* for Joburg's Rich Suburbs," *Sunday Times*, 19 May 1996.

33. Laurice Taitz, "It's Boom Time in a Suburb Once under Siege," *Sunday Times*, 14 March 1999; Sarah Oppler, "Partnership Policing Creates a United Front against Crime," *The Star*, 15 March 1997; and Anna Cox, "More Suburbs Want Fences and Booms."

34. Landman, "Man the Barricades!," 24–26; Mark Shaw, *Crime and Policing in Post-Apartheid South Africa: Transforming under Fire* (Bloomington: Indiana University Press, 2002), 102–18; and Sheree Rossouw, "Living behind the Barricades," *Mail & Guardian*, 12 January 2001. See also interview with Stewart Rider, 15 June 2012.

35. Margot Cohen, "Gated Communities at Loggerheads," *Financial Mail*, 6 July 2001, 33; and Simpiwe Piliso, "Just How Safe Are You Behind Your Boom Gate?," *Sunday Times*, 1 April 2001.

36. Fife, "Storming the Barricades"; Anna Cox, "'Laager Suburb' Must Drop Barriers," *The Star*, 12 June 2000; Claire Bénit-Gbaffou, "Unbundled Security Services and Urban Fragmentation in Post-Apartheid Johannesburg," *Geoforum* 39, no. 6 (2008): 1933–50 (esp. 1937–38); and Landman, *An Overview of Enclosed Neighbourhoods*, 9–10.

37. This quotation is from city councillor Judy Stockhill, cited in Cox and Banda, "Bang Go Those Booms." See also Claire Bénit-Gbaffou, Sophie Didier, and Marianne

Morange, "Communities, the Private Sector, and the State: Contested Forms of Security Governance in Cape Town and Johannesburg," *Urban Affairs Review* 43, no. 5 (2008): 691–717.

38. Anna Cox, "Boom Doom Looms in Gloomy Joburg Suburbs," *Saturday Star*, 11 April 2003; Michael Morris, "Rulebook to Check Blocking of Streets," *Cape Argus*, 23 January 2003; Thandiwe Mathibela, "Please Fence Us In!," *Sunday Times*, 27 May 2001; and Anna Cox, "Joburg Aims to Bring All Illegal Booms Down," *The Star*, 13 September 2002. In 2001, the Westdene, Auckland Park, Rossmore, Richmond, Melville, and Brixton Residents and Ratepayers Association (WARM) decided to erect boom gates on major access roads to protect this trendy nightclub and restaurant zone from rising crime. See Anna Cox, "Security Business in Melville Just Booming," *The Star*, 24 April 2001; and Staff Reporter, "Trendy Melville Wants the Nightlife without the Lowlife," *Sunday Times*, 1 April 2001.

39. Ian Fife, "The Rich Make Mischief'," *Financial Mail*, 18 April 2003, 50–51.

40. Michael Wines, "Speaking of Fences, Street Crime, and Ultimately, Race," *New York Times*, 28 October 2004.

41. The ideas for this paragraph are derived from Staff Reporter, "The Great Wall of Hyde Park," *Sunday Times*, 5 August 2001; Rossouw, "Living behind the Barricades"; Simpiwe Piliso, "Oh No, You Don't," *Sunday Times*, 15 September 2002; and Cohen, "Gated Communities at Loggerheads."

42. Gundrun Heckl, "Boom Gloom: The War between Residents of Two of Johannesburg's Wealthier Suburbs over Illegal Road Closure," *Sunday Times*, 23 February 2003; and Cox and Banda, "Bang Go Those Booms."

43. Ndlangisa, "Booming Battle Looms." Some information about Ekurhuleni is provided in interview with Paul Maseko, 8 June 2003.

44. Landman, "Man the Barricades!," 24–26; Fife, "Storming the Barricades"; and Landman, *An Overview of Enclosed Neighbourhoods*, 9–10.

45. Scores of letters to the editor in newspapers have reiterated these themes. See, for example, Brian Topic, "Freedom Can't Outweigh Security," *The Star*, 27 June 2003; Fred Bisschoff, "Closures: Reason behind Low Crime," *Citizen*, 24 July 2003; M. Robinson, "Access Control Makes Suburbs Safe," *The Star*, 8 July 2003; and Nick Karvelas, "Don't Restrict Our Freedom of Movement," *The Star*, 1 July 2003.

46. Anna Cox and Ndivhuwo Khangale, "Johannesburg Authorises Pointless Boom Gates," *The Star*, 29 November 2004.

47. Landman, *An Overview of Enclosed Neighbourhoods*, 5–9, 19–25; Staff Reporter, "Crime Buffers, or the New *Apartheid*?" *Cape Argus*, 10 July 2002; Piliso, "Just How Safe Are You?"; and interview with Stewart Rider, 15 June 2012.

48. Charlotte Lemanski, Karina Landman, and Matthew Durington, "Divergent and Similar Experiences of 'Gating' in South Africa: Johannesburg, Durban and Cape Town," *Urban Forum* 19, no. 2 (2008): 133–58.

49. Anna Cox, "High-Voltage Drama Surrounds 'Crime Cage,'" *The Star*, 9 April 2001; Anna Cox, "Electric Fence Switched On," *The Star*, 10 April 2001; and Anna Cox, "Electric Fence Switched On—For a Day," *The Star*, 11 April 2001.

50. Teresa Dirsuweit, "Between Ontological Security and the Right Difference:

Road Closures, Communitarianism, and Urban Ethics in Johannesburg, South Africa," *Autrepart* 42 (2007): 53–71; and Cox and Banda, "Bang Go Those Booms." Interviews with Wendy Voster-Robertson, 4 July 2014; Anthony Modena, 4 July 2014; and Vickie Drinkwater, 2 February 2016.

51. Anna Cox, "Boom Time for Sandton Has Motorists Outraged," *The Star*, 25 October 2002; and Cox and Banda, "Bang Go Those Booms."

52. Cox, "Joburg Aims"; and Staff Reporter, "Crime Buffers, or the New *Apartheid?*"

53. A trauma unit survey conducted by Johannesburg Hospital in 2004 estimated that the response time of ambulances and other emergency vehicles more than doubled. Consequently, the mortality and morbidity rate increased, because drivers were forced to take circuitous routes due to the unexpected presence of boom gates, barriers, and sentry points in suburban residential neighborhoods. See Anna Cox, "Security Booms Can Be the Death of You," *The Star*, 27 July 2004. See also O. Fabiyi Oluseyi, "Analysis of Inter-Connectivity Levels of Urban Street Networks and Social Interactions in Enclosed Neighbourhoods in Johannesburg RSA," *Humanity & Social Sciences Journal* 1, no. 1 (2006): 79–95.

54. Anna Cox, "Road Closure Is a Violation of My Rights," *The Star*, 3 April 2003; Anna Cox, "Legal Action Threatened in Road Closure Row," *The Star*, 7 April 2003; and Piliso, "Oh No, You Don't." In Durban, eThekwini municipal manager Mike Sutcliffe instructed city employers to tear down security gates on city streets. See Staff Reporter, "Tear Down Booms, or We'll Do It for You," *Sunday Independent*, 22 November 2002.

55. Cox, "Boom Time for Sandton"; Cox, "Legal Action Threatened"; Anna Cox, "Charges Could Spell Boom Doom in Joburg," *The Star*, 10 April 2003; and Simpiwe Piliso, "The Three Most Expensive Streets in Johannesburg," *Sunday Times*, 8 July 2001.

56. Anonymous, "Get Municipal Permission for Boom Gate," *SAPA*, 9 January 2003; Ndivhuwo Khangale and Anna Cox, "Moment of Truth Arrives for Illegal Booms," *The Star*, 18 July 2003; and Anna Cox, "Sandhurst Residents Face Trial over Booms," *The Star*, 24 July 2003; Sabelo Ndlangisa, "Boom Town Blues," *Sunday Times*, 18 May 2003; Noor-Jehan Yoro Badat, "Residents Angry over Costly Booms," *The Star*, 27 June 2003; and Anna Cox, "Gloom Looms as Booms Look Doomed," *The Star*, 11 July 2003.

57. Nano Mothibi, "Removal of Booms Angers Joburg Residents," *The Star*, 25 July 2003.

58. Mothibi, "Removal of Booms Angers Joburg Residents"; Khangale and Cox, "Moment of Truth Arrives"; and Anna Cox, "Joburg Booms: The Full Story," *The Star*, 27 November 2004.

59. Cox, "Sandhurst Residents Face Trial"; and Staff Reporter, "SA Security Gates Torn Down," *BBC News* (UK Edition), 25 July 2003.

60. Murray, "City of Layers," 179–96; and Czeglédy, "Villas of the Highveld," 21–42.

61. Harrison and Mabin, "Security and Space," 3–20; Dirsuweit and Wafer, "Maintenance of Privileged Control," 327–52; and Lemanski, Landman, and Durington, "'Gating' in South Africa," 133–58. See interviews with Daniel Marsay, 11 June 2012; and Brian Robertson, 12 June 2012.

62. Cox, "Gloom Looms." For the source of these ideas, see Mike Davis, *City of Quartz: Excavating the Future of Los Angeles* (New York: Vintage, 1992), 212–13, and 244–48. See also Brian Topic, "Freedom Can't Outweigh Security," *The Star*, 27 June 2003.

63. Karvelas, "Don't Restrict Our Freedom."

64. I. C. S. Melville, "There Is No Such Thing as an Open City," *The Star*, 27 June 2003.

65. Anna Cox, "Can Road Barriers Bring Down the Crime Rate?," *The Star*, 12 July 2004.

66. Felicity Jones, "Ratepayers Have a Right to Safety," *The Star*, 8 July 2003.

67. Robinson, "Access Control."

68. Staff Reporter, "Crime Buffers, or the New *Apartheid*?"; Simpiwe Piliso, "Neighbour vs Neighbour," *Sunday Times*, 4 March 2001; and interviews with Daniel Marsay, 11 June 2012; Brian Robertson, 12 June 2012; and Stewart Rider, 15 June 2012.

69. South African Human Rights Commission, *Report on the Issue of Road Closures, Security Booms and Related Measures* (Pretoria: South African Human Rights Commission, 2005).

70. Anna Cox, "Closed-Off Roads Are Dividing Communities," *The Star*, 23 March 2004; and Anna Cox, "Posh Suburb Targets Road-Closure Opponent," *The Star*, 17 March 2004.

71. Anna Cox, "Joburg Roads Closures Are About to Take Off with a Boom Again," *The Star*, 24 February 2011; and Bénit-Gbaffou, "Unbundled Security Services," 1939. See also Claire Bénit-Gbaffou, "Who Control the Streets? Crime, 'Community' and the State in Post-Apartheid Johannesburg," in *African Cities: Competing Claims on Urban Spaces*, ed. Francesca Locatelli and Paul Nugent (Leiden, NL: Brill, 2009), 55–79 (esp. 71).

72. Anonymous, "Joburg Plays Hardball over Bordeaux Access Restriction Structures," 15 July 2010, available at https//:www.IOLProperty.co.za.

73. Cox, "Joburg Roads Closures."

74. See Andy Clarno, "Rescaling White Space in Post-*Apartheid* Johannesburg," *Antipode* 45, no. 5 (2013): 1190–1212; Andy Clarno, "A Tale of Two Walled Cities: Neo-Liberalization and Enclosure in Johannesburg and Jerusalem," *Political Power and Social Theory* 19 (2008): 159–205; and Karina Landman and Willem Badenhorst, *The Impact of Gated Communities on Spatial Transformation in the Greater Johannesburg Area*, report series produced by the South African research chair in Development Planning and Modelling, School of Architecture and Planning (Johannesburg: University of the Witwatersrand, 2012).

75. Bénit-Gbaffou, "Who Control the Streets?," 63–64; Cox, "Joburg Booms"; and Sheree Bega, "Our Booms Are Saving Lives," *Saturday Star*, 22 May 2012.

76. See interviews with Anthony Modena, 4 July 2014; Ryan Rosaveare and Glenn du Toit, 2 July 2014; Wayne Minnaar, 9 July 2014; and Stewart Rider, 15 June 2012.

77. Anna Cox, "Suburban Boom Gates Policy Approved," *The Star*, 3 February 2014; and Staff Writer, "Boom Gates Get the Go-Ahead," *Randburg Sun*, 20 February 2014.

78. Amy Ingram, "Do You Know How to Apply for a Boom Gate?," *Roodeport Northsider*, 7 March 2017.

79. Staff Writer, "Joburg to Remove 'Illegal' Suburban Boom Gates," *Business Tech*, 13 December 2016.

80. Sinikiwe Mqadi, "City of Joburg Ordered to Restore Security Boom Gates," *702 Radio*, 21 December 2016; and Anna Cox, "City of Joburg Was 'Wrong to Remove Booms,'" *The Star*, 21 December 2016.

81. For the source of some of these ideas, see Lisa Benton-Short, "Bollards, Bunkers, and Barriers: Securing the National Mall in Washington, DC," *Environment & Planning D* 25, no. 3 (2007): 424–46 (esp. 442).

82. Cynthia Weber and Mark Lacy, "Securing by Design," *Review of International Studies* 37, no. 3 (2011): 1021–43 (esp. 1021). See also Mark Lacy, "Designer Security: MoMA's Safe: Design Takes on Risk and Control Society," *Security Dialogue* 39, nos. 2–3 (2008): 333–57.

83. Simone Tulumello, "From 'Spaces of Fear' to 'Fearscapes': Mapping for Re-Framing Theories about the Spatialization of Fear in Urban Space," *Space and Culture* 18, no. 3 (2015): 257–72.

84. Thandi Skade, "Homeowners Spend Bundles on Safety Features," *The Star*, 26 February 2008; and Sipho Mabena, "South Africans Spending More than the Police Budget on Own Security," *Sunday Times*, 15 February 2017. For a wider discussion of the concept of "grudge spending," see Ian Loader, Benjamin Goold, and Angélica Thumala, "Grudge Spending: The Interplay between Markets and Culture in the Purchase of Security," *The Sociological Review* 63, no. 4 (2015): 858–75.

85. It was reported in the mid-1990s that a fly-by-night entrepreneur was selling military-grade surplus landmines (including limpet mines and claymores for around thirty-two dollars apiece) to homeowners as a macabre crime-fighting deterrent to be placed along the perimeter of properties near high-security walls. See Anonymous, "Land Mines for Home Protection," *UPI Archives*, 5 November 1996, available at https://www.upi.com/Archives/1996/11/05/Land-mines-for-home-protection/4200847170000/.

86. Gill Moodie, "Crime Wave Robs Some, Pays Others," *Sunday Times*, 22 July 2001; and Derek Rodney, "It's Boom Time in a Suburb Once under Siege," *Sunday Times*, 14 March 1999.

87. Shaw, *Crime and Policing*, 102–18; Moodie, "Crime Wave Robs Some"; and Scott Calvert, "In Johannesburg Suburbs, an Obsession with Security," *Baltimore Sun*, 22 May 2005.

88. Samira Kawash, "Safe House? Body, Building, and the Question of Security," *Cultural Critique* 45 (2000): 185–221 (esp. 193).

89. Michele Rapoport, "Being a Body or Having One: Automated Domestic Technologies and Corporeality," *AI & Society: Journal of Knowledge, Culture, and Communication* 28 (2013): 209–18.

90. Skade, "Homeowners Spend Bundles."

91. Lerato Mbangeni, "Attacked at Home, Then Let Down by Police," *The Star*, 30 April 2015.

92. Lieven de Cauter, *The Capsular Civilization: On the City in the Age of Fear* (Rotterdam: NAi, 2004), 77–78; and Keller Easterling, *Enduring Innocence: Global Architecture and Its Political Masquerades* (Cambridge, MA: MIT Press, 2005), 1–5, 73.

93. Kristin Maurer, *Architectural Anxiety: The Perfect Safe Zone* (Raleigh, NC: Lulu Press, 2011), 17–18; and Anthony Vidler, *Warped Space: Art, Architecture, and Anxiety in Modern Culture* (Cambridge, MA: MIT Press, 2001), 26.

94. Thandi Skade, "A Security Alarm That Attacks Intruders?," *IOL*, 22 May 2009; David Smith, "Pepper-Spray Defence Means South Africa Robbers Face Loss of Balance

at Cash Machines," *The Guardian*, 12 July 2009. See also the Skunk corporate web page at http:/www.skunk.co.za/.

95. Guy Martin, "Desert Wolf Fitting RDM Grenades to Skunk UAV," *Defence Web*, 20 June 2017, available at http://www.defenceweb.co.za/index.php?option=com_content&view=article&id=48242&catid=74&Itemid=30.

96. Leo Kelion, "African Firm Is Selling Pepper-Spray Bullet Firing Drones," *BBC News*, 18 June 2014; David Smith, "Pepper-Spray Drone Offered to South African Mines for Strike Control," *The Guardian*, 20 June 2014; and Staff Reporter, "Christmas Drones' Flight Warning," *Saturday Star*, 24 December 2016.

97. Bert de Muynck, "The Prosthetic Paradox," in *Angst & Ruimte/Fear & Space*, ed. Theo Hauben and Marco Vermeulen with Veronique Patteeuw (Rotterdam: NAi, 2004), 8–15 (esp. 8).

98. See Anthony Vidler, *The Architectural Uncanny: Essays in the Modern Unhomely* (Cambridge, MA: MIT Press, 1992): 157, 168.

99. Staff Writer, "Fidelity ADT Launches New Smart Home Security Products," *Business Tech*, 26 February 2018.

100. Ideas for this and the following paragraphs are derived from a reading of Kawash, "Safe House?," 185–221.

101. See Svetlana Boym, *The Future of Nostalgia* (New York: Basic Books, 2001), xiii.

102. See Boym, *Future of Nostalgia*, 5, 55, 355; and Vidler, *Architectural Uncanny*, 11–13, 143, 167–68.

103. Murray, *City of Extremes*, 41–44; and Czeglédy, "Villas of the Highveld," 21–42.

104. Czeglédy, "Villas of the Highveld," 21–42.

105. Alan Mabin, "In the Forest of Transformation: The 'Northern Suburbs' of Johannesburg," in *Spatial Transformations in Johannesburg*, ed. Graeme Gotz et al. (Johannesburg: Wits University Press, 2014), 395–417 (esp. 399–400); and Eric Petersen, "The Life Cycle of Johannesburg Suburbs," in *Suburbanization in Global Society*, Research in Urban Sociology, vol. 10, ed. Mark Clapson and Ray Hutchison (Bingley, UK: Emerald Group, 2010), 179–204, and Murray, "City of Layers," 179–96.

106. Ronald Atkinson and Sarah Blandy, "Panic Rooms: The Rise of Defensive Home Ownership," *Housing Studies* 22, no. 4 (2007): 443; and Michele Rapoport, "The Home under Surveillance: A Tripartite Assemblage," *Surveillance & Society* 10, nos. 3/4 (2012): 320–33.

107. Kawash, "Safe House?," 185–86.

108. Atkinson and Blandy, "Panic Rooms," 443, 444.

109. See Keller Easterling, *Organization Space: Landscapes, Highways, and Houses in America* (Cambridge, MA: MIT Press, 1999), 129–30.

110. Hook and Vrdoljak, "Heterotopia and a 'Rights' of Privilege," 201, 202. See also Bremner, "Crime and the Emerging Landscape," 48–93.

111. Landman and Badenhorst, *Impact of Gated Communities*," 1–15, 17–25, 40–48. See also Murray, "City of Layers," 179–96; and Parker, "Effects of Walls," 1–5, 25–40.

112. Atkinson and Blandy, "Panic Rooms," 445. See also Rapoport, "Being a Body or Having One," 209–18.

113. Kawash, "Safe House?," 186. See also Davis, *City of Quartz*, 238.

114. Weber and Lacy, "Securing by Design," 1022; and De Cauter, *Capsular Civilization*, 60–64.

115. Kawash, "Safe House?," 186.

116. See Nan Ellin, "At Home and Everywhere: Making Place in the Global Village," in *Culture, Environmental Action, and Sustainability*, ed. Ricardo García Mira, José Camaselle, and José Martinez(Cambridge, MA: Hogrefe & Huber, 2003), 61–68 (esp. 62).

117. Kawash, "Safe House?," 185.

118. For the use of this phrase, see Patricia Leigh Brown, "Designs for a Land of Bombs and Guns," *New York Times*, 28 May 1995. See also Greg Mills, "Walls and Warriors: Speculations on the Relationship of Urban Design and Crime in the New South Africa," *Urban Forum* 2, no. 2 (1991): 89–93.

119. Kawash, "Safe House?," 187.

120. See Vidler, *Architectural Uncanny*, 167–68.

121. Kawash, "Safe House?," 188, 189. See also Rapoport, "Being a Body or Having One," 209–18.

122. Rapoport, "Home under Surveillance," 320.

123. Rapoport, "Home under Surveillance," 321; and Michele Rapoport, "Domestic Surveillance Technologies and a New Visibility," in *Rethinking Surveillance and Control: Beyond the "Security versus Privacy" Debate*, ed. Elisa Orrù, Maria Grazia Porcedda, and Sebastian Weydner-Volkmann (Baden-Baden, DE: Nomos, 2017), 217–38.

124. Taken almost verbatim from Rapoport, "Domestic Surveillance Technologies," 217.

125. Rapoport, "Home under Surveillance," 321; and Rapoport, "Domestic Surveillance Technologies," 220–22.

126. Kawash, "Safe House?," 189. See Liisa Mäkinen, "Surveillance ON/OFF. Examining Home Surveillance Systems from the User's Perspective," *Surveillance and Society* 14, no. 1 (2016), 59–77.

127. Peter Adey, "Surveillance at the Airport: Surveilling Mobility/Mobilising Surveillance," *Environment and Planning A* 36, no. 8 (2004): 1365–80 (esp. 1375, 1376).

128. Ayse Ceyhan, "Technologization of Security: Management of Uncertainty and Risk in the Age of Biometrics," *Surveillance & Society* 5, no. 2 (2008): 102.

129. See Paul Virilio, *Popular Defence and Ecological Struggles* (New York: Semiotext(e), 1990), 61.

130. Rapoport, "Being a Body or Having One," 209. See also Steven Flusty "Building Paranoia," in *Architecture of Fear*, ed. Nan Ellin (New York: Princeton Architectural Press, 1997), 48–52; and Scott Baldauf, "Backstory: In South Africa, Home Sweet Fortress," *The Christian Science Monitor*, 6 December 2006.

131. Anonymous, "South Africa: Murder and Siege Architecture," *The Economist*, 15 July 1995, 27–28; and Siyabulela Ooza, "Wall-to-Wall Security," *Financial Mail*, 5 March 1999, 64.

132. Kawash, "Safe House?," 207.

133. Tamara Vukov and Mimi Sheller, "Border Work: Surveillant Assemblages, Virtual Fences, and Tactical Counter-Media," *Social Semiotics* 23, no. 2 (2013): 225.

134. See Clark, "Security Assemblages," 53, 69. See interviews with Andrew Seldon,

13 June 2012; Ryan Nortmann, 19 June 2012; Ingo Mutinelli, 1 July 2014; Gareth Williams, 1 July 2014; and Jack Edery, 1 July 2014.

135. See Zygmunt Bauman, *Liquid Modernity* (Cambridge, UK: Polity, 2000).

136. Weber and Lacy, "Securing by Design," 1023–24, 1027.

137. Dennis Judd, "The Rise of the New Walled Cities," in *Spatial Practices: Critical Explorations in Social/Spatial Theory*, ed. Helen Liggett and David Perry (Thousand Oaks, CA: Sage, 1995), 144–66 (esp. 161).

138. Interviews with Patrick Frimat, 19 June 2012; Frederic Lancelin, 19 June 2012; and Jack Edery, 19 June 2012, and 1 July 2014.

139. See Operations meeting for "Safe Parkview" Security Initiative, 11 June 2012; Station Crime Combating Forum (SCCF) Meeting, 8 February 2016. See interview with Vickie Drinkwater, 2 February 2016. See also Stephen Graham, *Cities under Siege: The New Military Urbanism* (London: Verso, 2010), 302–56.

140. Alice Crawford, "Security Moms and Smart Homes: Information Technology and Domestic Surveillance in the 'Age of Terrorism,'" *The International Journal of Technology, Knowledge, and Society* 1, no. 1 (2005/2006): 94. See also interviews with Patrick Frimat, 19 June 2012; Frederic Lancelin, 19 June 2012; and Jack Edery, 19 June 2012, and 1 July 2014.

141. Crawford, "Security Moms and Smart Homes," 95.

142. See interviews with Jack Edery, 19 June 2012, and 1 July 2014; Ingo Mutinelli, 1 July 2014; and Gareth Williams, 1 July 2014.

143. Iris Marion Young, "House and Home: Feminist Variations on a Theme," chap. 7 in *Intersecting Voices: Dilemmas of Gender, Political Philosophy, and Policy* (Princeton, NJ: Princeton University Press, 1997), 134–64.

144. Crawford, "Security Moms and Smart Homes," 95.

145. Elisabetta Brighi, "Beyond the Gaze: The Changing Architecture of Security between Seduction and Camouflage," in *The Urban Invisibles: Explorations in Space and Society No. 35*, ed. Andrea Pavoni and Andrea Mubi Brighenti (Athens: Professional Dreamers, March 2015), 27. See also Trevor Boddy, "Architecture Emblematic: Hardened Sites and Softened Symbols," in *Indefensible Space: The Architecture of the National Insecurity State*, ed. Michael Sorkin (New York: Routledge, 2008), 277–304.

146. Roy Behrens, *Art and Camouflage: Concealment and Deception in Nature, Art and War* (Cedar Falls: University of Northern Iowa, 1981), 14.

147. See Rafael Gomez-Moriana, "Everyday Camouflage in the City," *Criticalista*, January 13, 2006, https://criticalista.com/2006/01/13/everyday-camouflage-in-the-city/.

148. See Davis, *City of Quartz*, 238.

149. Paul Virilio, *The Vision Machine*, trans. Julie Rose (Bloomington: Indiana University Press, 1994).

150. See Anne Bottomley and Nathan Moore, "From Walls to Membranes: Fortress Polis and the Governance of Urban Public Space in 21st Century Britain," *Law and Critique* 18, no. 2 (2007): 171–206 (esp. 195); and Roy Coleman, "Surveillance in the City: Primary Definition and Urban Spatial Order," *Crime, Media, Culture* 1, no. 2 (2005): 131–48.

151. Sheila Jasanoff, "Future Imperfect: Science, Technology, and the Imaginations of Modernity," in *Dreamscapes of Modernity: Sociotechnical Imaginaries and the Fabrication*

of Power, ed. Sheila Jasanoff and Sang-Hyun Kim (Chicago: University of Chicago Press, 2015), 1.

152. Lacy, "Designer Security," 340.

153. Interviews with Jack Edery, 1 July 2014; Patrick Frimat, 19 June 2012; Justin Hydes, 19 June 2012; Ingo Mutinelli, 1 July 2014; and Ryan Nortmann, 19 June 2012.

154. Graham, *Cities under Siege*, 116. See also Mike Crang and Stephen Graham, "Sentient Cities, Ambient Intelligence, and the Politics of Urban Space," *Information, Communication & Society* 10, no. 6 (2007): 789–817.

155. See, for example, David Lyon, "9/11, Synopticon, and Scopophilia: Watching and Being Watched," in *The New Politics of Surveillance and Visibility*, ed. Richard Victor Ericson and Kevin Haggerty (Toronto: University of Toronto Press, 2006), 35–54.

156. Nigel Thrift, "Movement-Space: The Changing Domain of Thinking Resulting from the Development of New Kinds of Spatial Awareness," *Economy & Society* 33, no. 4 (2004), 584.

157. Priyesh Jagjivan, *Perimeter Protection: The Invisible Fence Becomes Reality* (Johannesburg: Elvey Security Technologies, April 2012).

158. See Rohit Khokher and Ram Chandra Singh, "Footprint-Based Personal Recognition Using Scanning Technique," *Indian Journal of Science and Technology* 9, no. 44 (2016): 1–10.

159. Memorandum, "The Power Is in Your Hands!," July 2012, Elvey Security Technologies.

160. Graham, *Cities under Siege*, xiii–xvi, 60–88; Eyal Weizman, *Hollow Land: Israel's Architecture of Occupation* (New York: Verso, 2007); and Rafi Segal, David Tartakover, and Eyal Weizman, eds., *A Civilian Occupation: The Politics of Israeli Architecture* (New York: Verso, 2003).

161. Lacy, "Designer Security," 333.

162. Beatriz Colomina, *Domesticity at War* (Cambridge, MA: MIT Press, 2007), 12.

163. Stephen Graham, "Cities as Battlespace: The New Military Urbanism," *City* 13, no. 4 (2009): 383–402.

164. Benton-Short, "Bollards, Bunkers, and Barriers," 431.

165. Graham, *Cities under Siege*, 22, 27, 60–88.

CHAPTER 4

1. Karina Landman, *A National Survey of Gated Communities in South Africa*, Project Number: BP 565 (Pretoria: CSIR Council for Scientific and Industrial Research, Building and Construction Technology, 2003). See also Karina Landman and Martin Schönteich, "Gated Communities as a Reaction to Crime," *South African Security Review* 11, no. 1 (2002): 71–85; Jennifer Wood and Clifford Shearing, *Imagining Security* (New York: Routledge, 2007); Stephen Laufer, "The Politics of Fighting Crime in South Africa since 1994," in *Crime Wave: The South African Underworld and Its Foes*, ed. Jonny Steinberg (Johannesburg: Wits University Press, 2001), 14–23; and Jonny Steinberg, "Crime Prevention Goes Abroad: Policy Transfer and Policing in Post-Apartheid South Africa," *Theoretical Criminology* 15, no. 4 (2011): 349–64.

2. Anthony Minnaar, "Private–Public Partnerships: Private Security, Crime Preven-

tion and Policing in South Africa," *Acta Criminologica: Southern African Journal of Criminology* 18, no. 1 (2005): 85–114 (esp. 100–105). See also interviews with David de Lima, 28 June 2012; Jack Edery, 19 June 2012, and 1 July 2014; Patrick Frimat, 19 June 2012; Frederic Lancelin, 19 June 2012; Ingo Mutinelli, 1 July 2014; Gareth Williams, 1 July 2014; and Ryan Nortmann, 19 June 2012.

3. Claire Bénit-Gbaffou, Sophie Didier, and Elisabeth Peyroux, "Circulation of Security Models in Southern African Cities: Between Neoliberal Encroachment and Local Power Dynamics," *International Journal of Urban and Regional Research* 36, no. 5 (2012): 877–89; Julie Berg, "Private Policing in South Africa: The Cape Town City Improvement District—Pluralisation in Practice," *Society in Transition* 35, no. 2 (2005): 224–50; Julie Berg, "Seeing Like Private Security: Evolving Mentalities of Public Space Protection in South Africa," *Criminology and Criminal Justice* 10, no. 3 (2010): 287–301; and Sophie Didier, Elisabeth Peyroux, and Marianne Morange, "The Spreading of the City Improvement District Model in Johannesburg and Cape Town: Urban Regeneration and the Neoliberal Agenda in South Africa," *International Journal of Urban and Regional Research* 36, no. 5 (2012): 915–35.

4. Steve Herbert and Elizabeth Brown, "Conceptions of Space and Crime in the Punitive Neoliberal City," *Antipode* 38, no. 4 (2006): 755–77; Ian Loader, "Fall of the 'Platonic Guardians': Liberalism, Criminology and Political Responses to Crime in England and Wales," *British Journal of Criminology* 46, no. 4 (2006): 561–86; James Sidaway, "Enclave Space: A New Metageography of Development?," *Area* 39, no. 3 (2007): 331–39; Bryan Turner, "The Enclave Society: Towards a Sociology of Immobility," *European Journal of Social Theory* 10, no. 2 (2007): 287–304; Richard Yarwood, "An Exclusive Countryside? Crime Concern, Social Exclusion and Community Policing in Two English Villages," *Policing and Society* 20, no. 1 (2010): 61–78; and Jock Young, *The Exclusive Society: Social Exclusion, Crime and Difference in Late Modernity* (London: Sage, 1999).

5. See Sonia Bookman and Andrew Woolford, "Policing (by) the Urban Brand: Defining Order in Winnipeg's Exchange District," *Social and Cultural Geography* 14, no. 3 (2013): 314.

6. See Clifford Shearing and Philip Stenning, "Modern Private Security: Its Growth and Implications," *Crime and Justice* 3 (1981): 193–245 (esp. 193–94).

7. George Rigakos and David Greener, "Bubbles of Governance: Private Policing and the Law of Canada," *Canadian Journal of Law and Society* 15, no. 1 (2000): 145–85 (esp. 147–48); Trevor Jones and Tim Newburn, "Urban Change and Policing: Mass Private Property Re-considered," *European Journal on Criminal Policy and Research* 7, no. 2 (1999): 225–44; and Lindsay Bremner, "Bounded Spaces: Demographic Anxieties in Post-Apartheid Johannesburg," *Social identities* 10, no. 4 (2004): 455–68. For comparative purposes, see Mark Button, "Private Security and the Policing of Quasi-Public Space," *International Journal of the Sociology of Law* 31, no. 3 (2003): 227–37.

8. Nan Ellin, "Thresholds of Fear: Embracing the Urban Shadow," *Urban Studies Review* 38, nos. 5–6 (2001): 869–83. See also Nan Ellin, "Shelter from the Storm or Form Follows Fear and Vice Versa," in *Architecture of Fear*, ed. Nan Ellen (New York: Princeton Architectural Press, 1997), 13–46.

9. Julie Berg, "Governing Security in Public Spaces: Improvement Districts in South

Africa," in *Policing Cities: Urban Securitization and Regulation in a 21st Century World*, ed. Randy Lippert and Kevin Walby (New York: Routledge, 2013), 161–75; Julie Berg and Clifford Shearing, "New Authorities: Relating State and Non-State Security Auspices in South African Improvement Districts," in *On the Politics of Ordering: Insecurity, Power and Policing on City Frontiers*, ed. Helene Maria Kyed and Peter Albrecht (New York: Routledge, 2014), 91–107; Alison Wakefield, *Selling Security: The Private Policing of Public Space* (Cullompton, UK: Willan, 2003); and Minnaar, "Private–Public Partnerships," 96–97.

10. For nodal governance, see Randy Lippert and Daniel O'Connor, "Security Intelligence Networks and the Transformation of Private Security, *Policing and Society* 16, no. 1 (2006): 49–65; Daniel O'Connor et al., "Seeing Private Security Like a State," *Criminology and Criminal Justice* 8, no. 2 (2008): 203–26; and Clifford Shearing and Jennifer Wood, "Nodal Governance, Democracy, and the 'New Denizens,'" *Journal of Law and Society* 30, no. 3 (2003): 400–419.

11. Anthony Altbeker, *The Dirty Work of Democracy: A Year on the Streets with the SAPS* (Johannesburg: Jonathan Ball, 2005); Anthony Altbeker, *A Country at War with Itself: South Africa's Crisis of Crime* (Cape Town: Jonathan Ball, 2007); and Teresa Dirsuiweit and Alex Wafer, "Scale, Governance and the Maintenance of Privileged Control: The Case of Road Closures in Johannesburg's Northern Suburbs," *Urban Forum* 17, no. 4 (2006): 327–52. See interviews with Anthony Altbeker, 28 June 2011; Ivor Chipkin, 26 June 2014; and Jenny Reid, 11 July 2014.

12. Michael Kempa, Philip Stenning, and Jennifer Wood, "Policing Communal Spaces: A Reconfiguration of the 'Mass Private Property' Hypothesis," *British Journal of Criminology* 44, no. 4 (2004): 562–81.

13. Altbeker, *Dirty Work of Democracy*, 15–31; Anne-Marie Singh, *Policing and Crime Control in Post-Apartheid South Africa* (Burlington, VT: Ashgate, 2008); William Scharg, "Bombs, Bungles and Politic Transformation: When Is the SAPS Going to Get Smarter?," in *Crime Wave: The South African Underworld and Its Foes*, ed. Jonny Steinberg (Johannesburg: Wits University Press, 2001), 50–64.

14. Jarkko Pyysiäinen, Darren Halpin, and Andrew Guilfoyle, "Neoliberal Governance and 'Responsibilization' of Agents: Reassessing the Mechanisms of Responsibility-Shift in Neoliberal Discursive Environments," *Distinktion: Journal of Social Theory* 18, no. 2 (2017): 215–35.

15. Dhananjayan Sriskandarajah, "Both Rich and Poor Are Losing Faith in the State," *Mail & Guardian*, 19 December 2014. See also Staff Reporter, "It Pays to Support Private Security Initiatives," *Weekend Argus*, 16 February 2014.

16. See, among other sources, Mary Nel, "Crime as Punishment: A Legal Perspective on Vigilantism in South Africa" (PhD diss., Stellenbosch University, 2016); and Mark Gross, "Vigilante Violence and 'Forward Panic' in Johannesburg's Townships," *Theory & Society* 45, no. 3 (2016): 239–63.

17. Candice Bailey, "Gangs Attack Parents," *Argus Weekend*, 1 February 2009; and Graeme Hosken and Candice Bailey, "Schools Use Private Firms for Security after Spate of Attacks," *Pretoria News*, 31 January 2009.

18. R. W. Johnson, "Nobel Writer Nadine Gordimer Attacked and Robbed," *Sunday*

Times (London), 29 October 2006; and Andrew Meldrum, "Gordimer's Sorrow for Men Who Robbed Her," *The Guardian* (London), 2 November 2006.

19. Staff Reporter, "Breaking News: Shootout between Guards and Robbers," *Randburg Sun*, 25 July 2015; and Christa Eybers, "Suspect Dies after Shoot-Out during Randburg Cash-in-Transit Heist," *Eyewitness News*, 6 March 2018.

20. Staff Reporter, "Reign of Fear," *The Star*, 14 October 2008.

21. Sthembiso Sithole, "Armed Homeowners Kill Four Assailants," *The Star*, 7 May 2018; Matthew Savides, "Bullets Fly in 'Scary as Hell' Clash between Hijackers and Security Guards in Joburg," *Sunday Times*, 8 July 2018; and Chantelle Fourie and Citizen Reporter, "Dramatic Footage of Northcliff Shootout," *The Citizen*, 5 July 2018.

22. Berg, "Seeing Like Private Security," 287–301 (esp. 295).

23. Operations meeting for "Safe Parkview" security initiative, 11 June 2012. See also interviews with Vickie Drinkwater, 2 February 2016; Don Benson, 14 June 2012; Tanya Greenburg and Mark van Jaarsveld, 15 June 2012; Cheryl Labuschagne and Jenny Clark, 13 June 2012; and Wendy Voster-Robertson, 4 July 2014.

24. Interviews with Geoff Schapiro, 12 February 2016; Tanya Greenburg and Mark van Jaarsveld, 15 June 2012; and Rocky Scafer, 16 July 2014.

25. Interviews with Grant Moulder, 21 June 2012; Mark Notelovitz, 26 June 2012; Rocky Scafer, 16 July 2014; Geoff Schapiro, 12 February 2016; Juri Vos, 12 February 2016; David de Lima and Andre Viljeon, 28 June 2012; and Amir Ben David, 11 July 2014.

26. Dirsuiweit and Wafer, "Maintenance of Privileged Control," 327–52; Lindsay Bremner, "Crime and the Emerging Landscape of Post-Apartheid Johannesburg," in *Blank___: Architecture, Apartheid, and After*, ed. Hilton Judin and Ivan Vladislavić (Rotterdam: NAi, 1999), 48–63; and Alan Lipman and Howard Harris, "Fortress Johannesburg," *Environment and Planning B* 26, no. 5 (1999): 732–33.

27. Proactive private security companies accused their competitors (particularly, well-known international companies) of practicing conventional reactive policing tactics. While they dismissed their rivals as relaxing in their vehicles in the shade and eating donuts, the proactive tactical units claimed that they aggressively pursued the "bad guys." See interviews with David de Lima and Andre Viljeon, 28 June 2012; Grant Moulder, 21 June 2012; and focus group with 7 Arrows Security, 25 June 2012.

28. Karina Landman, "Privatizing Public Space in Post-Apartheid South African Cities through Neighborhood Enclosures," *GeoJournal* 66, nos. 1–2 (2006): 133–46; and Karina Landman, "Gated Neighbourhoods in South Africa: An Appropriate Urban Design Approach?," *Urban Design International* 13, no. 4 (2008): 227–40.

29. Phillip Harrison and Alan Mabin, "Security and Space: Managing the Contradictions of Access Restriction in Johannesburg," *Environment and Planning B* 33, no. 1 (2006): 3–20; and Dirsuiweit and Wafer, "Maintenance of Privileged Control," 327–52.

30. For the shifting contours of the built environment, see Martin J. Murray, "City of Layers: The Making and Shaping of Affluent Johannesburg after *Apartheid*," in *Urban Governance in Post-Apartheid Cities*, ed. Marie Huchzermeyer and Christoph Haferburg (Stuttgart: Schweizerbart, 2014): 179–96.

31. Interviews with Daniel Marsay, 11 June 2012; Don Benson, 14 June 2012; Stewart

Rider, 15 June 2012; Karen Dodo, 15 June 2012; and Carl Chemaly, Steve Lenahan, and Andre Viljoen, 11 June 2012.

32. Interviews with representatives from numerous neighborhood associations, but particularly Tessa Turvey, 11 June 2012; Jonathan Hackner and Elton Hill, 20 June 2012; and Glenda Hancock, 20 June 2012.

33. Interviews with representatives from numerous neighborhood associations, but particularly Tessa Turvey, 11 June 2012; Daniel Marsay, 11 June 2012; and Brian Robertson, 12 June 2012.

34. Interviews with representatives from numerous residents associations, but particularly Vickie Drinkwater, 2 February 2016; and Jonathan Hackner and Elton Hill, 20 June 2012.

35. Interviews with Tiaan Joubert, 26 June 2012; Johan Van Ben Berg, 26 June 2012; Grant Moulder, 21 June 2012; and Geoff Schapiro, 12 February 2016; and focus group with 7 Arrows Security, 25 June 2012.

36. Interviews with Karen Dodo, 15 June 2012; and representatives from numerous private security companies and their clients, particularly Mark Notelovitz, 26 June 2012; Grant Moulder, 21 June 2012; and Geoff Schapiro, 12 February 2016; and focus groups with 7 Arrows Security, 25 June 2012.

37. Interviews with representatives from many neighborhood associations, but particularly Cheryl Labuschagne and Jenny Clark, 13 June 2012; Beverley Markgraaff and Zenda Stravino, 20 June 2012; Daniel Marsay, 11 June 2012; Eve Jammy, 4 July 2014; and Vickie Drinkwater, 2 February 2016.

38. Interviews with representatives from many private security companies, particularly Mark Notelovitz, 26 June 2012; Grant Moulder, 21 June 2012; Rocky Scafer, 16 July 2014; and Geoff Schapiro, 12 February 2016; and focus groups with 7 Arrows Security, 25 June 2012. See also interview with Don Benson, 14 June 2012.

39. See Oldrich Bures and Helena Carrapico, "Private Security beyond Private Military and Security Companies: Exploring Diversity within Private-Public Collaborations and Its Consequences for Security Governance," *Crime, Law and Social Change* 67, no. 3 (2017): 229–43.

40. For example, two doors away from where I was staying in Melville, four armed robbers broke into a house with the goal of stealing whatever they could. The homeowner returned unexpectedly and confronted the thieves. The four men overpowered the homeowner and stole his car. An armed-response patrol vehicle arrived almost immediately but still too late to chase the getaway cars. The private security officers noticed two stationary guards (one armed with a rifle) watching over another home about fifty meters away. In a conversation I overheard, these two stationary guards responded to the query "Did you see anything?" with this answer: "Yes, we saw the confrontation but decided to do nothing since we were not paid to protect the home that was robbed."

41. Chief Rabbi Warren Goldstein, "Crime Can Be Beaten—The CAP Story of Hope," available at http://www.chiefrabbi.co.za/?p=1704&upm. See also Bobby Jordan, "Israel's Holy Warrior," *Sunday Times*, 8 March 2009; and interviews with Don Benson, 14 June 2012; and Tanya Greenburg and Mark van Jaarsveld, 15 June 2012.

42. See Jonny Steinberg and Monique Marks, "The Labyrinth of Jewish Security Arrangements in Johannesburg: Thinking through a Paradox about Security," *British Journal of Criminology* 54, no. 2 (2014): 244–59.

43. Beverley Dirmeik, "Others Would Do Well to Follow Our Lead," *Sunday Times,* 21 October 2007.

44. Martin J. Murray, *City of Extremes: The Spatial Politics of Johannesburg* (Durham, NC: Duke University Press, 2011), 269–73, 275–78.

45. Rita Lewis, "A Big 'Yes' for a Glenhazel CID," *South African Jewish Report* 11, no. 42 (16 November 2007). See also Anonymous, "Residential CIDs Get Support," official website of the City of Johannesburg, 14 August 2008. Available at http://www.joburg.org.za/index.

46. Sandown-Strathavon Community Active Protection Website. Available at https://secure.apsys.co.za/scap/Introduction.html.

47. Goldstein, "Crime Can Be Beaten."

48. Benjamin Moshatama and Isaac Mahlangu, "Coughing Up for Crime," *Sunday Times*, 12 October 2007.

49. Interviews with Tanya Greenburg and Mark van Jaarsveld, 15 June 2012; Karen Dodo, 15 June 2012; and Lionel Stein, 1 July 2014.

50. Interviews with Tanya Greenburg and Mark van Jaarsveld, 15 June 2012; Lionel Stein, 1 July 2014; Karen Dodo, 15 June 2012; and Don Benson, 14 June 2012.

51. Gill Clifford, "Communities Don Crime-Prevention Cap," *The Star*, 11 September 2007.

52. Michael Mopasa and Philip Stenning, "Tools of the Trade: The Symbolic Power of Private Security—An Exploratory Study," *Policing and Society* 11, no. 1 (2001): 69. See also Ian Loader, "Policing the Social: Questions of Symbolic Power," *British Journal of Sociology* 48, no. 1 (1997), 1–18.

53. Interviews with Tanya Greenburg and Mark van Jaarsveld, 15 June 2012; Amir Ben David, 11 July 2014; and Mark Notelovitz, 26 June 2012. See Lara Greenberg, "For Anton, Gap Was More than a Job," *South African Jewish Report* 11, no. 21 (08–15 June 2007).

54. In a particularly provocative intervention, security expert Julie Berg posed this question about CAP-style policing: "Reassurance policing or vigilantism by proxy?" See Berg, "Seeing Like Private Security," 287–301 (esp. 292).

55. Clifford, "Communities Don Crime-Prevention Cap."

56. CAP, "Building a Safer Community Together," accessed 14 April 2016, available at http://www.capgroup.org.za/#!about-us/ct05. See also Staff Reporter, "Project Calls on Former Cops, Soldiers," *The Star*, 17 February 2009; and interviews with Tanya Greenburg and Mark van Jaarsveld, 15 June 2012; and Don Benson, 14 June 2012.

57. Administration, "Armed Response—The Solution to Seeking Reliable Security," Stallion Security, South Africa Israel Chamber of Commerce, 2 December 2014, available at http://saicc.co.za/the-importance-of-armed-response/. See Ian Cook and Mary Whowell, "Visibility and the Policing of Public Space," *Geography Compass* 5, no. 8 (2011): 610–22.

58. Steinberg and Marks, "Labyrinth of Jewish Security Arrangements," 253.

59. Interviews with Tanya Greenburg and Mark van Jaarsveld, 15 June 2012; and Mark Notelovitz, 26 June 2012.

60. Steinberg and Marks, "Labyrinth of Jewish Security Arrangements," 253.

61. Steinberg and Marks, 253–54.

62. Steinberg and Marks. See Staff Reporter, "Project Calls"; and interviews with Amir Ben David, 11 July 2014; Mark Notelovitz, 26 June 2012; and Mark Notelovitz and Rayyaan Majiet, 18 July 2011. For a promotional video that provides an emotional eyewitness testimonial, see the *CAP website, available* at http://www.capgroup.org.za /#!about1/ckv8.

63. Andie Miller, "Walking the Talk," *Sunday Independent*, 28 September 2008.

64. Moshatama and Mahlangu, "Coughing Up for Crime"; Michelle Swart, "Tudor-Style Splendor," *Business Day*, 18 April 2008; and Staff Reporter, "Sandringham Grows in Size and Popularity," *The Star*, 22 June 2013.

65. Steinberg and Marks, "Labyrinth of Jewish Security Arrangements," 246. See also interviews with Lionel Stein, 1 July 2014; and Amir Ben David, 11 July 2014.

66. Yuri Slezkine, *The Jewish Century* (Princeton, NJ: Princeton University Press, 2004). For the origins of these ideas, see Steinberg and Marks, "Labyrinth of Jewish Security Arrangements," 249. Mark Notelovitz is the founder and director of the private security company Core Tactical. See Lethu Nxumalo, "Guards Save the Day," *Rosebank Killarney Gazette*, 3 February 2017.

67. Steinberg and Marks, "Labyrinth of Jewish Security Arrangements," 246. See interview with Amir Ben David, 11 July 2014.

68. See Phyllis Steinberg, "Judaism Is Thriving in South Africa," *Jewish Journal*, 11 September 2014; and Steve Lipman, "Letter from Johannesburg," *Jewish Action* (Winter 2011), available at https://www.ou.org/jewish_action/12/2011/letter_from_south _africa/.

69. Steinberg and Marks, "Labyrinth of Jewish Security Arrangements," 254.

70. See Marcel Mauss, *The Gift: The Form and Reason for Exchange in Archaic Societies*, trans. W. D. Halls (London: Routledge, 1990).

71. For the source of this idea in this and the following paragraphs, see Antina Von Schnitzler, *Democracy's Infrastructure: Techno-Politics and Protest after Apartheid* (Princeton, NJ: Princeton University Press, 2016), 75.

72. Angélica Thumala, Benjamin Goold, and Ian Loader, "A Tainted Trade? Moral Ambivalence and Legitimation Work in the Private Security Industry," *British Journal of Sociology* 62, no. 2 (2011): 285.

73. Von Schnitzler, *Democracy's Infrastructure*, 75.

74. Thumala, Goold, and Loader, "A Tainted Trade?," 299.

75. Thumala, Goold, and Loader, 298.

76. Steinberg and Marks, "Labyrinth of Jewish Security Arrangements," 244.

77. Steinberg and Marks, 256.

78. Thumala, Goold, and Loader, "A Tainted Trade?," 283, 298–99.

79. Anonymous, "Observatory Residents on the Warpath against Crime," *Northeastern Tribune* (local community newspaper), 5 November 2014.

80. Interview with Tanya Greenburg and Mark van Jaarsveld, 15 June 2012.

81. Thandi Skade, "Should Private Guns Take Security into Their Hands? The Fine Line between Protection and Vigilantism," *The Star*, 20 November 2007.

82. Goldstein, "Crime Can Be Beaten."

83. CAP website, available at http://www.capgroup.org.za/#!blank/ca88.

84. CAP website.

85. Anonymous, "Observatory Residents on the Warpath." See also Rabbi Ari Taback, "Cruise Control," *Mishpasha*, 27 February 2013, available at http://www.mishpacha.com/Browse/Article/2991/Cruise-Control.

86. Interviews with Tanya Greenburg and Mark van Jaarsveld, 15 June 2012; Karen Dodo, 15 June 2012; and Lionel Stein, 1 July 2014.

87. Anna Cox, "Houghton Residents Raise R7,5m in Bid to Boost War on Crime," *The Star*, 23 October 2007.

88. Interview with Penny Steyn, 22 June 2012; and on-site observation of training session, 22 June 2012.

89. CAP, "Building a Safer Community Together."

90. Mandy Yachad, quoted in Clifford, "Communities Don Crime-Prevention Cap."

91. Berg, "Seeing Like Private Security," 293. For a journalistic description of CAP, see Kevin Bloom, *Ways of Staying* (London: Portobello, 2010).

92. See Carl Klockars, "The Dirty Harry Problem," *Annals of the American Academy of Political and Social Science* 452, no. 1 (1980): 44. This idea is borrowed from Berg, "Seeing Like Private Security," 293. See interviews with Karen Dodo, 15 June 2012; and Tanya Greenburg and Mark van Jaarsveld, 15 June 2012.

93. Gill Gilford, "Cap Patrol Unit Comes to the Rescue of a Victim," *The Star*, 11 September 2007. See also interview with Don Benson, 14 June 2012.

94. CAP website, available at http://www.capgroup.org.za/#!blank/ca88. See interviews with Don Benson, 14 June 2012; and Tanya Greenburg and Mark van Jaarsveld, 15 June 2012.

95. CAP website, available at http://www.capgroup.org.za/#!blank/ca88.

96. CAP website, available at http://www.capgroup.org.za/#!blank/ca88.

97. CAP website, available at http://www.capgroup.org.za/#!blank/ca88.

98. Interview with Don Benson, 14 June 2012; and focus group with Hi-Tech Security Solutions, 29 June 2011.

99. Interviews with Tanya Greenburg and Mark van Jaarsveld, 15 June 2012; and Karen Dodo, 15 June 2012.

100. Mike Levi and David Wall, "Technologies, Security, and Privacy in the Post-9/11 European Information Society," *Journal of Law and Society* 31, no. 2 (2004): 200). See Roger Clarke, "Dataveillance: Delivering '1984,'" in *Framing Technology: Society, Choice and Change*, ed. Leila Green and Roger Guinery (London: Routledge, 1994): 117–30; and Roger Clarke, "Information Technology and Dataveillance," *Communications of the ACM* 31, no. 5 (1988): 498–511.

101. Sheree Bega, "Feeling Safe in Saxonwold," *The Star*, 22 September 2012.

102. For a broad discussion of flexible borderlands, see Deljana Iossifova, "Borderland Urbanism: Seeing between Enclaves," *Urban Geography* 36, no. 1 (2015): 90–108.

103. Berg, "Seeing Like Private Security," 295–96.

104. Loren Landau, "Immigration and the State of Exception: Security and Sovereignty in East and Southern Africa," *Millennium: Journal of International Studies* 34, no. 2 (2005): 329.

105. Staff Reporter, "Security Company Director Arrested," *The Citizen*, 15 November 2007; and Skade, "Should Private Guns Take Security into Their Hands?"

106. Staff Writer, "Private Cops Not the Answer," *The Star*, 25 October 2007.

107. Chief Rabbi Warren Goldstein, "Chief Rabbi's Report" (report presented at the biennial conference of Union of Orthodox Jewish Synagogues, 21 August 2011), available at http://www.uos.co.za/biennial/chief.asp. See also Lerato Diale, "Cap Creating a Culture of Safety First," *The Star*, 11 November 2011. CAP areas include Bryanston Riverclub North, Emmarentia, Greenside, Glenhazel, Greater Lombardy, Greater Oaklands Orchards, Gresswold, Highlands North, Houghton, Melrose Birdhaven, Norwood, Sandhurst, Sandown-Strathavon, Savoy and Waverley, Saxonwold, Senderwood Linksfield, Victory Park, and Emmarentia-Greenside.

108. Ant Katz, "SA Organizations," *South African Jewish Report*. 15 July 2015. Available at http://www.sajr.co.za/sa/organisations/2015/07/15/cso-and-cap-go-their-separate-ways.

109. Berg, "Seeing Like Private Security," 296–97.

110. See, for example, Ingrid Estha Marais, "Public Space/Public Sphere: An Ethnography of Joubert Park, Johannesburg" (PhD diss., University of Johannesburg, 2013).

111. Iris Marion Young, *Justice and the Politics of Difference* (Princeton, NJ: Princeton University Press, 1990), 238.

112. Doreen Massey, *For Space* (Thousand Oaks, CA: Sage, 2005), 152–53.

113. Alexandra Fanghanel, "The Trouble with Safety: Fear of Crime, Pollution and Subjectification in Public Space," *Theoretical Criminology* 20, no. 1 (2016): 58. See also Bernd Belina, "Evicting the Undesirables: The Idealism of Public Space and the Materialism of the Bourgeois State," *Belgeo* 1 (2003): 47–62.

114. Debra Livingston, "Police Discretion and the Quality of Life in Public Places: Courts, Communities, and the New Policing," *Columbia Law Review* 97, no. 3 (1997): 551–672; and Allen Feldman, "Securocratic Wars of Public Safety: Globalized Policing as Scopic Regime," *Interventions: The International Journal of Postcolonial Studies* 6, no. 3 (2004): 330–50.

115. For comparative work, see Rodrigo Meneses-Reyes, "Out of Place, Still in Motion: Shaping (Im)Mobility through Urban Regulation," *Social and Legal Studies* 22, no. 3 (2013): 335.

116. See, for example, Tony Roshan Samara, "Policing Development: Urban Renewal as Neo-Liberal Security Strategy," *Urban Studies* 47, no. 1 (2010): 197–214; and Tony Roshan Samara, "State Security in Transition: The War on Crime in Post-*Apartheid* South Africa," *Social Identities* 9, no. 2 (2003): 277–312.

117. Focus group with 7 Arrows Security, 25 June 2012; and interview with Grant Moulder, 21 June 2012. On a sunny Saturday morning in January 2016, I observed firsthand one and then three more CSS tactical vehicles converge at a commercial corner in Melville. All in all, eight private security personnel confronted, harassed, and then es-

corted away two poorly dressed young men. Passersby approvingly remarked that this crime prevention tactic protected the neighborhood from thieves.

118. See Herbert and Brown, "Conceptions of Space and Crime," 755–77.

119. Focus group with Hi-Tech Security Solutions, 13 June 2012; and interview with Grant Moulder, 21 June 2012.

120. In both official SAPS internal memorandums and in open conversation, public police officials and private security officers routinely refer, without hesitation or apology, to two or more black males as "bravos." See focus group with Hi-Tech Security Solutions, 13 June 2012; interview with Don Benson, 14 June 2012; and Meeting with representatives from SAPS (including Superintendent Foulds), Johannesburg Municipal Police Department, Omega Risk Solutions (CCTV Surveillance), and representatives of private security companies, 20 June 2012. See also Tessa Diphoorn, "The 'Bravo Mike Syndrome': Private Security Culture and Racial Profiling in South Africa," *Policing and Society* 27, no. 5 (2017): 525–40.

121. For a wider treatment, see Jackie Wang, *Carceral Capitalism* (South Pasadena, CA: Semiotext(e), 2018), especially chapter 5, "The Cybernetic Cop: RoboCop and the Future of Policing."

122. Rhys Jones and Peter Merriman, "Network Nation," *Environment and Planning A* 44, no. 4 (2012): 937–53 (esp. 937).

123. Stuart Elden, "Land, Terrain, Territory," *Progress in Human Geography* 34, no. 6 (2010): 799–817 (esp. 799, 810).

124. Michel Foucault, "Questions of Geography," trans. Colin Gordon, in *Space, Knowledge, and Power: Foucault and Geography*, ed. Jeremy Crampton and Stuart Elden (Burlington, VT: Ashgate, 2007), 176.

125. Faranak Miraftab, "Colonial Present: Legacies of the Past in Contemporary Urban Practices in Cape Town, South Africa," *Journal of Planning History* 11, no. 4 (2012): 283–307 (esp. 284).

126. Zoltán Glück, "Piracy and the Production of Security Space," *Environment and Planning D* 33, no. 4 (2015): 649.

127. For an analogous situation, see Markus Kienscherf, "Security Assemblages and Spaces of Exception: The Production of (Para-) Militarized Spaces in the U.S. War on Drugs," *Radical Criminology* 1, no. 1 (2012): 19–35.

128. Till Paasche, Richard Yarwood, and James Sidaway, "Territorial Tactics: The Socio-Spatial Significance of Private Policing Strategies in Cape Town," *Urban Studies* 51, no. 8 (2014): 1559–75 (esp. 1571).

129. Rigakos and Greener, "Bubbles of Governance," 145–85.

130. See Till Paasche, "Creating Parallel Public Spaces through Private Governments: A South African Case Study," *South African Geographical Journal* 94, no. 1 (2012): 46–59.

131. Paasche, Yarwood, and Sidaway, "Territorial Tactics," 1567.

132. See Steve Herbert, *Policing Space: Territoriality and the Los Angeles Police Department* (Minneapolis: University of Minnesota Press, 1997), esp. 59–78.

133. Goldstein, "Crime Can Be Beaten."

134. For comparative purposes, see Merav Amir, "The Making of a Void Sover-

eignty: Political Implications of the Military Checkpoints in the West Bank," *Environment & Planning D* 31, no. 2 (2013): 227–44.

135. Eyal Weizman, "The Geometry of Occupation" (lecture, Centre of Contemporary Culture of Barcelona, 1 March 2004), available at http://www.publicspace.org/es /texto-biblioteca/eng/a024-the-geometry-of-occupation.

136. See, for example, Edward Casey, "Border versus Boundary at La Frontera," *Environment and Planning D: Society and Space* 29, no. 3 (2011): 384–98.

137. Choon-Piew Pow, "Consuming Private Security: Consumer Citizenship and Defensive Urbanism in Singapore," *Theoretical Criminology* 17, no. 2 (2013): 179–96.

138. Paasche, Yarwood, and Sidaway, "Territorial Tactics," 1571.

139. Paasche, Yarwood, and Sidaway, 1571.

140. Paasche, Yarwood, and Sidaway, 1559.

CHAPTER 5

1. Stuart Elden, "Terror and Territory," *Antipode* 39, no. 5 (2007): 821–45; and Stuart Elden, *Terror and Territory: The Spatial Extent of Sovereignty* (Minneapolis: University of Minnesota Press, 2009), 139–70. See also Mark Salter, "When the Exception Becomes the Rule: Borders, Sovereignty and Citizenship," *Citizenship Studies* 12, no. 4 (2008): 365–80.

2. See Nasser Hussain, *The Jurisprudence of Emergency: Colonialism and the Rule of Law* (Ann Arbor: University of Michigan Press, 2003), 16. See also Robert Kaiser and Elena Nikiforova, "Borderland Spaces of Identification and Dis/location: Multiscalar Narratives and Enactments of Seto Identity and Place in the Estonian-Russian Borderlands," *Ethnic and Racial Studies* 29, no. 5 (2006): 928–58.

3. Till Paasche, Richard Yarwood, and James Sidaway, "Territorial Tactics: The Socio-Spatial Significance of Private Policing Strategies in Cape Town," *Urban Studies* 51, no. 8 (2014): 1559–75 (esp. 1572); and Keith Hayward, *City Limits: Crime, Consumer Culture and the Urban Experience* (London: Glasshouse Press, 2004), 114–15; and Keith Hayward, "Five Spaces of Cultural Criminology," *British Journal of Criminology* 52, no. 3 (2012): 441–62 (esp. 453–55).

4. Elaine Campbell, "Policing and Its Spatial Imaginaries," *Journal of Theoretical & Philosophical Criminology* 8, no. 2 (2016): 71.

5. See Clifford Shearing and Jennifer Wood, "Nodal Governance, Democracy, and the New 'Denizens,'" *Journal of Law and Society* 30, no. 3 (2003): 400–419.

6. Benoît Dupont, "Security in the Age of Networks," *Policing and Society* 14, no. 1 (2004): 76–91 (esp. 84).

7. Lucia Zedner, *Security* (New York: Routledge, 2009), 61.

8. Campbell, "Policing and Its Spatial Imaginaries," 71.

9. Darren Palmer and Ian Warren, "The Pursuit of Exclusion through Banning," *Australian and New Zealand Journal of Criminology* 47, no. 3 (2013): 429–46 (esp. 430).

10. Richard Yarwood, "The Geographies of Policing," *Progress in Human Geography* 31, no. 4 (2007): 447–65.

11. See Bernd Belina, "Evicting the Undesirables: The Idealism of Public Space and the Materialism of the Bourgeois State," *Belgeo* 1 (2003): 47–62.

12. Sally Engle Merry, "Spatial Governmentality and the New Urban Social Order:

Controlling Gender Violence through Law," *American Anthropologist* 103, no. 1 (2001): 16–29.

13. John Carr, Elizabeth Brown, and Steve Herbert, "Inclusion under the Law as Exclusion from the City: Negotiating the Spatial Limitation of Citizenship in Seattle," *Environment and Planning A* 41, no. 8 (2009): 1962–78 (esp. 1962); David Lyon, "Surveillance as Social Sorting: Computer Codes and Mobile Bodies," in *Surveillance as Social Sorting: Privacy, Risk and Digital Discrimination*, ed. David Lyon (New York: Routledge, 2003), 13–30. For how aesthetics works to secure space in Durban, see Christine Hentschel, "Outcharming Crime in (D)urban Space," *Social Dynamics* 37, no. 1 (2011): 148–64.

14. Miriam Ticktin, "Policing and Humanitarianism in France: Immigration and the Turn to Law as State of Exception," *Interventions* 7, no. 3 (2005): 348.

15. See Ticktin, "Policing and Humanitarianism in France," 348–49; and Anku Datta, "Rethinking Spaces of Exception: Notes from a Forced Migrant Camp in Jammu and Kashmir," *International Journal of Migration and Border Studies* 2, no. 2 (2016): 162–75.

16. For the source of these metaphors, see Felicity Scott, *Outlaw Territories: Environments of Insecurity/Architectures of Counterinsurgency* (Cambridge, MA: MIT Press, 2016).

17. Reece Jones, "Agents of Exception: Border Security and the Marginalization of Muslims in India," *Environment and Planning D* 27, no. 5 (2009): 879–97 (esp. 882–83); and Salter, "When the Exception Becomes the Rule," 365–66. See also Sandro Mezzadra and Brett Neilson, "Between Inclusion and Exclusion: On the Topology of Global Space and Borders," *Theory, Culture and Society* 29, nos. 4–5 (2012): 58–75.

18. David Newman, "On Borders and Power: A Theoretical Framework," *Journal of Borderland Studies* 18, no. 1 (2003): 13–25 (esp. 15); and Jeremy Packer, "Becoming Bombs: Mobilizing Mobility in the War on Terror," *Cultural Studies* 20, nos. 4–5 (2006): 378–99 (esp. 381).

19. See Roxanne Doty, "States of Exception on the Mexico-U.S. Border: Security, 'Decisions' and Civilian Border Patrols," *International Political Sociology* 1, no. 2 (2007): 113–37.

20. Campbell, "Policing and Its Spatial Imaginaries," 72.

21. Salter, "When the Exception Becomes the Rule," 374.

22. Jones, "Agents of Exception," 882.

23. Dominic Corva, "Neoliberal Globalization and the War on Drugs: Transnationalizing Illiberal Governance in the Americas," *Political Geography* 27, no. 2 (2008): 176–93 (esp. 177).

24. Andy Clarno and Martin J. Murray, "Policing in Johannesburg after Apartheid," *Social Dynamics* 39, no. 2 (2013): 210–27.

25. Markus Kienscherf, "Security Assemblages and Spaces of Exception: The Production of (Para-) Militarized Spaces in the U.S. War on Drugs," *Radical Criminology* 1, no. 1 (2012): 19–35 (esp. 21).

26. Eyal Weizman, *Hollow Land: Israel's Architecture of Occupation* (New York: Verso, 2007), 106.

27. Mark Salter, "The Global Airport: Managing Space, Speed, and Security," in *Politics at the Airport*, ed. Mark Salter (Minneapolis: University of Minnesota Press, 2008), 1–28 (esp. 1–2).

28. Packer, "Becoming Bombs," 381.

29. See, for example, Steven Flusty, "The Banality of Interdiction: Surveillance, Control, and the Displacement of Diversity," *International Journal of Urban and Regional Research* 25, no. 3 (2001): 658–64.

30. Kienscherf, "Security Assemblages and Spaces of Exception," 27.

31. Ticktin, "Policing and Humanitarianism in France," 365.

32. Kienscherf, "Security Assemblages and Spaces of Exception," 23–24.

33. David Bewley-Taylor, "US Concept Wars, Civil Liberties and the Technologies of Fortification," *Crime Law and Social Change* 43, no. 1 (2005): 104. Ideas from this paragraph are borrowed from Kienscherf, "Security Assemblages and Spaces of Exception," 23–24.

34. Allen Feldman, "Securocratic Wars of Public Safety: Globalized Policing as Scopic Regime," *Interventions: The International Journal of Postcolonial Studies* 6, no. 3 (2004): 331.

35. Kienscherf, "Security Assemblages and Spaces of Exception," 30. See also Michael Dean, "Liberal Government and Authoritarianism," *Economy & Society* 31, no. 1 (2000): 37–61.

36. Roy Coleman and Joe Sim, "Contemporary Statecraft and the 'Punitive Obsession': A Critique of the New Penology Thesis," in *The New Punitiveness: Trends, Theories, Perspectives*, ed. John Pratt et al. (Cullompton, UK: Willan, 2005), 108.

37. See Ole Jensen, *Staging Mobilities* (New York: Routledge, 2013).

38. Gillian Fuller, "Life in Transit: Between Airport and Camp," *Borderlands E-Journal* 2, no. 1 (2003): 13, available at http://www.borderlands.net.au/vol2no1_2003/fuller_transit.html.

39. Morten Frølund, "Becoming Capital: A Journey through the Political Economic Space of Copenhagen Airport," *ACME: An International E-Journal for Critical Geographies* 15, no. 1 (2016): 248.

40. Steve Herbert and Elizabeth Brown, "Conceptions of Space and Crime in the Punitive Neoliberal City," *Antipode* 38, no. 4 (2006): 755–77 (esp. 756).

41. Nassar Hussain, "Beyond Norm and Exception: Guantánamo," *Critical Inquiry* 33, no. 4 (2007): 734–53 (esp. 739).

42. Hussain, "Beyond Norm and Exception," 735.

43. Oren Gross, "Chaos and Rules: Should Responses to Violent Crises Always Be Constitutional?" *Yale Law Journal* 112, no. 5 (2003): 1022.

44. In numerous interviews with leaders of residential neighborhood associations, I was told that they just did not want to know what private security operatives did in the shadowy world of policing, as long as the residents were safe.

45. Information derived in part from interview with Margaret Gichanga, 10 July 2014. Oversight agencies include such organizations as the Independent Complaints Directorate, Secretariats for Safety and Security, and Civilian Oversight Committees (responsible for overseeing the Metro Police) as well as watchdog bodies such as the Human Rights Commission and the Public Protector. See Julie Berg, "Holding South Africa's Private Security Industry Accountable: Mechanisms of Control and Challenges to Effective Oversight," *Acta Criminologica* 21, no. 1 (2008): 87–96; and Julie Berg, *The Ac-*

countability of South Africa's Private Security Industry: Mechanisms of Control and Challenges to Effective Oversight (Cape Town: Criminal Justice Initiative of the Open Society Foundation for South Africa, 2007), 7.

46. See Robert Davis et al., "The Public Accountability of Private Police: Lessons from New York, Johannesburg, and Mexico City," *Policing and Society* 13, no. 2 (2003): 197–210; and Julie Berg, "The Private Security Industry in South Africa: A Review of Applicable Legislation," *South African Journal of Criminal Justice* 16, no. 2 (2003): 178–96.

47. Taken almost verbatim from Philip Stenning, "Powers and Accountability of Private Police," *European Journal on Criminal Policy and Research* 8, no. 3 (2000): 331.

48. Daniel Nira and Stuart Russell, "Policing 'By Any Means Necessary': Reflections on Privatisation, Human Rights and Police Issues—Considerations for Australia and South Africa," *Australian Journal of Human Rights* 3, no. 2 (1997): 157–82; and Berg, *Accountability of South Africa's Private Security Industry*, 7–8.

49. Anne-Marie Singh, *Policing and Crime Control in Post-Apartheid South Africa* (Burlington, VT: Ashgate, 2008), 50; and interview with Tony Botes, 25 June 2014.

50. Stenning, "Powers and Accountability of Private Police," 331.

51. Interviews with Nazira Cachalia, 24 June 2011; J. M. Tau, 25 June 2012; and Margaret Gichanga, 10 July 2014.

52. Stenning, "Powers and Accountability of Private Police," 331.

53. See, for example, Tessa Diphoorn, "'It's All about the Body': The Bodily Capital of Armed Response Officers in South Africa," *Medical Anthropology* 34, no. 4 (2015): 336–52.

54. Thomas Scott and Marlys McPherson, "The Development of the Private Sector of the Criminal Justice System," *Law and Society Review* 6, no. 2 (1971): 272.

55. Stenning, "Powers and Accountability of Private Police," 331; and Philip Stenning, "Governance and Accountability in a Plural Policing Environment: The Story So Far," *Policing* 3, no. 1 (2009), 22–33.

56. Berg, *Accountability of South Africa's Private Security Industry*, 8–11.

57. For the source of this phrase, see Veena Das, "The Signature of the State: The Paradox of Illegibility," in *Anthropology in the Margins of the State*, ed. Veena Das and Deborah Poole (Santa Fe: School of American Research Press, 2004), 225.

58. Interviews with Rocky Scafer, 16 July 2014; Geoff Schapiro, 12 February 2016; Johan Van Ben Berg, 26 June 2012; Carl Chemaly, Steve Lenahan, and Andre Viljoen, 11 June 2012; Cynthia Rose, 9 July 2014; and Danyle Nuñes, 14 June 2018. See also Tessa Diphoorn, *Twilight Policing: Private Security and Violence in Urban South Africa* (Berkeley: University of California Press, 2016); Christine Hentschel and Julie Berg, "Policing South African Cities: Plural and Spatial Perspectives," in *Police, Policing, Policy and the City in Europe*, ed. Marc Cools et al. (The Hague: Eleven International Publishing, 2010) 147–73; and Christine Hentschel, *Security in the Bubble: Navigating Crime in Urban South Africa* (Minneapolis: University of Minnesota Press, 2015).

59. For the source of these ideas (even though I fashion them to my own purposes), see Steve Herbert, "Policing the Contemporary City: Fixing Broken Windows or Shoring Up Neo-Liberalism?," *Theoretical Criminology* 5, no. 4 (2001), 445–66 (esp. 445).

60. Interviews with Anthony Modena, 4 July 2014; Mark Notelovitz, 26 June 2012;

Amir Ben David, 11 July 2014; David de Lima and Andre Viljeon, 28 June 2012; and Geoff Schapiro, 12 February 2016.

61. See interviews with Mark Notelovitz, 26 June 2012; David de Lima and Andre Viljeon, 28 June 2012; and Geoff Schapiro, 12 February 2016. See Neil Smith, "Giuliani Time: The Revanchist 1990s," *Social Text* 57 (1998): 1–20; James Q. Wilson and George Kelling, "Broken Windows: The Police and Neighborhood Safety," *Atlantic Monthly* 249, no. 3 (1982): 29–37; Robert Sampson and Stephen Raudenbush, "Seeing Disorder: Neighborhood Stigma and the Social Construction of 'Broken Windows,'" *Social Psychology Quarterly* 67, no. 4 (2004): 319–42; Bernd Belina and Gesa Helms, "Zero Tolerance for the Industrial Past and Other Threats: Policing and Urban Entrepreneurialism in Britain and Germany," *Urban Studies* 40, no. 9 (2003): 1845–67; and Herbert, "Policing the Contemporary City," 445–66.

62. Interviews with Margaret Gichanga, 10 July 2014; and Tony Botes, 25 June 2014; and focus group with 7 Arrows Security, 25 June 2012.

63. Steve Herbert, "The Normative Ordering of Police Territoriality: Making and Marking Space with the Los Angeles Police Department," *Annals of the Association of American Geographers* 86, no. 3 (1996): 567–82; Steve Herbert, "The Geopolitics of the Police: Foucault, Disciplinary Power and the Tactics of the Los Angeles Police Department," *Political Geography* 15, no. 1 (1996): 47–59; Steve Herbert, "Territoriality and the Police," *The Professional Geographer* 49, no. 1 (1997): 86–94; Steve Herbert, "The End of the Territorially-Sovereign State? The Case of Crime Control in the United States," *Political Geography* 18, no. 2 (1999): 149–72; and Herbert and Brown, "Conceptions of Space and Crime," 755–77.

64. Interviews with Gareth Newman, 11 July 2011; Vickie Drinkwater, 2 February 2016; Cheryl Labuschagne and Jenny Clark, 13 June 2012; Eve Jammy, 4 July 2014; Cynthia Rose, 9 July 2014; Ryan Roseveare and Glenn du Toit, 2 July 2014; Wendy Voster-Robertson, 4 July 2014; and Danyle Nuñes, 14 June 2018; focus group with Hi-Tech Security Solutions, 13 June 2012; and focus group with 7 Arrows Security, 25 June 2012. One Saturday morning as I was having coffee at a popular café near Melville, I noticed a private security vehicle pull up. Two private security personnel exited the vehicle and were greeted at the door by the owner/manager. He pointed in the direction of a parking lot across the road where two young black men were standing near the entrance without apparent purpose. These two young men—in their late teens or early twenties—were dressed in ways that resembled the legions of underemployed or unemployed people who traverse the streets of middle-class residential neighborhoods. The two private security operatives approached the young men in a fashion that reflected military training—spread twenty yards apart and moving one in front and one behind and to the side. Both had their hands on their pistols in their hip holsters. By the time the security personnel reached the young men, first one and then another and then another private security vehicle screeched to a halt in front of the café. Within thirty seconds, the two disheveled young men were surrounded by eight private security personnel. Shouting loudly, the security personnel pushed the young men, forcing them to leave the spots on the public pavement where they had been standing. As the two young men walked away, a private security vehicle followed them at a discreet dis-

tance. I asked the owner/manager what had just happened. He told me that he figured the two young men were going to break into and rob the cars in the parking lot. He said he suspected that the car guard who was supposed to be watching the cars in the lot was part of the robbery plot.

65. See interviews with Tessa Turvey, 11 June 2012; Beverley Markgraaff and Zenda Stravino, 20 June 2012; and Jonathan Hackner and Elton Hill, 20 June 2012.

66. Interviews with Grant Moulder, 21 June 2012; Tiaan Joubert, 26 June 2012; and Johan Van Der Berg, 26 June 2012. See also Monique Marks and Jennifer Wood, "South African Policing at a Crossroads," *Theoretical Criminology* 14, no. 3 (2010): 311–29.

67. For the use of this term, see Karen Malone, "Street Life: Youth, Culture and Competing Uses of Public Space," *Environment and Urbanization* 14, no. 2 (2002): 157–68.

68. Interviews with Mark Notelovitz, 26 June 2012; Geoff Schapiro, 12 February 2016; and Juri Vos, 12 February 2016.

69. Focus group with 7 Arrows Security, 25 June 2012. See also Natalie Jaynes, "Flying below the Radar: The Armed Private Security Sector in South Africa" (Criminal Justice Initiative, occasional paper no. 11, Open Society Foundation for South Africa, Pinelands, ZA, 2012), 1–43 (esp. 21).

70. Focus group with 7 Arrows Security, 25 June 2012; and interviews with Mark Notelovitz and Rayyaan Majiet, 18 July 2011; and Rocky Scafer, 16 July 2014.

71. Interviews with Grant Moulder, 21 June 2012; Geoff Schapiro, 12 February 2016; and Juri Vos, 12 February 2016.

72. Focus group with 7 Arrows Security, 25 June 2012. Interviews with Amir Ben David, 11 July 2014; David de Lima and Andre Viljeon, 28 June 2012; Mark Notelovitz and Rayyaan Majiet, 18 July 2011; and Mark Notelovitz, 26 June 2012. In an interview, a manager of one private security company who had served in a branch of the intelligence service in the Israeli Defense Force continually blurred the distinction between criminal suspects and "terrorists."

73. Interviews with Juri Vos, 12 February 2016; Amir Ben David, 11 July 2014; and David de Lima and Andre Viljeon, 28 June 2012; and focus group with 7 Arrows Security, 25 June 2012. See also Andy Clarno, *Neoliberal Apartheid: Palestine/Israel and South Africa after 1994* (Chicago: University of Chicago Press, 2017), 139–40.

74. Interviews with Juri Vos, 12 February 2016; and Geoff Schapiro, 12 February 2016. In an interview, one woman who headed the security portfolio of her neighborhood association talked about how she volunteered to approve all the tactical officers working with the private security company under contract in her area. She insisted that they all have military training. When asked if military service in the South African National Defense Force offered sufficient qualifications, she vehemently objected, remarking that the South African army did not have any actual combat experience.

75. At the end of a meeting with five owners/managers of well-known private security companies, we asked what their operatives were instructed to do when they detained persons in the act of armed robbery or house break-ins. They laughed and began one after the other bragging about how they "taught them a lesson," "got them ready for the police," and the like. In order to demonstrate his toughness, one manager/owner pulled out his cell phone and proudly displayed a photograph of a badly

beaten man dressed in a police uniform. He told us that his operatives pummeled the suspected criminal who was caught inside a private home. This gang of house-breakers impersonated police officers responding to a panic alarm as a ploy to trick their way into homes.

76. Interviews with Jonathan Hackner and Elton Hill, 20 June 2012; and Daniel Marsay, 11 June 2012; and focus groups with Hi-Tech Security Solutions, 29 June 2011, and 13 June 2012; and 7 Arrows Security, 25 June 2012.

77. Interviews with Daniel Marsay, 11 June 2012; Stewart Rider, 15 June 2012; Brian Robertson, 12 June 2012; Jonathan Hackner and Elton Hill, 20 June 2012; and Glenda Hancock, 20 June 2012.

78. Thomas Blom Hansen, "Performers of Sovereignty: On the Privatization of Security in Urban South Africa," *Critique of Anthropology* 26, no. 3 (2006): 290. See also Tony Roshan Samara, "Order and Security in the City: Producing Race and Policing Neoliberal Spaces in South Africa," *Ethnic and Racial Studies* 33, no. 4 (2010): 637–55; Tony Roshan Samara, "Policing Development: Urban Renewal as Neo-Liberal Security Strategy," *Urban Studies* 47, no. 1 (2010): 197–214; and Jonny Steinberg, *Thin Blue: The Unwritten Rules of Policing South Africa* (Cape Town: Jonathan Ball, 2008); and Tessa Diphoorn, "The 'Bravo Mike Syndrome': Private Security Culture and Racial Profiling in South Africa," *Policing and Society* 27, no. 5 (2017): 525–40. See interviews with Geoff Schapiro, 12 February 2016; Don Benson, 14 June 2012; and Grant Moulder, 21 June 2012; and meeting with representatives from SAPS, 20 June 2012.

79. Simpiwe Piliso, "Just How Safe Are You Behind Your Boom Gate?," *Sunday Times*, 1 April 2001. Information derived from focus groups with Hi-Tech Security Solutions, 29 June 2011, and 13 June 2012; and 7 Arrows Security, 25 June 2012. See also interviews with Tony Botes, 25 June 2014; and David de Lima and Andre Viljoen, 28 June 2012.

80. Focus groups with Hi-Tech Security Solutions, 29 June 2011, and 13 June 2012; and 7 Arrows Security, 25 June 2012. See interviews with Tony Botes, 25 June 2014; David de Lima and Andre Viljeon, 28 June 2012; Lionel Stein, 1 July 2014; and Geoff Schapiro, 12 February 2016.

81. Interviews with Geoff Schapiro, 12 February 2016; and Vickie Drinkwater, 2 February 2016.

82. Paul T. Clarke, "Security Assemblages: Enclaving, Private Security, and New Materialism in Suburban Johannesburg" (master's thesis, University of the Witwatersrand, 2016), 7.

83. Interview with Tanya Greenburg and Mark van Jaarsveld, 15 June 2012; and Don Benson, 14 June 2012.

84. See Mariana Valverde, "Targeted Governance and the Problem of Desire," in *Risk and Morality*, ed. Richard Victor Ericson and Aaron Doyle (Toronto: University of Toronto Press, 2003), 438–58.

85. Wendy Larner and William Walters, eds., introduction to *Global Governmentality: Governing International Spaces* (London: Routledge, 2004), 1–19 (esp. 15).

86. Hiroyuki Tosa, "Anarchical Governance: Neoliberal Governmentality in Reso-

nance with the State of Exception," *International Political Sociology* 3, no. 4 (2009): 414–30 (esp. 422).

87. Judith Butler, *Precarious Life: The Powers of Mourning and Violence* (New York: Verso, 2004), 56. See also Jones, "Agents of Exception," 881.

88. See Sarah Jane Cooper-Knock and Olly Owen, "Between Vigilantism and Bureaucracy: Improving Our Understanding of Police Work in Nigeria and South Africa," *Theoretical Criminology* 19, no. 3 (2015): 355–75 (esp. 365).

89. Walter Benjamin, *Reflections* (New York: Schoken Books, 1986), 277–87 (esp. 287).

90. Ticktin, "Policing and Humanitarianism in France," 354, 364.

91. Butler, *Precarious Life*, p. 60.

92. Ticktin, "Policing and Humanitarianism in France," 365, 366.

93. Ticktin, 354.

94. Interviews with Barbara Holtman, 28 June 2011; Anthony Altbeker, 28 June 2011; and Gareth Newman, 11 July 2011.

95. Anthony Altbeker, *The Dirty Work of Democracy: A Year on the Streets with the SAPS* (Johannesburg: Jonathan Ball, 2005); Julia Hornberger, "'My Police—Your Police': The Informal Privatization of the Police in Inner City Johannesburg," *African Studies* 63, no. 2 (2004): 213–30; Steinberg, *Thin Blue*; and Jonny Steinberg, "Crime Prevention Goes Abroad: Policy Transfer and Policing in Post-Apartheid South Africa," *Theoretical Criminology* 15, no. 4 (2011): 349–64.

96. Samara, "Order and Security in the City," 637–55; Samara, "Policing Development," 197–214; Altbeker, *Dirty Work of Democracy*, 128–45; Hornberger, "My Police—Your Police," 213–30; and Steinberg, *Thin Blue*, 100–116.

97. One egregious example of this 'swarming' tactic can be found in circumstances in which Wozani Security (the notorious "Red Ants") are called on to carry out evictions of unauthorized squatters from occupied buildings. The sheer presence of a large number of private security operatives in their distinctive red overalls serves to intimate those who are forcibly removed from their places of residence with their belongings piled unceremoniously on the street.

98. Julie Berg, "Seeing Like Private Security: Evolving Mentalities of Public Space Protection in South Africa," *Criminology & Criminal Justice* 10, no. 3 (2010): 287–301 (esp. 293). For a journalistic description of CAP, see Kevin Bloom, *Ways of Staying* (London: Portobello, 2010).

99. Interviews with Grant Moulder, 21 June 2012; Mark Notelovitz, 26 June 2012; Rocky Scafer, 16 July 2014; and Geoff Schapiro, 12 February 2016.

100. Focus group with 7 Arrows Security, 25 June 2012; and interviews with Glenda Hancock, 20 June 2012; Jonathan Hackner and Elton Hill, 20 June 2012; Rocky Scafer, 16 July 2014; Nazira Cachalia, 24 June 2011; and Geoff Schapiro, 12 February 2016. See also Clarno and Murray, "Policing in Johannesburg after Apartheid."

101. Focus groups with Hi-Tech Security Solutions, 29 June 2011, and 13 June 2012; and 7 Arrows Security, 25 June 2012.

102. Focus group with 7 Arrows Security, 25 June 2012; and interviews with Jona-

than Hackner and Elton Hill, 20 June 2012; Beverley Markgraaff and Zenda Stravino, 20 June 2012; and Glenda Hancock, 20 June 2012.

103. While they often do not express it so bluntly, this view is widely shared among private security managers.

104. Ügen Vos, "Hijacker Killed in 'Mini War' in Joburg Suburb," *News24*, 1 February 2017.

105. See Michael Wines, "Crime in South Africa Grows More Vicious," *New York Times*, 23 September 2005; Gerald Young, "Robber Shot Dead in Armed Robbery," *The Citizen*, 21 April 2017; Amanda Watson and Wendy Nyoni, "Nowhere to Hide for Hijackers," *The Citizen*, 9 January 2015; Staff Reporter, "Two Suspected Hijackers Shot Dead in Riverlea," *E News Channel Africa*, 19 November 2016; Alex Patrick, "Police Arrest Hijackers after Shootout in Joburg Suburb," *Sowetan Live*, May 15, 2017; and Lizeka Tandwa, "Several Injured in Joburg Shootout between Police and Hijackers," *News24*, 27 March 2017.

106. Ian Cook and Mary Whowell, "Visibility and the Policing of Public Space," *Geography Compass* 5, no. 8 (2011): 610–22.

107. Alex Vitale, "Innovation and Institutionalization: Factors in the Development of 'Quality of Life' Policing in New York City," *Policing & Society* 15, no. 2 (2005): 99–124 (esp. 100).

108. See Berg, "Seeing Like Private Security," 292–94; and Bloom, *Ways of Staying*, chap. 3; and Jonny Steinberg and Monique Marks, "The Labyrinth of Jewish Security Arrangements in Johannesburg: Thinking through a Paradox about Security," *British Journal of Criminology* 54, no. 2 (2014): 244–59. Interviews with Tanya Greenburg and Mark van Jaarsveld, 15 June 2012; and Cheryl Labuschagne and Jenny Clark, 13 June 2012.

109. Sanchia Temkin, "NYPD on Patrol to Protect the 'Bronx of the North,'" *Business Day*, 6 June 2008.

110. George Rigakos, "Hyperpanoptics as Commodity: The Case of the Parapolice," *Canadian Journal of Sociology/Cahiers Canadiens de Sociologie* 24, no. 1 (1999): 381.

111. There are exceptions. In private, off-the-record conversations, some private security managers bragged of paying off a Nigerian criminal syndicate to stay away from (and to physically prevent other syndicates from filling the void) the areas in which they have been paid by commercial proprietors to provide protection. Other private security managers proudly showed photographs of suspected criminals whom they had beaten. Still others boasted of burning down the shacks of homeless squatters and driving them away with sjamboks or of forcing unwanted persons into their vehicles and dropping them off miles away from where they were "arrested." Some private security managers claimed to have hired criminal gang members to help in the recovery of stolen vehicles in the townships.

112. Focus groups with Hi-Tech Security Solutions, 29 June 2011, and 13 June 2012; and interviews with Grant Moulder, 21 June 2012; and Amir Ben David, 11 July 2014.

113. Focus groups with Hi-Tech Security Solutions, 29 June 2011, and 13 June 2012.

114. Rowland Atkinson, "Domestication by Cappuccino or a Revenge on Urban

Space? Control and Empowerment in the Management of Public Spaces," *Urban Studies* 40, no. 9 (2003): 1829–43.

115. See Don Mitchell, "The Annihilation of Space by Law: The Roots and Implications of Anti-homeless Laws in the United States," *Antipode* 29, no. 3 (1997): 303–35; and Don Mitchell, *The Right to the City: Social Justice and the Fight for Public Space* (London: Guildford Press, 2003).

116. Roy Coleman, "Surveillance in the City: Primary Definition and Urban Social Order," *Crime, Media, Culture* 1, no. 2 (2005): 131–48; Cindy Katz, "Hiding the Target: Social Reproduction in the Privatized Urban Environment," in *Postmodern Geography: Theory and Practice*, ed. Claudio Minca (London: Routledge, 2001), 93–110; and Hentschel, *Security in the Bubble*, 57–88.

117. For a wider view, see John Paul Catungal and Eugene McCann, "Governing Sexuality and Park Space: Acts of Regulation in Vancouver, B.C.," *Social and Cultural Geography* 11, no. 1 (2010): 75–94; Phil Hubbard, "Cleansing the Metropolis: Sex Work and the Politics of Zero Tolerance," *Urban Studies* 41, no. 9 (2004): 1687–1702; and Kate Swanson, "Revanchist Urbanism Heads South: The Regulation of Indigenous Beggars and Street Vendors in Ecuador," *Antipode* 39, no. 4 (2007): 708–28.

118. Don Mitchell, *The Lie of the Land: Migrant Workers and the California Landscape* (Minneapolis: University of Minnesota Press, 1996); and David Lyon, *Surveillance Studies: An Overview* (Cambridge, UK: Polity, 2007).

119. Cook and Whowell, "Visibility and the Policing of Public Space," 610–22.

120. Berg, "Seeing Like Private Security," 288.

121. Clifford Shearing and Philip Stenning, "Snowflakes or Good Pinches? Private Security's Contribution to Modern Policing," in *The Maintenance of Order in Society*, ed. Rita Donelan (Ottawa: Canadian Police College, 1982), 96–105 (esp. 88).

122. Berg, "Seeing Like Private Security," 287–301.

123. For the source of these quotations, see Clark, "Security Assemblages," p. 15. See interviews with Gibbon Schickering, 19 June 2012; and Russell Thomas, 15 July 2008.

124. See Anthony Vidler, *The Architectural Uncanny: Essays in the Modern Unhomely* (Cambridge, MA: MIT Press, 1992), 23.

125. Christine Hentschel, "Making (In)Visible: CCTV, 'Living Cameras,' and Their Objects in a Post-Apartheid Metropolis," *International Criminal Justice Review* 17, no. 4 (2007): 289–303; and Niles Zurawski, "Video Surveillance and Everyday Life: Assessments of Closed-Circuit Television and the Cartography of Socio-Spatial Imaginations," *International Criminal Justice Review* 17, no. 4 (2007): 269–88.

126. Randy Lippert and Daniel O'Connor, "Security Intelligence Networks and the Transformation of Contract Private Security," *Policing and Society* 16, no. 1 (2006): 50–66 (esp. 50–51).

127. Dupont, "Security in the Age of Networks," 84.

128. Tim Hope, "Inequality and the Clubbing of Private Security," in *Crime, Risk and Insecurity: Law and Order in Everyday Life and Political Discourse*, ed. Tim Hope and Richard Sparks (London: Routledge, 2000), 83–106.

129. Lippert and O'Connor, "Transformation of Contract Private Security," 63.

130. Interviews with Vickie Drinkwater, 2 February 2016; Cheryl Labuschagne and Jenny Clark, 13 June 2012; Don Benson, 14 June 2012; and Carl Chemaly, Steve Lenahan, and Andre Viljoen, 11 June 2012.

131. Focus groups with Hi-Tech Security Solutions, 29 June 2011, and 13 June 2012; and 7 Arrows Security, 25 June 2012. See interviews with Tony Botes, 25 June 2014; David de Lima and Andre Viljeon, 28 June 2012; Lionel Stein, 1 July 2014; Karen Dodo, 15 June 2012; and Geoff Schapiro, 12 February 2016. See also Clarno, *Neoliberal Apartheid*, 144.

132. In a candid conversation, an owner of a private security company confided that one of their tactical teams had "lost" an assault weapon in a firefight with a gang of housebreakers. Following the leads of several informants, the private security company owner identified the leader of the gang. Private security operatives got word to the suspected criminal leader that they knew where he lived, what his comings and goings were, and where his children attended school. Suggesting in broad terms that kidnapping was an option, the owner boastfully said that he was confident his company would recover the weapon.

133. Interviews with Karen Dodo, 15 June 2012; and Geoff Schapiro, 12 February 2016. See also Clarno, *Neoliberal Apartheid*, 143.

134. Focus groups with Hi-Tech Security Solutions, 29 June 2011, and 13 June 2012; and 7 Arrows Security, 25 June 2012. Interviews with Don Benson, 14 June 2012; David de Lima and Andre Viljoen, 28 June 2012; Karen Dodo, 15 June 2012; and Tanya Greenburg and Mark van Jaarsveld, 15 June 2012.

135. Information derived from interviews with more than one private security company. Interviews with Geoff Schapiro, 12 February 2016; Mark Notelovitz, 26 June 2012; Rocky Scafer, 16 July 2014; and Grant Moulder, 21 June 2012; and focus groups with Hi-Tech Security Solutions, 29 June 2011, and 13 June 2012; and 7 Arrows Security, 25 June 2012.

136. Major General Bushie Engelbrecht took early retirement from the SAPS after completing more than forty-three years of public service. In 2002, he was appointed as deputy provincial commissioner for Detective and Crime Intelligence Services in Gauteng. At the time of his retirement, he was the commander of the Alexandra Cluster. Information derived from Staff Reporter, "Top Cops Join Private Security Company," *Gauteng Business News*, available at www.gbn.co.za/business/news/0175/0333 .htm. See also interviews with Grant Moulder, 21 June 2012; Jonathan Hackner and Elton Hill, 20 June 2012; Don Benson, 14 June 2012; and Mark Notelovitz, 26 June 2012.

137. Herbert, "Normative Ordering of Police Territoriality," 567–82.

138. Interviews with Stewart Rider, 15 June 2012; Brian Robertson, 12 June 2012; Ryan Roseveare and Glenn du Toit, 2 July 2014; and Tessa Turvey, 11 June 2012.

139. Lisa Wedeen, "Seeing Like a Citizen, Acting Like a State: Exemplary Events in Unified Yemen," *Comparative Studies in Society and History* 45, no. 4 (2003): 680–713.

140. Sarah-Jane Cooper-Knock, "Behind Closed Gates: Everyday Policing in Durban, South Africa," *Africa* 86, no. 1 (2016): 107.

141. These ideas are derived from candid interviews with leaders of residential associations.

142. Cooper-Knock, "Behind Closed Gates," 98.

143. Berg, "Seeing Like Private Security," 293–94.

144. See, for example, John Manzo, "The Folk Devil Happens to Be Our Best Customer: Security Officers' Orientations to 'Youth' in Three Canadian Shopping Malls," *International Journal of the Sociology of Law* 32, no. 3 (2004): 251.

145. Focus groups with Hi-Tech Security Solutions, 29 June 2011, 13 June 2012; and 7 Arrows Security, 25 June 2012.

146. Interview with Carl Chemaly, Steve Lenahan, and Andre Viljoen, 11 June 2012; Tessa Turvey, 11 June 2012; Anthony Modena, 4 July 2014; and Stewart Rider, 15 June 2012.

147. Interview with Carl Chemaly, Steve Lenahan, and Andre Viljoen, 11 June 2012; Daniel Marsay, 11 June 2012; Brian Robertson, 12 June 2012; Cynthia Rose, 9 July 2014; and Ryan Roseveare and Glenn du Toit, 2 July 2014.

148. Interviews with Geoff Schapiro, 12 February 2016; and Grant Moulder, 21 June 2012.

149. Tessa Diphoorn and Julie Berg, "Typologies of Partnership Policing: Case Studies from Urban South Africa," *Policing & Society* 24, no. 4 (2014): 425.

150. Bruce Baker, *Security in Post-Conflict Africa: The Role of Nonstate Policing* (Boca Raton: FL: CLC Press, 2010), 35. This idea is taken from Diphoorn, *Twilight Policing*, 131.

151. Focus groups with Hi-Tech Security Solutions, 29 June 2011, 13 June 2012; and interviews with Beverley Markgraaff and Zenda Stravino, 20 June 2012; Stewart Rider, 15 June 2012; Brian Robertson, 12 June 2012; Cynthia Rose, 9 July 2014; and Ryan Roseveare and Glenn du Toit, 2 July 2014.

152. Diphoorn and Berg, "Typologies of Partnership Policing," 431. See also interview with Don Benson, 14 June 2012.

153. Diphoorn, *Twilight Policing*, 131–32.

154. Interviews with J. M. Tau, 25 June 2012; Geoff Schapiro, 12 February 2016; Grant Moulder, 21 June 2012; and Amir Ben David, 11 July 2014; and focus group with Hi-Tech Security Solutions, 29 June 2011 and 13 June 2012.

155. Interviews with Nazira Cachalia, 30 May 2006, and 24 June 2011; Earl Stoles, 20 June 2012; and Earl Stoles and Zane Callaghan, 9 July 2008.

156. See Clarno, *Neoliberal Apartheid*, 148. See also focus groups with Hi-Tech Security Solutions, 13 June 2012; and 7 Arrows Security, 25 June 2012; and interviews with Don Benson, 14 June 2012; Tiaan Joubert, 26 June 2012; Johan Van Ben Berg, 26 June 2012; Colonel Kobus Lategan, 20 June 2012; Nazira Cachalia, 24 June 2011; Brigadier Danie Louw, 27 June 2011; Grant Moulder, 21 June 2012; Mark Notelovitz, 26 June 2012; Wendy Voster-Robertson, 4 July 2014; and Geoff Schapiro, 12 February 2016.

157. Interviews with J. M. Tau, 25 June 2012; Wendy Voster-Robertson, 4 July 2014; and Brigadier P. P. Billings, 4 July 2014.

158. Raenette Taljaard, "Private and Public Security in South Africa," in *The Private Security Sector in Africa*, ed. Sabelo Gumedze, monograph series, no. 146 (Pretoria: Institute for Security Studies, 2008), 69–98. See interviews with Colonel Kobus Lategan, 20 June 2012; Nazira Cachalia, 24 June 2011; and Brigadier Danie Louw, 27 June 2011.

159. Interviews with J. M. Tau, 25 June 2012; Brigadier P. P. Billings, 4 July 2014; and Wayne Minnaar, 9 July 2014.

160. Interviews with Vickie Drinkwater, 2 February 2016; Wendy Voster-Robertson, 4 July 2014; Eve Jammy, 4 July 2014; and Carl Chemaly, Steve Lenahan, and Andre Viljoen, 11 June 2012.

161. Interviews with Colonel Kobus Lategan, 20 June 2012; and Grant Moulder, 21 June 2012.

162. Focus groups with Hi-Tech Security Solutions, 29 June 2011, and 13 June 2012; and interviews with Wayne Minnaar, 9 July 2014; Mark Notelovitz, 26 June 2012; and Carl Chemaly, Steve Lenahan, and Andre Viljoen, 11 June 2012.

163. Focus group with 7 Arrows Security, 25 June 2012; and Hi-Tech Security Solutions, 29 June 2011 and 13 June 2012; and interviews with J. M. Tau, 25 June 2012; and Margaret Gichanga, 10 July 2014.

164. Salter, "Global Airport," 8.

165. Interviews with Cheryl Labuschagne and Jenny Clark, 13 June 2012; Jonathan Hackner and Elton Hill, 20 June 2012; Glenda Hancock, 20 June 2012; and Lornette Joseph, 10 July 2014.

166. Interviews with Barbara Holtman, 28 June 2011; Gareth Williams, 1 July 2014; Jenny Reid, 11 July 2014; and Ryan Roseveare and Glenn du Toit, 2 July 2014.

167. Johan Burger, "Crime Combating in Perspective: A Strategic Approach to Policing and the Prevention of Crime in South Africa," *Acta Criminologica* 19, no. 2 (2006): 105–18; Johan Burger, *Strategic Perspectives on Crime and Policing in South Africa* (Pretoria: Van Schaik, 2007); Martin Schönteich, *Unshackling the Crime Fighters: Increasing Private Security Involvement in South Africa's Criminal Justice System* (Johannesburg: South African Institute of Race Relations, 1999); and Taljaard, "Private and Public Security in South Africa," 69–106.

168. Focus groups with Hi-Tech Security Solutions, 29 June 2011, and 13 June 2012; and 7 Arrows Security, 25 June 2012; and interviews with Karen Dodo, 15 June 2012; and Stewart Rider, 15 June 2012.

169. Ideas for this paragraph derived from Logan Puck, "Uneasy Partners against Crime: The Ambivalent Relationship between the Police and the Private Security Industry in Mexico," *Latin American Politics and Society* 59, no. 1 (2017): 74–95.

170. Angélica Thumala, Benjamin Goold, and Ian Loader, "A Tainted Trade? Moral Ambivalence and Legitimation Work in the Private Security Industry," *British Journal of Sociology* 62, no. 2 (2011): 294; and Adam White, *The Politics of Private Security: Regulation, Reform and Re-Legitimation* (New York: Palgrave Macmillan, 2010).

171. Adam White, "The New Political Economy of Private Security," *Theoretical Criminology* 16, no. 1 (2012): 89. See also Julie Ayling and Clifford Shearing, "Taking Care of Business: Public Police as Commercial Security Vendors," *Criminology and Criminal Justice* 8, no. 1 (2008): 27–50; and Diphoorn, "It's All about the Body," 336–52.

172. Cooper-Knock, "Behind Closed Gates," 107; and White, "The New Political Economy of Private Security," 89 (source of second quotation).

173. Thumala, Goold, and Loader, "A Tainted Trade?" (294, source of first quotation); and White, "New Political Economy of Private Security," 90.

174. See Diphoorn and Berg, "Typologies of Partnership Policing," 430, 431–33.

See also interviews with Brigadier P. P. Billings, 4 July 2014; Nazira Cachalia, 30 May 2006, and 24 June 2011; Brigadier Danie Louw, 27 June 2011; and Colonel Kobus Lategan, 20 June 2012.

175. Interviews with Don Benson, 14 June 2012; Vickie Drinkwater, 2 February 2016; Brian Robertson, 12 June 2012; Tanya Greenburg and Mark van Jaarsveld, 15 June 2012; and Tessa Turvey, 11 June 2012.

176. Interviews with numerous private security companies and public policing agencies.

177. Monique Marks and Jenny Fleming, "As Unremarkable as the Air They Breathe? Reforming Police Management in South Africa," *Current Sociology* 52, no. 5 (2004): 784–808; Monique Marks and Jennifer Wood, "South African Policing at a Crossroads," *Theoretical Criminology* 14, no. 3 (2010): 311–29; and interview with Geoff Schapiro, 12 February 2016.

178. Interview with Margaret Gichanga, 10 July 2014; and Tony Botes, 25 June 2014. See also Tessa Diphoorn, "'Surveillance of the Surveillers': Regulation of the Private Security Industry in South Africa and Kenya," *African Studies Review* 59, no. 2 (2016): 161–82.

179. Interviews with Jack Edery, 19 June 2012, and 1 July 2014; Patrick Frimat, 19 June 2012; Ryan Nortmann, 19 June 2012; and Ingo Mutinelli, 1 July 2014.

180. Berg, "Private Security Industry in South Africa," 178–96; and Berg, *Accountability of South Africa's Private Security Industry*, 7–10. Interviews with Jenny Reid, 11 July 2014; Margaret Gichanga, 10 July 2014; and Tony Botes, 25 June 2014.

CHAPTER 6

1. Gareth Millington, "Book Review: Gordon Hughes, *The Politics of Crime and Community*," *Theoretical Criminology* 13, no. 3 (2009): 383–87 (esp. 383).

2. David Garland, "Ideas, Institutions, and Situational Crime Prevention," in *Ethical and Social Perspectives on Situational Crime Prevention*, ed. Andrew Von Hirsch, David Garland, and Alison Wakefield (Oxford, UK: Hart Publishing, 2000): 1–16 (esp. 1).

3. Mary Tuck, "Crime Prevention: A Shift in Concept," *Home Office Research and Planning Unit Research Bulletin*, occasional paper no. 24 (London: Home Office, 1988), 5–8.

4. Adam Crawford, "Community Safety Partnerships: Managerialist Tensions and Threats," *Criminal Justice Matters* 33, no. 1 (1998): 4.

5. Crawford, "Community Safety Partnerships," 4. See also Adam Crawford, "The Partnership Approach to Community Crime Prevention: Corporatism at the Local Level?," *Social & Legal Studies* nos. 3–4 (1994): 497–519; and Adam Crawford and Karen Evans, "Crime Prevention and Community Safety," in *The Oxford Handbook of Criminology*, 5th ed., ed. Mick Maguire, Rodney Morgan, and Robert Reiner (Oxford: Oxford University Press, 2012), 769–805.

6. See also Lucia Zedner, "Pre-Crime and Post-Criminology," *Theoretical Criminology* 11, no. 2 (2007): 261–81 (especially 362).

7. David Garland, *The Culture of Control: Crime and Social Order in Contemporary Society* (Oxford, UK: Oxford University Press, 2001), 171.

8. Adam Crawford, "The Preventative Turn in Europe," in *Crime Prevention Poli-*

cies in Comparative Perspective, ed. Adam Crawford (Cullompton, UK: Willan, 2009), xv–xxvii (esp. xv).

9. Garland, *Culture of Control*, 16.

10. Millington, "Book Review," 383. See also Alex Butchard and Mohamed Seedat, "Within and Without: Images of Community and Implications for South African Psychology," *Social Science Medicine* 31, no. 10 (1990): 1093–1102.

11. Bill Edwards, Mark Goodwin, Simon Pemberton, and Michael Woods, "Partnerships, Power and Scale in Rural Governance," *Environment and Planning C* 19, no. 2 (2001): 295.

12. Tessa Diphoorn and Julie Berg, "Typologies of Partnership Policing: Case Studies from Urban South Africa," *Policing and Society* 24, no. 4 (2014): 425–42. See also Wendy Larner and David Craig, "After Neoliberalism? Community Activism and Local Partnerships in Aotearoa New Zealand," *Antipode* 37, no. 3 (2005): 402–24.

13. Steve Herbert, "The Trapdoor of Community," *Annals of the Association of American Geographers* 95, no. 4 (2005): 850. As Raymond Williams put it, *community* is a "warmly persuasive word . . . [that] never seems to be used unfavorably, and never [seems] to be given any positive opposing or distinguishing term." *Keywords* (Oxford: Oxford University Press, 1973), 76.

14. For the source of this term, see Jonathan Davies, "Network Governance Theory: A Gramscian Critique," *Environment and Planning A* 44, no. 11 (2012): 2687–2704 (esp. 2690).

15. Herbert, "Trapdoor of Community," 850; and Julia Elyachar, *Markets of Dispossession: NGOs, Economic Development, and the State in Cairo* (Durham, NC: Duke University Press, 2005), 15. See also Michael Watts, "Antinomies of Community: Some Thoughts on Geography, Resources, and Empire," *Transactions of the Institute of British Geographers* 29, no. 2 (2004): 195–216.

16. See Fran Tonkiss, "The Ethics of Indifference: Community and Solitude in the City," *International Journal of Cultural Studies* 6, no. 3 (2003): 297–311.

17. See Butchard and Seedat, "Within and Without," 1093–1102.

18. David Harvey, "The New Urbanism and the Communitarian Trap," *Harvard Design Magazine* 1 (1997): 3. See also Miranda Joseph, *Against the Romance of Community* (Minneapolis: University of Minnesota Press, 2002), 1–20; and Morris Fiorina, "Extreme Voices: A Dark Side of Civic Engagement," in *Civic Engagement in American Democracy*, ed. Theda Skocpol and Morris Fiorina (Washington DC: Brookings Institution Press, 1999), 395–425.

19. Ade Kearns, "Active Citizenship and Local Governance: Political and Geographical Dimensions," *Political Geography* 14, no. 2 (1995): 155–75; and Michael Marinetto, "Who Wants to be an Active Citizen? The Politics and Practice of Community Involvement," *Sociology* 37, no. 1 (2003): 103–20.

20. For Johannesburg, see interviews with Nazira Cachalia, 30 May 2006, and 24 June 2011; Earl Stoles and Zane Callaghan, 9 July 2008; and Wayne Minnaar, 9 July 2014.

21. Millington, "Book Review," 383.

22. For comparative purposes, see Jennifer Carlson, *Citizen-Protectors: The Everyday*

Politics of Guns in an Age of Decline (New York: Oxford University Press, 2015); and Jennifer Carlson, "States, Subjects and Sovereign Power: Lessons from Global Gun Cultures," *Theoretical Criminology* 18, no. 3 (2014): 335–53.

23. Barry Schofield, "Partners in Power: Governing the Self-Sustaining Community," *Sociology* 36, no. 3 (2002): 664; and Watts, "Antinomies of Community," 196.

24. See Nikolas Rose, "Governing 'Advanced' Liberal Democracies," in Foucault and Political *Reason: Liberalism, Neo-Liberalism, and Rationalities of Government*, ed. Andrew Barry, Thomas Osborne, and Nikolas Rose (Chicago: University of Chicago Press, 1996): 37–64; and Nikolas Rose, "Government and Control," *British Journal of Criminology* 40, no. 2 (2000): 321–39.

25. Dominique Wisler and Ihekwoaba Onwudiwe, "Community Policing in Comparison," *Police Quarterly* 11, no. 4 (2008): 427–46. For South Africa, see Sizakele Nkosi-Malobane, "Community Policing Relations Key to Safety," *Saturday Star*, 17 July 2018.

26. Claire Bénit-Gbaffou, "Community Policing and Disputed Norms for Local Social Control in Post-Apartheid Johannesburg," *Journal of Southern African Studies* 34, no. 1 (2008): 93–109; and Claire Bénit-Gbaffou, "Policing Johannesburg Wealthy Neighborhoods: The Uncertain 'Partnerships' between Police, Communities and Private Security Companies," *Trialog* 89 (2006): 21–26.

27. Patrick O'Malley and Darren Palmer, "Post-Keynesian Policing," *Economy and Society* 25, no. 2 (1996): 137–55; Kevin Stenson, "Community Policing as Governmental Technology," *Economy & Society* 22, no. 3 (1993): 373–89; and Kevin Stenson, "Crime Control, Governmentality and Sovereignty," in *Governable Places: Readings on Governmentality and Crime Control*, ed. Russell Smandych (Aldershot, UK: Dartmouth, 1999), 45–73.

28. Michael Kempa and Anne-Marie Singh, "Private Security, Political Economy and the Policing of Race: Probing Global Hypotheses through the Case of South Africa," *Theoretical Criminology* 12, no. 3 (2008): 336. See also Michael Kempa et al., "Reflections on the Evolving Concept of 'Private Policing,'" *European Journal on Criminal Policy and Research* 7, no. 2 (1999): 197–224; Anne-Marie Singh, "Private Security and Crime Control," *Theoretical Criminology* 9, no. 2 (2005): 153–74; and Adam Crawford, "Policing and Security as 'Club Goods': The New Enclosures?," in *Democracy, Society and the Governance of Security*, ed. Jennifer Wood and Benoît Dupont (Cambridge, UK: Cambridge University Press, 2006), 111–38.

29. Boyane Tshehla, "Barricaded in the Suburbs: Private Security via Road Closures," *South African Crime Quarterly* 6 (2003): 17–20; and Claire Bénit-Gbaffou, Laurent Fourchard, and Alex Wafer, "Local Politics and the Circulation of Community Security Initiatives in Johannesburg," *International Journal of Urban and Regional Research* 36, no. 5 (2012): 936–57.

30. Adam Edwards and Gordon Hughes, "Public Safety Regimes: Negotiated Orders and Political Analysis in Criminology," *Criminology and Criminal Justice* 12, no. 4 (2012): 433–58.

31. Claire Bénit-Gbaffou, "Police-Community Partnerships and Responses to Crime: Lessons from Yeoville and Observatory, Johannesburg," *Urban Forum* 17, no. 4 (2006): 301–26; and Claire Bénit-Gbaffou, Sophie Didier, and Marianne Morange, "Com-

munities, the Private Sector, and the State: Contested Forms of Security Governance in Cape Town and Johannesburg," *Urban Studies Review* 43, no. 5 (2008): 691–717.

32. For example, see "Safeparkview," newsletter 144 (9 January 2019), available at https//safe@parkview.org.za/. See also interviews with Vickie Drinkwater, 2 February 2016; Beverley Markgraaff and Zenda Stravino, 20 June 2012; and Stewart Rider, 15 June 2012.

33. Adam Edwards and Gordon Hughes, "The Preventive Turn and the Promotion of Safer Communities in England and Wales: Political Inventiveness and Governmental Instabilities," in *Crime Prevention Policies in Comparative Perspective*, ed. Adam Crawford (London: Willan, 2009), 62–85 (esp. 67).

34. For the inspiration for this idea, see Daniel Goldstein, *The Spectacular City* (Durham, NC: Duke University Press, 2015), 29.

35. Ralph Ellison, *Invisible Man* (New York: Random House, 1952).

36. Stenson, "Community Policing as Governmental Technology," 373–89.

37. Pablo Piccato, *City of Suspects: Crime in Mexico City, 1900–1931* (Durham, NC: Duke University Press, 2001), 11.

38. Piccato, *City of Suspects*, 3, 4.

39. See Richard Shorey, "Neighbourhood Watch," *Sunday Times*, 14 January 2003; and Staff Reporter, "The Fight against Crime Has a New Face," *Sunday Independent*, 4 May 2002.

40. Oscar Newman, *Defensible Space: Crime Prevention through Urban Design* (New York: Macmillan, 1972).

41. For an early statement, see Richard Yarwood and Bill Edwards, "Voluntary Action in Rural Areas: The Case of Neighbourhood Watch," *Journal of Rural Studies* 11, no. 4 (1995): 447–59.

42. Bénit-Gbaffou, "Community Policing and Disputed Norms," 93–95; and Johan van Graan, "Multi-Sector Cooperation in Preventing Crime: The Case of a South African Neighbourhood Watch as an Effective Crime Prevention Model," *Police Practice and Research* 17, no. 2 (2016): 136–48.

43. Bénit-Gbaffou, "Community Policing and Disputed Norms," 98; and Teresa Dirsuweit, "Johannesburg: Fearful City," *Urban Forum* 13, no. 3 (2002): 4–19.

44. Mark Shaw, "Crime, Police and Public in Transitional Societies," *Transformation* 49 (2002): 1–24.

45. Bénit-Gbaffou, "Community Policing and Disputed Norms," 93–109.

46. Bénit-Gbaffou, "Community Policing and Disputed Norms," 108. See interviews with Nhlanhla Sydney Radebe, 11 July 2014, and 26 February 2016.

47. Rob Shields, "Social Spatialization and the Built Environment: the West Edmonton Mall," *Environment and Planning D* 7, no. 2 (1989): 147–64.

48. O'Malley and Palmer, "Post-Keynesian Policing," 137–39. See also Adam Crawford, "Networked Governance and the Post-Regulatory State? Steering, Rowing and Anchoring the Provision of Policing and Security," *Theoretical Criminology* 10, no. 4 (2006): 449–79.

49. These ideas are taken almost verbatim from Edwards and Hughes, "Preventive Turn," 68.

50. Adam Crawford, "Joined-Up but Fragmented: Contradiction, Ambiguity, and Ambivalence at the Heart of New Labour's 'Third Way,'" in *Crime, Disorder and Community Safety: A New Agenda?*, ed. Roger Matthews and John Pitts (New York: Routledge, 2001), 60. See also Adam Crawford, "The Governance of Crime and Insecurity in an Anxious Age: The Trans-European and the Local," in *Crime and Insecurity*, ed. Adam Crawford (Cullompton, UK: Willian, 2002): 31–32).

51. Marcia England (with Stephanie Simon), "Scary Cities: Urban Geographies of Fear, Difference, and Belonging," *Social & Cultural Geography* 11, no. 3 (2010): 204.

52. See also Marcia Rae England, "Citizens on Patrol: Community Policing and the Territorialization of Public Space in Seattle, Washington" (PhD diss., University of Kentucky, 2006), 33–35.

53. Layla Skinns, "Responsibility, Rhetoric, and Reality: Practitioners' Views on Their Responsibility for Crime and Disorder in Community Policing Partnerships" (selected papers from the British Criminology Conference, vol. 6, Bangor, 2003, 2, available at http://www.britsoccrim.org/v6htm.

54. Edwards and Hughes, "Preventive Turn," 67.

55. Edwards and Hughes, "Preventive Turn," 72. For Johannesburg, see Darshan Vigneswaran, "Protection and Conviviality: Community Policing in Johannesburg," *European Journal of Cultural Studies* 17, no. 4 (2014): 471–86. See also Roy Coleman, "Surveillance in the City: Primary Definition and Urban Spatial Order," *Crime, Media, Culture* 1, no. 2 (2005): 131–48.

56. Roy Coleman, Joe Sim, and Dave Whyte, "Power, Politics and Partnerships: The State of Crime Prevention on Merseyside," in *Crime Control and Community: The New Politics of Public Safety*, ed. Gordon Hughes and Adam Edwards (Cullompton, UK: Willan, 2002), 86–108 (esp. 96).

57. With 5,200 individual properties in the neighborhood, Kensington is perhaps the largest residential suburb in Johannesburg. See interview with Lornette Joseph, 10 July 2014; and the Kensington Residents and Rate Payers Association web page, available at https://krra.org.za/about/.

58. See interview with Lornette Joseph, 10 July 2014; and "Kensington Residents and Rate Payers Association" web page, available at https://krra.org.za/about/.

59. Interview with Cynthia Rose, 9 July 2014. See also Anthony Settipani, "Spate of Attacks at Melville Koppies," *Saturday Star*, 30 May 2015.

60. Melville is a mixed-use suburb that combines commercial activities, around 1,200 individual residences, and some high-rise apartment complexes. Interview with Danyle Nuñes, 14 June 2018; and email correspondence with Danyle Nuñes, 9 October 2018. See also Melville Security Initiative web page, available at https://msi.ilove melville.co.za/.

61. Interview with Cynthia Rose, 9 July 2014. See also Staff Writer, "Melville Koppies in Danger," *North Cliff Melville Times*, 29 September 2015; and Blake Sobczak, "Lengthy Jail Time for Melville Koppies Robbers," *The Star*, 16 May 2011.

62. David Bayley and Clifford Shearing, "The Future of Policing," *Law and Society Review* 30, no. 3 (1996): 585–606 (esp. 587–88).

63. Bayley and Shearing, "Future of Policing," 588.

64. Carlson, "States, Subjects and Sovereign Power," 335, 336, 344. See also David Garland, "The Limits of the Sovereign State: Strategies of Crime Control in Contemporary Society," *British Journal of Criminology* 36, no. 4 (1996): 445–71; and Patrick O'Malley, "Risk, Power and Crime Prevention," *Economy and Society* 21, no. 3 (1992): 252–75.

65. Singh, "Private Security and Crime Control," 170.

66. See Lucia Zedner, "Security, the State, and the Citizen: The Changing Architecture of Crime Control," *New Criminal Law Review* 13, no. 2 (2010): 391, 392. See also Mariana Valverde, "Practices of Citizenship and Scales of Governance," *New Criminal Law Review* 13, no. 2 (2010): 216–40.

67. Christine Hentschel, *Security in the Bubble: Navigating Crime in Urban South Africa* (Minneapolis: University of Minnesota Press, 2015), 11, 43, 113.

68. See Dawn Moore and Hideyuki Hirai, "Outcasts, Performers and True Believers: Responsibilized Subjects of Criminal Justice," *Theoretical Criminology* 18, no. 1 (2014): 5–19 (esp. 6).

69. Les Johnston and Clifford Shearing, *Governing Security: Explorations in Policing and Justice* (London: Routledge, 2003), 11–12. See also Steven Hutchinson and Daniel O'Connor, "Policing the New Commons: Corporate Security Governance on a Mass Private Property in Canada," *Policing and Society* 15, no. 2 (2005): 125–44.

70. Johnston and Shearing, *Governing Security*, 33, 149; and Ronald van Steden et al., "The Many Faces of Nodal Policing: Team Play and Improvisation in Dutch Community Safety," *Security Journal* 29, no. 3 (2016): 327–39.

71. These ideas are derived from a critical reading of Ayona Datta, "Encounters with Law and Critical Urban Studies: Reflections on Amin's Telescopic Urbanism," *City* 17, no. 4 (2013): 518, 519. For the idea of a culture of legality, see Jean Comaroff and John Comaroff, *Law and Disorder in the Postcolony* (Chicago: University of Chicago Press, 2006), viii.

72. For the source of these ideas, see Marinetto, "Who Wants to Be an Active Citizen?," 103–120, esp. 108.

73. Taken almost verbatim from Millington, "Book Review," 383.

74. Anne-Marie Singh, *Policing and Crime Control in Post-Apartheid South Africa* (Burlington, VT: Ashgate, 2008), 5–6.

75. Ian Loader, Benjamin Goold, and Angélica Thumala, "The Moral Economy of Security," *Theoretical Criminology* 18, no. 4 (2014): 470. Thanks to Jonny Steinberg for pointing out this compelling line of reasoning.

76. Margaret Jane Radin, *Contested Commodities* (Cambridge, MA: Harvard University Press, 1996). See Loader, Goold, and Thumala, "Moral Economy of Security," 475.

77. Benoît Dupont, "Private Security Regimes: Conceptualizing the Forces that Shape the Private Delivery of Security," *Theoretical Criminology* 18, no. 3 (2014): 264.

78. These ideas are taken almost verbatim from Loader, Goold, and Thumala, "Moral Economy of Security," 485. See also Jonny Steinberg and Monique Marks, "The Labyrinth of Jewish Security Arrangements in Johannesburg: Thinking through a Paradox about Security," *British Journal of Criminology* 54, no. 2 (2014): 244–59.

79. Interview with Ryan Roseveare and Glenn du Toit, 2 July 2014. See also Staff Reporter, "iSentry Implemented in Craighall and Craighall Park," *Rosebank-Killarney Gazette*, 8 May 2015.

80. Interview with Penny Steyn, 22 June 2012; and on-site observation of training session, 22 June 2012.

81. Claire Bénit-Gbaffou, "Unbundled Security Services and Urban Fragmentation in Post-Apartheid Johannesburg," *Geoforum* 39, no. 6 (2008): 1933–50 (esp. 1937–38); and Bénit-Gbaffou, "Community Policing and Disputed Norms," 7.

82. Simpiwe Piliso, "Boom Blitz," *Sunday Times*, 17 March 2002.

83. Mark Andrejevic, "The Discipline of Watching: Detection, Risk, and Lateral Surveillance," *Critical Studies in Media Communication* 23, no. 5 (2006): 391–407.

84. Some of these ideas taken almost verbatim from Mark Andrejevic, "The Work of Watching One Another: Lateral Surveillance, Risk, and Governance," *Surveillance & Society* 2, no. 4 (2005): 485.

85. Nikolas Rose, *Powers of Freedom: Reframing Political Thought* (Cambridge, UK: Cambridge University Press, 1999), 249–50.

86. Andrejevic, "Work of Watching One Another," 479, 485–86.

87. Focus groups with Hi-Tech Security Solutions, 29 June 2011, and 13 June 2012; and interview with Geoff Schapiro, 12 February 2016.

88. Focus groups with Hi-Tech Security Solutions; and interview with Geoff Schapiro.

89. Focus groups with Hi-Tech Security Solutions; and interview with Geoff Schapiro.

90. See interviews with Geoff Schapiro, 12 February 2016; Cheryl Labuschagne and Jenny Clark, 13 June 2012; and Danyle Nuñes, 14 June 2018.

91. Jennifer Wolch, "The Shadow State: Transformations in the Voluntary Sector," in *The Power of Geography*, ed. Jennifer Wolch and Michael Dear (Boston: Unwin Hyman, 1989), 197–221.

92. Herbert, "Trapdoor of Community," 852.

93. Nancy Fraser, "Rethinking the Public Sphere: A Contribution to the Critique of Actually Existing Democracy," in *The Phantom Public Sphere*, ed. Bruce Robbins (Minneapolis: University of Minnesota Press, 1993), 20.

94. Interviews with Carl Chemaly, Steve Lenahan, and Andre Viljoen, 11 June 2012; Cheryl Labuschagne and Jenny Clark, 13 June 2012; Jonathan Hackner and Elton Hill, 20 June 2012; Glenda Hancock, 20 June 2012; and Carine Hartman, 10 July 2008.

95. Interviews with Vickie Drinkwater, 2 February 2016; Beverley Markgraaff and Zenda Stravino, 20 June 2012; and Tessa Turvey, 11 June 2012.

96. Interviews with Stewart Rider, 15 June 2012; Brian Robertson, 12 June 2012; and Cynthia Rose, 9 July 2014. For a wider view, see also Mark Purcell, "Neighborhood Activism among Homeowners as a Politics of Space," *The Professional Geographer* 53, no. 2 (2001): 178–94.

97. Rapule Tabane, "Homeless Devalue Property—Gauteng Residents," *The Star*, 6 August 2000.

98. See interviews with Vickie Drinkwater, 2 February 2016; Daniel Marsay, 11 June 2012; Stewart Rider, 15 June 2012; Brian Robertson, 12 June 2012; Danyle Nuñes, 14 June 2018; and Grant Moulder, 21 June 2012.

99. See Andy Merrifield and Erik Swyngedouw, "Social Justice and the Urban Experience," and Neil Smith, "Social Justice and the New American Urbanism: The *Revan-*

chist City," in *The Urbanization of Injustice*, ed. Andy Merrifield and Erik Swyngedouw (New York: New York University Press, 1997), 1–17, and 117–36, respectively.

100. Sally Engle Merry, "Spatial Governmentality and the New Urban Social Order: Controlling Gender Violence through Law," *American Anthropologist* 103, no. 1 (2001): 16–29 (esp. 16–17).

101. Mapogo a Mathamaga web page, available at http://mapogoafrica.co.za/. See also Tim Butcher, "Black Vigilantes Dispense Rough Justice at a Price," *Telegraph*, 25 June 2001.

102. Nancy Scheper-Hughes, "Dangerous and Endangered Youth: Social Structures and Determinants of Violence," *Annals New York Academy of Sciences* 1036 (2004): 13. See also Paul Farmer, "An Anthropology of Structural Violence," *Current Anthropology* 45, no. 3 (2004): 305–30.

103. Quotation from Scheper-Hughes, "Dangerous and Endangered Youth," 14. See Paul Farmer, *Pathologies of Power: Health, Human Rights and the New War on the Poor* (Berkeley: University of California Press, 2003).

104. Rapule Tabane, "Homeless Devalue Property."

105. René Hoenderdos, "The Social Dynamics of Community Development in a Suburban Johannesburg Public Open Space: Verity Park," *Urban Environment* 10 (2016), available at http://eue.revues.org.proxy.lib.umich.edu/1437.

106. Mike Crang and Stephen Graham, "Sentient Cities: Ambient Intelligence and the Politics of Urban Space," *Information, Communication & Society* 10, no. 6 (2007): 789.

107. Andrejevic, "Work of Watching One Another," 479–97.

108. Jenna Etheridge, "How South Africans Are Fighting Crime in Their Hoods—With an App," *News24*, 9 July 2015.

109. Crang and Graham, "Sentient Cities," 789–801.

CHAPTER 7

1. Zygmut Bauman, *Liquid Fear* (Cambridge, UK: Polity Press, 2006), 2.

2. Linda Green, "Fear as a Way of Life," *Cultural Anthropology* 9, no. 2 (1994): 231.

3. Lieven De Cauter, *The Capsular Civilization: On the City in the Age of Fear* (Rotterdam: NAi, 2004), 80–81.

4. See also Lars Svendson, *A Philosophy of Fear* (London: Reaktion, 2008), 48.

5. Alexandra Parker, *Urban Film and Everyday Practice: Bridging Divisions in Johannesburg* (South Bend, IN: University of Notre Dame Press, 2016), 1–2, 193.

6. These ideas and phraseology are borrowed from Hannah Appel, "Toward an Ethnography of the National Economy," *Current Anthropology* 32, no. 2 (2017): 294.

7. See Joel Modiri, "The Grey Line in-between the Rainbow: (Re) Thinking and (Re) Talking Critical Race Theory in Post-*Apartheid* Legal and Social Discourse," *South African Public Law* 26, no. 1 (2011): 177–201.

8. Green, "Fear as a Way of Life," 227.

9. For a similar argument taken from another context, see Wil Pansters, "Zones of State-Making: Violence, Coercion, and Hegemony in Twentieth-century Mexico," in *Violence, Coercion, and State-Making in Twentieth-Century Mexico: The Other Half of the Centaur*, ed. Wil Pansters (Palo Alto, CA: Stanford University Press, 2012), 3–39 (esp. 6, 8, 10, 19).

10. See Antina Von Schnitzler, *Democracy's Infrastructure: Techno-Politics and Protest after Apartheid* (Princeton, NJ: Princeton University Press, 2016), 10.

11. See Jean Comaroff and John Comaroff, *The Truth about Crime: Sovereignty, Knowledge, Power* (Chicago: University of Chicago Press, 2017), 11.

12. Christopher McMichael, "Urban Pacification and 'Blitzes' in Contemporary Johannesburg," *Antipode* 47, no. 5 (2015): 1261–78; and Christopher McMichael, "Police Wars and State Repression in South Africa," *Journal of Asian and African Studies* 51, no. 1 (2016): 3–16.

13. Claire Bénit-Gbaffou, "Unbundled Security Services and Urban Fragmentation in Post-Apartheid Johannesburg," *Geoforum* 39, no. 6 (2008): 1933–50.

14. Staff Reporter, "Rioters and Police Clash in Johannesburg Protest," *Associated Press*, 9 May 2017; and Steven Tau, "Protest Anarchy Breaks Out in Gauteng, North West," *The Citizen*, 26 April 2017.

15. The ideas behind this paragraph are borrowed from Dennis Rodgers, "The State as a Gang: Conceptualizing the Governmentality of Violence in Contemporary Nicaragua," *Critique of Anthropology* 26, no. 3 (2006): 325.

EPILOGUE

1. The research for this epilogue was done via street patrols with public police officers and members of Community Policing Forums (CPFs), impromptu ride-alongs with South African Police Service (SAPS) officers, informal and semistructured interviews with key informants, and firsthand observations of street encounters.

2. These ideas were taken almost verbatim from Veena Das and Deborah Poole, "State and Its Margins: Comparative Ethnographies," in *Anthropology in the Margins of the State*, ed. Veena Das and Deborah Poole (Santa Fe: School of American Research Press, 2004): 3–34 (esp. 4).

3. João Biehl, "Ethnography in the Way of Theory," *Cultural Anthropology* 28, no. 4 (2013): 573–97; and James Ferguson, "Novelty and Method: Notes on Global Fieldwork," in *Multi-Sited Ethnography: Problems and Possibilities in the Translocation of Research Methods*, ed. Simon Coleman and Pauline von Hellermann (New York: Routledge, 2011): 194–208.

4. Lee Ann Fujii, "Fives Stories of Accidental Ethnography: Turning Unplanned Moments in the Field into Data," *Qualitative Research* 15, no. 4 (2015): 525–39.

5. Margarethe Kusenbach, "Street Phenomenology: The Go-Along as Ethnographic Research Tool," *Ethnography* 4, no. 3 (2003): 463.

6. Kusenbach, "Street Phenomenology," 455.

7. See Ramolobi Louis Gemane Matlala, "Implementation of Sector Policing in Hillbrow," *Academic Journal of Interdisciplinary Studies* 4, no. 3 (2015): 135–36.

8. During the time between 2012 and 2016 in which we carried out research in Hillbrow, the numbers of CPF volunteers fluctuated from a small handful to several dozen. For "shadow state," see also Katharyne Mitchell, "Transnationalism, Neo-Liberalism, and the Rise of the Shadow State," *Economy & Society* 30, no. 2 (2001): 165–89; and Dan Trudeau, "Towards a Relational View of the Shadow State," *Political Geography* 27, no. 6 (2008): 669–90.

9. Darshan Vigneswaran, The Contours of Disorder: Crime Maps and Territo-

rial Policing in South Africa," *Environment and Planning D: Society and Space* 31, no. 1 (2014): 101.

10. Antonio Pezzano, "'Integration' or 'Selective Incorporation'? The Modes of Governance in Informal Trading Policy in the Inner City of Johannesburg," *Journal of Development Studies* 52, no. 4 (2016): 498–513.

11. Claire Bénit Gbaffou,"Do Street Traders Have the 'Right to the City'? The Politics of Street Trader Organisations in Inner City Johannesburg, Post-Operation Clean Sweep," *Third World Quarterly* 37, no. 6 (2016): 1102–29.

12. Christian Rogerson, "Progressive Rhetoric, Ambiguous Policy Pathways: Street Trading in Inner-City Johannesburg, South Africa," *Local Economy* 31, nos. 1–2 (2016): 204–18; and Richard Grant and Daniel Thompson, "City on Edge: Immigrant Businesses and the Right to Urban Space in Inner-City Johannesburg," *Urban Geography* 36, no. 2 (2015): 181–200.

13. The vignettes assembled here are a composite drawn from several nighttime excursions with volunteers from the CPF attached to the Hillbrow Police Station. We have taken the liberty of altering some of the temporal sequences, merging some of the episodes, and juxtaposing disparate events in the spirit of narrative clarity.

14. See Richard Sparks, "States of Insecurity: Punishment, Populism and Contemporary Political Culture," in *The Use of Punishment*, ed. Seán McConville Cullompton, UK: Willan, 2003), 149.

15. Verashni Pillay, "Hillbrow: Where Cops Do the Work for Drug Lords," *Mail & Guardian*, 20 September 2013.

16. Stuart Elden, "Terror and Territory," *Antipode* 39, no. 5 (2007): 821–45.

17. Nir Gazit and Robert Latham, "Spatial Alternatives and Counter-Sovereignties in Israel/Palestine," *International Political Sociology* 8, no. 1 (2014): 63.

18. Gazit and Latham, "Spatial Alternatives and Counter-Sovereignties," 75.

19. Darshan Vigneswaran, "Protection and Conviviality: Community Policing in Johannesburg," *European Journal of Cultural Studies* 17, no. 4 (2014): 479–80.

Bibliography

PRIMARY MATERIALS

INTERVIEWS WITH AUTHOR

(References to interviews, focus-group sessions, and on-site visits are abbreviated in the footnotes.)

Neighborhood Residential Associations

Adler, Josie (social development consultant), and Chris Zenferna. Ekhaya Neighbourhood Precinct, Hillbrow, 11 June 2012.

Benson, Don (chair, Houghton Residents Association). Houghton, 14 June 2012.

Chemaly, Carl, Steve Lenahan, and Andre Viljoen (24/7 Security Company). Parkview Residents' Association ("Safe Parkview" Section 21 company), Parkview, 11 June 2012.

Dodo, Karen (executive committee, Melrose-Birdhaven Community Active Protection). Melrose, 15 June 2012.

Drinkwater, Vickie (manager, "Safeparkview" [Security Initiative of Parkview Residents Association]). Parkview, 2 February 2016.

Hackner, Jonathan, and Elton Hill (Athol, Illovo, Inanda, Winston Ridge Residents Association). Athol, 20 June 2012.

Hancock, Glenda (3rd Avenue Illovo Residents Association). Illovo, 20 June 2012.

Hartman, Carine (Observatory Ratepayers Association). Observatory, 10 July 2008.

Jammy, Eve (chair, Rosebank Community Policing Forum). Rosebank Mall, 4 July 2014.

Joseph, Lornette (chairperson, I Love Kensington Association). Eastgate Mall, 10 July 2014.

Labuschagne, Cheryl (chair, Parkhurst Residents and Business Owners Association), and Jenny Clark (lead safety cluster, Parkhurst Residents and Business Owners Association). Parkhurst, 13 June 2012.

Markgraaff, Beverley, and Zenda Stravino (Sandhurst Heritage Foundation). Sandhurst, 20 June 2012.

Marsay, Daniel (chair, Hurlingham Manor North Residents Association). Hurlingham, 11 June 2012.

Modena, Anthony (chairperson, Section Two, Sandton Community Policing Forum). Sandton Police Station, 4 July 2014.

Nuñes, Danyle (Melville neighborhood security forum). Melville, 14 June 2018.

Rider, Stewart (chair, Morningside Extension 40 Residents Association). Morningside, 15 June 2012.

Robertson, Brian (executive manager, Parkmore Community Association). Parkmore, 12 June 2012.

Rose, Cynthia (chair, Melville Community Policing Forum). Melville, 9 July 2014.

Roseveare, Ryan (chairperson), and Glenn du Toit (security team). Craighall and Craighall Park Community Policing Forum, Craighall Park, 2 July 2014.

Stein, Lionel (Sandringham Community Policing Forum). Sandringham, 1 July 2014.

Turvey, Tessa (Saxonwold and Parkwood Residents Association). Parkwood, 11 June 2012.

Voster-Robertson, Wendy (chairperson, Sandton Community Policing Forum). Sandton Police Station, 4 July 2014.

Private Security Companies

Ben David, Amir (chief executive officer, Megan Security). Highland North, 11 July 2014.

De Lima, David (managing director, 24/7 Security Services), and Andre Viljeon (armed reaction and fleet manager, 24/7 Security Services). Wynberg, 28 June 2012.

Edery, Jack (chief executive officer, Elvey Security Technologies). Gallagher Convention Centre, 19 June 2012; and Greenstone Hill, Edenvale, 1 July 2014.

Frimat, Patrick (chief executive officer, RSI Video Technologies). Gallagher Convention Centre, 19 June 2012.

Greenburg, Tanya (head of operations, Intelligence, Control, and Command Centre; Community Active Protection), and Mark van Jaarsveld (chief executive, Intelligence, Control, and Command Centre; Community Active Protection). Melrose, 15 June 2012.

Hydes, Justin (product sales, Spectrum Communications). Gallagher Convention Centre, 19 June 2012.

Joubert, Tiaan (EHS advisor, central region, ATD Security—a division of Tyco International). Sandton, 26 June 2012.

Lancelin, Frederic (Videofield). Gallagher Convention Centre, 19 June 2012.

Moulder, Grant (operations manager, CSS Tactical). Craighall, 21 June 2012.

Mutinelli, Ingo (sales director, Elvey Security Technologies). Greenstone Hill, Edenvale, 1 July 2014.

Nortmann, Ryan (Elvey Security Technologies). Gallagher Convention Centre, 19 June 2012.

Notelovitz, Mark (chief executive officer, Core Tactical). Head office, Riviera/Kilarney, 26 June 2012.

Notelovitz, Mark (chief executive officer, Core Tactical), and Rayyaan Majiet (manager, Core Tactical). Head office, Riviera/Kilarney, 18 July 2011.

Scafer, Rocky (chief executive officer, Saber Tactical). Sandton, 16 July 2014.

Schapiro, Geoff (operations director, 24/7 Security Services). Head office, Wynberg, 12 February 2016.

Schickerling, Gibbon (cost and design engineer, Omega Risk Solutions). Gallagher Convention Centre, 19 June 2012.

Thomas, Russell (general manager operations, Central Johannesburg Partnership, Operational Headquarters, CCTV Surveillance System, Omega Risk Solutions). 1 Rissik Street, 15 July 2008.

Van Ben Berg, Johan (community security manager, ADT Security—a division of Tyco International). Sandton, 26 June 2012.

Vos, Juri (training and recruitment manager, 24/7 Security Services). Head office, Wynberg, 12 February 2016.

Williams, Gareth (regional sales manager, Pentagon Services, Elvey Security Technologies). Greenstone Hill, Edenvale, 1 July 2014.

Focus Groups with Private Security Companies

Hi-Tech Security Solutions, Head Office, Randburg, 29 June 2011. Present: Geoff Shapiro (group managing director, Specialised Service Group, Randburg), Roy Alves (AXIS Security), and Sasha Bonheim (AXIS Security).

Hi-Tech Security Solutions, Head Office, Randburg, 13 June 2012. Present: Dean Paterson (managing executive, Labour Guard, Randburg), Conrad van der Merve (director, Justicia Investigations, Randburg), and Geoff Schapiro (group managing director, Specialised Service Group, Randburg).

7 Arrows Security, Savoy Estate, 25 June 2012. Present: Mike Sears (managing director), Jason Mordecai (operations manager), and Victor Tortora (tactical director).

Security-Related Organizations

Altbeker, Anthony (research and projects executive, Centre for Development and Enterprise). Parktown, 28 June 2011.

Botes, Tony (secretary and administrator at the Security Services Employers Association; administrator, Security Association of South Africa; chief executive officer, Ingulule Consultancy Services; and past trustee at Private Security Provident Fund). Melville, 25 June 2014.

Chipkin, Ivor (executive director, Public Affairs Research Institute). Parktown West Office, 26 June 2014.

Holtman, Barbara (vice president, International Centre for Prevention of Crime). Melville, 28 June 2011.

Loedolf, Cecile (public relations officer, ABSA Precinct). Johannesburg, 7 July 2008.

Minnaar, Anthony (Department of Criminology and Security Science, University of South Africa). Pretoria, 6 July 2011.

Newman, Gareth (Institute for Security Studies). Pretoria, 11 July 2011.

Penberthy, John (executive director, Business against Crime Surveillance Technology). Rosebank, 19 June 2003.

Reid, Jenny (Security Association of South Africa; editor, iFacts website). Skype interview, Melville, 11 July 2014.

Seldon, Andrew (editor, *Hi-Tech Security Solutions* magazine). Randburg, 13 June 2012.

Steyn, Penny (Domestic Watch Programme; and Making a Difference). Parktown North, Parktown, 22 June 2012.

Public Policing Agencies

Billings, Brigadier P. P. (Sandton police commissioner, South African Police Service). Sandton Police Station, 4 July 2014.

Cachalia, Nazira (city safety and security, Johannesburg Municipal Police Department). Police headquarters, Martindale, 30 May 2006, and 24 June 2011.

Lategan, Colonel Kobus (central senior superintendent, South African Police Services). 1 Rissik Street, Penmore Towers, 20 June 2012.

Louw, Brigadier Danie (South African Police Service). Jeppes Police Station, 27 June 2011.

Minnaar, Wayne (chief superintendent, Johannesburg Municipal Police Department). Martindale, 9 July 2014.

Mohlanga, Major M. S. (South African Police Service). Parkview SAPS Station, 8 February 2016.

Radebe, Nhlanhla Sydney (Hillbrow Community Policing Forum). Hillbrow SAPS Station, 11 July 2014, and 26 February 2016.

Stoles, Earl (Johannesburg City Safety Programme, Johannesburg Metropolitan Police Department). 1 Rissik Street, Penmore Towers, 20 June 2012.

Stoles, Earl, and Zane Callaghan (inner-city GFA coordinators, Johannesburg City Safety Programme). Johannesburg Metropolitan Police Department headquarters, Martindale, 9 July 2008.

Tau, J. M. (superintendent, head of Client Service Centre, South African Police Service). Bramley Precinct, 25 June 2012.

Municipal Officials

Gichanga, Margaret (director's office, Private Security Industry Regulatory Authority). Eco Park, Centurion, 10 July 2014.

Maseko, Paul (city manager, Ekurhuleni Metropolitan Municipality). Ekurhuleni Municipal Offices, 8 June 2003.

On-Site Visits

City of Johannesburg Crime Prevention Forum Meeting. Omega Risk Solutions boardroom, third floor, Penmore Towers (1 Rissik Street). With Omega Risk Solutions operations staff, 20 June 2012.

Community Policing Forum nighttime patrol. Inner city (Hillbrow, Berea, Joubert Park). With volunteer patrollers, 27 June 2014, and 16 February 2016.

Head Office Command Centre, 24/7 Security Services. Philo Road, Wynberg. With Juri Vos (training and recruitment manager), 12 February 2016.

Head Offices. eKahaya Neighborhood, Hillbrow. With Josie Adler and staff, 11 June 2012.

IFSEC South Africa 2012 Exhibition. Gallagher Convention Centre, Midrand, 19–21 June 2012. (This is the largest commercial and residential security, homeland security, and fire exhibition on the African continent, with over 800 company displays.)

Meeting with representatives from SAPS. South African Police Service (SAPS), Johannesburg headquarters, Penmore Building, 1 Rissik Street. With Superintendent Foulds, Johannesburg Municipal Police Department, Omega Risk Solutions (CCTV Surveillance), and representatives of private security companies, 20 June 2012.

Operational Headquarters, Bad Boyz Security. Corner of Wolmarans and Quartz Street, Hillbrow. With operations staff (including visit to CCTV Operations Room and ride-along with private security officer), 29 June 2011, and 6 July 2014.

Operational Headquarters, CCTV Control Room, Omega Risk Solutions. Penmore Towers (1 Rissik Street), Johannesburg central city. With Richard Frederick Witte (chief superintendent, CCTV Operations), 20 June 2012.

Operational Headquarters, CCTV Control Room, RSS Security Services. Prism Office Park, Fourways. Meeting with Sean Mooney (managing director), and Brett Fisher (manager, RSS Security Services), 12 July 2011.

Operational Headquarters, CCTV Surveillance System. Carlton Centre (Commissioner Street). With Omega Risk Solutions operations staff, 19 June 2003.

Operational Headquarters, CCTV Surveillance System, Omega Risk Solutions. Penmore Towers (1 Rissik Street), Johannesburg central city. With Russell Thomas (general manager of operations, Central Johannesburg Partnership), and Kobus Van Deventer, 15 July 2008.

Operational Headquarters, Omega Risk Solutions. Penmore Towers (1 Rissik Street). With Richard Frederick Witte (chief superintendent, CCTV Operations), 27 June 2011.

Operations meeting for "Safe Parkview" Security Initiative. Parkview, 11 June 2012.

Station Crime Combating Forum (SCCF) meeting. Parkview SAPS boardroom. With SAPS, JMPD, private security companies, and neighborhood association representatives, 8 February 2016.

Training session. Parktown. With Penny Steyn (Domestic Watch Programme; and Making a Difference, Parktown North), 22 June 2012.

SECONDARY SOURCES
Books and Articles

Abrahamsen, Rita, and Michael Williams. "Privatization, Globalization, and the Politics of Protection in South Africa." In *The Politics of Protection: Sites of Insecurity and Political Agency*, edited by Jef Huysmans, Andrew Dobson, and Raia Prokhovnik, 34–47. New York: Routledge, 2006.

———. "Securing the City: Private Security Companies and Non-State Authority in Global Governance." *International Relations* 21, no. 2 (2007): 237–53.

———. *Security beyond the State: Private Security in International Politics*. Cambridge, UK: Cambridge University Press, 2011.

———. "Security Privatization and Global Security Assemblages." *Brown Journal of World Affairs* 18, no. 1 (2011): 153–62.

Adey, Peter. "Surveillance at the Airport: Surveilling Mobility/Mobilising Surveillance." *Environment and Planning A* 36, no. 8 (2004): 1365–80.

Ahmad, Aijaz. *In Theory: Classes, Nations, Literature* (New York: Verso, 1992).

Ahmed, Sara. "Affective Economies." *Social Text* 79 [22, 2] (2004): 117–39.

Akpome, Aghogho. "'Zones of Indistinction' and Visions of Post-Reconciliation South Africa in *District 9*." *Sarafundi: The Journal of South African and American Studies* 18, no. 1 (2017): 85–97.

Albert, D. "New Security Company Identifies Niche Market." *Security Focus* 22, no. 1 (2004): 56.

Allen, Danielle Burger. "Race Crime and Social Exclusion: A Qualitative Study of White Women's Fear of Crime in Johannesburg." *Urban Forum* 13, no. 3 (2002): 53–79.

Altbeker, Anthony. *A Country at War with Itself: South Africa's Crisis of Crime*. Cape Town: Jonathan Ball, 2007.

————. *The Dirty Work of Democracy: A Year on the Streets with the SAPS*. Johannesburg: Jonathan Ball, 2005.

————. "Puzzling Statistics: Is South Africa Really the World's Crime Capital?" *SA Crime Quarterly* 11 (2005): 1–8.

Amir, Merav. "The Making of a Void Sovereignty: Political Implications of the Military Checkpoints in the West Bank." *Environment & Planning D* 31, no. 2 (2013): 227–44.

Andrejevic, Mark. "The Discipline of Watching: Detection, Risk, and Lateral Surveillance." *Critical Studies in Media Communication* 23, no. 5 (2006): 391–407.

————. "The Work of Watching One Another: Lateral Surveillance, Risk, and Governance." *Surveillance & Society* 2, no. 4 (2005): 479–97.

Appadurai, Arjun. *Modernity at Large: Cultural Dimensions of Globalization*. Minneapolis: University of Minnesota Press, 1996.

Appel, Hannah. "Toward an Ethnography of the National Economy." *Current Anthropology* 32, no. 2 (2017): 294–322.

Atkinson, Ronald, and Sarah Blandy. "Panic Rooms: The Rise of Defensive Home Ownership." *Housing Studies* 22, no. 4 (2007): 443–58.

Atkinson, Rowland. "Domestication by Cappuccino or a Revenge on Urban Space? Control and Empowerment in the Management of Public Spaces," *Urban Studies* 40, no. 9 (2003): 1829–43.

Ayling, Julie, and Clifford Shearing. "Taking Care of Business: Public Police as Commercial Security Vendors." *Criminology and Criminal Justice* 8, no. 1 (2008): 27–50.

Baker, Bruce. "Living with Non-State Policing in South Africa: The Issues and Dilemmas." *Journal of Modern African Studies* 40, no. 1 (2002): 29–53.

————. *Multi-Choice Policing in Africa*. Uppsala, SE: Nordiska Afrikainstitutet, 2008.

————. *Security in Post-Conflict Africa: The Role of Nonstate Policing*. Boca Raton: FL: CLC Press, 2010.

Bardhan, Pranap. *The Role of Governance in Economic Development*. Paris: OECD Development Center, 1997.

Barthes, Roland. *Mythologies*. New York: Hill and Wang, 1972.

Bartov, Omar. "Defining Enemies, Making Victims: Germans, Jews, and the Holocaust." *American Historical Review* 103, no. 3 (1998): 771–816.

Baucom, Ian. *Out of Place: Englishness, Empire and the Locations of Identity* Princeton, NJ: Princeton University Press, 1999.

Bauman, Zygmunt. *Liquid Fear*. Cambridge, UK: Polity Press, 2006.

————. *Liquid Modernity*. Cambridge, UK: Polity, 2000.

Bayley, David, and Clifford Shearing. "The Future of Policing." *Law and Society Review* 30, no. 3 (1996): 585–606.

Behrens, Roy. *Art and Camouflage: Concealment and Deception in Nature, Art and War*. Cedar Falls: University of Northern Iowa, 1981.

Belina, Bernd. "Evicting the Undesirables: The Idealism of Public Space and the Materialism of the Bourgeois State." *Belgeo* 1 (2003): 47–62.

Belina, Bernd, and Gesa Helms. "Zero Tolerance for the Industrial Past and Other Threats: Policing and Urban Entrepreneurialism in Britain and Germany." *Urban Studies* 40, no. 9 (2003): 1845–67.

Bénit-Gbaffou, Claire. "Community Policing and Disputed Norms for Local Social Control in Post-Apartheid Johannesburg." *Journal of Southern African Studies* 34, no. 1 (2008): 93–109.

———. "Do Street Traders Have the 'Right to the City'? The Politics of Street Trader Organisations in Inner City Johannesburg, Post-Operation Clean Sweep." *Third World Quarterly* 37, no. 6 (2016): 1102–29.

———. "Police-Community Partnerships and Responses to Crime: Lessons from Yeoville and Observatory, Johannesburg." *Urban Forum* 17, no. 4 (2006): 301–26.

———. "Policing Johannesburg Wealthy Neighborhoods: The Uncertain 'Partnerships' between Police, Communities and Private Security Companies." *Trialog* 89 (2006): 21–26.

———. "Unbundled Security Services and Urban Fragmentation in Post-Apartheid Johannesburg." *Geoforum* 39, no. 6 (2008): 1933–50.

———. "Who Control the Streets? Crime, 'Community' and the State in Post-Apartheid Johannesburg." In *African Cities: Competing Claims on Urban Spaces*, edited by Francesca Locatelli and Paul Nugent, 55–79. Leiden, NL: Brill, 2009.

Bénit-Gbaffou, Claire, Sophie Didier, and Marianne Morange. "Communities, the Private Sector, and the State: Contested Forms of Security Governance in Cape Town and Johannesburg." *Urban Affairs Review* 43, no. 5 (2008): 691–717.

Bénit-Gbaffou, Claire, Sophie Didier, and Elisabeth Peyroux. "Circulation of Security Models in Southern African Cities: Between Neoliberal Encroachment and Local Power Dynamics." *International Journal of Urban and Regional Research* 36, no. 5 (2012): 877–89.

Bénit-Gbaffou, Claire, Laurent Fourchard, and Alex Wafer. "Local Politics and the Circulation of Community Security Initiatives in Johannesburg." *International Journal of Urban and Regional Research* 36, no. 5 (2012): 936–57.

Benjamin, Walter. *The Arcades Project.* Translated by Howard Eiland and Kevin McLaughlin. Cambridge, MA: Belknap Press, 1999.

———. *Reflections.* New York: Schoken Books, 1986.

Benton-Short, Lisa. "Bollards, Bunkers, and Barriers: Securing the National Mall in Washington, DC." *Environment & Planning* D 25, no. 3 (2007): 424–46.

Berg, Julie. "Challenges to a Formal Private Security–SAPS Partnership: Lessons from the Western Cape." *Society in Transition* 35, no. 1 (2004): 105–24.

———. "Governing Security in Public Spaces: Improvement Districts in South Africa." In *Policing Cities: Urban Securitization and Regulation in a 21st Century World*, edited by Randy Lippert and Kevin Walby, 161–75. New York: Routledge, 2013.

———. "Holding South Africa's Private Security Industry Accountable: Mechanisms of Control and Challenges to Effective Oversight." *Acta Criminologica* 21, no. 1 (2008): 87–96.

———. "Private Policing in South Africa: The Cape Town City Improvement District— Pluralisation in Practice." *Society in Transition* 35, no. 2 (2004): 224–50.

———. "The Private Security Industry in South Africa: A Review of Applicable Legislation." *South African Journal of Criminal Justice* 16, no. 2 (2003): 178–96.

———. "Seeing Like Private Security: Evolving Mentalities of Public Space Protection in South Africa." *Criminology & Criminal Justice* 10, no. 3 (2010): 287–301.

Berg, Julie, and Jean-Pierre Nouveau. "Towards a Third Phrase of Regulation: Re-Imagining Private Security in South Africa." *SA Crime Quarterly* 38 (2011): 23–32.

Berg, Julie, and Clifford Shearing. "New Authorities: Relating State and Non-State Security Auspices in South African Improvement Districts." In *On the Politics of Ordering: Insecurity, Power and Policing on City Frontiers*, edited by Helene Maria Kyed and Peter Albrecht, 91–107. New York: Routledge, 2014.

Bergin, Victor. *Some Cities*. Berkeley: University of California Press, 1996.

Bewley-Taylor, David. "US Concept Wars, Civil Liberties and the Technologies of Fortification." *Crime Law and Social Change* 43, no. 1 (2005): 81–111.

Beyes, Timon, and Chris Steyeart. "Strangely Familiar: The Uncanny and Unsiting Organizational Analysis." *Organizational Studies* 34, no. 10 (2013): 1445–65.

Biehl, João. "Ethnography in the Way of Theory." *Cultural Anthropology* 28, no. 4 (2013): 573–97.

Blaustein, Jarrett, "The Space Between: Negotiating the Contours of Nodal Security Governance through 'Safer Communities' in Bosnia-Herzegovina." *Policing & Society* 24, no. 1 (2014): 44–62.

Bloom, Kevin. *Ways of Staying*. London: Portobello, 2010.

Boddy, Trevor. "Architecture Emblematic: Hardened Sites and Softened Symbols." In *Indefensible Space: The Architecture of the National Insecurity State*, edited by Michael Sorkin, 277–304. New York: Routledge, 2008.

Boels, Dominique, and Antoinette Verhage. "Plural Policing: A State-of-the-Art Review." *Policing: An International Journal of Police Strategies & Management* 39, no. 1 (2016): 2–18.

Boholm, Asa. "Situated Risk: An Introduction." *Ethnos: Journal of Anthropology* 68, no. 2 (2003): 157–58.

Bookman, Sonia, and Andrew Woolford. "Policing (by) the Urban Brand: Defining Order in Winnipeg's Exchange District." *Social and Cultural Geography* 14, no. 3 (2013): 300–317.

Boyer, M. Christine. *The City of Collective Memory: Its Historical Imagery and Architectural Entertainments*. Cambridge, MA: MIT Press, 1996.

———. "Twice Told Stories: The Double Erasure of Times Square." In Borden, Kerr, and Rendell, with Pivaro, *Unknown City*, 30–52.

Borden, Iain, Jane Rendell, Joe Kerr, and Alicia Pivaro. "Things, Flows, Filters, Tactics." In Borden, Kerr, and Rendell, with Pivaro, *Unknown City*, 2–28.

Borden, Iain, Joe Kerr, and Jane Rendell, with Alicia Pivaro, eds., *The Unknown City: Contesting Architecture and Social Space*. Cambridge, MA: MIT Press, 2001.

Bottomley, Anne, and Nathan Moore. "From Walls to Membranes: Fortress Polis and the Governance of Urban Public Space in 21st Century Britain." *Law and Critique* 18, no. 2 (2007): 171–206.

Bourdieu, Pierre. *The Logic of Practice*. Translated by Richard Nice. Cambridge, UK: Cambridge University Press, 1990.

———. *Outline of a Theory of Practice* (New York: Cambridge University Press, 1977).

Boym, Svetlana. *The Future of Nostalgia*. New York: Basic Books, 2001.

Bremner, Lindsay. "Bounded Spaces: Demographic Anxieties in Post-Apartheid Johannesburg." *Social Identities* 10, no. 4 (2004): 455–68.

———. "Closure, Simulation, and 'Making Do' in the Contemporary Johannesburg Landscape." In *Under Siege: Four African Cities. Freetown, Johannesburg, Kinshasa, Lagos. Documenta 11_Platform 4*, edited by Okwui Enwezor, Carlos Basualdo, Ute Meta Bauer, Susanne Ghez, Sarat Maharaj, Mark Nash, and Octavio Zaya, 153–72. Ostfildern-Ruit, DE: Hatje Catnz, 2002.

———. "Crime and the Emerging Landscape of Post-*Apartheid* Johannesburg." In *Blank___: Architecture, Apartheid and After*, edited by Hilton Judin and Ivan Vladislavić, 48–63. Rotterdam: NAi, 1998.

———. "Remaking Johannesburg." In *Future City*, edited by Stephen Read, Jürgen Rosemann, and Job van Eldijk. London: Spon, 2005, 32–47.

Brighi, Elisabetta. "Beyond the Gaze: The Changing Architecture of Security between Seduction and Camouflage." In *The Urban Invisibles: Explorations in Space and Society No. 35*, edited by Andrea Pavoni and Andrea Mubi Brighenti, 27–30. Athens: Professional Dreamers, March 2015.

Brodeur, Jean-Paul. *The Policing Web*. Oxford, UK: Oxford University Press, 2010.

Bures, Oldrich, and Helena Carrapico. "Private Security beyond Private Military and Security Companies: Exploring Diversity within Private-Public Collaborations and Its Consequences for Security Governance." *Crime, Law and Social Change* 67, no. 3 (2017): 229–43.

Burger, Johan. "Crime Combating in Perspective: A Strategic Approach to Policing and the Prevention of Crime in South Africa." *Acta Criminologica* 19, no. 2 (2006): 105–18.

———. *Strategic Perspectives on Crime and Policing in South Africa*. Pretoria: Van Schaik, 2007.

Butchard, Alex, and Mohamed Seedat. "Within and Without: Images of Community and Implications for South African Psychology." *Social Science Medicine* 31, no. 10 (1990): 1093–1102.

Butler, Judith. *Precarious Life: The Powers of Mourning and Violence*. New York: Verso, 2004.

Button, Mark. *Doing Security: Critical Reflections and an Agenda for Change*. New York: Palgrave Macmillan, 2008.

———. "Private Security and the Policing of Quasi-Public Space." *International Journal of the Sociology of Law* 31, no. 3 (2003): 227–37.

Buur, Lars, and Steffen Jensen. "Vigilantism and the Policing of Everyday Life in South Africa." *African Studies* 63, no. 2 (2004): 139–52.

Caldeira, Teresa. *City of Walls: Crime, Segregation, and Citizenship in São Paulo*. Berkeley: University of California Press, 2000.

———. "Fortified Enclaves: The New Urban Segregation," *Public Culture* 8 (1996): 303–28.

Calvino, Italo. *Invisible Cities*. London: Farber & Farber, 1972.

Campbell, Elaine. "Policing and Its Spatial Imaginaries." *Journal of Theoretical & Philosophical Criminology* 8, no. 2 (2016): 71–89.

Caparini, Marina. "Applying a Security Governance Perspective to the Privatisation of Security." In *Private Actors and Security Governance*, edited by Alan Bryden and Marina Caparini, 263–82. Münster: LIT Verlag, 2006.

Carlson, Jennifer. *Citizen-Protectors: The Everyday Politics of Guns in an Age of Decline.* New York: Oxford University Press, 2015.

———. "States, Subjects and Sovereign Power: Lessons from Global Gun Cultures." *Theoretical Criminology* 18, no. 3 (2014): 335–53.

Carr, John, Elizabeth Brown, and Steve Herbert. "Inclusion under the Law as Exclusion from the City: Negotiating the Spatial Limitation of Citizenship in Seattle." *Environment and Planning A* 41, no. 8 (2009): 1962–78.

Carrier, Ryan. "Dissolving Boundaries: Private Security and Policing in South Africa." *African Security Review* 8, no. 6 (1999): 37–43.

Casey, Edward. "Border versus Boundary at La Frontera." *Environment and Planning D: Society and Space* 29, no. 3 (2011): 384–98.

Catungal, John Paul, and Eugene McCann. "Governing Sexuality and Park Space: Acts of Regulation in Vancouver, B.C." *Social and Cultural Geography* 11, no. 1 (2010): 75–94.

Ceyhan, Ayse. "Technologization of Security: Management of Uncertainty and Risk in the Age of Biometrics." *Surveillance & Society* 5, no. 2 (2008): 102–23.

Chipkin, Clive. *Johannesburg Transition: Architecture & Society from 1950.* Johannesburg: STE Publishers, 2008.

Claassen, Rutger. "The Marketization of Security Services." *Public Reason* 3, no. 2 (2011): 124–45.

Clarke, Roger. "Dataveillance: Delivering '1984.'" In *Framing Technology: Society, Choice and Change,* edited by Leila Green and Roger Guinery, 117–30. London: Routledge, 1994.

———. "Information Technology and Dataveillance." Communications of the ACM 31, no. 5 (1988): 498–511.

Clarno, Andy. *Neoliberal Apartheid: Palestine/Israel and South Africa after 1994.* Chicago: University of Chicago Press, 2017.

———. "Rescaling White Space in Post-Apartheid Johannesburg." *Antipode* 45, no. 5 (2013): 1190–1212.

———. "A Tale of Two Walled Cities: Neo-Liberalization and Enclosure in Johannesburg and Jerusalem." *Political Power and Social Theory* 19 (2008): 159–205.

Clarno, Andy, and Martin J. Murray. "Policing in Johannesburg after Apartheid." *Social Dynamics* 39, no. 2 (2013): 210–27.

Clay, Grady. *Close-Up: How to Read the American City.* Chicago: University of Chicago Press, 1973.

Coaffee, Jon. "Urban Renaissance in the Age of Terrorism: *Revanchism,* Automated Social Control or the End of Reflection?" *International Journal of Urban and Regional Research* 29, no. 2 (2005): 447–54.

Coffin, Judy. "Artisans of the Sidewalk." *Radical History Review* 26 (1982): 89–101.

Cohen, Stanley. *Folk Devils and Moral Panics* (New York: Routledge, 2011).

Coleman, Roy. "Surveillance in the City: Primary Definition and Urban Spatial Order." *Crime, Media, Culture* 1, no. 2 (2005): 131–48.

Coleman, Roy, and Joe Sim. "Contemporary Statecraft and the 'Punitive Obsession': A Critique of the New Penology Thesis." In *The New Punitiveness: Trends, Theories, Perspectives,* edited by John Pratt, Wayne Morrison, Simon Hallsworth, Mark Brown, and David Brown, 101–120. Cullompton, UK: Willan, 2005.

Coleman, Roy, Joe Sim, and Dave Whyte. "Power, Politics and Partnerships: The State of Crime Prevention on Merseyside." In *Crime Control and Community: The New Politics of Public Safety*, edited by Gordon Hughes and Adam Edwards, 86–108. Cullompton, UK: Willan, 2002.

Collier, Stephen. "Topologies of Power: Foucault's Analysis of Political Government beyond 'Governmentality.'" *Theory, Culture & Society* 26, no. 6 (2009): 78–108.

Colomina, Beatriz. *Domesticity at War.* Cambridge, MA: MIT Press, 2007.

Comaroff, Jean, and John Comaroff. "Alien-Nation: Zombies, Immigrants, and Millennial Capitalism," *The South Atlantic Quarterly* 101, no. 4 (2002): 779–805.

———. "Criminal Justice, Cultural Justice: The Limits of Liberalism and the Pragmatics of Difference in the New South Africa." *American Ethnologist* 31, no. 2 (2004): 188–204.

———. "Criminal Obsessions, after Foucault: Postcoloniality, Policing, and the Metaphysics of Disorder." *Critical Inquiry* 30, no. 4 (2004): 800–824.

———. "Figuring Crime: Quantifacts and the Production of the Un/Real." *Public Culture* 18, no. 1 (2006): 209–46.

———. *Law and Disorder in the Postcolony.* Chicago: University of Chicago Press, 2006.

———. "Naturing the Nation: Aliens, Apocalypse and the Postcolonial State." *Journal of Southern African Studies* 27, no. 3 (2001): 627–51.

———. "Policing Culture, Cultural Policing: Law and Social Order in Postcolonial South Africa," *Law and Social Inquiry* 29, no. 3 (2004): 513–46.

———. *The Truth about Crime: Sovereignty, Knowledge, Social Order.* Chicago: University of Chicago Press, 2016.

Cook, Ian, and Mary Whowell. "Visibility and the Policing of Public Space." *Geography Compass* 5, no. 8 (2011): 610–22.

Cooper, Brenda. *Magical Realism in West African Fiction: Seeing with a Third Eye.* London: Routledge, 1998.

Cooper-Knock, Sarah Jane. "Behind Closed Gates: Everyday Policing in Durban, South Africa." *Africa* 86, no. 1 (2016): 98–121.

Cooper-Knock, Sarah Jane, and Olly Owen. "Between Vigilantism and Bureaucracy: Improving Our Understanding of Police Work in Nigeria and South Africa." *Theoretical Criminology* 19, no. 3 (2015): 355–75.

Corva, Dominic. "Neoliberal Globalization and the War on Drugs: Transnationalizing Illiberal Governance in the Americas." *Political Geography* 27, no. 2 (2008): 176–93.

Crang, Mike, and Stephen Graham. "Sentient Cities: Ambient Intelligence and the Politics of Urban Space." *Information, Communication & Society* 10, no. 6 (2007): 789–817.

Crawford, Adam. "Community Safety Partnerships: Managerialist Tensions and Threats." *Criminal Justice Matters* 33, no. 1 (1998): 4–5.

———. *Crime Prevention and Community Safety: Politics, Policies and Practices.* Harlow, UK: Addison Wesley Longman, 1998.

———, ed. "The Governance of Crime and Insecurity in an Anxious Age: The Trans-European and the Local." In *Crime and Insecurity*, 27–51. Cullompton: Willan Publishing, 2002.

———. "Joined-Up but Fragmented: Contradiction, Ambiguity, and Ambivalence at the

Heart of New Labour's 'Third Way.'" In *Crime, Disorder and Community Safety: A New Agenda?*, edited by Roger Matthews and John Pitts, 54–80. London: Routledge, 2001.

———. *The Local Governance of Crime: Appeals to Community and Partnerships*. London: Clarendon Press, 1997.

———. "Networked Governance and the Post-Regulatory State: Steering, Rowing, and Anchoring the Provision of Policing and Security." *Theoretical Criminology* 10, no. 4 (2006): 449–79.

———. "The Partnership Approach to Community Crime Prevention: Corporatism at the Local Level?" *Social & Legal Studies* nos. 3–4 (1994): 497–519.

———. "The Pattern of Policing in the UK: Policing beyond the Police." In *Handbook of Policing*, edited by Tim Newburn, 136–69. Cullompton, UK: Willan, 2003.

———. "Plural Policing in the UK: Policing beyond the Police." In *Handbook of Policing*, 2nd ed., edited by Tim Newburn, 147–81. New York: Routledge, 2008.

———. "Policing and Security as 'Club Goods': The New Enclosures?" In *Democracy, Society, and the Governance of Security*, edited by Jennifer Wood and Benoît Dupont, 111–38. Cambridge, UK: Cambridge University Press, 2006.

———. "The Preventative Turn in Europe." In *Crime Prevention Policies in Comparative Perspective*, edited by Adam Crawford, xv–xxvii. Cullompton, UK: Willan, 2009.

Crawford, Adam, and Karen Evans. "Crime Prevention and Community Safety." In *The Oxford Handbook of Criminology*, 5th ed., edited by Mick Maguire, Rodney Morgan, and Robert Reiner, 769–805. Oxford, UK: Oxford University Press, 2012.

Crawford, Adam, and Stuart Lister. "Additional Security Patrols in Residential Areas: Notes from the Marketplace." *Policing & Society* 16, no. 2 (2006): 164–88.

———. "The Patchwork Shape of Reassurance Policing in England and Wales: Integrated Local Security Quilts or Frayed, Fragmented and Fragile Tangled Webs?" *Policing: An International Journal of Police Strategies & Management* 27, no. 3 (2004): 413–30.

Crawford, Adam, Stuart Lister, Sarah Blackburn, and Jonathan Burnett. *Plural Policing: The Mixed Economy of Visible Patrols in England and Wales* (Bristol, UK: Policy Press, 2005).

Crawford, Alice. "Security Moms and Smart Homes: Information Technology and Domestic Surveillance in the 'Age of Terrorism.'" *The International Journal of Technology, Knowledge, and Society* 1, no. 1 (2005/2006): 93–96.

Czeglédy, André. "Villas of the Highveld: A Cultural Perspective on Johannesburg and Its 'Northern Suburbs.' in Tomlinson et al., *Emerging Johannesburg*, 21–42.

Daniel, E. Valentine. "Tea Talk: Violent Measures in the Discursive Practices of Sri Lanka's Estate Tamils." *Comparative Studies in Society and History* 35, no. 3 (1993): 568–600.

Das, Veena. "The Signature of the State: The Paradox of Illegibility." In *Anthropology in the Margins of the State*, edited by Veena Das and Deborah Poole, 225–52. Santa Fe: School of American Research Press, 2004.

Das, Veena, and Deborah Poole. "State and Its Margins: Comparative Ethnographies." In *Anthropology in the Margins of the State*, edited by Veena Das and Deborah Poole, 3–34. Santa Fe: School of American Research Press, 2004.

Datta, Anku. "Rethinking Spaces of Exception: Notes from a Forced Migrant Camp in Jammu and Kashmir." *International Journal of Migration and Border Studies* 2, no. 2 (2016): 162–75.

Datta, Ayona. "Encounters with Law and Critical Urban Studies: Reflections on Amin's Telescopic Urbanism." *City* 17, no. 4 (2013): 517–22.

Davies, Jonathan. "Network Governance Theory: A Gramscian Critique." *Environment and Planning A* 44, no. 11 (2012): 2687–2704.

Davis, Mike. *City of Quartz: Excavating the Future of Los Angeles.* New York: Vintage, 1992.

———. "Fortress Los Angeles: The Militarization of Urban Space." In *Variations on a Theme Park: The New American City and the End of Public Space,* edited by Michael Sorkin, 154–180. New York: Hill and Wang, 1992.

Davis, Robert, Christopher Ortiz, Sarah Dadusyh, Jenny Irish, Arturo Alvarado, and Diane Davis. "The Public Accountability of Private Police: Lessons from New York, Johannesburg, and Mexico City." *Policing and Society* 13, no. 2 (2003): 197–210.

Dean, Michael. "Liberal Government and Authoritarianism." *Economy & Society* 31, no. 1 (2000): 37–61.

De Cauter, Lieven. *The Capsular Civilization: On the City in the Age of Fear.* Rotterdam: NAi, 2004.

De Certeau, Michel. *The Practice of Everyday Life.* Translated by Steven Rendall. Berkeley: University of California Press, 1984.

De Kock, Leon. "From the Subject of Evil to the Evil Subject: 'Cultural Difference' in Postapartheid South African Crime Fiction." *Safundi* 16, no. 1 (2015): 28–50.

De Lint, Willem. "A Post-Modern Turn in Policing: Policing as Pastiche?" *International Journal of the Sociology of Law* 27 (1999): 127–52.

De Muynck, Bert. "The Prosthetic Paradox." In *Angst & Ruimte/Fear & Space,* edited by Theo Hauben and Marco Vermeulen with Veronique Patteeuw, 8–15. Rotterdam: NAi, 2004.

Deutsche, Rosalyn. *Evictions: Art and Spatial Politics.* Cambridge, MA: MIT Press, 1996.

Didier, Sophie, Elisabeth Peyroux, and Marianne Morange. "The Spreading of the City Improvement District Model in Johannesburg and Cape Town: Urban Regeneration and the Neoliberal Agenda in South Africa." *International Journal of Urban and Regional Research* 36, no. 5 (2012): 915–35.

Diphoorn, Tessa. "The 'Bravo Mike Syndrome': Private Security Culture and Racial Profiling in South Africa." *Policing and Society* 27, no. 5 (2017): 525–40.

———. "'It's All about the Body': The Bodily Capital of Armed Response Officers in South Africa." *Medical Anthropology* 34, no. 4 (2015): 336–52.

———. "'Surveillance of the Surveillers': Regulation of the Private Security Industry in South Africa and Kenya." *African Studies Review* 59, no. 2 (2016): 161–82.

———. *Twilight Policing: Private Security and Violence in Urban South Africa.* Berkeley: University of California Press, 2016.

———. "Twilight Policing: Private Security Practices in South Africa." *British Journal of Criminology* 56, no. 2 (2016): 313–31.

Diphoorn, Tessa, and Julie Berg. "Typologies of Partnership Policing: Case Studies from Urban South Africa." *Policing & Society* 24, no. 4 (2014): 425–42.

Diphoorn, Tessa, and Helene Maria Kyed. "Entanglements of Private Security and Community Policing in South Africa and Swaziland." *African Affairs* 115, no. 461 (2016): 710–32.

Dirsuweit, Teresa. "Between Ontological Security and the Right Difference: Road Closures, Communitarianism and Urban Ethics in Johannesburg, South Africa." *Autrepart* 2 (2007): 53–71.

———. "Johannesburg: Fearful City." *Urban Forum* 13, no. 3 (2002): 3–19.

Dirsuweit, Teresa, and Alex Wafer. "Scale, Governance, and the Maintenance of Privileged Control: The Case of Road Closures in Johannesburg's Northern Suburbs." *Urban Forum* 17, no. 4 (2006): 327–52.

Donald, James. *Imagining the Modern City*. Minneapolis: University of Minnesota Press, 1999.

———. "This, Here, Now: Imagining the Modern City." In *Imagining Cities: Scripts, Signs, Memory*, edited by Sallie Westwood and John Williams, 181–201. London: Routledge, 1997.

Doty, Roxanne. "States of Exception on the Mexico-U.S. Border: Security, 'Decisions' and Civilian Border Patrols." *International Political Sociology* 1, no. 2 (2007): 113–37.

Douglas, Mary. *Purity and Danger: An Analysis of the Concepts of Pollution and Taboo*. London: Routledge and Kegan Paul, 1966.

———. *Risk and Blame: Essays in Cultural Theory*. London: Routledge, 1992.

Dovey, Lindiwe. "Redeeming Features: From *Tsotsi* (1980) to *Tsotsi* (2006)." *Journal of African Cultural Studies* 19, no. 2 (2007): 143–64.

Dupont, Benoît. "Private Security Regimes: Conceptualizing the Forces that Shape the Private Delivery of Security." *Theoretical Criminology* 18, no. 3 (2014): 263–81.

———. "Security in the Age of Networks." *Policing and Society* 14, no. 1 (2004): 76–91.

Easterling, Keller. *Enduring Innocence: Global Architecture and Its Political Masquerades*. Cambridge, MA: MIT Press, 2005.

———. *Organization Space: Landscapes, Highways, and Houses in America*. Cambridge, MA: MIT Press, 1999.

Edwards, Adam, and Gordon Hughes. "The Preventive Turn and the Promotion of Safer Communities in England and Wales: Political Inventiveness and Governmental Instabilities." In *Crime Prevention Policies in Comparative Perspective*, edited by Adam Crawford, 62–85. London: Willan, 2009.

———. "Public Safety Regimes: Negotiated Orders and Political Analysis in Criminology." *Criminology and Criminal Justice* 12, no. 4 (2012): 433–58.

Edwards, Bill, Mark Goodwin, Simon Pemberton, and Michael Woods. "Partnerships, Power and Scale in Rural Governance." *Environment and Planning C* 19, no. 2 (2001): 289–310.

Elden, Stuart. "Land, Terrain, Territory." *Progress in Human Geography* 34, no. 6 (2010): 799–817.

———. "Terror and Territory." *Antipode* 39, no. 5 (2007): 821–45.

———. *Terror and Territory: The Spatial Extent of Sovereignty*. Minneapolis: University of Minnesota Press, 2009.

Ellin, Nan. "At Home and Everywhere: Making Place in the Global Village." In *Culture,*

Environmental Action, and Sustainability, edited by Ricardo García Mira, José Cama-selle, and José Martinez, 61–68. Cambridge, MA: Hogrefe & Huber, 2003.

———. "Fear and City Building." *The Hedgehog Review* 5, no. 3 (2003): 43–61.

———. "Shelter from the Storm or Form Follows Fear and Vice Versa." In *Architecture of Fear,* edited by Nan Ellin, 13–45. New York: Princeton Architectural Press, 1997.

———. "Thresholds of Fear: Embracing the Urban Shadow." *Urban Studies Review* 38, nos. 5–6 (2001): 869–83.

Ellison, Ralph. *Invisible Man.* New York: Random House, 1952.

Elyachar, Julia. *Markets of Dispossession: NGOs, Economic Development, and the State in Cairo.* Durham, NC: Duke University Press, 2005.

England, Marcia (with Stephanie Simon). "Scary Cities: Urban Geographies of Fear, Difference, and Belonging." *Social & Cultural Geography* 11, no. 3 (2010): 201–7.

Ericson, Richard. *Crime in an Insecure World.* Cambridge, UK: Polity Press, 2007.

———. "The Division of Expert Knowledge in Policing and Security." *British Journal of Sociology* 45, no. 2 (1994): 149–75.

Ericson, Richard, and Kevin Haggerty. *Policing the Risk Society.* Toronto: University of Toronto Press, 1997.

Fanghanel, Alexandra. "The Trouble with Safety: Fear of Crime, Pollution and Subjectification in Public Space." *Theoretical Criminology* 20, no. 1 (2016): 57–74.

Farish, Matthew. "Cities in Shade: Urban Geography and the Uses of *Noir.*" *Environment and Planning D* 23, no. 1 (2005): 95–118.

Farmer, Paul. "An Anthropology of Structural Violence." *Current Anthropology* 45, no. 3 (2004): 305–30.

———. *Pathologies of Power: Health, Human Rights and the New War on the Poor.* Berkeley: University of California Press, 2003.

Faull, Andrew. "Need or Greed? Corruption and Integrity Management in a Gauteng Police Station." *SA Crime Quarterly* 28 (2009): 11–19.

Feeley, Malcolm, and Jonathan Simon. "Actuarial Justice: The Emerging New Criminal Law." In *The Futures of Criminology,* edited by David Nelken, 173–201. London: Sage, 1994.

———. "The Form and the Limits of the New Penology." In *Punishment and Social Control,* enlarged 2nd ed., edited by Thomas G. Blomberg and Stanley Cohen, 75–94. New York: Aldine de Gruyter, 2003.

———. "The New Penology: Notes on the Emerging Strategy of Corrections and Its Implications." *Criminology* 30, no. 4 (1992): 449–74.

Feldman, Allen. "Securocratic Wars of Public Safety: Globalized Policing as Scopic Regime." *Interventions: The International Journal of Postcolonial Studies* 6, no. 3 (2004): 330–50.

Ferguson, James. "Novelty and Method: Notes on Global Fieldwork." In *Multi-Sited Ethnography: Problems and Possibilities in the Translocation of Research Methods,* edited by Simon Coleman and Pauline von Hellermann, 194–208. New York: Routledge, 2011.

Fiorina, Morris, "Extreme Voices: A Dark Side of Civic Engagement." In *Civic Engagement in American Democracy,* edited by Theda Skocpol and Morris Fiorina, 395–425. Washington DC: Brookings Institution Press, 1999.

Flusty Steven. "The Banality of Interdiction: Surveillance, Control, and the Displacement of Diversity." *International Journal of Urban and Regional Research* 25, no. 3 (2001): 658–64.

———. "Building Paranoia." In *Architecture of Fear*, edited by Nan Ellin, 48–52. New York: Princeton Architectural Press, 1997.

Foucault, Michel. *Discipline and Punish: The Birth of the Prison*. Translated by Alan Sheridan. New York: Vintage, 1991.

———. "Questions of Geography." Translated by Colin Gordon. In *Space, Knowledge, and Power: Foucault and Geography*, edited by Jeremy Crampton and Stuart Elden, 173–84. Burlington, VT: Ashgate, 2007.

Fraser, Nancy. "Rethinking the Public Sphere: A Contribution to the Critique of Actually Existing Democracy." In *The Phantom Public Sphere*, edited by Bruce Robbins, 1–32. Minneapolis: University of Minnesota Press, 1993.

Fregonese, Sara. "Beyond the Weak State: Hybrid Sovereignties in Beirut." *Environment and Planning D* 30, no. 4 (2012): 655–74.

Freilich, Joshua, and Graeme Newman. "Regulating Crime: The New Criminology of Crime Control." *The Annals of the American Academy of Political and Social Science* 679, no. 1 (2018): 8–18.

———. "Transforming Piecemeal Social Engineering into Grand Crime Prevention Policy: Toward a New Criminology of Social Control." *Journal of Criminal Law & Criminology* 105, no. 1 (2016): 203–32.

Frølund, Morten. "Becoming Capital: A Journey through the Political Economic Space of Copenhagen Airport." *ACME: An International E-Journal for Critical Geographies* 15, no. 1 (2016): 230–52.

Fu, Albert, and Martin J. Murray. "Cinema and the Edgy City: Johannesburg, Carjacking, and the Postmetropolis." *African Identities* 5, no. 2 (2007): 279–89.

Fujii, Lee Ann. "Five Stories of Accidental Ethnography: Turning Unplanned Moments in the Field into Data." *Qualitative Research* 15, no. 4 (2015): 525–39.

Gabriel, Yiannis. "The Narrative Veil: Truth and Untruths in Storytelling." In *Myths, Stories and Organizations: Premodern Narratives for our Times*, 17–31. Oxford, UK: Oxford University Press, 2004.

Garland, David. *The Culture of Control: Crime and Social Order in Contemporary Society*. Oxford, UK: Oxford University Press, 2001.

———. "Ideas, Institutions, and Situational Crime Prevention." In *Ethical and Social Perspectives on Situational Crime Prevention*, edited by Andrew Von Hirsch, David Garland, and Alison Wakefield, 1–16. Oxford, UK: Hart Publishing, 2000.

———. "The Limits of the Sovereign State: Strategies of Crime Control in Contemporary Society." *British Journal of Criminology* 36, no. 4 (1996): 445–71.

Gazit, Nir, and Robert Latham. "Spatial Alternatives and Counter-Sovereignties in Israel/Palestine." *International Political Sociology* 8, no. 1 (2014): 63–81.

Giddens, Anthony. *The Consequences of Modernity*. Cambridge, UK: Polity Press, 1990.

Gilfoyle, Timothy. "Prostitutes in History: From Parables of Pornography to Metaphors of Modernity," *American Historical Review* 104, no. 1 (1999): 117–41.

Gilloch, Graeme. *Myth and Metropolis: Walter Benjamin and the City*. London: Polity Press, 1996.

Girling, Evi, Ian Loader, and Richard Sparks. "A Telling Tale: A Case of Vigilantism and Its Aftermath in an English Town." *British Journal of Sociology* 49, no. 3 (1998): 474–90.

Glassner, Barry. *The Culture of Fear*. New York: Basic Books, 1999.

Glück, Zoltán. "Piracy and the Production of Security Space." *Environment and Planning D* 33, no. 4 (2015): 642–59.

Goldstein, Daniel. *The Spectacular City*. Durham, NC: Duke University Press, 2015.

Gomel, Elana. "Aliens among Us: Fascism and Narrativity." *Journal of Narrative Theory* 30, no. 1 (2000): 127–62.

Goode, Erich, and Nachman Ben-Yehuda. "Moral Panics: Culture, Politics, and Social Construction." *Annual Review of Sociology* 20 (1994): 149–71.

———. *Moral Panics: The Social Construction of Deviance* (Cambridge, MA: Blackwell, 1994).

Gordimer, Nadine. *Jump and Other Stories*. New York: Penguin, 1991.

Goris, Peter, and Reece Walters. "Locally-Orientated Crime Prevention and the 'Partnership Approach.'" *Policing* 22, no. 4 (1999): 633–45.

Gould, Chandre, Johan Burger, and Gareth Newham. "The SAPS Crime Statistics: What They Tell Us—and What They Don't." *South African Crime Quarterly* 42 (2014): 3–12.

Graham, Stephen. "Cities as Battlespace: The New Military Urbanism." *City* 13, no. 4 (2009): 383–402.

———. *Cities under Siege: The New Military Urbanism*. London: Verso, 2010.

———. "The Urban 'Battlespace.'" *Theory, Culture & Society* 26, nos. 7–8 (2009): 278–88.

———. "When Life Itself Is War: On the Urbanization of Military and Security Doctrine." *International Journal of Urban and Regional Research* 36, no. 1 (2012): 136–55.

Grant, Evadne. "Private Policing." In *Acta Juridica*, edited by Thomas Bennett, Derry Devine, Dale Hutchison, Solly Leeman, and Dirk Van Zyl Smit, 92–117. Cape Town: Juta, 1989.

Grant, Richard, and Daniel Thompson. "City on Edge: Immigrant Businesses and the Right to Urban Space in Inner-City Johannesburg." *Urban Geography* 36, no. 2 (2015): 181–200.

Green, Linda. "Fear as a Way of Life." *Cultural Anthropology* 9, no. 2 (1994): 227–56.

Greenberg, Lara. "For Anton, Gap Was More than a Job." *South African Jewish Report* 11, no. 21 (08–15 June 2007).

Gregory, Marshall. "Fictions, Facts, and the Fact(s) of (in) Fictions." *Modern Language Studies* 28, nos. 3–4 (1998): 3–40.

Gross, Mark. "Vigilante Violence and 'Forward Panic' in Johannesburg's Townships." *Theory & Society* 45, no. 3 (2016): 239–63.

Gross, Oren. "Chaos and Rules: Should Responses to Violent Crises Always Be Constitutional?" *Yale Law Journal* 112, no. 5 (2003): 1011–34.

Gumedze, Sabelo. "Regulating the Private Security Sector in South Africa." *Social Justice* 34, nos. 3–4 [109–110] (2007): 195–207.

Hansen, Thomas Blom. "Performers of Sovereignty: On the Privatization of Security in Urban South Africa." *Critique of Anthropology* 26, no. 3 (2006): 279–95.

Haraway, Donna. *Primate Visions: Gender, Race, and Nature in the World of Modern Science.* New York: Routledge, 1989.

Harrison, Philip, and Alan Mabin. "Security and Space: Managing the Contradictions of Access Restriction in Johannesburg." *Environment & Planning B* 33, no. 1 (2006): 3–20.

Harvey, David. "The New Urbanism and the Communitarian Trap." *Harvard Design Magazine* 1 (1997): 1–3.

———. *Spaces of Hope.* Berkeley: University of California Press, 2000.

Hayward, Keith. *City Limits: Crime, Consumer Culture and the Urban Experience.* London: Glasshouse Press, 2004.

———. "Five Spaces of Cultural Criminology." *British Journal of Criminology* 52, no. 3 (2012): 441–62.

Hentschel, Christine. "Making (In)Visible: CCTV, 'Living Cameras,' and Their Objects in a Post-Apartheid Metropolis." *International Criminal Justice Review* 17, no. 4 (2007): 289–303.

———. "Outcharming Crime in (D)urban Space." *Social Dynamics* 37, no. 1 (2011): 148–64.

———. *Security in the Bubble: Navigating Crime in Urban South Africa.* Minneapolis: University of Minnesota Press, 2015.

Hentschel, Christine. and Julie Berg. "Policing South African Cities: Plural and Spatial Perspectives." In *Police, Policing, Policy and the City in Europe,* edited by Marc Cools, Sophie De Kimpe, Arne Dormaels, Marleen Easton, Els Enhus, Paul Ponsaers, Gudrun Van de Walle, and Antoinette Verhage, 147–73. The Hague: Eleven International Publishing, 2010.

———. *Security in the Bubble: Navigating Crime in Urban South Africa.* Minneapolis: University of Minnesota Press, 2015.

Herbert, Steve. "The End of the Territorially-Sovereign State? The Case of Crime Control in the United States," *Political Geography* 18, no. 2 (1999): 149–72.

———. "The Geopolitics of the Police: Foucault, Disciplinary Power and the Tactics of the Los Angeles Police Department." *Political Geography* 15, no. 1 (1996): 47–59.

———. "The Normative Ordering of Police Territoriality: Making and Marking Space with the Los Angeles Police Department." *Annals of the Association of American Geographers* 86, no. 3 (1996): 567–82.

———. *Policing Space: Territoriality and the Los Angeles Police Department.* Minneapolis: University of Minnesota Press, 1997.

———. "Policing the Contemporary City: Fixing Broken Windows or Shoring Up Neo-Liberalism?" *Theoretical Criminology* 5, no. 4 (2001): 445–66.

———. "Territoriality and the Police." *The Professional Geographer* 49, no. 1 (1997): 86–94.

———. "The Trapdoor of Community." *Annals of the Association of American Geographers* 95, no. 4 (2005): 850–65.

Herbert, Steve, and Elizabeth Brown. "Conceptions of Space and Crime in the Punitive Neoliberal City." *Antipode* 38, no. 4 (2006): 755–77.

Hershatter, Gail. *Dangerous Pleasures: Prostitution and Modernity in Twentieth-Century Shanghai.* Berkeley: University of California Press, 1997.

Hier, Sean. "Conceptualizing Moral Panic through a Moral Economy of Harm." *Critical Sociology* 28, no. 3 (2002): 311–34.

———. "Thinking beyond Moral Panic: Risk, Responsibility, and the Politics of Moralization." *Theoretical Criminology* 12, no. 2 (2008): 173–90.

Hills, Alice. "The Unavoidable Ghettoization of Security in Iraq." *Security Dialogue* 41, no. 3 (2010): 301–21.

Hinton, Mercedes. *The State on the Streets: Police and Politics in Argentina and Brazil.* Boulder, CO: Lynne Rienner, 2006.

Hobsbawm, Eric. "Introduction: Inventing Traditions." In *The Invention of Tradition*, edited by Eric Hobsbawm and Terence Ranger, 1–14. Cambridge and New York: Cambridge University Press, 1983.

Hook, Derek, and Michele Vrdoljak. "Fear and Loathing in Northern Johannesburg: The Security Park as Heterotopia." *Psychology in Society* 27 (2001): 61–83.

———. "Gated Communities, Heterotopia and a 'Rights' of Privilege: A 'Heterotopology' of the South African Security-Park." *Geoforum* 33, no. 2 (2002): 195–219.

Hope, Tim. "Inequality and the Clubbing of Private Security." In *Crime, Risk and Insecurity: Law and Order in Everyday Life and Political Discourse*, edited by Tim Hope and Richard Sparks, 83–106. London: Routledge, 2000.

Hornberger, Julia. "'My Police—Your Police': The Informal Privatization of the Police in Inner City Johannesburg." *African Studies* 63, no. 2 (2004): 213–30.

———. *Policing and Human Rights: The Meaning of Violence and Justice in the Everyday Policing of Johannesburg.* New York: Routledge, 2011.

Hubbard, Phil. "Cleansing the Metropolis: Sex Work and the Politics of Zero Tolerance." *Urban Studies* 41, no. 9 (2004): 1687–1702.

Hughes, Gordon, Eugene McLaughlin, and John Muncie. *Crime Prevention and Community Safety: New Directions.* London: Sage, 2001.

Hunt, Arnold. "'Moral Panic' and Moral Language in the Media." *British Journal of Sociology* 48, no. 4 (1997): 629–48.

Hussain, Nasser. "Beyond Norm and Exception: Guantánamo." *Critical Inquiry* 33, no. 4 (2007): 734–53.

———. *The Jurisprudence of Emergency: Colonialism and the Rule of Law.* Ann Arbor: University of Michigan Press, 2003.

Hutchinson, Steven, and Daniel O'Connor. "Policing the New Commons: Corporate Security Governance on a Mass Private Property in Canada." *Policing and Society* 15, no. 2 (2005): 125–44.

Ingenschay, Dieter, and Joan Ramon Resina. Preface to *After-Images of the City*, edited by Joan Ramon Resina and Dieter Ingenschay, xi–xvii. London: Cornell University Press, 2003.

Iossifova, Deljana. "Borderland Urbanism: Seeing between Enclaves." *Urban Geography* 36, no. 1 (2015): 90–108.

Jaguaribe, Beatriz. "Cities without Maps: Favelas and the Aesthetics of Realism." In *Urban Imaginaries: Locating the Modern City*, edited by Alev Çinar and Thomas Bender, 100–120. Minneapolis: University of Minnesota Press, 2007.

Jasanoff, Sheila. "Future Imperfect: Science, Technology, and the Imaginations of Modernity." In *Dreamscapes of Modernity: Sociotechnical Imaginaries and the Fabrication of Power*, edited by Sheila Jasanoff and Sang-Hyun Kim, 1–33. Chicago: University of Chicago Press, 2015).

Jay, Martin. *Downcast Eyes: The Degeneration of Vision in Twentieth Century French Thought.* Berkeley: University of California Press, 1993.

Jeganathan, Pradeep. "Checkpoint: Anthropology, Identity, and the State." In *Anthropology in the Margins of the State*, edited by Veena Das and Deborah Poole, 67–80. Santa Fe, NM: School of American Research Press, 2004.

Jensen, Ole. *Staging Mobilities*. New York: Routledge, 2013.

Johnston, Les. "Crime, Fear and Civil Policing." *Urban Studies* 38, nos. 5–6 (2001): 959–76.

———. "From 'Pluralization' to 'the Police Extended Family': Discourses on the Governance of Community Policing in Britain." *International Journal of the Sociology of Law* 31, no. 3 (2003): 185–204.

———. *Policing Britain: Risk, Security, and Governance*. Harlow: Longman, 2000.

———. "Policing Diversity: The Impact of the Public-Private Complex in Policing." In *Core Issues in Policing*, edited by Frank Leisham, Barry Loveday, and Stephen Savage, 54–70. London: Longman, 1996.

———. "Private Policing in Context." *European Journal on Criminal Policy and Research* 7, no. 2 (1999): 175–96.

———. "Privatization and the Police Function: From 'New Police' to 'New Policing.'" In *Beyond Law and Order: Criminal Justice Policy and Politics in the 1990s*, edited by Robert Reiner and Malcolm Cross, 18–40. Basingstoke, UK: Macmillan, 1991.

———. *The Rebirth of Private Policing*. New York: Routledge, 1992.

Johnston, Les, and Clifford Shearing. *Governing Security: Explorations in Policing and Justice*. London: Routledge, 2003.

Jones, Reece. "Agents of Exception: Border Security and the Marginalization of Muslims in India." *Environment and Planning D* 27, no. 5 (2009): 879–97.

Jones, Rhys, and Peter Merriman. "Network Nation." *Environment and Planning A* 44, no. 4 (2012): 937–53.

Jones, Trevor, and Tim Newburn, eds. *Plural Policing: A Comparative Perspective*. New York: Routledge, 2006.

———. *Private Security and Public Policing*. Oxford, UK: Clarendon, 1998.

———. "The Transformation of Policing? Understanding Trends in Policing Systems." *British Journal of Criminology* 42, no. 1 (2002): 129–46.

———. "Urban Change and Policing: Mass Private Property Re-considered." *European Journal on Criminal Policy and Research* 7, no. 2 (1999): 225–44.

Joseph, Miranda. *Against the Romance of Community*. Minneapolis: University of Minnesota Press, 2002.

Judd, Dennis. "The Rise of the New Walled Cities." In *Spatial Practices: Critical Explorations in Social/Spatial Theory*, edited by Helen Liggett and David Perry, 144–66. Thousand Oaks, CA: Sage, 1995.

Jürgens, Ulrich, and Martin Gnad. "Gated Communities in South Africa: Experiences from Johannesburg." *Environment and Planning B* 29, no. 3 (2002: 337–53.

Jürgens, Ulrich, Martin Gnad, and Jürgen Bahr. "New Forms of Class and Racial Segregation: Ghettos or Ethnic Enclaves?" In Tomlinson et al., *Emerging Johannesburg*, 56–70.

Kaiser, Robert, and Elena Nikiforova. "Borderland Spaces of Identification and Dis/location: Multiscalar Narratives and Enactments of Seto Identity and Place in the Estonian-Russian Borderlands." *Ethnic and Racial Studies* 29, no. 5 (2006): 928–58.

Katz, Cindy. "Hiding the Target: Social Reproduction in the Privatized Urban Environment." In *Postmodern Geography: Theory and Practice*, edited by Claudio Minca, 93–110. London: Routledge, 2001.

Kawash, Samira. "The Homeless Body." *Public Culture* 10, no. 2 (1998): 319–40.

———. "Safe House? Body, Building, and the Question of Security." *Cultural Critique* 45 (2000): 185–221.

Kearns, Ade. "Active Citizenship and Local Governance: Political and Geographical Dimensions." *Political Geography* 14, no. 2 (1995): 155–75.

Keil, Roger. "The Urban Future Revisited: Politics and Restructuring in Los Angeles after Fordism," *Strategies* 3 (1990): 105–29.

Kempa, Michael, Ryan Carrier, Jennifer Wood, and Clifford Shearing. "Reflections on the Evolving Concept of 'Private Policing.'" *European Journal on Criminal Policy and Research* 7, no. 2 (1999): 197–223.

Kempa, Michael, and Clifford Shearing. "Microscopic and Macroscopic Responses to Inequalities in the Governance of Security: Respective Experiments in South Africa and Northern Ireland." *Transformation* 29, no. 2 (2002): 25–54.

Kempa, Michael, and Anne-Marie Singh. "Private Security, Political Economy and the Policing of Race: Probing Global Hypotheses through the Case of South Africa." *Theoretical Criminology* 12, no. 3 (2008): 333–54.

Kempa, Michael, Philip Stenning, and Jennifer Wood. "Policing Communal Spaces: A Reconfiguration of the 'Mass Private Property' Hypothesis." *British Journal of Criminology* 44, no. 4 (2004): 562–81.

Kennedy, David. *Deterrence and Crime Prevention: Reconsidering the Prospect of Sanction*. London: Routledge, 2008.

Kennedy, Liam. "Alien Nation: White Male Paranoia and Imperial Culture in the United States." *Journal of American Studies* 30, no. 1 (1996): 87–100.

Khokher, Rohit, and Ram Chandra Singh. "Footprint-Based Personal Recognition Using Scanning Technique." *Indian Journal of Science and Technology* 9, no. 44 (2016): 1–10.

Kienscherf, Markus. "Security Assemblages and Spaces of Exception: The Production of (Para-) Militarized Spaces in the U.S. War on Drugs." *Radical Criminology* 1, no. 1 (2012): 19–35.

Kligmann, Anna. *Brandscapes: Architecture in the Experience Economy*. Cambridge, MA: MIT Press, 2007.

Klockars, Carl. "The Dirty Harry Problem." *Annals of the American Academy of Political and Social Science* 452, no. 1 (1980): 33–47.

Kruger, Loren. "Filming the Edgy City: Cinematic Narrative and Urban Form in Post-apartheid Johannesburg." *Research in African Literatures* 37, no. 2 (2006): 141–63.

Kusenbach, Margarethe. "Street Phenomenology: The Go-Along as Ethnographic Research Tool." *Ethnography* 4, no. 3 (2003): 455–85.

Lacy, Mark. "Designer Security: MoMA's Safe: Design Takes on Risk and Control Society." *Security Dialogue* 39, nos. 2–3 (2008): 333–57.

Landau, Loren. "Immigration and the State of Exception: Security and Sovereignty in East and Southern Africa." *Millennium: Journal of International Studies* 34, no. 2 (2005): 325–48.

Landman, Karina. "Exploring the Impact of Gated Communities on Social and Spatial Justice and Its Relation to Restorative Justice and Peace-Building in South Africa." *Acta Juridica* 7 (2007): 134–55.

———. "Gated Communities in South Africa: Tensions between the Planning Ideal and Practice." *Town and Regional Planning* 61 (2012): 1–9.

———. "Gated Minds, Gated Places: The Impact and Meaning of Hard Boundaries in South Africa." In *Gated Communities: Social Sustainability in Contemporary and Historical Gated Developments*, edited by Samer Bagaeen and Ola Uduku, 49–62. London: Earthscan, 2010.

———. "Gated Neighbourhoods in South Africa: An Appropriate Urban Design Approach?" *Urban Design International* 13 (2008): 227–40.

———. "Man the Barricades! Gated Communities in South Africa." *Crime & Conflict* 21 (Spring 2000): 24–26.

———. "Privatizing Public Space in Post-Apartheid South African Cities through Neighborhood Enclosures." *GeoJournal* 66, nos. 1–2 (2006): 133–46.

———. "Reconsidering Crime and Urban Fortification in South Africa." In *The Urban Fabric of Crime and Fear*, edited by Vania Ceccato, 239–66. New York: Springer, 2012.

Landman, Karina, and Martin Schönteich. "Gated Communities as a Reaction to Crime." *South African Security Review* 11, no. 1 (2002): 71–85.

———. "Urban Fortresses: Gated Communities as a Reaction to Crime." *African Security Review* 11, no. 4 (2002): 71–85.

Larner, Wendy, and David Craig, "After Neoliberalism? Community Activism and Local Partnerships in Aotearoa New Zealand." *Antipode* 37, no. 3 (2005): 402–24.

Larner, Wendy, and William Walters, eds. Introduction to *Global Governmentality: Governing International Spaces*, 1–19. London: Routledge, 2004.

Laufer, Stephen, "The Politics of Fighting Crime in South Africa since 1994." In *Crime Wave: The South African Underworld and Its Foes*, edited by Jonny Steinberg, 14–23. Johannesburg: Wits University Press, 2001.

Lefebvre, Henri. *The Production of Space*. Translated by Donald Nicholson-Smith. Oxford, UK: Blackwell, 1991.

Lemanski, Charlotte, Karina Landman, and Matthew Durington. "Divergent and Similar Experiences of 'Gating' in South Africa: Johannesburg, Durban and Cape Town." *Urban Forum* 19, no. 2 (2008): 133–58.

Lenta, Patrick. "'Everyday Abnormality': Crime and In/security in Ivan Vladislavić's *Portrait with Keys*." *The Journal of Commonwealth Literature* 44, no. 1 (2009): 117–33.

Levi, Mike, and David Wall. "Technologies, Security, and Privacy in the Post-9/11 European Information Society." *Journal of Law and Society* 31, no. 2 (2004): 194–220.

Lianos, Michalis, and Mary Douglas. "Dangerization and the End of Deviance: The Institutional Environment." In *Criminology and Social Theory*, edited by David Garland and Richard Sparks, 103–26. Oxford, UK: Oxford University Press, 2000.

Lipman, Alan, and Howard Harris. "Fortress Johannesburg." *Environment and Planning B* 26, no. 5 (1999): 727–40.

Lippert, Randy, and Daniel O'Connor. "Security Intelligence Networks and the Transformation of Contract Private Security." *Policing and Society* 16, no. 1 (2006): 49–65.

Livingston, Debra. "Police Discretion and the Quality of Life in Public Places: Courts, Communities, and the New Policing." *Columbia Law Review* 97, no. 3 (1997): 551–672.

Livingstone, Ken, and Jerry Hart. "The Wrong Arm of the Law? Public Images of Private Security." *Policing and Society* 13, no. 2 (2003):. 159–70.

Loader, Ian. "Consumer Culture and the Commodification of Policing and Security." *Sociology* 33, no. 2 (1999): 373–92.

———. "Fall of the 'Platonic Guardians': Liberalism, Criminology and Political Responses to Crime in England and Wales." *British Journal of Criminology* 46, no. 4 (2006): 561–86.

———. "Plural Policing and Democratic Governance." *Social & Legal Studies* 9, no. 3 (2000): 323–45.

———. "Policing the Social: Questions of Symbolic Power." *British Journal of Sociology* 48, no. 1 (1997): 1–18.

———. "Private Security and the Demand for Protection in Contemporary Britain." *Policing and Society* 7 (1997): 143–62.

Loader, Ian, Benjamin Goold, and Angélica Thumala. "Grudge Spending: The Interplay between Markets and Culture in the Purchase of Security." *The Sociological Review* 63, no. 4 (2015): 858–75.

———. "The Moral Economy of Security." *Theoretical Criminology* 18, no. 4 (2014): 469–88.

Loader, Ian, and Neil Walker. *Civilizing Security.* Cambridge, UK: Cambridge University Press, 2007.

———. "Policing as a Public Good: Reconstituting the Connections between Policing and the State." *Theoretical Criminology* 5, no. 1 (2001): 9–35.

Loś, Maria. "Post-Communist Fear of Crime and the Commercialization of Security." *Theoretical Criminology* 6, no. 2 (2002): 165–88.

Low, Setha, and Neil Smith, eds. *The Politics of Public Space.* New York: Routledge, 2006.

Lynch, Kevin. *The Image of the City.* Cambridge, MA: Harvard University Press, 1960.

Lyon, David. "9/11, Synopticon, and Scopophilia: Watching and Being Watched." In *The New Politics of Surveillance and Visibility*, edited by Richard Victor Ericson and Kevin Haggerty, 35–54. Toronto: University of Toronto Press, 2006.

———. "Surveillance as Social Sorting: Computer Codes and Mobile Bodies." In *Surveillance as Social Sorting: Privacy, Risk and Digital Discrimination*, edited by David Lyon, 13–30. New York: Routledge, 2003.

———. *Surveillance Studies: An Overview.* Cambridge, UK: Polity, 2007.

Mabin, Alan. "In the Forest of Transformation: The 'Northern Suburbs' of Johannesburg." In *Spatial Transformations in Johannesburg*, edited by Graeme Gotz, Philip Harrison, Alison Todes and Chris Wray, 395–417. Johannesburg: Wits University Press, 2014.

———. "Suburbanisation, Segregation, and Government of Territorial Transformations." *Transformation: Critical Perspectives on Southern Africa* 57 (2005): 41–63.

Macfarlane, Roy. "The Private Sector Security Industry in South Africa." *African Defence Review* 19 (1994): 25–29.

Mäkinen, Liisa. "Surveillance ON/OFF. Examining Home Surveillance Systems from the User's Perspective." *Surveillance and Society* 14, no. 1 (2016): 59–77.

Malkki, Liisa. *Purity and Exile: Violence, Memory, and National Cosmology among Hutu Refugees in Tanzania.* Chicago: University of Chicago Press, 1995.

Malone, Karen. "Street Life: Youth, Culture and Competing Uses of Public Space." *Environment and Urbanization* 14, no. 2 (2002): 157–68.

Manzo, John. "The Folk Devil Happens to Be Our Best Customer: Security Officers' Orientations to 'Youth' in Three Canadian Shopping Malls." *International Journal of the Sociology of Law* 32, no. 3 (2004): 243–61.

Marcus, George, and Angela Rivas Gamboa. "Contemporary Cities with Colonial Pasts and Global Futures: Some Aspects of the Relations between Governance, Order, and Decent, Secure Life." In *Postcolonial Urbanism: Southeast Asian Cities and Global Processes*, edited by Ryan Bishop, John Phillips, and Wei-Wei Yeo, 227–42. New York: Routledge, 2003.

Marinetto, Michael. "Who Wants to Be an Active Citizen? The Politics and Practice of Community Involvement." *Sociology* 37, no. 1 (2003): 103–20.

Marks, Monique, and Jenny Fleming. "As Unremarkable as the Air They Breathe? Reforming Police Management in South Africa." *Current Sociology* 52, no. 5 (2004): 784–808.

Marks, Monique, and Jennifer Wood. "South African Policing at a Crossroads." *Theoretical Criminology* 14, no. 3 (2010): 311–29.

Marks, Monique, Jennifer Wood, and Clifford Shearing. "A Thin or Thick Blue Line? Exploring Alternative Models for Community Policing and the Police Role in South Africa." In *Community Policing and Peacekeeping*, edited by Peter Grabosky, 153–68. New York: CRC Press, 2009.

Marotta, Vince. "The Stranger and Social Theory." *Thesis Eleven* 62 (2000): 121–34.

Marx, Leo. "The American Ideology of Space." In *Denatured Visions: Landscape and Culture in the Twentieth Century*, edited by Stuart Wrede and William Howard Adams, 62–78. New York: The Museum of Modern Art, 1991.

Massey, Doreen. *For Space.* Thousand Oaks, CA: Sage, 2005.

Matlala, Ramolobi Louis Gemane. "Implementation of Sector Policing in Hillbrow." *Academic Journal of Interdisciplinary Studies* 4, no. 3 (2015): 135–42.

Maurer, Kristin. *Architectural Anxiety: The Perfect Safe Zone.* Raleigh, NC: Lulu Press, 2011.

Mauss, Marcel. *The Gift: The Form and Reason for Exchange in Archaic Societies.* Translated by W. D. Halls. London: Routledge, 1990.

Mayfield, David, and Susan Thorne. "Social History and Its Discontents: Gareth Stedman Jones and the Politics of Language," *Social History* 17, no. 2 (1992): 165–88.

Mbembe, Achille. "Aesthetics of Superfluity." *Public Culture* 16, no. 3 (2004): 373–405 (esp. 380–81, 383).

Mbembe, Achille, and Sarah Nuttall. "Writing the World from an African Metropolis," *Public Culture* 16, no. 3 (2004): 347–72.

McFarlane, Colin. "Assemblage and Critical Urbanism." *City* 15, no. 2 (2011): 204–24.

McLaughlin, Eugene. "Walled Cities: Surveillance, Regulation and Segregation." In *Unruly Cities?*, edited by Steve Pile, Christopher Brook, and Gerry Mooney, 96–136. London: Routledge, 2000.

McLaughlin, Eugene, and Karim Murji. "The End of Public Policing? Police Reform and the 'New Managerialism.'" In *Contemporary Issues in Criminology*, edited by Leslie Noaks, Michael Levi, and Mike Maguire, 110–127. Cardiff: University of Wales Press, 1995.

———. "Lost Connections and New Directions: Neo-liberalism, New Public Managerialism, and the 'Modernization' of the British Police." In *Crime, Risk, and Justice: The Politics of Crime Control in Liberal Democracies*, edited by Kevin Stenson and Robert Sullivan, 104–121. Cullompton, UK: Willan, 2001.

———. "The Postmodern Condition of the Police." *Liverpool Law Review* 21 (1999): 217–40.

McMichael, Christopher. "Police Wars and State Repression in South Africa." *Journal of Asian and African Studies* 51, no. 1 (2016): 3–16.

———. "Urban Pacification and 'Blitzes' in Contemporary Johannesburg." *Antipode* 47, no. 5 (2015): 1261–78.

Meagher, Kate. "The Strength of Weak States? Non-State Security Forces and Hybrid Governance in Africa." *Development and Change* 43, no. 5 (2012): 1073–1101.

Mendlesohn, Farah. *Rhetorics of Fantasy*. Middletown, CT: Wesleyan University Press, 2008.

Meneses-Reyes, Rodrigo. "Out of Place, Still in Motion: Shaping (Im)Mobility through Urban Regulation." *Social and Legal Studies* 22, no. 3 (2013): 335–56.

Merrifield, Andy, and Erik Swyngedouw. "Social Justice and the Urban Experience." In *The Urbanization of Injustice*, edited by Andy Merrifield and Erik Swyngedouw, 1–17. New York: New York University Press, 1997.

Merry, Sally Engle. "Spatial Governmentality and the New Urban Social Order: Controlling Gender Violence through Law." *American Anthropologist* 103, no. 1 (2001): 16–29.

Mezzadra, Sandro, and Brett Neilson. "Between Inclusion and Exclusion: On the Topology of Global Space and Borders." *Theory, Culture and Society* 29, nos. 4–5 (2012): 58–75.

Millington, Gareth. "Book Review: Gordon Hughes, *The Politics of Crime and Community*." *Theoretical Criminology* 13, no. 3 (2009): 383–87.

Mills, Greg. "Walls and Warriors: Speculations on the Relationship of Urban Design and Crime in the New South Africa." *Urban Forum* 2, no. 2 (1991): 89–93.

Minnaar, Anthony. "Crime Prevention, Partnership Policing and the Growth of Private Security: The South African Experience." In *Policing in Central and Eastern Europe: Dilemmas of Contemporary Criminal Justice*, edited by Gorazd Mesko, Milan Pagon, and Bojan Dobovsek, 1–25. Maribor, SI: University of Maribor, 2004).

———. "Private–Public Partnerships: Private Security, Crime Prevention and Policing in South Africa." *Acta Criminologica: Southern African Journal of Criminology* 18, no. 1 (2005): 85–114.

Miraftab, Faranak. "Colonial Present: Legacies of the Past in Contemporary Urban Practices in Cape Town, South Africa." *Journal of Planning History* 11, no. 4 (2012): 283–307.

Mitchell, Don. "The Annihilation of Space by Law: The Roots and Implications of Anti-Homeless Laws in the United States." *Antipode* 29, no. 3 (1997): 303–35.

———. *The Lie of the Land: Migrant Workers and the California Landscape*. Minneapolis: University of Minnesota Press, 1996.

———. *The Right to the City: Social Justice and the Fight for Public Space*. London: Guildford Press, 2003.

Mitchell, Katharyne. "Transnationalism, Neo-Liberalism, and the Rise of the Shadow State." *Economy & Society* 30, no. 2 (2001): 165–89.

Modiri, Joel. "The Colour of Law, Power and Knowledge: Introducing Critical Race Theory in (Post-) Apartheid South Africa." *South African Journal on Human Rights* 28 (2012): 405–36.

———. "The Grey Line in-between the Rainbow: (Re) Thinking and (Re) Talking Critical Race Theory in Post-Apartheid Legal and Social Discourse." *South African Public Law* 26, no. 1 (2011): 177–201.

Moore, Dawn, and Hideyuki Hirai. "Outcasts, Performers and True Believers: Responsibilized Subjects of Criminal Justice." *Theoretical Criminology* 18, no. 1 (2014): 5–19.

Mopasa, Michael, and Philip Stenning. "Tools of the Trade: The Symbolic Power of Private Security—An Exploratory Study." *Policing and Society* 11, no. 1 (2001): 67–97.

Morris, Rosalind. "Style, *Tsotsi*-Style and *Tsotsitaal*: The Histories, Politics and Aesthetics of a South African Figure." *Social Text* 103 [28, 2] (2010): 85–112.

Moses, Michael Valdez, Lucy Valerie Graham, John Marx, Gerald Gaylard, Ralph Goodman, and Stefan Helgesson. "*District 9*: A Roundtable." *Sarafundi: The Journal of South African and American Studies* 11, nos. 1–2 (2010): 155–75.

Murray, Martin J. "Alien Strangers in Our Midst: The Dreaded Foreign Invasion and 'Fortress South Africa,'" *Canadian Journal of African Studies* 37, nos. 2–3 (2003): 440–66.

———. "The City in Fragments: Kaleidoscopic Johannesburg after *Apartheid*." In *The Spaces of the Modern City: Imaginaries, Politics, and Everyday Life*, edited by Gyan Prakash and Kevin Kruse, 144–78. Princeton, NJ: Princeton University Press, 2008.

———. *City of Extremes: The Spatial Politics of Johannesburg*. Durham, NC: Duke University Press, 2011.

———. "City of Layers: The Making and Shaping of Affluent Johannesburg after Apartheid." In *Urban Governance in Post-Apartheid Cities*, edited by Marie Huchzermeyer and Christoph Haferburg, 179–96. Stuttgart: Schweizerbart, 2014.

———. *Taming the Disorderly City: the Spatial Politics of Johannesburg after Apartheid* (Ithaca: Cornell University Press, 2008).

Murray, Susan. "A Spy, a Shill, a Go-Between, or a Sociologist: Unveiling the 'Observer' in Participant Observer." *Qualitative Sociology* 3, no. 3 (2003): 377–95.

Nel, Adéle. "The Repugnant Appeal of the Abject: Cityscape and Cinematic Corporality in *District 9*." *Critical Arts* 26, no. 4 (2012): 547–69.

Newburn, Tim. "The Commodification of Policing: Security Networks in the Late Modern City." *Urban Studies* 38, nos. 5–6 (2001): 829–48.

Newburn, Tim, and Robert Reiner. "Policing and the Police." In *The Oxford Handbook of Criminology*, edited by Mike Maguire, Rod Morgan, and Robert Reiner, 910–52. Oxford: Clarendon Press, 1997.

Newman, David. "On Borders and Power: A Theoretical Framework." *Journal of Borderland Studies* 18, no. 1 (2003): 13–25.

Newman, Oscar. *Creating Defensible Space*. Washington, DC: Department of Housing and Urban Development, 1996.

———. *Defensible Space: Crime Prevention through Urban Design*. New York: Macmillan, 1972.

Nira, Daniel, and Stuart Russell. "Policing 'By Any Means Necessary': Reflections on Privatisation, Human Rights and Police Issues—Considerations for Australia and South Africa." *Australian Journal of Human Rights* 3, no. 2 (1997): 157–82.

Oc, Taner, and Steven Tiesdell. "Urban Design Approaches to Safer City Centres: The Fortress, the Panoptic, the Regulatory, and the Animated." In *Landscapes of Defense*, edited by John Gold and George Revill, 188–208. Harlow, UK: Pearson Educational Press, 2000.

O'Connor, Daniel, Randy Lippert, Dale Spencer and Lisa Smylie. "Seeing Private Security Like a State." *Criminology and Criminal Justice* 8, no. 2 (2008): 203–26.

Oluseyi, O. Fabiyi. "Analysis of Inter-Connectivity Levels of Urban Street Networks and Social Interactions in Enclosed Neighbourhoods in Johannesburg RSA." *Humanity & Social Sciences Journal* 1, no. 1 (2006): 79–95.

O'Malley, Patrick. "Policing Crime Risks in the Neo-Liberal Era." In *Crime, Risk and Justice*, edited by Kevin Stenson and Robert Sullivan, 89–103. Cullompton, UK: Willan Publishing, 2001.

———. "Risk and Responsibility." In *Foucault and Political Reason: Liberalism, Neo-liberalism, and Rationalities of Government*, edited by Nikolas Rose, Thomas Osborne, and Andrew Barry, 189–207. Chicago: University of Chicago Press, 1996.

———. "Risk, Power and Crime Prevention." *Economy & Society* 21, no. 3 (1992): 252–75.

O'Malley, Patrick, and Darren Palmer. "Post-Keynesian Policing." *Economy & Society* 25, no. 2 (1996): 137–55.

Ophir, Adi, Michal Givoni, and Sari Hanafi, eds. Introduction to *The Power of Inclusive Exclusion: Anatomy of Israeli Rule in the Occupied Palestinian Territories*, 15–30. New York: Zone Books, 2009.

Paasche, Till. "Creating Parallel Public Spaces through Private Governments: A South African Case Study." *South African Geographical Journal* 94, no. 1 (2012): 46–59.

Paasche, Till, Richard Yarwood, and James Sidaway. "Territorial Tactics: The Socio-Spatial Significance of Private Policing Strategies in Cape Town." *Urban Studies* 51, no. 8 (2014): 1559–75.

Packer, Jeremy. "Becoming Bombs: Mobilizing Mobility in the War on Terror." *Cultural Studies* 20, nos. 4–5 (2006): 378–99.

Palmer, Darren, and Ian Warren. "The Pursuit of Exclusion through Banning." *Australian and New Zealand Journal of Criminology* 47, no. 3 (2013): 429–46.

Pansters, Wil. "Zones of State-Making: Violence, Coercion, and Hegemony in Twentieth-Century Mexico." In *Violence, Coercion, and State-Making in Twentieth-Century Mexico:*

The Other Half of the Centaur, edited by Wil Pansters, 3–39. Palo Alto, CA: Stanford University Press, 2012.

Park, Robert. "The City: Suggestions for Investigation of Human Behavior in the Urban Environment." In *The City: Suggestions for Investigation of Human Behavior in the Urban Environment*, edited by Robert Park, Ernest Burgess, and Roderick McKenzie, 1–46. Chicago: University of Chicago Press, 1925.

Parker, Alexandra. *Urban Film and Everyday Practice: Bridging Divisions in Johannesburg*. South Bend, IN: University of Notre Dame Press, 2016.

Petersen, Eric. "The Life Cycle of Johannesburg Suburbs." In *Suburbanization in Global Society*, Research in Urban Sociology, vol. 10, edited by Mark Clapson and Ray Hutchison, 179–204. Bingley, UK: Emerald Group, 2010.

Pezzano, Antonio. "'Integration' or 'Selective Incorporation'? The Modes of Governance in Informal Trading Policy in the Inner City of Johannesburg." *Journal of Development Studies* 52, no. 4 (2016): 498–513.

Piccato, Pablo. *City of Suspects: Crime in Mexico City, 1900–1931*. Durham, NC: Duke University Press, 2001.

Pile, Steve. *Real Cities: Modernity, Space and the Phantasmagoria of City Life*. Thousand Oaks, CA: Sage, 2005.

———. "The Un(known) City . . . or, an Urban Geography of What Lies Buried Below the Surface." In Borden, Kerr, and Rendell, with Pivaro, *Unknown City*, 262–79.

Pillay, Kris. "Repositioning the Private Security Industry in South Africa in the 21st Century." *Acta Criminologica* 14, no. 3 (2001): 66–74.

Pillay, Suren. "Crime, Community and the Governance of Violence in Post-Apartheid South Africa." *Politikon* 35, no. 2 (2008): 141–58.

Pinder, David. "Subverting Cartography: The Situationists and Maps of the City," *Environment and Planning A* 28, no. 3 (1996): 405–27.

Podalsky, Laura. *Specular City: Transforming Culture, Consumption, and Space in Buenos Aires, 1955–1973*. Philadelphia: Temple University Press, 2004.

Pow, Choon-Piew. "Consuming Private Security: Consumer Citizenship and Defensive Urbanism in Singapore." *Theoretical Criminology* 17, no. 2 (2013): 179–96.

Puck, Logan. "Uneasy Partners against Crime: The Ambivalent Relationship between the Police and the Private Security Industry in Mexico." *Latin American Politics and Society* 59, no. 1 (2017): 74–95.

Purcell, Mark. "Neighborhood Activism among Homeowners as a Politics of Space." *The Professional Geographer* 53, no. 2 (2001): 178–94.

Pyysiäinen, Jarkko, Darren Halpin, and Andrew Guilfoyle. "Neoliberal Governance and 'Responsibilization' of Agents: Reassessing the Mechanisms of Responsibility-Shift in Neoliberal Discursive Environments." *Distinktion: Journal of Social Theory* 18, no. 2 (2017): 215–35.

Raban, Jonathan. *Soft City: A Documentary Exploration of Metropolitan Life*. London: Picador, 1974.

Radin, Margaret Jane. *Contested Commodities*. Cambridge, MA: Harvard University Press, 1996.

Ramadan, Adam, and Sara Fregonese. "Hybrid Sovereignty and the State of Exception in the Palestinian Refugee Campus in Lebanon." *Annals of the American Association of Geographers* 107, no. 4 (2017): 949–63.

Rapoport, Michele. "Being a Body or Having One: Automated Domestic Technologies and Corporeality." *AI & Society: Journal of Knowledge, Culture, and Communication* 28 (2013): 209–18.

———. "Domestic Surveillance Technologies and a New Visibility." In *Rethinking Surveillance and Control: Beyond the "Security versus Privacy" Debate,* edited by Elisa Orrù, Maria Grazia Porcedda, and Sebastian Weydner-Volkmann, 217–38. Baden-Baden, DE: Nomos, 2017.

———. "The Home under Surveillance: A Tripartite Assemblage." *Surveillance & Society* 10, nos. 3/4 (2012): 320–33.

Reichman, Nancy. "Managing Crime Risks: Towards an Insurance Based Model of Social Control." *Research in Law and Social Control* 8 (1986): 151–72.

Reiner, Robert. "Policing a Postmodern Society." *Modern Law Review* 55, no. 5 (1992): 761–78.

Rendell, Jane. "'Bazaar Beauties' or 'Pleasure Is Our Pursuit': A Spatial Story of Exchange." In Borden, Kerr, and Rendell, with Pivaro, *Unknown City,* 104–21.

Rigakos, George. "Hyperpanoptics as Commodity: The Case of the Parapolice." *Canadian Journal of Sociology/Cahiers Canadiens de Sociologie* 24, no. 1 (1999): 381–409.

———. *The New Parapolice: Risk Markets and Commodified Social Control.* Toronto: University of Toronto Press, 2002.

Rigakos, George, and David Greener. "Bubbles of Governance: Private Policing and the Law of Canada." *Canadian Journal of Law and Society* 15, no. 1 (2000): 145–85.

Robins, Kevin. "Prisoners of the City: Whatever Could a Postmodern City Be?" In *Space and Place: Theories of Identity and Location,* edited by Erica Carter, James Donald, and Judith Squires, 303–30. London: Laurence & Wishart, 1993.

Rodgers, Dennis. "The State as a Gang: Conceptualizing the Governmentality of Violence in Contemporary Nicaragua." *Critique of Anthropology* 26, no. 3 (2006): 315–30.

Rogerson, Christian. "Progressive Rhetoric, Ambiguous Policy Pathways: Street Trading in Inner-City Johannesburg, South Africa." *Local Economy* 31, nos. 1–2 (2016): 204–18.

Roitman, Janet. *Fiscal Disobedience: An Anthropology of Economic Regulation in Central Africa.* Princeton, NJ: Princeton University Press, 2005.

Rose, Nikolas. "Governing 'Advanced' Liberal Democracies." In *Foucault and Political Reason: Liberalism, Neo-Liberalism, and Rationalities of Government,* edited by Andrew Barry, Thomas Osborne, and Nikolas Rose, 37–64. Chicago: University of Chicago Press, 1996.

———. "Governing Cities, Governing Citizenship." In *Democracy, Citizenship and the Global City,* edited by Engin Isin, 95–101. New York: Routledge, 2000.

———. "Government and Control." *British Journal of Criminology* 40, no. 2 (2000): 321–39.

———. *Powers of Freedom: Reframing Political Thought.* Cambridge, UK: Cambridge University Press, 1999.

Ruddick, Susan. *Young and Homeless in Hollywood: Mapping Social Identities.* New York: Routledge, 1996.

Rude, George. Introduction to *The Great Fear of 1789: Rural Panic in Revolutionary France*, by Georges Lefebvre, ix–xvi. Princeton, NJ: Princeton University Press, 1982.

Rundell, John. "Imagining Cities, Others: Strangers, Contingency and Fear." *Thesis Eleven* 121, no. 1 (2014): 9–22.

Salter, Mark. "The Global Airport: Managing Space, Speed, and Security." In *Politics at the Airport*, edited by Mark Salter, 1–28. Minneapolis: University of Minnesota Press, 2008.

———. "When the Exception Becomes the Rule: Borders, Sovereignty, and Citizenship." *Citizenship Studies* 12, no. 4 (2008): 365–80.

Samara, Tony Roshan. "Order and Security in the City: Producing Race and Policing Neoliberal Spaces in South Africa." *Ethnic and Racial Studies* 33, no. 4 (2010): 637–55.

———. "Policing Development: Urban Renewal as Neo-Liberal Security Strategy." *Urban Studies* 47, no. 1 (2010): 197–214.

———. "State Security in Transition: The War on Crime in Post-Apartheid South Africa." *Social Identities* 9, no. 2 (2003): 277–312.

Sampson, Robert, and Stephen Raudenbush. "Seeing Disorder: Neighborhood Stigma and the Social Construction of 'Broken Windows.'" *Social Psychology Quarterly* 67, no. 4 (2004): 319–42.

Samuel, Raphael. "Reading the Signs." *History Workshop* 32 (1991): 88–109.

Scandura, Jani. *Down in the Dumps: Place, Modernity, American Depression*. Durham, NC: Duke University Press, 2008.

Scharg, William. "Bombs, Bungles and Politic Transformation: When Is the SAPS Going to Get Smarter?" In *Crime Wave: The South African Underworld and Its Foes*, edited by Jonny Steinberg, 50–64. Johannesburg: Witwatersrand University Press, 2001.

Scheper-Hughes. Nancy. "Dangerous and Endangered Youth: Social Structures and Determinants of Violence." *Annals New York Academy of Sciences* 1036 (2004): 13–46.

———. *Death without Weeping: The Violence of Everyday Life in Brazil*. Berkeley: University of California Press, 1992.

Schofield, Barry. "Partners in Power: Governing the Self-Sustaining Community." *Sociology* 36, no. 3 (2002): 663–83.

Schönteich, Martin. "Fighting Crime with Private Muscle: The Private Sector and Crime Prevention." *African Security Review* 8, no. 5 (1999): 65–75.

———. *Unshackling the Crime Fighters: Increasing Private Security Involvement in South Africa's Criminal Justice System*. Johannesburg: South African Institute of Race Relations, 1999.

Scott, Felicity. *Outlaw Territories: Environments of Insecurity/Architectures of Counterinsurgency*. Cambridge, MA: MIT Press, 2016.

Scott, James. *Seeing Like a State: How Certain Schemes to Improve the Human Condition Have Failed*. New Haven, CT: Yale University Press, 1998.

Scott, Thomas, and Marlys McPherson. "The Development of the Private Sector of the Criminal Justice System." *Law and Society Review* 6, no. 2 (1971): 267–88.

Segal, Rafi, David Tartakover, and Eyal Weizman, eds. *A Civilian Occupation: The Politics of Israeli Architecture*. New York: Verso, 2003.

Shamir, Boas, and Eyal Ben-Ar. "Challenges of Military Leadership in Changing Armies." *JPMS: Journal of Political and Military Sociology* 28, no. 1 (2000): 43–59.

Shaw, Mark. *Crime and Policing in Post-Apartheid South Africa: Transforming under Fire.* Bloomington: Indiana University Press, 2002.

———. "Crime, Police and Public in Transitional Societies." *Transformation* 49 (2002): 1–24.

Shearing, Clifford. "Nodal Governance." *Police Quarterly* 8, no. 1 (2005): 57–63.

———. "Policing: Relationships between Its Public and Private Forms." In *Alternative Policing Styles: Cross-Cultural Perspectives*, edited by Mark Findlay and Uglješa Zvekić, 203–28. Cambridge, MA: Kluwer Law and Taxation Publishers, 1993.

Shearing, Clifford, and Philip Stenning. "Modern Private Security: Its Growth and Implications." *Crime & Justice* 3 (1981): 193–245.

———. "Private Security: Implications for Social Control." *Social Problems* 30, no. 5 (1983): 493–506.

———. "Snowflakes or Good Pinches? Private Security's Contribution to Modern Policing." In *The Maintenance of Order in Society*, edited by Rita Donelan, 96–105. Ottawa: Canadian Police College, 1982.

Shearing, Clifford, and Jennifer Wood. "Nodal Governance, Democracy, and the New 'Denizens.'" *Journal of Law and Society* 30, no. 3 (2003): 400–419.

Shearing, Clifford, and Jennifer Wood (in collaboration with John Cartwright and Madeleine Jenneker). "Nodal Governance, Denizenship & Communal Space: Challenging the Westphalian Ideal." In *Limits to Liberation after Apartheid: Citizenship, Governance & Culture*, edited by Steven Robins, 97–112. Athens: Ohio University Press, 2005.

Sheptycki, James. "Book Review: A. Crawford, S. Lister, S. Blackburn and J. Burnett, *Plural Policing: The Mixed Economy of Visible Patrols in England and Wales.*" *Social Legal Studies* 17, no. 1 (2008): 147.

———. "Policing Postmodernism and Transnationalization." *British Journal of Criminology* 38, no. 3 (1998): 485–503.

Shields, Rob. "Social Spatialization and the Built Environment: The West Edmonton Mall." *Environment and Planning D* 7, no. 2 (1989): 147–64.

———. "Visualicity." *Visual Culture in Britain* 5, no. 1 (2004): 23–36.

Sidaway, James. "Enclave Space: A New Metageography of Development?" *Area* 39, no. 3 (2007): 331–39.

Sihlongonyane, Mfaniseni Fana. "The Rhetorical Devices for Marketing and Branding Johannesburg as a City: a Critical Review." *Environment & Planning A* 47, no. 10 (2015): 2134–52.

Simone, AbdouMaliq. "Straddling the Divides: Remaking Associational Life in the Informal City." *International Journal of Urban and Regional Research* 25, no. 1 (2001): 102–17.

Singh, Anne-Marie. *Policing and Crime Control in Post-Apartheid South Africa.* Burlington, VT: Ashgate, 2008.

———. "Private Security and Crime Control." *Theoretical Criminology* 9, no. 2 (2005): 153–74.

Slezkine, Yuri. *The Jewish Century.* Princeton, NJ: Princeton University Press, 2004.

Smit, Trudi, Karina Landman, and Christoffel Venter. "The Impact of Crime and Neighbourhood Enclosures on Travel Behaviour and Transport Patterns in South

Africa." In *Safety and Security in Transit Environments: Crime Prevention and Security Management*, edited by Vania Ceccato and Andrew Newton, 234–50. New York: Palgrave Macmillan, 2015.

Smith, Carl. *Urban Disorder and the Shape of Belief: The Great Chicago Fire, the Haymarket Bomb, and the Model Town of Pullman* (Chicago: University of Chicago Press, 1995).

Smith, Jay. "No More Language Games." *American Historical Review* 102, no. 5 (1997): 1413–40.

Smith, Neil. "Giuliani Time: The Revanchist 1990s." *Social Text* 57 (1998): 1–20.

———. "Social Justice and the New American Urbanism: The *Revanchist* City." In *The Urbanization of Injustice*, edited by Andy Merrifield and Erik Swyngedouw, 117–36. New York: New York University Press, 1997

Smith, Susan. "Police Accountability and Local Democracy." *Area* 18, no. 2 (1986): 99–107.

Soguk, Nevzat. *States and Strangers: Refugees and Displacements* (Minneapolis: University of Minnesota Press, 1998).

Sparks, Richard. "States of Insecurity: Punishment, Populism and Contemporary Political Culture." In *The Use of Punishment*, edited by Seán McConville, 149–74. Cullompton, UK: Willan, 2003).

Sparks, Richard, Evi Girling, and Ian Loader. "Fear and Everyday Urban Lives." *Urban Studies* 38, nos. 5–6 (2001): 885–98.

Spiegel, Gabrielle. "History, Historicism, and the Social Logic of the Text in the Middle Ages." *Speculum* 65, no. 1 (1990): 59–86.

Steinberg, Jonny. "Crime Prevention Goes Abroad: Policy Transfer and Policing in Post-Apartheid South Africa." *Theoretical Criminology* 15, no. 4 (2011): 349–64.

———. *Thin Blue: The Unwritten Rules of Policing South Africa*. Cape Town: Jonathan Ball, 2008.

Steinberg, Jonny, and Monique Marks. "The Labyrinth of Jewish Security Arrangements in Johannesburg: Thinking through a Paradox about Security." *British Journal of Criminology* 54, no. 2 (2014)" 244–59.

Stenning, Phillip. "Governance and Accountability in a Plural Policing Environment: The Story So Far." *Policing* 3, no. 1 (2009): 22–33.

———. "Powers and Accountability of Private Police." *European Journal on Criminal Policy and Research* 8, no. 3 (2000): 325–52.

Stenson, Kevin. "Community Policing as Governmental Technology." *Economy & Society* 22, no. 3 (1993): 373–89.

———. "Crime Control, Governmentality and Sovereignty." In *Governable Places: Readings on Governmentality and Crime Control*, edited by Russell Smandych, 45–73. Aldershot, United Kingdom: Dartmouth, 1999.

Super, Gail. *Governing through Crime in South Africa: The Politics of Race and Class in Neoliberalizing Regimes*. New ed. New York: Routledge, 2016.

———. "The Spectacle of Crime in the 'New' South Africa: A Historical Perspective (1976–2004)." *British Journal of Criminology* 50, no. 2 (2010): 165–84.

———. "Volatile Sovereignty: Governing Crime through the Community in Khayelitsha." *Law and Society Review* 50, no. 2 (2016): 450–83.

Svendson, Lars. *A Philosophy of Fear*. London: Reaktion, 2008.

Swanson, Kate. "Revanchist Urbanism Heads South: The Regulation of Indigenous Beggars and Street Vendors in Ecuador." *Antipode* 39, no. 4 (2007): 708–28.

Swanson, Maynard. "Sanitation Syndrome: Bubonic Plague and Urban Native Policy in the Cape Colony, 1900–1909," *Journal of African History* 18, no. 3 (1977): 387–410.

Thomas, W. I., and D. S. Thomas. *The Child in America: Behavior Problems and Programs*. New York: Knopf, 1928.

Thrift, Nigel. "Movement-Space: The Changing Domain of Thinking Resulting from the Development of New Kinds of Spatial Awareness." *Economy & Society* 33, no. 4 (2004): 582–604.

Thumala, Angélica, Benjamin Goold, and Ian Loader. "A Tainted Trade? Moral Ambivalence and Legitimation Work in the Private Security Industry." *British Journal of Sociology* 62, no. 2 (2011): 283–303.

Ticktin, Miriam. "Policing and Humanitarianism in France: Immigration and the Turn to Law as State of Exception." *Interventions* 7, no. 3 (2005): 346–68.

Tijerino, Roger. "Civil Spaces: A Critical Perspective of Defensible Space." *Journal of Architectural and Planning Research* 15, no. 4 (1998): 321–37.

Tilly, Nick. "Privatizing Crime Control." *The Annals of the American Academy of Political and Social Science* 679, no. 1 (2018): 55–71.

Todes, Alison, Dylan Weakley, and Philip Harrison. "Densifying Johannesburg: Context, Policy and Diversity." *Journal of Housing and the Built Environment* 33, no. 2 (2018): 281–99.

Tomlinson, Richard, Robert Beauregard, Lindsay Bremner, and Xolela Mangcu, eds. *Emerging Johannesburg: Perspectives on the Post-Apartheid City*. New York, Routledge, 2003.

Tonkiss, Fran. "The Ethics of Indifference: Community and Solitude in the City." *International Journal of Cultural Studies* 6, no. 3 (2003): 297–311.

Tosa, Hiroyuki. "Anarchical Governance: Neoliberal Governmentality in Resonance with the State of Exception." *International Political Sociology* 3, no. 4 (2009): 414–30.

Trudeau, Dan. "Towards a Relational View of the Shadow State." *Political Geography* 27, no. 6 (2008): 669–90.

Tshehla, Boyane. "Barricaded in the Suburbs: Private Security via Road Closures." *South African Crime Quarterly* 6 (2003): 17–20.

Tulumello, Simone. "From 'Spaces of Fear' to 'Fearscapes': Mapping for Re-Framing Theories about the Spatialization of Fear in Urban Space." *Space and Culture* 18, no. 3 (2015): 257–72.

Turner, Bryan. "The Enclave Society: Towards a Sociology of Immobility." *European Journal of Social Theory* 10, no. 2 (2007): 287–304.

Valverde, Mariana. "Practices of Citizenship and Scales of Governance." *New Criminal Law Review* 13, no. 2 (2010): 216–40.

———. "Targeted Governance and the Problem of Desire." In *Risk and Morality*, edited by Richard Victor Ericson and Aaron Doyle, 438–58. Toronto: University of Toronto Press, 2003.

Van Buuren, Jelle. *Security as a Commodity: The Ethical Dilemmas of Private Security Services*. INEX Policy Brief, paper 6. Oslo: International Peace Research Institute, 2010.

Van Graan, Johan. "Multi-Sector Cooperation in Preventing Crime: The Case of a

South African Neighbourhood Watch as an Effective Crime Prevention Model." *Police Practice and Research* 17, no. 2 (2016): 136–48.

Van Steden, Ronald, Jennifer Wood, Clifford Shearing, and Hans Boutellier. "The Many Faces of Nodal Policing: Team Play and Improvisation in Dutch Community Safety." *Security Journal* 29, no. 3 (2016): 327–39.

Vidler, Anthony. *The Architectural Uncanny: Essays in the Modern Unhomely.* Cambridge, MA: MIT Press, 1992.

———. *Warped Space: Art, Architecture, and Anxiety in Modern Culture.* Cambridge, MA: MIT Press, 2001.

Vigneswaran, Darshan. "The Contours of Disorder: Crime Maps and Territorial Policing in South Africa." *Environment and Planning D: Society and Space* 31, no. 1 (2014): 91–107.

———. "Protection and Conviviality: Community Policing in Johannesburg." *European Journal of Cultural Studies* 17, no. 4 (2014): 471–86.

Virilio, Paul. *City of Panic.* Translated by Julie Rose. New York: Berg, 2005.

———. *Popular Defence and Ecological Struggles.* New York: Semiotext(e), 1990.

———. *The Vision Machine.* Translated by Julie Rose. Bloomington: Indiana University Press, 1994.

Vitale, Alex. "Innovation and Institutionalization: Factors in the Development of 'Quality of Life' Policing in New York City." *Policing & Society* 15, no. 2 (2005): 99–124.

Von Schnitzler, Antina. *Democracy's Infrastructure: Techno-Politics and Protest after Apartheid.* Princeton, NJ: Princeton University Press, 2016.

Vukov, Tamara, and Mimi Sheller. "Border Work: Surveillant Assemblages, Virtual Fences, and Tactical Counter-Media." *Social Semiotics* 23, no. 2 (2013): 225–41.

Wakefield, Alison. *Selling Security: The Private Policing of Public Space.* Cullompton, UK: Willan, 2003.

Wang, Jackie. *Carceral Capitalism.* South Pasadena, CA: Semiotext(e), 2018.

Warren, Robert. "Situating the City and September 11th: Military Urban Doctrine, 'Pop-Up' Armies and Spatial Chess." *International Journal of Urban and Regional Research* 26, no. 3 (2002): 614–19.

Waters, Chris. "'Dark Strangers' in Our Midst: Discourses of Race and Nation in Britain, 1947–1963." *Journal of British Studies* 36, no. 2 (1997): 207–38.

Watts, Michael. "Antinomies of Community: Some Thoughts on Geography, Resources, and Empire." *Transactions of the Institute of British Geographers* 29, no. 2 (2004): 195–216.

Weber, Cynthia, and Mark Lacy. "Securing by Design." *Review of International Studies* 37, no. 3 (2011): 1021–43.

Wedeen, Lisa. "Seeing Like a Citizen, Acting Like a State: Exemplary Events in Unified Yemen." *Comparative Studies in Society and History* 45, no. 4 (2003): 680–713.

Weizman, Eyal. *Hollow Land: Israel's Architecture of Occupation.* New York: Verso, 2007.

White, Adam. "The New Political Economy of Private Security." *Theoretical Criminology* 16, no. 1 (2012): 85–101.

———. *The Politics of Private Security: Regulation, Reform and Re-Legitimation* (New York: Palgrave Macmillan, 2010).

White, Louise. *Speaking with Vampires: Rumor and History in Colonial Africa*. Berkeley: University of California Press, 2000.

———. "Vampire Priests of Central Africa: African Debates about Labor and Religion in Colonial Northern Zambia." *Comparative Studies in Society and History* 35, no. 4 (1993): 746–47.

Wickham, Chris. "Gossip and Resistance among the Medieval Peasantry," *Past & Present* 160 (1998): 3–24.

Williams, Raymond. *Keywords*. Oxford, UK: Oxford University Press, 1973.

Williams, Richard. *The Anxious City*. New York: Routledge, 2004.

Wilson, James Q., and George Kelling. "Broken Windows: The Police and Neighborhood Safety." *Atlantic Monthly* 249, no. 3 (1982): 29–37.

Wisler, Dominique, and Ihekwoaba Onwudiwe. "Community Policing in Comparison." *Police Quarterly* 11, no. 4 (2008): 427–46.

Wolch, Jennifer. "The Shadow State: Transformations in the Voluntary Sector." In *The Power of Geography*, edited by Jennifer Wolch and Michael Dear, 197–221. Boston: Unwin Hyman, 1989.

Wollen, Peter. "*Blade Runner*: 'Ridleyville' and Los Angeles." In *The Hieroglyphics of Space: Reading and Experiencing the Modern Metropolis*, edited by Neil Leach, 236–43. New York: Routledge, 2002.

Wood, Jennifer, and Clifford Shearing. *Imagining Security*. New York: Routledge, 2007.

Yang, Arnand. "'A Conversation of Rumors': The Language of Popular *Mentalités* in Late Nineteenth-Century Colonial India." *Journal of Social History* 20, no. 3 (1987): 485–505.

Yarwood, Richard. "An Exclusive Countryside? Crime Concern, Social Exclusion and Community Policing in Two English Villages." *Policing and Society* 20, no. 1 (2010): 61–78.

———. "The Geographies of Policing." *Progress in Human Geography* 31, no. 4 (2007): 447–65.

Yarwood, Richard, and Bill Edwards. "Voluntary Action in Rural Areas: The Case of Neighbourhood Watch." *Journal of Rural Studies* 11, no. 4 (1995): 447–59.

Young, Iris Marion. "House and Home: Feminist Variations on a Theme." Chap. 7 in *Intersecting Voices: Dilemmas of Gender, Political Philosophy, and Policy*. Princeton, NJ: Princeton University Press, 1997.

———. *Justice and the Politics of Difference*. Princeton, NJ: Princeton University Press, 1990.

Young, Jock. *The Exclusive Society: Social Exclusion, Crime and Difference in Late Modernity*. London: Sage, 1999.

———. *The Vertigo of Late Modernity*. Thousand Oaks, CA: Sage, 2007.

Zaloom, Caitlin. "The Productive Life of Risk." *Cultural Anthropology* 19, no. 3 (2004): 365–91.

Zedner, Lucia. "The Concept of Security: An Agenda for Comparative Analysis." *Legal Studies* 23, no. 1 (2003): 153–75.

———. "Liquid Security: Managing the Market for Crime Control." *Criminology & Criminal Justice* 6, no. 3 (2006): 267–88.

———. "Policing before and after the Police." *British Journal of Criminology* 46, no. 1 (2006): 78–96.

———. "Pre-Crime and Post-Criminology." *Theoretical Criminology* 11, no. 2 (2007): 261–81.

———. "The Pursuit of Security." In *Crime, Risk, and Insecurity*, edited by Tim Hope and Richard Sparks, 200–214. London: Routledge, 2000.

———. *Security.* New York: Routledge, 2009.

———. "Security, the State, and the Citizen: The Changing Architecture of Crime Control." *New Criminal Law Review* 13, no. 2 (2010): 379–403.

———. "Too Much Security?" *International Journal of the Sociology of Law* 31, no. 3 (2003): 155–84.

Zivin, Erin Graff. *The Wandering Signifier: Rhetoric of Jewishness in the Latin American Imaginary.* Durham, NC: Duke University Press 2008.

Zukin, Sharon. "Space and Symbols in an Age of Decline." In *Re-presenting the City*, edited by Anthony King, 43–59. New York: Macmillan, 1996.

Zurawski, Niles. "Video Surveillance and Everyday Life: Assessments of Closed-Circuit Television and the Cartography of Socio-Spatial Imaginations." *International Criminal Justice Review* 17, no. 4 (2007): 269–88.

Newspapers, Magazines, and Television Sources

Anonymous, "City Fears Fuel Security Boom," *Cape Argus* (Cape Town), 24 May 2001.

———. "Crime Comes Calling." *Cape Argus* (Cape Town), 26 May 1999.

———. "Crime in South Africa: It Won't Go Away," *Economist* (London), 1 October 2009.

———. "The Fight against Crime Has a New Face." *Sunday Independent* (Johannesburg), 4 May 2002.

———. "Get Municipal Permission for Boom Gate." *SAPA* (Johannesburg), 9 January 2003.

———. "Government Use of Crime Statistics Undermines Credibility." *Business Day* (Johannesburg), 10 February 1998.

———. "If You Get Mugged, Don't Bother Reporting It." *The Star* (Johannesburg), 2 May 1998.

———. "Mufamadi Explains Crime-Count Disparity." *The Star* (Johannesburg), 6 March 1998.

———. "Observatory Residents on the Warpath against Crime." *Northeastern Tribune* (Observatory, Johannesburg), 5 November 2014.

———. "Press, Opposition Challenge Crime Statistics." *BBC Worldwide Monitoring* (London), 7 February 2001.

———. "South Africa 'a Country at War' as Murder Rate Soars to Nearly 49 a Day." *The Guardian* (London), 29 September 2015.

———. "South Africa: Murder and Siege Architecture." *The Economist* (London), 15 July 1995, 27–28.

Araie, Farouk. "Crime Out of Control." *Saturday Star* (Johannesburg), 27 March 2017.

Badat, Noor-Jehan Yoro. "Residents Angry over Costly Booms." *The Star* (Johannesburg), 27 June 2003.

Bailey, Candice. "Gangs Attack Parents." *Argus Weekend* (Cape Town), 1 February 2009.

Baldauf, Scott. "Backstory: In South Africa, Home Sweet Fortress." *The Christian Science Monitor*, 6 December 2006.

Bega, Sheree. "Feeling Safe in Saxonwold." *The Star* (Johannesburg), 22 September 2012.

———. "Our Booms Are Saving Lives." *Saturday Star* (Johannesburg), 22 May 2012.

Bisschoff, Fred. "Closures: Reason behind Low Crime." *Citizen* (Pretoria), 24 July 2003.

Brown, Patricia Leigh. "Designs for a Land of Bombs and Guns." *New York Times*, 28 May 1995.

Butcher, Tim. "Black Vigilantes Dispense Rough Justice at a Price." *Telegraph* (London), 25 June 2001.

Calvert, Scott. "In Johannesburg Suburbs, an Obsession with Security." *Baltimore Sun*, 22 May 2005.

Cauvin, Henri. "Homegrown Guards." *New York Times*, 9 October 2001.

Citizen Reporter. "57 South Africans Murdered a Day—Crime Statistics." *The Citizen* (Pretoria), 11 September 2018.

Cohen, Margot. "Gated Communities at Loggerheads." *Financial Mail* (Johannesburg), 6 July 2001.

Collins, Gary. "Back to the *Laager* for Joburg's Rich Suburbs." *Sunday Times* (Johannesburg), 19 May 1996.

Conley, Euan. "South Africa: A Really Attractive White-Collar Crime Venue for Criminals." *Global Investigations Review* (New York), 13 October 2016.

Cox, Anna. "Boom Doom Looms in Gloomy Joburg Suburbs." *Saturday Star* (Johannesburg), 11 April 2003.

———. "Boom Time for Sandton Has Motorists Outraged." *Saturday Star* (Johannesburg), 25 October 2002.

———. "Can Road Barriers Bring Down the Crime Rate?" *The Star* (Johannesburg), 12 July 2004.

———. "Charges Could Spell Boom Doom in Joburg." *The Star* (Johannesburg), 10 April 2003.

———. "City of Joburg Was 'Wrong to Remove Booms.'" The Star (Johannesburg), 21 December 2016.

———. "Closed-Off Roads Are Dividing Communities." *The Star*, (Johannesburg), 23 March 2004.

———. "Electric Fence Switched On." *The Star* (Johannesburg), 10 April 2001.

———. "Electric Fence Switched On—For a Day." *The Star* (Johannesburg), 11 April 2001.

———. "Gloom Looms as Booms Look Doomed," *The Star* (Johannesburg), 11 July 2003.

———. "High-Voltage Drama Surrounds 'Crime Cage.'" *The Star* (Johannesburg), 9 April 2001.

———. "Houghton Residents Raise R7,5m in Bid to Boost War on Crime." *The Star* (Johannesburg), 23 October 2007.

———. "Joburg Aims to Bring All Illegal Booms Down." *The Star* (Johannesburg), 13 September 2002.

———. "Joburg Booms: The Full Story." *The Star* (Johannesburg), 27 November 2004.

———. "Joburg Road Closures Are About to Take Off with a Boom Again." *The Star* (Johannesburg), 24 February 2011.

———. "'Laager Suburb' Must Drop Barriers." *The Star* (Johannesburg), 12 June 2000.

———. "Legal Action Threatened in Road Closure Row." *The Star* (Johannesburg), 7 April 2003.

———. "More Suburbs Want Fences and Booms," *The Star* (Johannesburg), 23 March 1998.

———. "Posh Suburb Targets Road-Closure Opponent." *The Star* (Johannesburg), 17 March 2004.

———. "Road Closure Is a Violation of My Rights." *The Star* (Johannesburg), 3 April 2003.

———. "Sandhurst Residents Face Trial over Booms." *The Star* (Johannesburg), 24 July 2003.

———. "Security Booms Can Be the Death of You." *The Star* (Johannesburg), 27 July 2004.

———. "Security Business in Melville Just Booming." *The Star* (Johannesburg), 24 April 2001.

———. "Suburban Boom Gates Policy Approved." *The Star* (Johannesburg), 3 February 2014.

Cox, Anna, and Chimaimba Banda. "Bang Go Those Booms if Joburg Gets Its Way." *The Star* (Johannesburg), 31 March 2003.

Cox, Anna, and Ndivhuwo Khangale. "Johannesburg Authorises Pointless Boom Gates." *The Star* (Johannesburg), 29 November 2004.

De Lange, Ilse. "Inmate Set for R200K Private Prison Payout." *The Citizen* (Pretoria), 19 May 2016.

Diale, Lerato. "Cap Creating a Culture of Safety First." *The Star* (Johannesburg), 11 November 2011.

Dirmeik, Beverley. "Others Would Do Well to Follow Our Lead." *Sunday Times* (Johannesburg), 21 October 2007.

DuPlessis, Carlen. "Private Security Costs Cops 121m Rands." *The Star* (Johannesburg), 14 March 2009.

Eliseev, Alex. "Cop Held over Guns for Guards." *The Star* (Johannesburg), 4 December 2009.

Eloff, Corné. "Understanding Trio Robbery Crimes through Spatial Analysis." *PositionIT* (November/December 2010): 48–49.

Epstein, Helen. "The Mystery of AIDS in South Africa," *New York Review of Books*, 20 July 2000, 50–51.

Etheridge, Jenna. "How South Africans Are Fighting Crime in Their Hoods—With an App." *News24* (Johannesburg), 9 July 2015.

Eybers, Christa. "Suspect Dies after Shoot-Out during Randburg Cash-in-Transit Heist." *Eyewitness News* (Johannesburg), 6 March 2018.

Fife, Ian. "The Rich Make Mischief." *Financial Mail* (Johannesburg), 18 April 2003, 50–51.

———. "Storming the Barricades." *Financial Mail* (Johannesburg), 28 July 2000.

Forrest, Drew. "Reasons for Alarmist Fantasies Abound." *Business Day* (Johannesburg), 29 May 1998.

Fourie, Chantelle, and Citizen Reporter. "Dramatic Footage of Northcliff Shootout." *The Citizen* (Pretoria), 5 July 2018.

Gilford, Gill. "Cap Patrol Unit Comes to the Rescue of a Victim." *The Star* (Johannesburg), 11 September 2007.

———. "Communities Don Crime-Prevention Cap." *The Star* (Johannesburg), 11 September 2007.

Gous, Nico. "US, Canada, Britain Warn about Travelling to South Africa after Crime Stats Release." *Sowetan*, 14 September 2018.

Gruzd, Steven. "White-Collar Crime Thrives When Ethics Aren't Enforced." *South African Jewish Report* (Johannesburg), 15 March 2018.

Haffajee, Ferial. "Suburbs Search for Better Private Security Service." *Financial Mail* (Johannesburg), 8 September 2000.

Hans, Bongani. "Privatizing Prison 'Was a Huge Mistake.'" *Business Day* (Johannesburg), 6 November 2013.

Harrison, Rebecca. "Witness: Pizza and Machetes: Living with Crime in Johannesburg." *Reuters* (New York), 19 April 2007.

Hartley, Wyndham. "Ndebele Acknowledges Failure of Private Prisons." *Business Day* (Johannesburg), 6 November 2013.

Heckl, Gundrun. "Boom Gloom: The War between Residents of Two of Johannesburg's Wealthier Suburbs over Illegal Road Closure." *Sunday Times* (Johannesburg), 23 February 2003.

Hosken, Graeme. "Fear Rules Joburg, but Cape Town Is Murder Capital." *Sunday Times* (Johannesburg), 29 June 2016.

Hosken, Graeme, and Candice Bailey. "Schools Use Private Firms for Security after Spate of Attacks." *Pretoria News*, 31 January 2009.

Ingram, Amy. "Do You Know How to Apply for a Boom Gate?" *Roodeport Northsider*, 7 March 2017.

Jacobs, C. "Locking Out the Criminals." *Sunday Times* (Johannesburg), 10 May 1998.

Jagmohan, Karinda, and Kwanda Njoli. "Citizens Spend R160bn on SAPS, Private Security." *Weekend Argus* (Cape Town), 16 September 2018.

Johnson, R. W. "Nobel Writer Nadine Gordimer Attacked and Robbed." *Sunday Times* (London), 29 October 2006.

Johnson, R. W., and Irina Filatova. "Analysis: Foreign Investors Threatened." *United Press International* (New York), 6 October 2001.

Jones, Felicity. "Ratepayers Have a Right to Safety." *The Star* (Johannesburg), 8 July 2003.

Joommal A. S. K. "Crime Decrease Claims Are Myths Designed to Lull the Public." *The Star* (Johannesburg), 28 February 1998.

Jordaan, Nomahlubi. "Three of Joburg's Police Districts Record Increase in Murders." *Sunday Times* (Johannesburg), 8 May 2018.

Jordan, Bobby. "Israel's Holy Warrior." *Sunday Times* (Johannesburg), 8 March 2009.

Karvelas, Nick. "Don't Restrict Our Freedom of Movement." *The Star* (Johannesburg), 1 July 2003.

Kelion, Leo. "African Firm Is Selling Pepper-Spray Bullet Firing Drones." *BBC News* (London), 18 June 2014.

Kempen, Annalise. "Private Security Alignment Initiative." *Servamus* (Johannesburg), 102, no. 1 (2009): 28–32.

Khangale, Ndivhuwo, and Anna Cox. "Moment of Truth Arrives for Illegal Booms." *The Star* (Johannesburg), 18 July 2003.

Laing, Aislinn. "Crime Is Never Far Away from You in Johannesburg." *The Telegraph* (London), 11 July 2015.

Lamont, James. "Concern at S. Africa Security Sector Plan." *Financial Times* (London), 4 October 2001.

Lewis, Rita. "A Big 'Yes' for a Glenhazel CID." *South African Jewish Report* (Johannesburg), 11, no. 42 (16 November 2007).

Mabena, Sipho. "South Africans Spending More than the Police Budget on Own Security." *Sunday Times* (Johannesburg), 15 February 2017.

Madondo, Bongani. "Send Task Force to Save Hillbrow!" *City Press* (Johannesburg), 20 April 1997.

Mahr, Krista. "High South African Crime Rates and Low Faith in Police Boost Private Security in Gauteng." *Financial Times* (London), 12 May 2017.

Mathibela, Thandiwe. "Please Fence Us In!" *Sunday Times* (Johannesburg), 27 May 2001.

Mbangeni, Lerato. "Attacked at Home, Then Let Down by Police." *The Star* (Johannesburg), 30 April 2015.

Mbanjwa, Xolani. "Experts in Limbo about New Anti-Crime Plan." *The Star* (Johannesburg), 31 October 2008.

Meldrum, Andrew. "Gordimer's Sorrow for Men Who Robbed Her." *The Guardian* (London), 2 November 2006.

Melville, I. C. S. "There Is No Such Thing as an Open City." *The Star* (Johannesburg), 27 June 2003.

Miller, Andie. "Walking the Talk." *Sunday Independent* (Johannesburg), 28 September 2008.

Mkhulisi, Mfundekelwa. "We Must Rein in Security Firms." *Sowetan*, 2 September 2010.

Moodie, Gill. "Crime Wave Robs Some, Pays Others." *Sunday Times* (Johannesburg), 22 July 2001.

Morris, Michael. "Rulebook to Check Blocking of Streets," *Cape Argus* (Cape Town), 23 January 2003.

Moshatama, Benjamin, and Isaac Mahlangu. "Coughing Up for Crime." *Sunday Times* (Johannesburg), 12 October 2007.

Mothibi, Nano. "Removal of Booms Angers Joburg Residents." *The Star* (Johannesburg), 25 July 2003.

Mqadi, Sinikiwe. "City of Joburg Ordered to Restore Security Boom Gates." *702 Radio* (Johannesburg), 21 December 2016.

Mufweba, Yolanda. "The Boom Comes Down on Illegal Road Closures." *The Star* (Johannesburg), 11 July 2003.

Mulholland, Stephen. "Crime Is a Problem for the Whole Country, Mr Mbeki." *The Star* (Johannesburg), 13 June 1999.

Nair, Nivashni. "First Food, Then Private Security." *The Times* (Johannesburg), 20 July 2015.

Ndlangisa, Sabelo. "Booming Battle Looms over Bid to Seal off Suburbs." *Sunday Times* (Johannesburg), 2 September 2001.

———. "Boom Town Blues." *Sunday Times* (Johannesburg), 18 May 2003.

Ngalo, Aphiwe, and Hlumela Dyantyi. "Murder, Attempted Murder and Robbery the Three Biggest Headaches for SAPS." *Daily Maverick*, 29 September 2018.

Ngqakamba, Sesona. "Joburg Man Gets Six Months for False Reporting of a Hyjacking." *News24* (Johannesburg), 20 June 2018.

Nkosi-Malobane, Sizakele. "Community Policing Relations Key to Safety." *Saturday Star* (Johannesburg), 17 July 2018.

Nussey, Wilf. "After Apartheid, Hope and Decay." *Guardian Weekly* (London), 19 November 1995.

Nxumalo, Lethu. "Guards Save the Day." *Rosebank-Killarney Gazette*, 3 February 2017.

Ooza, Siyabulela. "Wall-to-Wall Security." *Financial Mail* (Johannesburg), 5 March 1999, 64.

Oppler, Sarah. "Partnership Policing Creates a United Front against Crime." *The Star* (Johannesburg), 15 March 1997.

Padayachee, Nicki. "In the Line of Fire." *Sunday Times* (Johannesburg), 25 March 2001.

———. "The Price of Feeling Safe in the Suburbs." *Sunday Times*, 9 April 2000.

Patrick, Alex. "Police Arrest Hijackers after Shootout in Joburg Suburb." *Sowetan Live*, May 15, 2017.

Piliso, Simpiwe. "Boom Blitz." *Sunday Times* (Johannesburg), 17 March 2002.

———. "Just How Safe Are You Behind Your Boom Gate?" *Sunday Times* (Johannesburg), 1 April 2001.

———. "Neighbour vs Neighbour." *Sunday Times* (Johannesburg), 4 March 2001.

———. "Oh No, You Don't." *Sunday Times* (Johannesburg), 15 September 2002.

———. "The Three Most Expensive Streets in Johannesburg." *Sunday Times* (Johannesburg), 8 July 2001.

Pillay, Verashni. "Hillbrow: Where Cops Do the Work for Drug Lords." *Mail & Guardian* (Johannesburg), 20 September 2013.

Quintal, Angela. "Police 'Buying Protection' from Private Firms." *The Star* (Johannesburg), 8 December 2004.

Radebe, Sibonelo. "'Orphan' Police Station Has Guardian," *Business Day* (Johannesburg), 2 June 1999.

Reynolds, T. "South Africa's Security Business Is Booming." *Pretoria News*, 24 July 2004.

Robinson, M. "Access Control Makes Suburbs Safe." *The Star* (Johannesburg), 8 July 2003.

Rodney, Derek. "It's Boom Time in a Suburb Once under Siege." *Sunday Times* (Johannesburg), 14 March 1999.

Rossouw, Sheree. "Living behind the Barricades." *Mail & Guardian* (Johannesburg), 12 January 2001.

Savides, Matthew. "Bullets Fly in 'Scary as Hell' Clash between Hijackers and Security Guards in Joburg." *Sunday Times* (Johannesburg), 8 July 2018.

Settipani, Anthony. "Spate of Attacks at Melville Koppies." *Saturday Star* (Johannesburg), 30 May 2015.

Shaw, Mark, and Antoinette Louw. "Government Risks Undermining the Credibility of Crime Statistics by Using Them for Its Own Ends." *Business Day* (Johannesburg), 2 October 1998.

Shorey, Richard. "Neighbourhood Watch." *Sunday Times* (Johannesburg), 14 January 2003.

Sithole, Sthembiso. "Armed Homeowners Kill Four Assailants." *The Star* (Johannesburg), 7 May 2018.

Skade, Thandi. "Homeowners Spend Bundles on Safety Features." *The Star* (Johannesburg), 26 February 2008.

———. "A Security Alarm That Attacks Intruders?" *IOL* (Johannesburg), 22 May 2009.

———. "Security Guards 'Won't Have Police Powers.'" *The Star* (Johannesburg), 30 October 2008.

———. "Should Private Guns Take Security into Their Hands? The Fine Line between Protection and Vigilantism." *The Star* (Johannesburg), 20 November 2007.

Smith, David. "Pepper-Spray Defence Means South Africa Robbers Face Loss of Balance at Cash Machines." *The Guardian* (London), 12 July 2009.

———. "Pepper-Spray Drone Offered to South African Mines for Strike Control." *The Guardian* (London), 20 June 2014.

Sobczak, Blake. "Lengthy Jail time for Melville Koppies Robbers." *The Star* (Johannesburg), 16 May 2011.

Sriskandarajah, Dhananjayan. "Both Rich and Poor Are Losing Faith in the State." *Mail & Guardian* (Johannesburg), 19 December 2014.

Staff Reporter. "Breaking News: Shootout between Guards and Robbers." *Randburg Sun*, 25 July 2015.

———. "Calm Needed in Security Storm." *Business Day* (Johannesburg), 8 October 2001.

———. "Christmas Drones' Flight Warning." *Saturday Star* (Johannesburg), 24 December 2016.

———. "Count Us Out! Walls Keep the Rich Safe from Census." *Sunday Times* (Johannesburg), 14 October 2001.

———. "Crime Buffers, or the New Apartheid?" *Cape Argus* (Cape Town), 10 July 2002.

———. "Crime Stats Figures Released." *The Citizen* (Pretoria), 19 September 2014.

———. "The Fight against Crime Has a New Face." *Sunday Independent* (Johannesburg), 4 May 2002.

———. "Foreign Investor Ban Bid Dropped." *Business Day* (Johannesburg), 11 October 2001;

———. "The Great Wall of Hyde Park." *Sunday Times* (Johannesburg), 5 August 2001.

———. "The Guardian Angel of Soweto." *Star Business Report* (Johannesburg), 23 May 1999.

———. "An Industry Hijacked." *The Economist* (London), 6 October 2001.

———. "iSentry Implemented in Craighall and Craighall Park." *Rosebank-Killarney Gazette*, 8 May 2015.

———. "It Pays to Support Private Security Initiatives." *Weekend Argus* (Cape Town), 16 February 2014.

———. "Project Calls on Former Cops, Soldiers." *The Star* (Johannesburg), 17 February 2009.

———. "Reign of Fear." *The Star* (Johannesburg), 14 October 2008.

———. "Rioters and Police Clash in Johannesburg Protest." *Associated Press* (New York), 9 May 2017.

———. "Sandringham Grows in Size and Popularity." *The Star* (Johannesburg), 22 June 2013.

———. "SA Security Gates Torn Down." *BBC News* (UK edition), 25 July 2003.

———. "Security Company Director Arrested." *The Citizen* (Pretoria), 15 November 2007.

———. "Small Security Firms Endangered." *Star Business Report* (Johannesburg), 23 May 1999.

———. "South African Jews to Fund Johannesburg Police Station." *Jewish Telegraphic Agency* (Johannesburg), 21 April 1997.

———. "Tear Down Booms, or We'll Do It for You." *Sunday Independent* (Johannesburg), 22 November 2002.

———. "Two Suspected Hijackers Shot Dead in Riverlea." *E News Channel Africa* (Johannesburg), 19 November 2016.

———. "Trendy Melville Wants the Nightlife without the Lowlife." *Sunday Times* (Johannesburg), 1 April 2001.

Staff Writer. "The Biggest Types of Private Security Businesses in South Africa." *Business Tech* (Johannesburg), 16 November 2017.

———. "Boom Gates Get the Go-Ahead." *Randburg Sun*, 20 February 2014.

———. "Fidelity ADT Launches New Smart Home Security Products." *Business Tech* (Johannesburg), 26 February 2018.

———. "Joburg to Remove 'Illegal' Suburban Boom Gates." *Business Tech* (Johannesburg), 13 December 2016.

———. "Melville Koppies in Danger." *North Cliff-Melville Times*, 29 September 2015.

———. "Private Cops Not the Answer." *The Star* (Johannesburg), 25 October 2007.

———. "Private Security vs. Police Officer Numbers in South Africa." *Business Tech* (Johannesburg), 12 June 2018.

———. "Robbery, Hijacking and Break-In Crime Trends in South Africa in 2018." *Business Tech* (Johannesburg), 25 February 2018.

———. "This Is How Much Private Security Guards Now Earn in South Africa." *Business Tech* (Johannesburg), 15 October 2018.

Steinberg, Jonny. "Fortress Sandton Contributes Zero to the Rule of Law." *Business Day* (Johannesburg), 6 July 1998.

Steinberg, Phyllis. "Judaism Is Thriving in South Africa." *Jewish Journal* (Johannesburg), 11 September 2014.

Stephen, Janine. "Private Security: Blending in to Protect the Well-Heeled." *Business Day* (Johannesburg), 20 September 2017.

Swart, Michelle. "Tudor-Style Splendor." *Business Day* (Johannesburg), 18 April 2008.

Swingler, Shaun. "South Africa's R40bn Private Security Industry under Threat." *Daily Maverick*, 14 May 2017.

Tabane, Rapule. "Homeless Devalue Property—Gauteng Residents." *The Star* (Johannesburg), 6 August 2000.

Taitz, Laurice. "It's Boom Time in a Suburb Once under Siege." *Sunday Times* (Johannesburg), 14 March 1999.

Tandwa, Lizeka. "Several Injured in Joburg Shootout between Police and Hijackers." *News24* (Johannesburg), 27 March 2017.

Tau, Steven. "Protest Anarchy breaks out in Gauteng, North West." *The Citizen* (Pretoria), 26 April 2017.

Temkin, Sanchia. "NYPD on Patrol to Protect the 'Bronx of the North.'" *Business Day* (Johannesburg), 6 June 2008.

Topic, Brian. "Freedom Can't Outweigh Security." *The Star* (Johannesburg), 27 June 2003.

Van Rensburg, Dewald. "Private Security Amendment Bill 'the Enemy of SA Economy.'" *City Press* (Johannesburg), 11 October 2015.

Van Rooyen, Karen. "Private Guards Get More Powers to Police the Suburbs." *Sunday Times* (Johannesburg), 26 October 2008.

Vos, Ügen. "Hijacker Killed in 'Mini War' in Joburg Suburb." *News24* (Johannesburg), 1 February 2017.

Watson, Amanda. "South Africa's Choice: Private Security or Vigilantism." *The Citizen* (Pretoria), 24 September 2015.

Watson, Amanda, and Wendy Nyoni. "Nowhere to Hide for Hijackers." *The Citizen* (Pretoria), 9 January 2015.

Wines, Michael. "Crime in South Africa Grows More Vicious." *New York Times*, 23 September 2005.

———. "Speaking of Fences, Street Crime, and Ultimately, Race." *New York Times*, 28 October 2004.

Young, Gerald. "Robber Shot Dead in Armed Robbery." *The Citizen* (Pretoria), 21 April 2017.

Research Reports and Periodicals

Berg, Julie. *The Accountability of South Africa's Private Security Industry: Mechanisms of Control and Challenges to Effective Oversight*. Cape Town: Criminal Justice Initiative of the Open Society Foundation for South Africa, 2007.

Burt, Geoff, and Eric Muller. *Foreign Ownership Bans and Private Security: Protectionism or Security Sector Governance?* Kitchener, CA: Centre for Security Governance, July 2016.

Crawford, Adam, and Stuart Lister. *The Extended Policing Family: Visible Patrols in Residential Areas*. Centre for Criminal Justice Studies, University of Leeds. York: Joseph Roundtree Foundation, 2004.

Cronje, Frans. *FastFacts: They All Lived Together in a Crooked Little House*. Johannesburg: Institute of Race Relations and Centre for Risk Analysis, issue 289, no. 9, September 2015.

Elvey Security Technologies. "The Power Is in Your Hands!" Memorandum, July 2012.

Gumedze, Sabelo. "The Private Security Sector in Africa: The 21st Century's Major

Cause for Concern?" Occasional paper no. 133, 1–20. Pretoria: Institute for Security Studies, 2007.

Irish, Jenny. *Policing for Profit: The Future of South Africa's Private Security Industry*. Monograph 39, 1–27. Pretoria: Institute for Security Studies, 1999.

Jagjivan, Priyesh. *Perimeter Protection: The Invisible Fence Becomes Reality*. Johannesburg: Elvey Security Technologies, April 2012.

Jaynes, Natalie. "Flying below the Radar: The Armed Private Security Sector in South Africa." Criminal Justice Initiative, occasional paper no. 11. Open Society Foundation for South Africa, Pinelands, ZA, 2012, 1–43.

Landman, Karina. *A National Survey of Gated Communities in South Africa*. Project Number: BP 565. Pretoria: CSIR Council for Scientific and Industrial Research, Building and Construction Technology, 2003.

———. *An Overview of Enclosed Neighbourhoods in South Africa* (Pretoria: CSIR, 2000).

Landman, Karina, and Willem Badenhorst. *The Impact of Gated Communities on Spatial Transformation in the Greater Johannesburg Area*. Report series produced by the South African research chair in Development Planning and Modelling, School of Architecture and Planning. Johannesburg: University of the Witwatersrand, 2012.

Minnaar, Anthony. "Oversight and Monitoring of Non-State/Private Policing: The Private Security Practitioners in South Africa." In *Private Security in Africa: Manifestations, Challenges, and Regulations*, edited by Sabelo Gumedze, 128–49. Institute for Security Studies, monograph series, no. 139. Pretoria: Institute for Security Studies, 2007.

Minnaar, Anthony, and Duxita Mistry. "Outsourcing and the South African Police Service." In *Private Muscle: Outsourcing the Provision of Criminal Justice Services*, edited by Martin Schönteich, Anthony Minnaar, Duxita Mistry, and K. C. Goyer, 38–54. Monograph series, no. 93. Pretoria: Institute for Security Studies, 2004.

Napier, Mark, Chrisna du Plessis, Susan Liebermann, Tinus Kruger, Mark Shaw, Antoinette Louw, and Sarah Oppler. *Environmental Design for Safer Communities*. Pretoria: Council for Scientific and Industrial Research, 1998.

Oppler, Sarah. "Partners against Crime." In *Policing the Transition: Further Issues in South Africa's Crime Debate*, edited by Mark Shaw, Lala Camerer, and Dixita Misty, 50–65. Monograph series, no. 12. Pretoria: Institute for Security Studies, 1997.

Schönteich, Martin, Anthony Minnaar, Duxita Misty, and K. C. Goyer, eds. *Private Muscle: The Provision of Criminal Justice Services*. Monograph series, no. 93. Pretoria: Institute for Security Studies, 2004.

Shaw, Mark. "Crime in Transition." In *Policing the Transition: Further Issues in South Africa's Crime Debate*, edited by Mark Shaw, Lala Camerer, and Dixita Misty, 7–27. Monograph series, no. 12. Pretoria: Institute for Security Studies, 1997.

———. *Towards Safer Cities: The South African Debate on Options for Urban Safety*. Monograph series, no. 11, 1–25. Pretoria: Institute for Security Studies, 1997.

Shaw, Mark, and Antoinette Louw. *Environmental Design for Safer Communities: Preventing Crime in South Africa's Cities and Towns*. Monograph series, no. 24. Midrand, ZA: Institute for Security Studies, 1998.

South African Human Rights Commission. *Report on the Issue of Road Closures, Security*

Booms and Related Measures. Pretoria: South African Human Rights Commission, 2005.

Taljaard, Raenette. "Private and Public Security in South Africa." In *The Private Security Sector in Africa*, edited by Sabelo Gumedze, 69–106. Monograph series, no. 146. Pretoria: Institute for Security Studies, July 2008.

Tuck, Mary. "Crime Prevention: A Shift in Concept." *Home Office Research and Planning Unit Research Bulletin*, occasional paper no. 24. London: Home Office, 1988.

Van Rooyen, Conrad. "South Africa's Security Industry Boom." *Hi Tech Security Solutions Magazine*, October 2017.

Government Reports

Private Security Industry Regulatory Authority. *Annual Report 2010/2011*. Centurion, ZA: Private Security Industry Regulatory Authority, 2011.

South African Police Service. *Annual Report 2010/2011*. Pretoria, ZA: Government Printing Office, 2011.

Theses and Dissertations

Clark, Paul T. "Security Assemblages: Enclaving, Private Security, and New Materialism in Suburban Johannesburg." Master's thesis, University of the Witwatersrand, 2016.

Dieltiens, Nicolas. "The Making of the Criminal Subject in Democratic South Africa." Master's thesis, University of the Witwatersrand, 2011.

England, Marcia Rae. "Citizens on Patrol: Community Policing and the Territorialization of Public Space in Seattle, Washington." PhD diss., University of Kentucky, 2006.

Kole, Olaotse John. "Partnership Policing between the South African Police Service and Private Security Industry in Reducing Crime in South Africa." PhD diss., University of South Africa, June 2015.

Mabudusha, Sekgololo Angel. "The Policing of Illegal Squatting in the Greenbelts within Weltevreden Park Area." Master's thesis, University of South Africa, May 2010.

Marais, Ingrid Estha. "Public Space/Public Sphere: An Ethnography of Joubert Park, Johannesburg." PhD diss. University of Johannesburg, 2013.

Nel, Mary. "Crime as Punishment: A Legal Perspective on Vigilantism in South Africa." PhD diss., Stellenbosch University, 2016.

Parker, Alexandra. "The Effects of Walls in the Suburbs of Johannesburg." Master's thesis, faculty of Engineering and the Built Environment, University of the Witwatersrand, Johannesburg, 2008.

Internet Sources

Administration. "Armed Response—The Solution to Seeking Reliable Security." Stallion Security, South Africa Israel Chamber of Commerce, 2 December 2014. Available at http://saicc.co.za/the-importance-of-armed-response/.

Anonymous. "Joburg Plays Hardball over Bordeaux Access Restriction Structures." IOL (Johannesburg), 15 July 2010. Available at https/www.IOLProperty.co.za.

———. "Land Mines for Home Protection." *UPI Archives*, 5 November 1996. Available at https://www.upi.com/Archives/1996/11/05/Land-mines-for-home-protection/4200 847170000/.

———. "Residential CIDs get Support." Official website of the City of Johannesburg, 14 August 2008. Available at http://www.joburg.org.za/index.php?option=com_con tent&task=view&id=2847&Itemid=253.

Areff, Ahmed. "More Private Security than Police and Army Combined." *News24*, 23 September 2015. Available at http://www.news24.com/SouthAfrica/News/More -private-security-than-police-army-combined-SAIRR-20150923.

Ballard, Richard. "Bunkers for the Psyche: How Gated Communities Have Allowed the Privatisation of Apartheid in Democratic South Africa." Dark Roast Occasional Paper Series, no. 24, Isandla Institute, Cape Town, 2005. Available at http:/www .isandla.org.za.

CAP. "Building a Safer Community Together." Accessed 14 April 2016. Available at http://www.capgroup.org.za/#!about-us/ct05.

Cohen, Mike. "Crime-Busting G4S Faces South Africa Private Security Curbs." *Bloomberg News*, 7 April 2014. Available at http://www.bloomberg.com/news/articles/2014 -04-06/crime-busting-g4s-at-risk-as-south-africa-curbs-private-security.

Fuller, Gillian. "Life in Transit: Between Airport and Camp." *Borderlands E-Journal* 2, no. 1 (2003): 13. Available at http://www.borderlands.net.au/vol2no1_2003/fuller _transit.html.

Goldstein, Chief Rabbi Warren. "Chief Rabbi's Report." Report presented at the biennial conference of Union of Orthodox Jewish Synagogues, 21 August 2011. Available at http://www.uos.co.za/biennial/chief.asp.

———. "Crime Can Be Beaten—The CAP Story of Hope." Available at http://www .chiefrabbi.co.za/?p=1704&upm.

Gomez-Moriana, Rafael. "Everyday Camouflage in the City." *Criticalista*, January 13, 2006. Available at https://criticalista.com/2006/01/13/everyday-camouflage-in-the -city/.

Hoenderdos, René. "The Social Dynamics of Community Development in a Suburban Johannesburg Public Open Space: Verity Park." *Urban Environment* 10 (2016). Available at http://eue.revues.org.proxy.lib.umich.edu/1437.

Katz, Ant. "SA Organizations." *South African Jewish Report*, 15 July 2015. Available at http:// www.sajr.co.za/sa/organisations/2015/07/15/cso-and-cap-go-their-separate-ways.

Landman, Karina. "Serious about Safety." Paper presented at the Urban Planning & Environment Symposium, Pretoria, ZA, 5–9 April 1999. Available at https://research space.csir.co.za/dspace/bitstream/handle/10204/2824/Landman2_1999.pdf?se quence=1&isAllowed=y.

Lipman, Steve. "Letter from Johannesburg." *Jewish Action* (Winter 2011). Available at https://www.ou.org/jewish_action/12/2011/letter_from_south_africa/.

Martin, Guy. "Desert Wolf Fitting RDM Grenades to Skunk UAV." *Defence Web*, 20 June 2017. Available at http://www.defenceweb.co.za/index.php?option=com_content &view=article&id=48242&catid=74&Itemid=30.

Ministry of Police. "South Africa Has World's Largest Private Security Industry; Needs Regulation—Mthethwa." *Defence Web*, 30 October 2012. Available at https://www

.defenceweb.co.za/industry/industry-industry/south-africa-has-worlds-largest -private-security-industry-needs-regulation-mthethwa/.

News24 Wire. "Private Security Officers in SA Outnumber Police and Army." *Business Tech*, 23 September 2015. Available at http://businesstech.co.za/news/general/99248 /private-security-officers-outnumber-sa-police-and-army-combined/.

"Safeparkview." Newsletter 144 (9 January 2019). Available at http://www.parkview .org.za/.

Sandown Strathavon Community Active Protection Website. Available at https:// secure.apsys.co.za/scap/Introduction.html.

Skinns, Layla. "Responsibility, Rhetoric, and Reality: Practitioners' Views on Their Responsibility for Crime and Disorder in Community Policing Partnerships." Selected papers from the British Criminology Conference, vol. 6, Bangor, 2003. Available at http://www.britsoccrim.org/volume6/007.pdf.

Staff Reporter. "Top Cops Join Private Security Company." *Gauteng Business News*, 7 September 2010. Available at www.gbn.co.za/business/news/0175/0333.htm.

Staff Writer. "40,000 SA Police Do Not Have Firearm Competency Certificates." *Business Tech*, 11 September 2015. Available at http://businesstech.co.za/news/general/98135 /40000-sa-police-do-not-have-firearm-competency-certificates/.

Taback, Rabbi Ari. "Cruise Control." *Mishpasha*, 27 February 2013. Available at http:// www.mishpacha.com/Browse/Article/2991/Cruise-Control.

Weizman, Eyal. "The Geometry of Occupation." Lecture, Centre of Contemporary Culture of Barcelona, 1 March 2004. Available at http://www.publicspace.org/es /texto-biblioteca/eng/a024-the-geometry-of-occupation.

Email Correspondence

Gichanga, Margaret (researcher, Research and Development, PSIRA). 15 August 2015.

Nuñes, Danyle (chair, sector crime forum). Melville, 9 October 2018.

Pittman, Andrew, Paul Mills, and Eric van Gils. Melville Security Initiative, 15 and 21 October 2018, and 22 February 2019.

Reddy, Major-General O. D. (former cluster commander). Honeydew, South African Police Service, 14 August 2017.

Index